Refiguring Modernism

BONNIE KIME SCOTT

Refiguring Modernism

VOLUME ONE

The Women of 1928

INDIANA UNIVERSITY PRESS

Bloomington and Indianapolis

The paper used in this publication
meets the minimum requirements of American National Standard
for Information Sciences—Permanence of Paper
for Printed Library Materials,
ANSI Z39.48-1984.

™

Manufactured in the United States of America

Library of Congress Cataloging-in-Publication Data

Scott, Bonnie Kime, date
    Refiguring modernism / Bonnie Kime Scott.
      p.   cm.
    Includes bibliographical references (p.   ) and index.
    Contents: v. 1. The Women of 1928—v. 2. Postmodern feminist
readings of Woolf, West, and Barnes.
    ISBN 0-253-32936-1 (v. 1 : cl : alk. paper).—ISBN 0-253-20995-1 (v. 1 : pa : alk. paper).
    —ISBN 0-253-32937-X (v. 2 : cl : alk. paper).—ISBN 0-253-21002-X (v. 2 : pa : alk. paper)
    1. English fiction—20th century—History and criticism.
    2. Modernism (Literature)—Great Britain.
    3. Feminism and literature—Great Britain—History—20th century.
    4. Feminism and literature—United States—History—20th century.
    5. Women and literature—Great Britain—History—20th century.
    6. Women and literature—United States—History—20th century.
    7. Woolf, Virginia, 1882–1941—Criticism and interpretation.
    8. West, Rebecca, Dame, 1892—Criticism and interpretation.
    9. Barnes, Djuna—Criticism and interpretation.
    10. Modernism (Literature)—United States.   I. Title.
    PR888.M63S43   1995
823'.91099287—dc20   95-3579

1 2 3 4 5   00 99 98 97 96 95

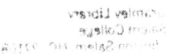

For
Tom

my lasting attachment

and
in search of

Bhima

Contents

Acknowledgments ix
Abbreviations xiii
Introduction xv

PART ONE: BEGINNINGS
1. (Dys)functional Families 3
2. Edwardian Uncles 19
3. Stretching the Scope of Suffrage 35
4. Midwives of Modernism 55

PART TWO: THE MEN OF 1914
5. Ezra Pound: Plunging Headlong into Female Chaos 84
6. Wyndham Lewis: Above the Line of Messy Femininity 100
7. T. S. Eliot: Playing Possum 113
8. James Joyce: Halting Female Pens with *Ulysses* 145
9. Lawrence, Forster, and Bloomsbury:
   Male Modernist Others 162

PART THREE: THE WOMEN OF 1928
10. Arranging Marriages, Partners, and Spaces 187
11. Becoming Professionals 209
12. Rallying round *The Well of Loneliness* 242

Notes 259
Bibliography 289
Index 309

Acknowledgments

I should like to thank the following institutions for access to their collections and permission to quote from manuscripts and reproduce images: BBC Written Archives Centre for quotations from letters by Christopher Salmon and Charles Bridge; British Library for letters of Rebecca West to George Bernard Shaw (Add MS 50519 f 228 and 50522 ff 169–172) and a letter from Shaw to West (Add MS 50518 ff 211–213) in the Shaw papers; Musée Carnavalet, Paris, for Romaine Brooks's painting of Natalie Barney; Cornell University Library for a photo of Violet Hunt, Ford Madox Ford, and Rebecca West; University of Delaware Library, Newark, for letters of Emily Coleman and Djuna Barnes and a photograph of Coleman in the Emily Coleman Papers; Jacques Doucet Library for letters of Djuna Barnes and Natalie Barney in its Natalie Barney Collection; The Houghton Library, Harvard University, for a letter of Rebecca West to Alexander Woollcott (bMS AM 1449 (485)–(494)); House of Lords Record Office for letters of Rebecca West and Lord Beaverbrook in the Beaverbrook Collection; Special Collections, University of Maryland at College Park Libraries (cited in this volume as Maryland), for letters and drawings of Djuna Barnes and drawings by Thelma Wood in the Papers of Djuna Barnes, for a photograph of Zadel Barnes Gustafson in the Barnes Family Papers, and for drawings by Thelma Wood in the Papers of Saxon Barnes; The National Portrait Gallery for a photograph of Virginia Woolf (NPG P221) and a Wyndham Lewis sketch of Rebecca West (NPG 5693); The New York Public Library, Astor, Lenox and Tilden Foundations for letters by T. S. Eliot and John Quinn in the Henry W. and Albert A. Berg Collection; The Manuscripts Division, Department of Rare Books and Special Collections, Princeton University Libraries, for letters of Rebecca West in Box 1, Folder 26 of the Dora Marsden Collection (cited in this volume as Princeton) and a photograph of Djuna Barnes and Mina Loy; University of Reading Library for letters of Leonard Woolf and Rebecca West in its Hogarth Press and Jonathan Cape collections; The Manuscripts Section, University of Sussex Library, for letters of Clive Bell and Leonard Woolf and scrapbooks in the Monk's House Papers; Harry Ransom Humanities Research Center of the University of Texas at Austin for letters of Rebecca

West and Ottoline Morrell; University of Tulsa for letters and manuscripts of Rebecca West in the Rebecca West Collection; The Beinecke Rare Book and Manuscript Library, Yale University, for letters of Rebecca West, a letter by Anthony West, and a sketch by H. G. Wells in the Rebecca West Collection. I am also grateful for the services of the Library of Congress, the British Council Archive, the Millicent Garrett Fawcett Library, the Lilly Library of Indiana University, the University of London Library, the University of Syracuse Library, and the Wellesley College Library.

I have made a concerted effort to contact holders of copyrights and apologize for any that are missing. Djuna Barnes extracts copyright by the Authors League Fund, 330 West 42nd Street, New York, NY 10036, as Literary Executor of the Estate of Djuna Barnes; Clerk of the Records, the House of Lords Record Office, acting on behalf of the Beaverbrook Foundation Trustees; Georgina Berkeley for the Literary Estate of Stella Benson; Joseph Geraci, Literary Executor of Emily Holmes Coleman; Quentin Bell for the literary estates of Clive Bell and Virginia Woolf; Valerie Eliot, Literary Executor for T. S. Eliot; Laurence Pollinger Limited for the Literary Estate of D. H. Lawrence; Harold Ober Associates for permission to quote Naomi Michison; the literary executors of Ottoline Morrell; Artists Rights Society (ARS), New York, as agents for the Man Ray Trust, Paris, for photographs of Djuna Barnes and Barnes with Mina Loy; A. P. Watt Ltd. on behalf of The Literary Executors of the Estate of H. G. Wells; Lily West for permission to quote from a letter by Anthony West; Peters Fraser & Dunlop Group Ltd. for permission to publish extracts from Rebecca West; M. T. Parsons, Literary Executor for Leonard Woolf; Roma Woodnut for The Society of Authors for the Literary Estates of Clive Bell, G. B. Shaw, G. B. Stern, and Virginia Woolf; Ezra Pound Letter to Dora Marsden, copyright 1995 by the Trustees of the Ezra Pound Literary Property Trust, used by permission of New Directions Publishing Corporation, agents. I should also like to acknowledge permission to reprint passages from the published works of Virginia Woolf by Harcourt Brace Jovanovich and Hogarth Press.

Excerpts from *Mrs. Dalloway* by Virginia Woolf, copyright 1925 by Harcourt Brace & Company and renewed in 1953 by Leonard Woolf, reprinted by permission of the publisher.

Excerpts from *To the Lighthouse* by Virginia Woolf, copyright 1927 by Harcourt Brace & Company and renewed in 1954 by Leonard Woolf, reprinted by permission of the publisher.

Excerpts from *A Room of One's Own* by Virginia Woolf, copyright 1929 by Harcourt Brace & Company and renewed in 1957 by Leonard Woolf, reprinted by permission of the publisher.

Excerpts from *The Waves* by Virginia Woolf, copyright 1931 by Harcourt Brace & Company and renewed in 1959 by Leonard Woolf, reprinted by permission of Harcourt Brace & Company.

Excerpts from *Between the Acts* by Virginia Woolf, copyright 1941 by Harcourt Brace & Company and renewed in 1969 by Leonard Woolf, reprinted by permission of the publisher.

Excerpts from *Moments of Being* by Virginia Woolf, copyright © 1976 by Quentin Bell and Angelica Garnett, reprinted by permission of Harcourt Brace & Company.

Excerpts from *The Diary of Virginia Woolf*, Volume III: 1925–1930, copyright © 1976 by Quentin Bell and Angelica Garnett, reprinted by permission of Harcourt Brace & Company.

Excerpts from *The Diary of Virginia Woolf*, Volume V: 1936–41, copyright © 1984 by Quentin Bell and Angelica Garnett, reprinted by permission of Harcourt Brace & Company.

Several essays published previously are reworked here, and I thank the publishers for permitting me to draw from this material: "Jellyfish and Treacle: Joyce, Lewis, Gender and Modernism," published in *Coping with Joyce: Essays from the Copenhagen Symposium,* ed. Morris Beja and Shari Benstock, Ohio State University Press; " 'The Look in the Throat of a Stricken Animal': Joyce as Met by Djuna Barnes," published in *Joyce Studies Annual 1991,* University of Texas Press; "Refiguring the Binary, Breaking the Cycle: Rebecca West as Feminist Modernist," *Twentieth Century Literature* 37.2 (Summer 1991), Hofstra University; " 'The Word Split Its Husk': Woolf's Double Vision of Modernist Language," *Modern Fiction Studies* 32.3 (1988), Purdue University.

I am grateful to the University of Delaware for awarding me a year to work on this project as a fellow in its Center for Advanced Study. Archival research was made possible by travel grants from the Dean of Arts and Science and the General University Research Fund.

Finally, I am appreciative of colleagues who have provided resources, criticism, and encouragement: Jane Marcus, who shares a fascination with all three of my central authors, a depth of wisdom about them, and her own West archive; Mary Lynn Broe and Phil Herring for consultations on Barnes; Carl Rollyson, Victoria Glendinning, Loretta Stec, and Margaret Stetz as consultants on West; and Suzette Henke and Ann Ardis for reading early drafts. I thank Wayne Craven, who identified Zadel Gustafson's illustrator, and my brother, Milford Burton Kime, who restored a family photograph. I am grateful to all of the contributors to an earlier project, *The Gender of Modernism: A Critical Anthology,* who prepared the wider context I needed as a basis. Finally, my graduate students and honors students, including Shirley Peterson, Patience Phillips, Marylu Hill, Judith Allen, Donald Brown, Justyna Kostkowska, and Jennifer Johnson, have traversed little-read texts with me, casting their own light upon them.

Abbreviations

DJUNA BARNES

Ladies Almanack	*LA*
New York	*NY*
Ryder (St. Martin's Press)	*R*

REBECCA WEST

Black Lamb and Grey Falcon	*BL & GF*
Family Memories	*FM*
Saint Augustine	*SA*
The Strange Necessity	*SN*
The Young Rebecca	*YR*

VIRGINIA WOOLF

The Collected Essays of Virginia Woolf	*CE*
The Common Reader	*CR*
The Diary of Virginia Woolf	*D*
The Essays of Virginia Woolf	*E*
The Letters of Virginia Woolf	*L*
Moments of Being	*MB*
Orlando	*O*
A Passionate Apprentice	*PA*
A Room of One's Own	*ROOM*
Three Guineas	*3G*
To the Lighthouse	*TTL*
Virginia Woolf & Lytton Strachey: Letters	*VW & LS*
Women and Writing	*W & W*

Introduction

Fiction is like a spider's web, attached ever so lightly perhaps, but still attached to life at all four corners. Often the attachment is scarcely perceptible; Shakespeare's plays, for instance, seem to hang there complete by themselves. But when the web is pulled askew, hooked up at the edge, torn in the middle, one remembers that these webs are not spun in midair by incorporeal creatures, but are the work of suffering human beings, and are attached to grossly material things, like health and money and the houses we live in.

—Virginia Woolf, *A Room of One's Own* 43–44

Webs are favorite figures of speech in Western culture. They are widely cast, diversely interpreted, and frequently rewoven. Alexander Pope provides a companion quotation for Woolf's, admiring the rare sensitivity of the spider as it lives off the lines of its web:

The spider's touch, how exquisitely fine!
Feels at each thread, and lives along the line.
(*Essay on Man* ll. 217–218)

In noncanonical Native American writing, we encounter webs through "Thought-Woman, the spider" of Leslie Silko's novel *Ceremony*, or "Grandmother Spider" in Paula Gunn Allen's poetry. Ariadne's thread and the webs of Arachne, Philomela, and Penelope are cast anew in such modernist works as *Ulysses, The Waste Land*, and *Between the Acts*. Webs and comparable textiles such as knitting, quilts, lace, and tapestries serve the enabling feminist theories of Mary Daly, Rachel Blau DuPlessis, Carol Gilligan, Nancy K. Miller, Elaine Showalter, Adrienne Rich, Alice Walker, Judy Chicago, and many others.[1]

Together with the companion figure of the scaffolding, which I associated with accounts of canonical modernism, the web provided an enabling design in the early stages of writing this study. The web in the scaffolding (my working title) reappeared in unexpected forms, to the very end. Other types of figuring assumed equal importance, inviting a play on the words of the final title, *Refiguring Modernism*. Refiguring occurred as Virginia Woolf, Rebecca West, and Djuna Barnes were selected as central representatives of modernist writing, where typically a cluster of male figures have stood. Significant dates were recalculated and associated with events that had not previously been figured as important to modernism. The mental process of "figuring out" modernism shifted from genetic filiation to simultaneous attachments; the research investigated not just the figurative patterns in literary works, but also workable domestic and professional arrangements.[2]

Moving into the Web

Woolf's choice of the web for a complexly realized simile is hardly unusual. If her uses of the web seem surprising in a modernist, this is because we have only a limited sense of modernism. The web serves Woolf's analysis of the process rather than the product of writing, while it assists her exploration of new territories. She prefers this metaphoric mode to the hard, exact words called for in much-cited modernist manifestoes, such as Ezra Pound's prescriptions for imagism. She is intrigued by attachments, unlike T. S. Eliot in his poetics of depersonalization, or the New Critics, who largely governed the selection and reception of modernism along formalist lines. Woolf follows her figure of the web to surprisingly practical things, betraying an interest in material contexts. She also records the suffering of the artisan.

Woolf's reference to Shakespeare's plays makes the web a model of widely recognized achievement, applicable to men, as is the case in Pope's *Essay on Man*. In an earlier draft, however, Woolf argued that it was the woman writer whose web was most apt to have "strains & holes that to my mind still slightly disfigure" her work (*Women and Fiction* 65). This is compatible with the deadly strain placed on Shakespeare's imaginary sister, Judith, as sketched in Woolf's *A Room of One's Own*. Unlike the deceptively self-sufficient men's artifacts, women's webs encourage exploration of attachments and consider their difficulties. I infer that the female writer must strain, sometimes painfully, to reach existing supports. Her efforts may leave holes, remain incomplete, or be torn into by the critics who trivialize the woman writer. In Woolf's *The Voyage Out*, Helen Ambrose crafts a needlework version of the river-scape voyaged to by Rachel Vinrace, with deadly results. Mrs. Ramsay's sock, knitted through much of the first part of *To the Lighthouse*, is never delivered.

In both male and female figures of webbing, woman is the usual weaver

Plate 1. Virginia Woolf profile.

George Charles Beresford, 1902,

National Portrait Gallery.

and her work is often problematic. She might, like Ariadne, be punished for her outstanding achievement by a rival goddess. Or like Philomela's, her narrative may have been one of rape, with weaving providing her only communication once her tongue was slashed out by her ravisher. Feminist critics have accused Geoffrey Hartman of again silencing Philomela. His universalizing theory is said to rob her of agency and to obscure the crime of sexual abuse, meant to be read and avenged by her sister.[3] The task of the woman weaver often lacks agency, creativity, and pride—particularly as we move into the modern era, when "New Women" turned from domestic works; we are now wary of sweatshop sewing imposed on third world women. Djuna Barnes deliberately confuses a woman living in urban poverty with her machine-stitched garments:

> Still her clothing is less risky
> Than her body in its prime,
> They are chain-stitched and so is she
> Chain-stitched to her soul for time.
> Ravelling grandly into vice
> Dropping crooked into rhyme.
> Slipping through the stitch of virtue,
>   Into crime. (*The Book of Repulsive Women* 95)

The poem is titled, "Seen from the 'L.' " The woman is probably a prostitute, slipping through the fabric of society. The infamous scaffolding for urban transport, the "L," permits a fleeting gaze as our only contact with her life.

In male-based psychoanalytic theory, the metaphor of the web assigns woman to a masquerade of compensatory actions or erotic display. Freud sets women to weaving in order to hide supposed genital deficiency. The defining of woman in terms of lack, instead of possession, is sustained by Jacques Lacan. Working out of the French psycholinguistic tradition and toward a theory of the writing subject, Julia Kristeva offers a comparable metaphor of fabric. It is presided over by an attentive rather than an inventive weaver. Weaving a textile of male design achieves toleration. The mobile, creative act of the "other" is the attentiveness also marked by Pope.

> The negative awakens within the body and language of the other so as to weave a fabric in which your role is tolerated only if it resembles that of women in Sade, Joyce, and Bataille. But you most

Plate 2. Djuna Barnes profile. Man Ray,
copyright 1995 Artists Rights Society (ARS),
New York/ADAGP/Man Ray Trust, Paris.

certainly must not consider yourself either as the weaving or as the character against whom it is woven. What is important is to listen to it, in your own way, indefinitely, and to disappear within the movement of this attentiveness. (*Desire in Language* 166)

I have greater confidence in the ability of the modernist woman, however negative her reception, to shape language into a substantially different web. But with Kristeva's encouragement, I shall also monitor the woman writer's attentiveness. In an essay on feminist poetics notably titled "Arachnologies," Nancy K. Miller expresses interest in the "place of production that marks the spinner's attachment to her web" (288).[4] This trope is consistent with the function of actual webs, though it situates the spider on her thread rather than searching out her attachments.

Like a store of repeated metaphors used by Woolf, West, and Barnes, the web has helped me toward the approach I needed to study their part in modernism. In my web, as in Woolf's, there is the possibility of agency and selection for the weaver, within the structures of cultural and physical demands. Woolf's figure reminds us of the necessity of multiple attachment, making the creation of pattern and the collection of sustenance possible. Despite the supposed modernist preference for wholeness, she declares the completeness of the textual web an illusion. The cultural systems to which the web is, of necessity, attached include material, psycho-biographical, historical, and epistemological frames. Spiders spin a new web almost daily. I will re-view the attachments of the web for my authors at late Victorian, Edwardian, and modernist stages, as they move toward a period of highly successful literary production around 1928. Woolf's attitudes as an early reader of modernism—and she constantly deferred to readers—are instructive. She felt challenged to match the contemporary writer's intrepid ventures and physical dexterity with another web—the net: "Whenever there is life in them they will be casting their net out over some unknown abyss to snare new shapes, and we must throw our imaginations after them if we are to accept with understanding the strange gifts they bring back to us" ("Hours in the Library," 2 E 59). Great nets serve the affirmative ending of Zora Neale Hurston's *Their Eyes Were Watching God,* arguably a modernist text of the Harlem Renaissance. The women of modernism also ventured outside of the scaffolding, leaping through space to haul in beauty and life.

An unruly web assisted my introduction to the twenty-six authors of *The Gender of Modernism* (1990), where I became fascinated with the

Plate 3. Rebecca West profile.

Photograph given to Jane Marcus by Rebecca West.

writers' attachments to one another, strung by acquaintance or common literary interest. Arranging their names in a circle, I drew a line between authors every time one of my editors mentioned a significant contact. In reading the resultant "tangled mesh of modernists" (see Figure 1), I was surprised by some of the authors with the most numerous attachments. Marianne Moore, long famed for her privacy, tallied eleven connections—one of them to Djuna Barnes. Virginia Woolf, with thirteen lines of attachment, was second only to Ezra Pound, who had fifteen. Djuna Barnes, a supposed recluse, made nine attachments, and Rebecca West, ten. These figures compared well to T. S. Eliot and D. H. Lawrence, both with ten connections, and to James Joyce, who had eleven. To some extent attachments in this "mesh" reinforced old accounts of modernism. Thus Pound made many attachments as the hyperactive talent scout. Joyce's *Ulysses* was seized as the central experimental text. Connections accrue to Eliot for offering the criteria for entering an enduring tradition. Woolf is enlisted as the token woman, acceptable because most comparable in her experiments to the men. Still, the web of *The Gender of Modernism* showed a more diversely energized modernist field than I had known previously, with a lot more important players. I saw the need to look more deeply into the nature of these attachments. This was plausible with a small, strategic selection of women. For some time, I have had three candidates.

Woolf, West, and Barnes all emerged as valuable but neglected critics for me when I reviewed a history of feminist criticism of Joyce for my first book, *Joyce and Feminism.* I was struck by ways that their negative remarks on Joyce had been seized upon for mockery by early critics and turned toward their dismissal. The grounds were often personal—the supposed snobbery of Woolf, or the immaturity of West. Slighted or ignored in such dismissals were their unconventional critical methods, including the dramatization of criticism as a process. Though attached to the canonized masters, Woolf, West, and Barnes promised both different terms of attachment and a modernist weave of their own.

This is not, then, a purely gynocritical study focused on women's traditions, though by 1928 Woolf, West, and Barnes had some comparable professional arrangements and methods. Nor is it aimed at identifying feminine writing, as French feminists have defined it, though Woolf, West, and Barnes have formal similarities as well. Volume 1 is sensitive to a number of different scaffoldings available to this set of women. An understanding of the use these women make of Edwardian authority figures and "the men of 1914" is vital to our understanding of modernism, and

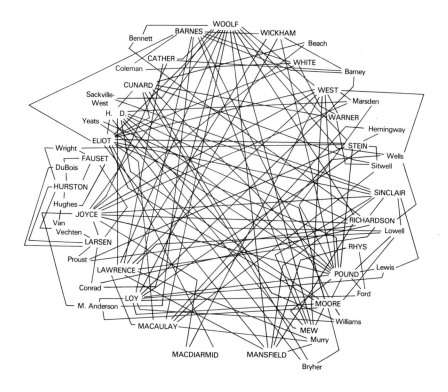

Figure 1. A Tangled Mesh of Modernists

is duly emphasized. But I also consider family structures and premodernist attachments to writers of both genders. Though I work in a much more practical and material way than Luce Irigaray, my project of moving from scaffolding to web has something in common with her strategy with the "masculine imaginary":

> I am trying . . . to go back through the masculine imaginary, to interpret the way it has reduced us to silence, to muteness, or mimicry, and I am attempting from that starting-point and at the same time, to (re)discover a possible space for the feminine imaginary. (Irigaray, *This Sex Which Is Not One* 165)

I also see some compatibility with a procedure suggested by Myra Jehlen in "Archimedes and the Paradox of Feminist Criticism." Each line of attachment that Woolf, West, or Barnes makes to a male modernist scaffolding provides a point for what Jehlen called "radical comparativism." Jehlen sought Archimedean leverage for feminist criticism that she found lacking in self-contained gynocritical accounts. This leverage, set along a boundary of male ground, could be used by the feminist critic to shift the world. But I prefer to work within a cultural sense of context—a surround rather than a radically divisive boundary. Many lines of attachment are routed clear of modernist and premodernist men. Tracking these has the excitement of an untold story. Much of my evidence of attachments comes from unpublished materials.

However rich the network I offer here, I must emphasize that the critical web has to be cast many more times before we will have an adequate set of designs, let alone the ability to read them. It is helpful in refiguring modernism that Woolf, West, and Barnes had diverse attachments to the historical events, early canonized works, and theories that provided the tentative scaffolding of high modernism. It is equally critical that their lines of interest ran beyond and askew from this limited but long-accepted frame. In a new web, I have traced many of these attachments (see Figure 2). An intriguing way to begin reading this web is to find mutual attachments, and the common interests they served.

Appropriating Modernist Scaffoldings

The scaffolding, the second component of my enabling metaphor for this study, evokes architectonic male modernist designs. The paintings of Wyndham Lewis are traversed in powerful diagonals by steel girders—

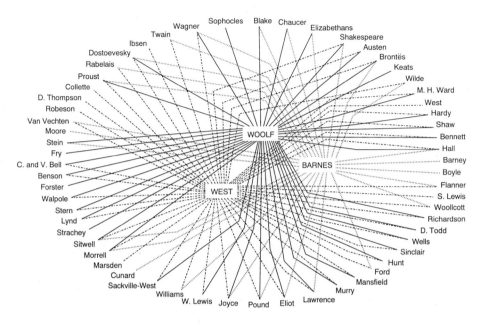

Figure 2. A Triple Web of Attachments

the defining matrices of modern architecture. In his 1922 endorsement of James Joyce's *Ulysses*, Ezra Pound used the figure of "a scaffold" to describe the use of Homeric correspondences, resulting in a "triumph in form, in balance, a main scheme which continues unweaving and arabesque" (*Literary Essays* 406). A firmer and more famous scaffolding for modernism is offered in Eliot's "*Ulysses*, Order and Myth," where he constructs a "mythic method" for Joyce. Eliot tries to improve upon what he sees as the usual limitations of scaffolding. Joyce's "manipulating a continuous parallel between contemporaneity and antiquity" is not an "amusing dodge, or scaffolding . . . of no interest in the completed structure" but a way of "controlling, of ordering, of giving a shape and a significance to the immense panorama of futility and anarchy which is contemporary history." Thus in 1919 Eliot set out an aesthetic of control through tradition, which only grew stronger in his later criticism. All of Joyce's major works lend themselves to systematic charts. Eliot derived his sense of Joyce's classical parallels from Valerie Larbaud's presentation of *Ulysses*. Few students now enter Joyce's *Ulysses* without Stuart Gilbert's "schema," devised with Joyce's help. This chart arrays classical parallels, bodily organs, colors, arts, and "technics" for each episode. In further harmony with scaffolding, Joyce was fond of metaphors related to the construction of buildings. *Ulysses* starts in a Norman tower intended for defense, though his artist soon loses his tenancy; the ill-fated tower of Ibsen's *The Master Builder* crops up time and again in *Finnegans Wake*. However, lest Joyce be confused with Eliot, it is well to remember that this last work is premised on Tim Finnegan's fall from a scaffolding (621). Guiding Harriet Shaw Weaver through *Ulysses*, Joyce turned from scaffolding to proclaim, "Circe has a vast web" (1 *Letters of James Joyce* 164).

One of Rebecca West's most engaging characters, Ellen Melville of *The Judge*, incorporates both web and scaffolding in her lover's description. Her various qualities evade feminine stereotypes; they are suggested by a scene that combines solitude, turbulent nature, and useful engineering—all considered beautiful:

> It was beautiful and solitary even as she was. The loch that stretched north-east from the narrow neck of water under the bridge was fretted to a majesty of rage by the winds that blew from the black hills around it; but it ended in a dam that was pierced in the middle with some metallic spider's web of engineering; even so would romantic and utilitarian Ellen have designed a loch. (106)

West told an interviewer, "I really write to find out what I know about something and what is to be known about something" (Plimpton 87). Typically, West brings a full range of aesthetic and philosophical resources to this process, including art, music, and theology. She also offers a rich fund of domestic experience, which she likes to present by way of analogy. Background research reveals "what is to be known." West's final product, delivered in a tone of authority, often locates her "something" within a philosophical or historical scaffolding, registering the effects of that structure, for good or ill.

Virginia Woolf admits an element of scaffolding in her work, though never in isolation. Early in *The Voyage Out*, the unworldly Rachel Vinrace takes refuge in her music: "In three minutes she was deep in a very difficult, very classical fugue in A, and over her face came a queer remote impersonal expression of complete absorption and anxious satisfaction . . . an invisible line seemed to string the notes together, from which rose a shape, a building" (57). But when Mrs. Dalloway bursts into the room, "the Bach fugue crashed to the ground" (57). The more mature Lily Briscoe in *To the Lighthouse* thinks, "The fabric must be clamped together with bolts of iron," as she also strives for a "feathery and evanescent" surface for her painting, "like the colours on a butterfly's wing" (171). She begins the second phase of her painting by "scoring her canvas with brown, nervous, running lines" (158). In a late essay Woolf declares that "moments of being" are her scaffolding (MB 73). But she discloses important reservations over the attention given to form and method in criticisms of Joyce, and in the critical approach of Percy Lubbock, a precursor of the New Critics. Lubbock's attention to method, which she compares to the x-ray, dissolves all but the bone. While he has the skeletal frame, then, he misses the process of production and the emotional connection to an audience (3 E 339–41). Woolf makes it her strategy to work around form, without allowing it to eliminate life. She lets it gradually emerge in the writing process. Thus she discovered that she had found a "tunneling process" for *Mrs. Dalloway* and scraps of poetry for *Between the Acts*.

Barnes's recourse to literary styles of the past suggests a scaffolding for her work. In his introduction to *Nightwood*, T. S. Eliot settles Barnes into Elizabethan tradition. But her apparent assumption of period styles—a song from Shakespeare or a scene from a Jacobean drama—also plays with cultural assumptions of the period. Barnes was a great spinner of stories and a twister of aphorisms that produce enigmas, challenging readers to define their psychological underpinnings, which are premised on marginal cultural positions. The historical scaffolding constructed by *Nightwood*'s Felix Volkbein, like the aristocratic figures he bows down to, are fake or crumbling. In a memorable scene from the same novel, Nora Flood dreams of "standing at the top of a house" in her grandmother's room, "looking down into the body of the house as if from a scaffold" (62). This vantage point, somehow connected to her grandmother, separates her surrealistically—like opera glasses turned the wrong way, and with "a speed that ran away with the two ends of the building" from her lover, Robin. The architectural scaffold brings with it a set of taboos regulating what may be touched or brought together. "Scaffold" in its short form reminds us of the classic Puritan device for persecution of those who break the rules. Barnes refers repeatedly to the Victorian and the Puritan structures in her nature.

Both the web and the scaffolding have companion figures in Woolf, West, and Barnes. Allied to the scaffolding are frequent references to towers (as we have seen for Joyce), temples, and chapels as structures where women have been denied entry or empowerment. Through Woolf, we have the inevitable beadle who turns a woman away from the lawn, library, and chapel of the famous men's college in *A Room of One's Own*. *Jacob's Room* and *Three Guineas* also attack the "sacred edifices of male education and administration," as Angela Ingram has noted. "The Leaning Tower" provides both title and metaphor for the position of male authors of the 1930s in one of Woolf's best known late essays. In a late diary entry (5 D 340), Woolf wrote of demolishing "queer little sand castles . . . Little boys making sand castles. . . . Each is weathertight and gives shelter to the occupant." In *The Judge*, West stages love scenes in a Greek garden temple, evoking goddess worship as the lover places his beloved in a statuary niche. But Ellen Melville thinks of the surrounding trees as a larger temple. Her love culminates on the very different terrain of an island in a tidal swamp. In heralding Woolf's *Orlando* as a "high fountain of genius," West makes a joyful combination of the tropes of water and tower for female writing success.[5] Barnes depicts women routinely going to and from churches, with little tangible result in both *Ryder* and *Nightwood* until Robin Vote finds her own unique rite to perform in the ruined and deserted chapel at the end of the latter work. Not just webs attached by an arachnid's skill and whim, or nets thrown into unknown territory, but woods and sea elaborate, defy, and even invade manmade structures and limitations.[6]

Gender and Metaphor

The metaphorical scheme of web in scaffolding could be viewed as a divisive, binary system, confined by master narratives of Western tradition. This would equate the feminine with nature (web, woods, or water) and the masculine with the technical products of culture (phallic erections of scaffolding, tower, or church), inevitably placing the masculine above the feminine in a hierarchy of value. This sort of division has been problematized as a device of patriarchy by a host of feminists and post-structuralists, including Hélène Cixous and Jacques Derrida—theory well summarized and extended by Alice Jardine in *Gynesis*, her study of the "putting into discourse of 'woman' " (72, 25). There are possibilities of contention and destruction between these figures. But the spider is more concerned with her own design than with the planned uses of scaffolding. Her actions of repeatedly attaching, launching out into the unknown, and landing for the next anchoring point suggest polyvalence, polyphony, independence, and the inclination and ability to make selective use of existing structures or to seek new ones—not all of them manmade.

Figurative language has long been played in games of gender. From the "great" male rationalists and realists of ancient Greece to present academe, the unreliability of tropes (taken from the Greek word for "turn") has been compared to the behavior of women. John Locke associated rhetoric with "the fair sex": It "has too prevailing beauties in itself to suffer itself ever to be spoken against. And it is in vain to find fault with those arts of deceiving wherein men find pleasure to be deceived."[7] Paul de Man suggests that the metaphor's penchant to proliferate and become mixed is what troubled Locke. In his own play with feminine gender, de Man likens the proliferation of metaphor to that of the Gothic drama of Anne Radcliffe and Mary Shelley (21), though he plays the part of deconstructing previous male anxieties.

Metaphor has its own history with feminist critics. Suzanne Clark suggests that "modernism wrote itself out in a metaphor of the subject" (41). She cites antidomestic and antisentimental use of metaphor as evidence of male modernist contempt for women—noting that the practice was perpetuated into the 1980s (41). Sandra Gilbert and Susan Gubar often use metaphor as a lively device in their writing, but I see their figural strategy as more divisive and ultimately less liberating than my metaphorical web work. They typically use linguistic levity as a weapon in sustaining the "war between the sexes" that serves as the controlling trope of the first two volumes of their study of modernism, which is militantly and metaphorically titled *No Man's Land*. Their mocking metaphor reverses the disposition of linguistic power within a hierarchy of gender, but maintains that system. Take, for example, one of their linguistic tricks on Joyce, as modernist master of logos: "At bottom, for Joyce, woman's scattered logos is a scatologos, a Swiftian language that issues from the many obscene mouths of the female body" (vol. 1, 232). If we agree to a war of words, we would tend to say touché. But they base their findings on a highly selective investigation of Joycean texts, neglecting in this case his widely dispersed scatological imagination.[8] Barnes's scatological imagination, applied to women and animals in particular, is at least a match for Joyce's.

To numerous feminist theorists, metaphor is suspect as part of a masculine system of language. Indeed, this can be rendered in figurative language as another manifestation of masculine scaffolding. Roman Jakobson constructed a scaffold-like arrangement for the world of language, working vertically through metonymy and horizontally through metaphor. Alienated by her studies with Lacan, Luce Irigaray denounced metaphor as an aspect of a masculine imaginary, teaming it with the additional masculine tendencies of conceptualization, naming, individualizing, the mechanics of solids, and the gaze. According to Irigaray, the feminine imaginary is better served by metonymy, association, gesture, and touch in a feminine imaginary (*This Sex Which Is Not One* 24–28). In order to make her assault on language, however, Irigaray constantly uses metaphors. It seems worth pointing out that the process of webbing is both fluid and solid; it facilitates touch and capture.[9]

Helena Michie makes the helpful suggestion that feminist suspicion of metaphor is "a synecdoche for feminist distrust and dis-ease with patriarchal language in general" (145). Jardine points out the risks of metaphor: "To accept a metaphorization, a semiosis of woman . . . means risking once again the absence of women as subjects in the struggles of modernity" (37). But then like Michie she suggests that the recent theoretical concern is part of a modern crisis over the breakdown of narrative, calling for a "wide-ranging reorganization of figurability." I should like to suggest that, in my mixed figure of the web in the scaffolding, I am out to capture that reorganization, as attempted by Woolf, West, and Barnes. I am also webbing a newer scaffolding of postmodern questions with feminist designs.

Feminism in a Postmodern Era

In "Modern Fiction," Virginia Woolf notes the disadvantages of her "vantage ground" on contemporary fiction—standing "on the flat, in the crowd, half blind with dust" (CR 150). This study is written amid considerable dust, in an anxious, self-conscious, yet ill-defined era of postmodern feminist theory. Whether all or any of the feminisms being practiced today are (or want to be) postmodern is a subject of lively debate that puts into question the utility of both terms. Too often, the discussion takes the destructive form of one-up*man*ship,[10] of being the latest and wisest about everyone else's earlier assumptions. This reminds me of the shadow of the "I" falling across the page that Woolf found so unappealing in male contemporaries (*Room* 103). It is at least partly generational. Feminism is more fractured now than it was a decade ago, when a major struggle occurred between French and Anglo-American feminisms. That episode was dramatized in Toril Moi's challenge to the dismissal of Virginia Woolf by Elaine Showalter. One of Moi's major objections to Showalter was that she was invested in the Cartesian "unified, integrated, self-identity" (7), a concept Moi dismissed as Western patriarchal philosophy. Given her investment in feminist progress, Showalter saw androgyny and aestheticism as a retreat.[11] This evaluation was understandable in a critic more interested in realist, activist expression than in the demanding delays of revolutionary language.[12]

The dismissal of a series of former feminist focuses and strategies has become a fairly standard preliminary to new work.[13] Androgyny, the autonomous self, and more recently a women's literary tradition, maternal affiliations, essentialism, and the category of gender have all been superseded. Adding to internal skirmishing, the new right, served by performers such as Camille Paglia, seeks to discredit feminist and deconstructionist critics alike by accusing them of enforcing narrow standards of political correctness. In postmodern and feminist practices, there are some comparable lines of attack on high modernism. These include increased interest in popular as opposed to "high" forms of writing, concern for political praxis rather than experimental innovation, and valorizing of textual gaps rather than patterns of transcendence or aesthetic wholeness, as expected in master narratives.[14] We will retest the traits of "high" modernism assigned to Woolf and to male modernists such as Eliot and Joyce. Though examples of what the New Critics emphasized in these texts can readily be found, it is important to do a sufficiently thorough reexamination, if only to have a better sense of the relations of women writers to these works. Rather than offering the next in a long series of intergenerational renunciations of feminist precursors, I am pursuing a strategy of strategic attachment, closer to the tactics of the women writers of modernism. This is designed most fundamentally to reattach to three modernist women writers—sufficiently distant in time to be our critical grandmothers, or even our great-grandmothers—from beyond the postmodern divide. That I skip over my own mother's generation to link with an earlier one is part of the complex cultural history of this waning century and worth its own study.[15]

The working space and dynamic suggested in the figure of the web in the scaffolding has affinity with several feminist and postmodern approaches. Quite likely it has emerged from my exposure to them. Although Michel Foucault's masculine pronouns are daunting and he displays a general neglect of differences deriving from gender, there is considerable resonance between Woolf's well-attached web and Foucault's account of the production of language and knowledge:

> In a general fashion, his corporeal existence interlaces him through and through with the rest of the living world; since he produces objects and tools, exchanges the things he needs, organizes a whole network of circulation along which what he is able to consume flows, and in which he himself is defined as an intermediary stage, he appears in his existence immediately interwoven with others; lastly, because he has a language, he can constitute a whole symbolic universe for himself, within which he has a relation to his past, to things, to other men, and on the basis of which he is able equally to build something like a body of knowledge. (*The Order of Things* 351)

Foucault points to the constructed nature of world and indeed personal order, as well as the contingency of language and knowledge upon the interlacing of connections. His account of the interested narrative, "a history of the past in the terms of the present" (*Discipline and Punish* 31), is a useful description of what we can hope to do (and all we can hope to do) in a critical practice that seeks to be aware of its own parameters.

Some critical tools and vocabulary used in this project are resonant with French feminist theory in its alliance with Derridean deconstruction and its appropriation of Lacan. My work joins a relatively new practice of applying these perspectives to female as well as male modernists.[16] Deconstruction encouraged the evaluation of the Western "philosophy of presence," in effect, as a scaffolding. We see it as a construction, premised on hierarchies, binaries, and phallogocentrism. Derrida has offered deconstructive strategies such as "decentering," the following of traces of the repressed "other" of language, and a mapping of "différance" among linguistic signs. These strategies encourage us to attach multiply and marginally in critical work. Julia Kristeva has appropriated the term *chora* from Plato for a prelinguistic concept. This matrix space of the Kristevan "semiotic" erupts into the symbolic even after a subject has entered into that later system, which is associated with the word of the father and the phallus as "transcendental signifier." The qualities of the *chora*, that "essential mobile and extremely provisional articulation constituted by movements and their ephemeral stases," come close to web-weaving in relation to scaffolding. Indeed, the possibility of attaching down, or back to the semiotic has become a much-used feminist strategy, anchoring the critical web. Web-work is suggested in Kristeva's description of discourse in relation to the *chora*: "Discourse moves with and against the *chora* in the sense that it simultaneously depends upon and refuses it" ("Revolution in Poetic Language," *Kristeva Reader* 93–94). Kristeva is also sympathetic with the theories of the carnival and the dialogic, which she construes as polyphonic, in the work of M. M. Bakhtin. The spider seems to me highly compatible with the carnival, just as it is a favorite player at Halloween. Its attachments figure the polyphonic. In reaction to Lacan's phallicism, and in another manifestation of the polyphonic, Luce Irigaray has posited a language of lesbian/female jouissance founded on the recognition that the female body has multiple erogenous zones (64); she is "not one," but not in the sense Lacan meant it, in denying her subjectivity. Her touch and attachment are multiple and physical, and thus compatible with my scheme.

The blend of psycho-biography and materialist history with closer textual reading, as practiced by American feminists such as Elizabeth Abel, Susan Stanford Friedman, Louise DeSalvo, and Jane Marcus, has encouraged attention to holes, gaps, and "versioning." These critics also offer the reading of metaphor as a code for the repressed and a channel for its return.[17] My interest in contexts and metaphors as formal strategies, along with my extensive use of manuscript materials and uncollected materials, has affinity here as well.

The concern of postmodern-era feminism over essentialism confronts the many French feminist definitions of feminine language, as well as maternally grounded theories of the female imaginary. It also seeks to take into account individual differences prompted by a widening compass of feminism that is more sensitive to diversity of class and ethnicity, postcolonial writing, economic systems, and complexities of defining sexuality. Even the concept of gender has been faulted by Judith Butler and Eve Sedgwick for its reliance on heterosexual arrangements and its perpetuation of binary thinking. Having developed a postmodern caution about difference, I am not going to propose a new, unifying concept of female modernism to be found in three authors. Even as I carry postmodern issues of essentialism and binarism back to their texts, I see these issues as factors in my attachment to them. I am not interested in proving my postmodern progress from them, or their postmodern precocity (both of which would be presumptuous), but in assessing cross-generational saving and sharing.

There have been a number of studies that detect common factors in the historical situation, the literary strategies, and the psychological makeup of modernist women writers. Several implicate Woolf, West, and/or Barnes. Sydney Janet Kaplan's *Feminist Consciousness in the Modern British Novel* casts Woolf, Dorothy Richardson, May Sinclair, Rosamond Lehmann, and Doris Lessing more positively than Showalter did in assigning them to aesthetic modernism, though still in an apolitical posture. Kaplan investigates ways that all of these writers depict the consciousness of women characters centrally as a literary strategy. Suzanne Clark, on the other hand, has reasserted the "sentimental modernism" of Edna St. Vincent Millay and others, analyzing the disfavor it found with the New Critics. She forces me to scrutinize Rebecca West's detection of sentimentality, even in Joyce, and West's knowledge that he would resist its detection. Djuna Barnes's rejection of the sugary sweet qualities of Kay Boyle's writing and her own acceptability to Eliot also pose challenges here. In *Writing for Their Lives,* Gillian Hanscombe and Virginia L. Smyers identify H. D., Bryher, Dorothy Richardson, Amy Lowell, Djuna Barnes, and Mary Butts as a hidden network of women for whom periodical and book publishing became a female profession—a project that has much in common with my construction of "Women of 1928." A network of modernist women's living and creating in Paris is carefully laid out in Shari Benstock's *Women of the Left Bank,* which also investigates experiments in language and attends to the importance of lesbian sexuality in modernist women writers. Recent collections highlight other historical and formal patterns: *The Voyage In: Fictions of Female Development,* edited by Elizabeth Abel; *Arms and the Woman,* edited by Helen M. Cooper, Adrienne Auslander Munich, and Susan Merrill Squier; *Women's Writing in Exile,* edited by Mary Lynn Broe and Angela Ingram; and *Breaking the Sequence: Women's Experimental Fiction,* edited by Ellen G. Friedman and Miriam Fuchs.

Sandra Gilbert and Susan Gubar group modernist women in numerous ontogenetic accounts and as authors of specific fantasy tropes. They have adjusted the psychodynamics of *The Madwoman in the Attic,* their outstanding analysis of nineteenth-century women writers, for the twentieth century. In a move that has something in common with my selective, spidery attachments, they define an "affiliation complex" which allows modernist women to "adopt" literary mothers. They distinguish this process from the male "belatedness" or "anxiety of influence" theorized by Harold Bloom, in which they find a stricter, biological imperative for literary descent from an originatory father. One of the ways that Gilbert and Gubar group women is by their method of resolving the Freudian Oedipus complex. In normative resolution, women writers remain anxious about the fragility of paternal power, or about usurping paternal primacy; they may fear male vengeance. Women who make a nonnormative resolution of the Oedipus complex, entering a "masculinity complex" (e.g., Gertrude Stein), may achieve autonomy, a new maternal relation, and the creative option of male mimicry. The anxious response of women who make the normative resolution, as described by Gilbert and Gubar's paradigm, is echoed by Marianne DeKoven, though in a more politically engaged modernism. DeKoven adapts Derrida's formulation of *sous-rature* to an unresolved contradiction between the terrifying appeal of movements for social change such as feminism and socialism, and gender-marked ambivalence. Her male modernists, resembling those of Gilbert and Gubar, "feared the loss of hegemony the change they desired might entail, while female modernists feared punishment for desiring that utter change" (4). It is not my purpose to adopt or adapt the Freudian accounts, though it is worth noting that Woolf, Barnes, and West had their own ways of coping with psychoanalysis, both as a narrative strategy and in riddling out their own problems. Only West underwent analysis.

Gilbert and Gubar find that the women of modernism construct feminist linguistic fantasies as a means to relate to language. This model grants intuitive primacy to the mother, rather than the father, in language acquisition—a more powerful position than the male-associated symbolic language central to Kristeva's analysis, and one which connects well with American feminist sociology, including the work of Nancy Chodorow and Carol Gilligan. Pamela Caughie's analysis of Virginia Woolf as a writer of process (a formula derived from Kristeva) is another attempt to investigate relation to language, useful when we turn to Woolf's relation to language in volume 2.

Offering another set of categories, Gilbert and Gubar devote portions of their works to women's tropes found in a variety of known and neglected texts: the femme fatale, the empowered woman vs. the no-man of World War I,[18] and transvestites and cross-dressers galore. Their findings are conveyed in a voice that grows ever more convinced of its own evidentiary momentum and energizing wit. With web and scaffolding, I have already engaged in comparable collection of tropes. My major concern, born of resistant reading to their all too engaging voice of discovery, is to beware of self-serving selectivity and the all too neat division they often make between failed male and superior female modernists. The existing scholarship on modernist women writers does convince me that the negotiation of connections, of shared tropes and ontogenies, is a historically and formally varied, fluid, but abiding strategy. It is adapted by Alice Walker, who splices Phillis Wheatley and the experience of working women into her connection with Woolf's *A Room of One's Own*.

Refigured History: 1914, 1928, 1939

As I have pulled at the webs woven by the fiction, essays, and letters of Woolf, West, and Barnes, and by Woolf's diaries, I have found common attachments to other literary persons, such as Joyce, Eliot, Pound, Janet Flanner, Edith Sitwell, and Ottoline Morrell. There are also common attachments to the "grossly material things" evoked in the epigraph, such as their need to make money as professional writers, or to cope with the censor over the issue of writing their own sexualities. These women attach to comparable aspects of history—women's suffrage and socialist movements, the crises of two world wars, and the advent of fascism. They collect and connect women's opinions.

Their web of work changes as the cultural environment does, and thus I have found it useful to provide temporally distinct discussions of "The Men of 1914," "The Women of 1928," and, as my conclusion to volume 2, "1939: The Ends of Modernism." It was the artist and writer Wyndham

Lewis who designated Pound, Joyce, Eliot, and himself as "The Men of 1914." The selection proved influential to canon formation, even if the date preceded the height of male modernism, which might be settled around 1922. Woolf, West, and Barnes were clearly affected by the men of 1914. I have noted the common critical interest in Joyce's *Ulysses*. To this should be added political interest in Eliot. Woolf and Barnes had affectionate relationships with Eliot and entered into publishing arrangements with him. West challenged Eliot's critical authority in print. All three knew the literary manifestoes of Ezra Pound. West and Barnes encountered him in different arenas of modernist entrepreneurship—West in London, Barnes in Paris. I discuss additional encounters of Woolf, West, and Barnes with men who are regarded as only slightly less central to modernism. The list includes Ford Madox Ford, D. H. Lawrence, and E. M. Forster. The slightly older Edwardian "uncles" of Woolf, West, and Barnes, including George Bernard Shaw, Arnold Bennett, and H. G. Wells, precede the modernist men in this study, exacting their own price as portals to modernism for a new generation of women.

"The Women of 1928" is my own term, calling attention to a second rise in modernism. It selects a year when Woolf, West, and Barnes were highly productive, having found strategies to succeed as professional writers and a degree of formal license. They had written their way out of some of their confining paternal, avuncular, and male modernist relationships and literary patterns. They had found women-made circles and journals. In building toward 1928, I acknowledge the powerful groundwork of new women in the suffrage movement, and midwives of modernism who brought forth women as well as men of modernism. Nineteen twenty-eight was also a year of cultural crisis over lesbian censorship occasioned by the trial of Radclyffe Hall's novel *The Well of Loneliness*—a debate involving Woolf, West, and Barnes both in argument and in creative writing. My conclusion, "1939: The Ends of Modernism," is saved for volume 2. It briefly investigates the sense of community and relation to tradition arrived at in works either written or situated in 1939, a year that has ushered in the end of modernism in most accounts.

Why Woolf, West, and Barnes?

In an era when identity politics are a major issue in the academy, I will concede that Woolf, West, and Barnes represent a narrow spectrum of the world's women, or even of the women of modernism. *The Gender of Modernism,* the critical anthology for which I served as general editor, offered a wider sweep that included African American writers, women from colonial settings, and writers less associated with formal experiment, though its range, too, could be greatly expanded. Woolf, West, and Barnes were all white, of varied British stock, and born to educated families. They do present subtle differences, useful in gaining a nuanced view of a portion of modernism. Woolf (born Virginia Stephen) was of an intellectual subset of the English upper middle class; she was not an aristocratic lady, as some would have her, and not wealthy, despite the £500 per year bequeathed by her aunt and made famous by *A Room of One's Own.* England was her place of residence and the primary setting of her works, though she revisits a family tradition of service to the empire in India and tests Oxbridge's cultural allegiance to Greece.

Rebecca West (by suggestive pseudonym; she was named Cicely Isabel Fairfield by her parents) was the child of educated, struggling middle-class British parents.[19] Her mother's Scottish and her father's Anglo-Irish backgrounds, as well as residence in Australia, made them marginal to English culture, despite years spent in London, where West was born. At various times she claimed both Slavic and Berber blood. West had a fondness for the United States, where she found a significant audience. The international range of her writing included political analysis of both Yugoslavia and South Africa.

Barnes was American, born into a bigamous household in the artistic enclave of Cornwall-on-Hudson in northern New York State. Her mother, Elizabeth Chappell Barnes, was born and reared in England. Her father, Wald, prided himself on procreation, music, and various inventions. The family's chief support was her grandmother, Zadel Barnes Buddington Gustafson, a successful writer and journalist, reputed to have run a London literary salon. During the twenties and thirties, Barnes was more in Paris and London than the U.S., thus meriting a place among the American expatriate generation. Much of her writing negotiates among European, English, and American cultures. Barnes began and ended her literary career in Greenwich Village, where she contributed to the Provincetown Players and the Theatre Guild group.

Though inhabitants of the urban capitals of modernism—London, Paris, and New York—Woolf, West, and Barnes all explored other regions in their lives and writing—France, Spain, Germany, the Balkans, Greece, Constantinople, and Africa. They all write of both urban and country settings, though Barnes's preference was clearly the city, perhaps because of her early initiation to her family's odd species of farming.[20]

There are some intriguing similarities in their early nurture—the details of which are reserved for the next chapter. All came from troubled families, by standards of both their own day and ours. Barnes and West had fathers who failed to support their households adequately, thus upsetting a basic expectation of the patriarchal family. Both Woolf and Barnes have been convincingly presented as incest survivors, and West may have been one as well. Literary and artistic talent existed in all three families: for Woolf, Sir Leslie Stephen (eminent biographer), Julia Stephen (writer of children's stories and articles on nursing), and Vanessa Bell (painter); for West, Charles Fairfield (journalist) and Isabella Fairfield (pianist); for Barnes, Zadel Barnes Gustafson (poet and journalist) and Wald Barnes (private inventor and musician).

The educations of Woolf, West, and Barnes owed much more to reading than to formal instruction. Though universities were open to women in their day, this form of education was denied them out of family preference or economic lack. Though she praised some of her teachers, West grew impatient with the courses offered at her secondary school, a working women's college. At nineteen she went off to London for dramatic training, to which she proved ill suited. Barnes's father defied the public school system to keep his children at home for their education. It was not until Barnes was on her own that she managed a few art classes at the Pratt Institute. Her habits as an autodidact continued late into life, when she immersed herself in her own copy of the OED. Woolf also had parental tutoring. Women's higher education was not a priority for the Stephen family. Later she had her celebrated run of her father's admirable library, a few language classes, and tutors in Greek and Latin. Woolf's father, her brothers, and their Bloomsbury male friends such as Clive Bell and Roger Fry regularly suggested what she should read, presenting her with books as gifts. The male penchant for recommending worthwhile reading comes in for satire in her first novel, *The Voyage Out*. Thus none of these women had a standard reading list or a set of approved approaches, though they all read voraciously. When called upon for a fairly typical first writing sample, the book or theater review, they began with few rules or assumptions.

In their mature lives, both Barnes and Woolf had important lesbian love relationships, while sustaining affectionate relationships with both homosexual and heterosexual men. They were working with lesbian identifications and expressive forms at a time when the "sexology" of Havelock Ellis and Edward Carpenter and the developmental theories of Freud were just becoming known, and long before their problematics were discussed in feminist terms.

West, on the other hand, had a heterosexual crisis, bequeathed in part by the sexual liberation of the new woman. She endured unwed maternity, lifelong identification as the mistress of the sexual libertarian H. G. Wells, and persecution as a bad mother by her only child, Anthony West. Maternity was much considered by all of these writers, both in looking back to their mothers and in considering their own choice of roles, which involved unconventional situating of maternal functions.

For too long, Virginia Woolf served as a solo representative of female modernists. She was the first to suggest to me that a new view of modernism was in order, and that the study of women needed to be conducted differently. Woolf will often yield to West or Barnes as we chart attachments in volume 1. Indeed, the evidence centered around 1928 suggests that West was much more active and wide-ranging in her associations, offering a better means for re-webbing modernism. But in addressing crucial questions about modernism, Barnes takes a more radical direction, leading to the most unusual findings. In volume 2 I look to each of these three writers, in turn, to answer questions about modernist concerns and form that seem most urgent in our postmodern era.

Rebecca West has offered a seemingly inexhaustible archive for this project, including thousands of letters and autobiographical manuscripts—some of the latter in print. With her there is a major problem of coping with different versions of the same relationship. Barnes remains the hardest figure to reach, having deliberately silenced herself in the twenties and resisted contacts with academics and biographers in her later years. Her archive, though rich, has lamentable holes in the late twenties period that interests me most, and her output was relatively small. Woolf's archive of letters, diaries, and drafts is much better known and relatively accessible in print, so that the problem here has been to use known materials in new ways, particularly as suggested in the three-author plan. All three say things that matter about both writing and modernism, in syntax that challenges and involves readers. They defy a unified account, even of their modernism, and certainly of modernism in general. They bring a long line of critical work to a new accounting.

En route to this book, I sat down for afternoon tea with Rebecca West in her Kensington apartment. She was then eighty-eight, a sturdy woman of middle height, assisted by, but not dependent upon, a walking stick. She wore comfortable-looking woolen slacks and a sweater—garb she apologized for, but which made her seem much more contemporary and approachable than the more formal dress I had equated with a Dame Commander of the British Empire. I had made the appointment that very morning, on the last day of a research trip to England, thanks to Richard Ellmann's suggestion and Samuel Hynes's directing me to a standard telephone directory. West rightly guessed that I had assumed she was dead. It amused her to offer a vigorous refutation. In some ways, West gave me what her biographer, Victoria Glendinning, describes as a fairly standard performance for her late years, complete with a vehement rejection of Shaw and Tolstoy and a description of her current writing of memoirs concerning her parents (organized posthumously as *Family Memories* by Faith Evans). By gesturing to paintings and sketches, West brought into the discussion her husband, who had purchased one painting out of penance for receiving a traffic summons, and a relative who did the sketches before disappearing into India, dying there at an early age.[21] However performative on her part, the meeting was also preconstructed on mine.

As I approached Rebecca West, walking down Hyde Park, I thought about a lost grandmother, Bhima, who would have been about her age. I experienced very little of "Grandma Bee." I dimly recall from my fourth year Bhima's brief appearance, made when she had an eye operation in New York City. She sat in a corner chair wearing dark glasses and hugged me, apologizing for not being able to offer a firmer embrace. Her watercolor paintings of seascapes in Maine and fighting skunks have come down to me, along with flapper jewelry and scrapbooks. Various photos show her marching with a plumed hat and a suffragette banner, entertaining pilots in 1917, and staying in Paris sometime in the 1920s. She had carefully preserved examples of German propaganda posted in Belgium at the outbreak of World War I. Bhima and my grandfather, who were later divorced, had some connection to the Provincetown Players in the early teens. But Bhima was largely erased from my childhood. She was described to me in hushed tones as an alcoholic. My mother had felt neglected by her as a child and imperiled as a young adult when they shared an apartment in New York. When Bhima died, we collected her things from an island cabin in the Adirondacks, where she had lived and painted

Plate 4. Bhima Husted Burton, 1908.

alone. In many ways, Bhima is more evocative of the reclusive, imbibing Djuna Barnes than Rebecca West. Her mystery flickers behind all the artistic young women of her age, who were hidden for a generation or more.

As we talked, Rebecca West asked about the writers I was reading, hoping to discover some new female talent in the U.S. She was eager to discuss the fortunes of feminism and of contemporary women writers: "I don't think women have much more opportunity now to write than they did in my youth. They can do many more practical things, but they are not advanced in writing." Women's advancement was something we valued in common. She mentioned women writers she would have liked to promote more in her reviewing and the satisfaction of getting commissions to review Virginia Woolf. She battled with two pairs of thick glasses hanging from cords around her neck, hunting for an article she had done on Harriet Shaw Weaver which would help with my research. She recalled circumstances at the feminist periodical where she worked, the *New Freewoman*—evidence useful in this study.

West had determination that was catching. She said that her regular book reviews were done "to rob age of its terrors." She talked about the indignities and horrors of a failing body—the outrage she felt when she was unable to bathe herself during an illness. She sought an explanation for seizures of a few minutes' duration, when she found herself making sounds without meaning. She considered her failures in hearing and seeing at least partly psychological, connecting them to upsetting circumstances. She avowed that she should will their control. "Consciousness is a battle," she said, "an exercise in will." Out of my brief connection to West, as part of my battle for consciousness of her generation, comes this effort of attachment.

Part One: *Beginnings*

1   (Dys)functional Families

> I was obsessed by them both, unhealthily; & writing of them was a neces-
> sary act.
>
> —Virginia Woolf of her parents, 3 D 208

> My sister really saw me as grotesquely ugly, badly behaved and stupid, as
> abnormal as an epileptic or a Mongolian idiot.
>
> —Rebecca West of Letitia Fairfield, *Family Memories* 202

> I always thought I was my grandmother.
>
> —Djuna Barnes, quoted in Broe, ed. 4

The family is typically the first ordering structure, or scaffolding, encountered in life. Whatever aptitudes we may be born with, the family soon
influences our self-esteem, creative expression, capacity to form relationships, and attitudes toward gender, sexuality, race, and class. In the twentieth century, the nuclear family, composed of the marital partners of
father and mother plus their offspring, was treated as a social and psychological norm, even as it became less pervasive. Freud saw the resolution of the Oedipus complex as the critical incident of libidinal and social development.[1] Post-Freudians worked out relations to language along
comparably gendered familial lines. To the late Victorians in the United
States as well as Britain, maintenance of the ideal of a peaceful family
sphere was a woman's assignment. Analyzing the family as a flawed institution decidedly was not. Yet Virginia Woolf, Rebecca West, and Djuna
Barnes all take on this shift in assignment, reifying it in autobiographical
writing.

Did skewed and stressed familial scaffoldings somehow condition or
provision the emergence of Woolf, West, and Barnes as highly original
writers? The Stephen, Fairfield, and Barnes families were compounded of
complex marital histories. Second marriages gave rise to half-brothers
and -sisters, complicating parental affiliations and sibling relations. The
three girls who became the central writers of this study were subject to
stern or eccentric controls. Their childhoods were fractured further by
illness, death, and abandonment. Shockingly, it is possible that all three

experienced incest. Their families all had exceptional members to contribute to the girls' inborn genius and to their intellectual and creative environments, but this was a mixed inheritance. Gifted relations of both sexes tormented Woolf, West, and Barnes with their extraordinary expectations and demands.

While the written accounts of Woolf, West, and Barnes can contribute to an understanding of their attachments to and detachments from the family, these are treacherous materials to work with. They exist in many versions, forms, and frames of time, presenting inconsistencies and contradictions, admitting fantasy and disguise. Relatively little work has been done leading to an understanding of Barnes's family; even less is available on West's. Louise DeSalvo's startling revision of Woolf's family history in terms of childhood sexual abuse is a dramatic example of how the Victorian familial ideal stands to be deconstructed, though hers is not the only model. DeSalvo has threaded the gap of previous accounts, giving new meaning to previously detected attachments, and detecting a code of abuse in Woolf's designs. However, abuse, as detected in all three families, is but one factor in the complex histories of Woolf, West, and Barnes.

Hyde Park Gate News

Adeline Virginia Stephen Woolf's family was fused from previous marriages, both Julia Jackson Duckworth and Sir Leslie Stephen having outlived their original spouses. Thus there were siblings of three different matches—children differing by as much as sixteen years in age. The Duckworth set—George, Stella, and Gerald—clung to values of the Victorian social elite. Vanessa, Thoby, Virginia, and Adrian, born in rapid succession between 1879 and 1883, turned toward intellectual and creative pursuits.[2] One of the earliest of these was their family paper, the *Hyde Park Gate News*, begun by Thoby and Virginia when she was nine. Laura, the sole child of Leslie Stephen's previous marriage, gradually faded from the picture. DeSalvo summarizes the evidence of stern parental discipline in response to Laura's tantrums, which often arose in reaction to home instruction (see chapter 1). Laura was at first kept apart from the younger children. Virginia referred to her in the *Hyde Park Gate News* in engulfing, Arthurian terms as "Our Lady of the Lake." She was eventually institutionalized as a "backward" child, the diagnosis advanced by Sir

Leslie. This is one of many judgments challenged by DeSalvo, who suggests that Laura's fate served as a threat to the younger Stephen girls.

Woolf's relationship to her brother, Thoby, has been ably described by Sara Ruddick in "Private Brother, Public World." Thoby led the expeditions for moths that survive in her novels, and shared his books on the Greeks and his love of Shakespeare with his youngest sister. On the more negative side, Ruddick suggests, he "most certainly refused to see or hear his sisters' justified anger at the restrictions imposed by their domestic world" (188). In a notebook kept around 1905, Woolf wrote of the "burden of G & G" (her elder half-brothers), with whom "Thoby and & A[drian] no help" while "V & I struggled together." She gives indications that, while Thoby resented his mother's authority, Adrian was her favorite.[3] Woolf's attachment to Thoby helped produce an understanding of herself and her culture. In *Moments of Being,* Woolf records the "violent shock," in the midst of their mutual pummeling on the lawn at St. Ives, when she asked herself, "Why hurt another person?" She then allowed herself to be beaten by Thoby (71).

By all accounts, the death of Julia Stephen in May 1885, when Virginia was thirteen, shattered the family structure. Woolf wrote "Reminiscences" around 1907 for Vanessa's first child, Julian, whose very name suggests their mother.[4] In this account, Woolf describes Julia Stephen as "impetuous and also a little imperious." Unwilling to trust someone else with her children's early education, and unable to delegate social projects and responsibilities, she eventually "sank like an exhausted swimmer" (*MB* 39). Thinking back through the sensibility of the teenagers she and Vanessa were in 1885, Woolf tells her young nephew that her mother's death was "the greatest disaster that could happen." And despite the earlier hint of her sternness, Woolf closes her account to Julian with a haunting note: "Now and again on more occasions than I can number, in bed at night, or in the street, or as I come into the room, there she is; beautiful, emphatic, with her familiar phrase and her laugh; closer than any of the living are, lighting our random lives as with a burning torch, infinitely noble and delightful to her children" (40). The first epigraph for this chapter reminds us of Woolf's exorcism of mother and father in *To the Lighthouse.* In "Professions for Women," written in 1931, the Julia-like angel in the house is assassinated lest she inhibit the critical voice of the professional woman writer (285–86). This detachment is comedic—the assault coming from a hurled ink bottle—but deliberate.[5]

"Reminiscences" thrusts the family into a "period of Oriental gloom" with the death of Julia—the phrase mildly mocking the mood (40). Leslie Stephen had lost his primary source of sympathy at a time when he had turned from his much-heralded biographical work. He was ill suited to single parenthood and thus depended upon his female relations. Woolf records Stella Duckworth's efforts to serve as handmaiden to her stepfather, noting that she had been equally angelic to their mother. As an aftershock to their mother's death, Stella died soon after marriage, when Virginia was fifteen. Following this second maternal loss, Vanessa appears heroic in "Reminiscences." Refusing to become the next "victim" of their father's "tyranny," she was Virginia's buffer and a model of alternate female conduct (56). In the same diary entry cited in the epigraph, written in 1928, on what would have been her deceased father's ninety-sixth birthday, Woolf imagines what her life would have been like if, "like other people one has known," Sir Leslie were still alive. "His life would have entirely ended mine. What would have happened? No writing, no books;— inconceivable" (3 D 208). Is this an exaggeration?

Leslie and Julia Stephen did permit Virginia and Vanessa creative work—Vanessa was early identified as the painter and attended art classes; Virginia was the writer. Her parents read the *Hyde Park Gate News* with apparent pleasure, despite its satirical edge, which often took digs at elder relations. Virginia was kept well stocked with serious, challenging reading material by her father, as is very evident in her earliest surviving diary, kept in 1897. Her "Reminiscences" seize at fleeting moments of value when he tried to help them use their sorrow "to quicken the feeling that remained," or was "exquisitely tender" (46), but finally admits that the gulf of age inhibited connection.

In the 1897 diary, Woolf began expressing her skepticism about the Victorian family ideals still held by much of her family. She gives a mocking account of Stella Duckworth's wedding, which was done with all the trappings of Victorian custom, at the behest of various aunts, Sir Leslie, and the Duckworth half-brothers. She expresses amazement at what they were wearing and doing, scrupulously setting down the details of errands, visits, receptions, purchases of clothing, a tagged displays of gifts, and copious acknowledgments. After a fitting, she reports being "forced to wear certain underclothing for the first time in my life" (PA 64). Of the final events she writes, "Good gracious what a week this unfortunate diary will have to contain!" (66). There is an amusing account of going to hear the banns, involving a series of half-compliances with religious ritual—a rummaging about the house for hymnals and prayer books and blundering through the service: "At certain parts we stood, then sat, and finally knelt—this last I refused to do. . . . Our prayers and psalms were rather guess work—but the hymns were splendid." She remarks that, to the announcement of the banns of Jack Waller Hills and Stella Duckworth, "no one pronounced any reason why etc. etc" (61), as if she'd have been happier with the dramatic turn of events in *Jane Eyre*. The final rite, urged by George Duckworth, was leaving some of Stella's flowers on their mother's grave at Highgate Cemetery. This accomplished, according to her own report, young Virginia turned eagerly to several volumes of Pepys, so as to get a new book from her father. Here was her own attachment, both to books and to her father's regard.

The diary hints at behavioral as well as authorial resistance to the constraints placed upon her activities. Young Virginia notes when she has been "tantrumical" and heads some entries with an "O," perhaps a code for the condition of her physical or mental health. A fictional aspect of herself, "Miss Jan," sometimes gets assigned the outraged behavior, as De-Salvo has noted. The records in Woolf's early diary make it clear that Stella was an agent of patriarchy in the family, carrying out the health regimen doctors had prescribed for Virginia after she suffered a mental breakdown in 1895. Accordingly, the aspiring writer was given a spade to dig in the garden instead of lessons. She accompanied the saintly Stella on tedious rounds of errands and visits. Stella "the old cow" was too mild to invite rebellion.

Memoirs of various time periods and forms provide the dramatic disclosure of incest perpetrated on Virginia Woolf by both of her half-brothers. When she was seven, Gerald Duckworth stood Virginia on a shelf in their St. Ives summer home and probed her vagina—an experience that left her with feelings of guilt. George used the excuse of offering comfort at the time of their mother's death to impose the erotic fondlings of a lover upon both Virginia and Vanessa. In his introduction to Woolf's early journals, Mitchell Leaska expresses the opinion that feminists have been too hard on George Duckworth as incest perpetrator. Leaska catalogues the many lunches and treats, such as "the most gorgeous strawberry ices" he provided, as evidence of a very different account from the one of sexual abuse that he dates at 1939, when Woolf wrote her most extended memoir, "A Sketch of the Past." George's strawberry ices are better read as a part of the system of control. Leaska speculates further, "The Duckworth brothers, guilty as they might have been of sexual interference, very probably became the despised objects on to which she could attach the deeply disturbing fantasies she herself harbored for her father" (xxxiv–xxxv). The "fantasies" go unidentified. It should be noted that Woolf's story of her half-brothers' passions began emerging long before 1939. There is the notation of the "burden of G & G" cited above from the 1905 notebook. George's peculiar affections are suggested in two places in the 1907 memoir. Woolf says in her third chapter, "George insisted upon a closer and more mature friendship; Gerald even became for the time serious and sentimental" (MB 44). She is less euphemistic toward the end of the memoir, when she compares the two "other" Duckworth brothers:

> Gerald, strange though it may seem, represented intellect in the contest. George was in truth, a stupid, good natured young man, of profuse, voluble affections, which during his mother's lifetime were kept in check. When she died however, some restraint seemed to have burst; he showed himself so sad, so affectionate, so boundlessly unselfish in his plans, that the voices of all women cried aloud in his praise, and men were touched by his modest virtues, at the same time that they were puzzled. . . . Thus, under the name of unselfishness he allowed himself to commit acts which a cleverer man would have called tyrannical, and, profoundly believing in the purity of his love, he behaved little better than a brute. (57–58)

In the early twenties, Woolf is more specific and outspoken about tyrannies and brutality in both letters and "Old Bloomsbury," a sketch written for presentation to the Memoir Club, answering some of the puzzled men (MB 160). Leaska suggests further that if Woolf "entrusted her first two novels" to Gerald Duckworth's publishing firm, she could not have been traumatized (xxxiv–xxxv). Instead, I see this pattern as proof of how difficult it was to escape the power structure of her literary family, and of sexually exploratory, directive Edwardian males, who become the topic of the next chapter.

21 Streatham Place

Rebecca West was the product of an apparently troubled marriage. One of three daughters, she was conceived six years after Winifred, her closest sibling in age. Winifred hypothesized that West's birth was the result of a brief parental reconciliation.[6] Charles Fairfield and Isabella

Mackenzie had met in Australia, where both had been seeking a turn in their fortunes. A talented pianist and formerly a musical governess, Isabella had come out from Edinburgh to recover from a romantic disappointment and to check up on a wayward, drunkard brother. By then middle-aged, Charles Fairfield had begun as a military man but turned toward journalism as his major occupation. Fairfield specialized in financial predictions and antisocialist politics, championing the ideals of Herbert Spencer, with whom he corresponded. On an early adventure in the United States, Fairfield had looked in on the Civil War. A marriage contracted in Virginia, discovered after his death, had apparently produced a son and a divorce. The latter event was perhaps in reaction to his decamping to Colorado, where he served for a brief interval as a sheriff.[7] Fairfield began his journalism in a remote mining town. In Australia he presented himself as a caricaturist and turned to writing financial and political articles for the Melbourne *Argus*. When their Australian fortunes faded, soon after the birth of Winifred, the Fairfields settled first in Glasgow, and then more permanently in south London, where Cicely Isabel Fairfield was born.

The first memories of this third daughter are of a functional family unit living at Streatham Place, the home idealized in her novel *The Fountain Overflows*. Its intellectual atmosphere was made up of a mother's music and a father's writing late into the night, of literary discussions between the parents, and books read by all. The values of this oddly impoverished family are seen as superior to the neighbors'. In the last book published in her lifetime, *1900*, West represents the family circa 1898, returning from a walk to a later home in Richmond-on-Thames. The parents conduct a pleasant and politically instructive dialogue relating to the recent death of William Ewart Gladstone—the last in a line of prime ministers who had the look of a "stern and wise and honoured father" (6). Their own family order was short-lived after that. In 1901 Fairfield left the family to seek a fortune in Sierra Leone. He never returned to them, dying in 1906, apparently alone and without possessions, in a Liverpool rooming house.

In a letter to her elder sister, Lettie, West reports that a "disguised father fixation" had been discovered in psychoanalytic sessions she underwent in 1927 (West letter to Letitia Fairfield, 1927, private). In her own notebook on the analysis, West gives fragmentary records and comments upon what she labeled a "father violation memory." She began with a "moderately painful" memory of her mother's applying a mustard plaster and preventing "infant's masturbation." Slowly other images emerged—a "memory of penis seen through cot bars uncovered," and days later "father exciting nipples and face of father during orgasm," and "offering tip of penis to mouth" and "masturbating beside child" (*Sunflower* notebook, Tulsa). She also recorded an "animal fantasy" sprung from a "suspicion of my father urinating in the grove in garden." It contained the logic "Animals free from taboos in sex. . . . If my father and I were animals we would be free to enjoy each other" (*Sunflower* notebook). What actually occurred is impossible to say. Even West speculated that, under the influence of her analyst, she might have imagined it all. Certainly she suffered from paternal abandonment and decidedly mixed emotions about her father's sexuality.

Over the years, West made many things of Charles Fairfield and his desertion of the family when she was only eight. Being deliberate, his departure instilled guilt in West. The event may have been even more traumatic than Woolf's loss of her mother. A poem West wrote at the time ended with "the anguish of a soul / that finds its twin has faithless been" ("Juvenilia" ms., Yale). As an adolescent, West apparently grew to hate her Aunt Sophie (wife of Charles Fairfield's brother, Arthur) for telling stories of her father's youthful vices.[8]

West's own account of her father in *Family Memories* begins romantically with the ebb and flow of Fairfield family fortunes in Ireland. The Fairfields had a small estate in County Kerry, a Dublin townhouse, and a London residence, all lost by her widowed grandmother. In establishing her own addresses in London and in the country, and in collecting fine furnishings and paintings, West approached the lost style of her ancestors. Though she never forgot her father's claim to gentility, she denounced his Protestant Irish snobbery. One peculiar proclamation of this exists in a letter written to another Anglo-Irish exile, George Bernard Shaw, in 1922: "He married my mother, who was a great pianist, and destroyed her musical genius and ruined her life with the most complete and well-mannered imperturbability, because she came of low people of peasant extraction" (Letter to Shaw, British Library). A family story credits Charles Fairfield with outdoing a much younger Shaw in an all-night debate at Conway Hall (*FM* 194). West attributes to her father a Shavian style that she may well have imitated (*FM* 164). West claimed that her father had received an extraordinary education from a French anarchist, Elie Reclus. She did not partake of Charles Fairfield's ideology, which was ardently antisocialist, though her own conservative notions of the state, expressed in the 1950s, may owe something to him.[9]

West closes her section on "My Father" in *Family Memories* with a scene from her early childhood. Charles Fairfield watched her as she disinterred chestnuts she had buried, playing at a God who had made people die so that she might have the fun of resurrecting them. As he went on looking at her "with a gusto which soon puzzled" her, she took this as an expression of love and ran to embrace him "round his neck and was swung up into his tobacco-ish warmth" (208). Years later her mother provided his thoughts, which were the prediction of "a great future for me rather on the lines of the atheist Popes of the middle ages" (208). More important than his love, she had his endorsement of her own mode of authority.

She also felt that she carried his curse, which was a denial of family. It began by his being "continually and frenetically unfaithful to my mother" (203) and ended with the desertion. Even as a child of five she sensed that something was amiss when he took her to an out-of-the-way cottage that displayed a sloppy sign advertising teas. Too young to have any "idea of the sexual mechanism," she could already read the ingredients of sexual seduction as he spoke to the handsome black-haired woman who offered the tea and "smirked under his eyes." West "never felt quite the same about my father again" (204). Late in life, she could generalize with a vengeance, having the experience of "a mistress—a silly word, it suggests a gaiety not at all relevant—and as a wife, which suggests a stability also not guaranteed":

> Men have nearly all such extra-marital relationships out of hostility to their wives, not that they have any personal hostility to them, but they dislike women in general, and a wife is one woman who has got the law on her side and they punish her by denying her sexual satisfaction. (FM 203)

West's ideas about deserting wives would adversely affect her relations with both her son and her grandson when they divorced.

Female-headed households were not a rarity in West's family. Isabella Mackenzie Fairfield and Charles Fairfield had both been reared by widowed mothers. West's maternal grandmother, Janet Campbell Mackenzie, was widowed with six children while still in her twenties. She became the successful proprietor of an Edinburgh lace shop, assisted with the children by one of her sisters. West summarizes this woman-trained family: "Armed with their own talents, they faced a world which they knew would guarantee their well-being only if they insisted, but this did not perturb them" (FM 31). West's *Family Memories*, assembled after her death

(Dys)functional Families 11

from many-versioned manuscripts, goes back through these single-parent mothers with care. West also attends to talent, recalling her grandfather's abilities on the violin, her mother's on the piano, and the eminence of her uncle Alick, who rose to president of the Royal Academy of Music in London. Always an analyst of family dynamics, she attributed his success to his being first-born (FM 19). She collects characters, such as the self-serving Mary Ironside, whose marriage to Uncle Alick supposedly destroyed the unity of the family, and her Australian aunt Lizzie, the proverbial prostitute with a heart of gold, who was essential to her mother's survival in Australia.

West's psychoanalysis suggested problems with the discipline of her household, which she attributed not to her father but to her mother and sisters. In a 1928 letter, West presents a Calvinist sensibility understandable from her mother's Edinburgh origins and the family's resettlement there:

> I have the type of mind that in less favourable conditions than mine would conceive the idea it had been guilty of the sin against the Holy Ghost. This disposition was intensified by my upbringing—I was the youngest of my family by nine years, and my mother and sisters were very fond and proud of me, and I was an infant prodigy. In order to prevent me from becoming conceited and spoiled they subjected me without cease to the most merciless criticism. (West letter to Hugh Walpole, 19 Sept. 1928, Texas)

The brunt of the early discovery of persecution was to be sustained by West's successful eldest sister,[10] Letitia Fairfield. Cordelia, the less talented, persecuting eldest child of *The Fountain Overflows* and its sequels, is often attributed to Lettie, though oddly that book was also dedicated to her. In *Family Memories* Lettie is offered as a case history of sibling rivalry—the sullen older sister who always regarded West as an intruder (201). West reports her childhood feeling: "If she denounced me she must be right. A burning sense of guilt brought me to tears. I was halfway on her side, and the seriousness of that can be judged from the fact that my sister really saw me as grotesquely ugly, badly behaved and stupid, as abnormal as an epileptic or a Mongolian idiot" (202). West's letters directed to her sister in 1908, when she was fifteen, are addressed to "Cow," in a startling echo of the name given to Virginia Woolf's much older half-sister, Stella Duckworth. West signs her adolescent letters "Your loving baby" or "Your affectionate baby," suggesting that her eldest sister took on the role of a

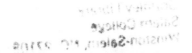

parent, with West playing the coddled infant.[11] That West was the petted youngest child has been suspected by Victoria Glendinning, based on a photograph that shows little Cissie being fed berries by her older sisters and female cousins. Both scenarios allow for authority wielded by the older sister. This the youngest child came to resent and learned to subvert in her writing.

Letitia Fairfield trained in medicine and law and was the author of four books.[12] She had a distinguished career in medical administration for the London County Council. In one interview, West lauds the feminist nature of the Fairfield household during her teen years, which was largely to Lettie's credit (Warner). With her interest in Fabian socialism and her pursuit of advanced education, Lettie helped to set the wide horizon of the professional woman for her younger sister. Lettie rallied to West's support on several occasions, including both the birth and the defection of West's son, Anthony. In later years, whenever she traveled, West maintained an active correspondence with Lettie, which now offers invaluable insights into her professional growth. But unlike Virginia Woolf's supervising sister, Stella Duckworth, Lettie was as headstrong and very possibly as intelligent as her younger sister. These Fairfield sisters had an enduring capacity to argue with one another, which Victoria Glendinning captures in the opening pages of her biography of West (5–6). One lasting source of envy must have been that Lettie had years longer to be a favorite with their father, who continued to use her as a go-between even after he left the family. Lettie's fatal flaw with her more dramatic, adventuresome younger sister was to constantly criticize, with an eye toward making West more presentable to the public. Lettie's bossiness has been confirmed by their niece, Alison Selford, and nephew, Norman Macleod. But Selford was shocked by West's portrayals of Lettie in fiction, and seems to have preferred her elder aunt.[13] In some ways Letitia and Cicily Fairfield were made for each other, bonded in argument for the duration of their long lives.

Cornwall-on-Hudson

The Introduction has already proclaimed the extraordinary fact that Djuna Barnes was born into a bigamous household—a remnant perhaps of numerous nineteenth-century rural utopian schemes in the United States, or freethinking encountered by elder generations in England. The family occupied a wooden two-story chalet on land owned by Wald Barnes's brother in Cornwall-on-Hudson. The family was composed of Wald, his British wife, Elizabeth Chappell Barnes, his mistress, Fannie Faulkner, and the two resulting sets of children. Wald's mother, Zadel Barnes Gustafson, was a frequent visitor. The children were all home-educated, in defiance of school authorities. Though insular, it was a creative environment. Wald composed never-performed operas and proffered unusual theories of gender and sexuality, most centered upon his own procreativity. Barnes's 1928 novel, *Ryder*, suggests that he played diverse instruments and told mythical stories of his own compounding. Zadel conducted educational seances, summoning her favorite authors, most often Oscar Wilde and Jack London, for her grandchildren's edification. She also sent books and domestic instructions to her eldest granddaughter, Djuna, whom she tried to use as a peacemaker between the Chappell and Faulkner factions. The family seems to have subsisted upon desultory farm operations, Zadel's income as a successful writer and journalist, and later her maternal applications to old friends for funds. Unlike Woolf and West, Barnes eschewed writing memoirs, though *Ryder* and *The Antiphon* have been mined for autobiographical content by her critics and biographers. Clues to her family situation are widely scattered in family letters (many of them preserved in the University of Maryland archive), Barnes's correspondence with friends, and these friends' recording of her rare disclosures.

Unlike Woolf and West, Barnes did not maintain regular or close sibling relationships. Given her father's emphasis upon fertility and the intimacy of the household, Barnes was much more aware than Woolf or West of the physical nature of childbirth. She witnessed numerous confinements and consequently was not eager to have children of her own. (She had an abortion when she was forty.) Barnes was closer to her mother's sons, Saxon, Shangar (who went by Charles), and Thurn, than to the offspring of Fannie Faulkner, Duane and Muriel. Though she was the second-eldest child, she resisted mothering her siblings, reserving this role for later relationships with female friends and intimates. As an adult, she alternately praises and resents Saxon in her letters. Perhaps in reaction to their unorthodox upbringing, Barnes's siblings became much more conventional than she. Saxon has cooperated with editors and biographers, and her half-brother Duane and his son Kerron have shared family archives, though Philip Herring suggests that the two sides of the family still do not communicate (111).

Zadel was probably the source of ideas about free love and an uncon-

Plate 5. Zadel Barnes (Buddington) Gustafson, 1891.
Barnes Family Papers, Special Collections,
University of Maryland at College Park Libraries.

ventional family structure perpetuated and adapted by her son. Her first marriage, to her Latin teacher, seems to have been precipitated by pregnancy. It ended in divorce, as did a second marriage to a Swede, Axel Gustafson, who made a name for himself (with Zadel's help) as a temperance writer. In addition to the temperance work, Zadel's political activism included militant unionism during the Civil War and support of the suffrage movement. She spoke at the 1888 International Council of Women Convention in Washington, D.C., and hosted a party for Elizabeth Cady Stanton that is recalled in Stanton's letters. Zadel had lived in London in the early 1880s and entertained stage and literary figures at Grosvenor Place. Barnes would call her establishment a salon, evoking it nostalgically to Natalie Barney, whose Paris salon Barnes inhabited: "I think of all of us with amazement and antique amused affection—hip boots, Russian hats, our capes, our polemics for and against freedom and love. And I recall my grandmother, and her salon and her friend Willie Wilde, Browning, Elizabeth Cady Stanton, and scandals of Stead and God knows what, and are the children then, today so mad? Or rather, when will inbred folly dis-prevail?" (Barnes letter to Barney, 10 Sept. 1967, Maryland). Speranza Wilde and Victoria Woodhull, who shared London with Zadel in the 1880s, may have been sources for her spiritualist, suffragist, and free-love ideals (Herring 110). It was during these London years that Wald Barnes met Elizabeth Chappell.

Zadel Barnes was the primary literary model for Djuna—the woman whom she confused with herself, as suggested in the epigraph and the letter to Barney. Zadel was a successful journalist in the 1870s and 1880s. Her many articles and verses for *Harper's Monthly Magazine* set a model of productivity for Djuna, even if she would strive for very different form and content. Among her articles were interviews with notables, including Swedish royalty, stories about disadvantaged child laborers, and fairytale fantasies, replete with little-girl characters, which were in particular demand for Christmas numbers. Zadel is the only family member to haunt *Nightwood*, where she has her counterpart in the grandmother who appears in a dream sequence. Zadel prefigures the lusty, crafty, and culturally connected grandmother, Sophia, of *Ryder*. She has a small part in the memory of adult brothers and sister in *The Antiphon*.

Djuna Barnes's story of incest is much more complex and calculated than Woolf's destructive encounters with Gerald and George Duckworth, though as with Woolf and even West, we encounter abuse in many versions over the years. Letters suggest that her first experience of physical love may have been with her grandmother. Barnes's mother also sent physically evocative letters when they were separated, however, and sexually suggestive discourse may have been the family custom. Zadel's letters written from 1905 to 1909 are densely coded and illustrated. They feature drawings of Zadel's "pink tops" or breasts and suggest other erotic zones and pleasures in "flitch" and "starbits" (see Broe, "My Art" 42, Herring 112, and particularly Dalton, whose article provides partial transcripts and reproduces two of the illustrations). Zadel looks forward to sharing a bed with Djuna when her granddaughter is well into her teens. Barnes's family-centered fiction suggests that Djuna was obsessed, inseparably, with both her father and grandmother, and aware of another close physical and mental bond between them.

Andrew Field has used Barnes's supposed hatred of her father as a central thesis of his biography, *Djuna: The Formidable Miss Barnes* (31). A doubly suppressed scenario of a daughter's sexual abuse by her father is suggested in censored early drafts of *The Antiphon*, and it is recorded at a double remove in the journal of one of her writer friends, Emily Holmes Coleman. At fifteen or sixteen, Barnes was probably forced to comply with her father's ideas of virginal sexual initiation, with the complicity of both her mother and grandmother, even as younger brothers looked on. In her typed diary, Coleman reports a rare disclosure:

> Djuna told me yesterday morning . . . all about her youth and adolescence—it is plain why she turned to a Lesbian love—sex was horrible to her—her father—a horror of the first water, what a terrible man—and she had to make love to his friend at 16 to please him, to start her off, supposed to marry him. Violence, fights and horror were all she knew in her childhood, no one loving her except her grandmother—whom she passionately loved. Her father when she was 16, behaved in a way so inconceivable that one does not know why such persons are not wiped off the earth. He tried to make love to her—she was washing dishes—he came out and said, "Now youre 16 Ive always wanted to know you then."

Coleman scribbles through the words "removed his organ from his trousers" and writes in pen "(I really can't see it)" (Ts Diary 425). The account continues, "Djuna fled to the barn where she was found screaming by her mother who went after her father with a meat-axe" (425).

Soon after this episode, Djuna was encouraged by her father and grandmother to accept as her mate Percy Faulkner, the fifty-two-year-old brother of her father's mistress, Fannie Faulkner. Zadel may have regarded it as a temporary arrangement, like her own first marriage, easing the family situation. Djuna went off with Faulkner to live in Bridgeport. Two years later, Elizabeth Barnes forced Wald to choose between spouses. He opted for Fannie, divorcing Elizabeth. Barnes stayed in contact with her mother, sharing an apartment with her at intervals when she returned to New York, first from Bridgeport and later, in the twenties through forties, from her sojourns in Paris and London. Elizabeth Barnes's interest in Christian Science was as hard for Djuna as the Calvinism of her maternal line was for West. Woolf, West, and Barnes were all fascinated with the mother as victim of a family structure she had not defined.

Writing many times over these family situations became both a cure and a literary resource, as will be evident in the more detailed tracing of the fictional designs of Woolf, West, and Barnes in volume 2.

The families that produced Woolf, West, and Barnes, and the familial structures they devised in later life, are as remarkable for their defects and ambivalence as for their rare and momentary supports. Woolf, West, and Barnes gradually remember the guilt, pain, and powerlessness of girlhood, deriving a cast of family ghosts and emotional situations for their later writing, and perhaps the need to burrow back in memory through a succession of ever more revealing images. Their autobiographical writing suggests that they learned through observation of custom and conversation, in families where intelligent and eccentric people had and expressed ideas. Deliberate instruction, whether at school or in the home, was probably less important than the availability of books, variously given and voraciously read. In touching upon their adult alternatives to the family, we get somewhat ahead of our account, for many of their selections came from the cultural matrices that lay beyond the family. It should be clear, however, that the maturing Woolf, West, and Barnes produced new stresses upon the normative family model. They did this in part by seeking affection from a number of partners—Woolf and Barnes choosing from various sexualities, West re-finding the heterosexual infidelity that had troubled her childhood. Their art required a connection to more remote and imaginary supports than the family.

2   Edwardian Uncles

Many men, of whom Mr. Wells is the chief spokesman . . . regard
[woman's] advance with mixed feelings, and face her with a neat dilemma.
Either, they say, you must go on being Helens and Cinderellas, or you must
drop all that and play the game, in so far as your disabilities allow, as we
play it. They look forward to the emergence of an army of civilized, docile
women, following modestly behind the vanguard of males at work upon
the business of reducing chaos to order.
                    —Dorothy Richardson, "Women and the Future" 412–13

The Edwardian uncle is a fictional relation created for critical purposes
by both Virginia Woolf and Rebecca West, and easily located in the experience of Djuna Barnes. We can interpret him as a bridge from the family
scaffoldings discussed in chapter 1 to the modern literary culture that
Woolf, West, and Barnes all aspired to. Typically uncles need not be taken
as seriously as parents, or even siblings. Some are uncles in name only—
close family friends rather than blood relations. They come on visits or
occupy remote reaches of the house, giving children the opportunity to
make fun of them in private—as young Virginia Woolf did her relations
in the *Hyde Park Gate News*. Such uncles may offer gifts of dubious merit
or unwanted advice. For Woolf, there is an "avuncular" tone to the voice
of the pedagogue who mixes criticism of sex incongruously with criticism of poetry, setting suitable limits if she is to claim "some shiny prize"
(*Room* 78). "Edwardian" is a historical tag, inviting this uncle's assignment to "progressive" attitudes that take him beyond the Victorian fathers
of Woolf, West, and Barnes. He may be well established in the literary
business of publishing or reviewing books. He is probably keen on social
improvements. He has met the new woman, heard doctrines of free sex,
and may seek to combine the two, as we have noted in the case of H. G.
Wells. As a half-brother and publisher, half a generation older than Virginia Woolf and privately mocked by her, Gerald Duckworth qualifies as an
Edwardian uncle. Once she made her appearance in Greenwich Village,
Djuna Barnes found Edwardian uncles in abundance, including Courtenay Lemon, her second commonlaw partner, and Guido Bruno, publish-

er of *The Book of Repulsive Women*—the pamphlet that was her first collected work.

In essays that prepared their way into literary modernism, Woolf, West, and Barnes used various means to address the Edwardian uncle, gradually moving out of his influence. Starting with her earliest writing for the *New Freewoman* (a periodical we hear more about in the next chapter), Rebecca West was willing and able to shock her audience with pronouncements about elder males. She makes forthright judgments on literary quality, accompanied by disarmingly original comparisons and educated assignments to social, religious, or philosophical categories. In contrast to this, Woolf's critical persona is more evocative, refusing to pressure her readers into accepting her views. She plays out the interests of the Edwardians through example, leaving the suggestion that they no longer serve the perceptions of the present age. She likes to set them in domestic spaces, noting their odd behavior in conversation or at the tea table. Lurking in the background is her quarrel with Arnold Bennett, whose 1923 essay "Is the Novel Decaying?" used *Jacob's Room* as an example of the failure of contemporary writers in the creation of characters that "vitally survive in the mind."[1] In her depictions of Edwardians, Barnes builds from odd details, typically collected in a conversation that she might turn to an interview, for profit. She makes exotic comparisons and shifts among a number of questions. It often takes re-reading for her meaning and wit to emerge.

Woolf, West, and Barnes have all been cited for some literary borrowing from the recent past: Woolf from Henry James; West from George Bernard Shaw and H. G. Wells; Barnes from Aubrey Beardsley and Oscar Wilde. But they looked to older classics for a sense of literary tradition: Shakespearean drama and opera were important to all. Montaigne, Austen, and the Brontës were shared by Woolf and West, with both of them writing travel essays on Hayworth Parsonage. Barnes and West were mutual admirers of a variegated list: the Bible, Blake, Rabelais, and Mark Twain. Chaucer and the Elizabethans were common interests of Barnes and Woolf. (See figure 2.)

The verdicts of Woolf and West on Henry James stand apart from their judgments of the Edwardians. Woolf encountered James repeatedly as a child, since he was a family friend. She and Vanessa appear to have made a bit of a joke over him. In a 1907 letter, Violet Dickinson received Woolf's description of his halting attempts at conversation, attributable mainly to old age. The label of writer, which he applied to her, seems to have sat uneasily. That James went back through two generations of patrimony may also have proved trying: "My dear Virginia, they tell me—they tell me—they tell me—that you—as indeed being your father's daughter—nay your grandfather's grandchild—the descendant I may say of a century—of a century of quill pens and ink—ink—ink pots, yes, yes, yes, they tell me—ahm m m—that you, that you, that you *write* in short" (1 L 306). Woolf's 1918 review of Joseph Warren Beach's study of James, "The Method of Henry James," brushes aside Beach's notion that James was "a portentous figure looming large and underlined in the consciousness of writers" (2 E 346). She suggests that, though gradual and concerted in his development, James may have been too devout about method—a category that remains controversial in her evaluation of the moderns: "His pursuit of his method was religious in its seriousness, religious in its sacrifices, and productive, as we see from his prefaces and sketches, of a solemn rejoicing such as one can imagine in a priest to whom a vision of the divinity has been vouchsafed at last" (2 E 348). James escapes the "materialist" label she attaches to Wells, Galsworthy, and Bennett. Yet owing to his status as an American and an "exile," he is suspected of something else. This is parasitism, seen in his affection for old furniture and afternoon tea: "Their attitude not only to furniture but to life is more that of the appreciative collector than of the undoubting possessor" (348). But Woolf insists upon James's intricacy, using his own favored image of the figures in the carpet, and she admires his mature powers of conception, the "weaving together of many themes into one theme, the making out of a design." Her own quotation of his design for *The Awkward Age* offers a pattern for the experimental illumination of character that Woolf was to pursue in *Jacob's Room*. It was the first of Woolf's novels to upset the Edwardian sense of form. Woolf credits James with the following design, which I think applies well to *Jacob's Room*:

> the neat figure of a circle consisting of a number of small rounds disposed at equal distances about a central object. The central object was my situation, my subject in itself, to which the thing would owe its title, and the small rounds represented so many distinct lamps, as I like to call them, the function of each of which would be to light with all due intensity one of its aspects. (348)[2]

Rebecca West's first book, published in 1916, was a study of the recently deceased James. This was a bold move in several ways. She had selected for a largely appreciative work a man who had repudiated the working methods of H. G. Wells. But neither did she offer pure adulation. The stodgy and somewhat old-fashioned Hugh Walpole found it intolerable that the young Rebecca West could presume to criticize James in tones of authority and irreverence. Despite her own relative youth, West declares that James lacked historical sense, partaking of a distaste for politics that she thinks was forced on cultured Americans in his youth. She finds that in his later work he had lost his passion for an international subject, which meant that his unconscious was failing to provide him with "hoarded riches in the form of the right word, the magic phrase, the clarifying incident" (52). The international subject was one she would never desert; indeed she shares the designation of travel writer with James. West expresses feminist irritation with "a persistent presentation of woman, not as a human, but as a sexual being. One can learn nothing of the heroine's beliefs and character for the hullabaloo that has been set up because she has come in too late or gone out too early or omitted to provide herself with that figure of questionable use . . . a chaperone" (53). Despite his Puritan traces, James does offer a "theme of interest to our generation," and one which she applies to her own later works: "the aptness of young persons possessed of that capacity for contagious enthusiasm which makes the good propagandist to be exploited by the mercenary and to deteriorate under the strain of public life" (71). It is a dark vision applicable to her own professional development. West also finds that James makes use of the lesson of the decadents, that "words are jewels which, wisely set, make by their shining, mental light" (82). This graceful praise for well-selected words would never grace her reviews of the writers generally settled into the group labeled Edwardians.

Woolf justifies her quarrel with the Edwardians on the basis of closeness, not opposition. They still visit. "By the mere fact of their existence in the flesh and their work has a living, breathing, everyday imperfection which bids us take what liberties with it we choose" ("Modern Novels," 3 E 31). She seeks to understand the place of the modern in a larger pattern of history that could prove circular, rather than progressive, as the Edwardians would demand.[3] If the Edwardian age is "just breaking off from our own," it is she who is doing the breaking, stepping back like an artist to "reduce Edwardian fiction to a view" (31).

In one such view, Max Beerbohm's essays "lie on the drawing-room table. There is no gin about; no strong tobacco; no puns, drunkenness, or insanity. Ladies and gentlemen talk together, and some things, of course are not said. . . . His age seems already a little distant, and the drawing-room table, as it recedes, begins to look rather like an altar where, once upon a time, people deposited offerings" (CR 223). Galsworthy's characters "have been out hunting all day for so many generations that they are now perpetually in this evening condition of physical well-being and spiritual simplicity" (2 E 152). Woolf also finds flaws in reasoning. Bennett, Galsworthy, and two relatively conventional Bloomsbury writers, E. M. Forster and Hugh Walpole, all create "a composite group of English families" under "a common belief that there is only one view of the world, and one family; and invariably at the end the mirrors break, and the new generation bursts in" (ibid.).

Woolf's most formidable charge against the Edwardians, derived from the Bennett quarrel, is that theirs was the age "when character disappeared or was mysteriously engulfed" (3 E 385). Woolf wrests character from its Edwardian conception and form, updating it to suit the interests of her own generation. Woolf's most frequently reprinted and best-known essays on Edwardians cite three men—John Galsworthy, Arnold Bennett, and H. G. Wells—as she turns over the leaf of literary history upon their form as "materialists." Arnold Bennett is the consummate workman, losing his characters in the solid fabric of buildings, towns, and first-class railway carriages. Woolf has a more complicated and sustained reaction to H. G. Wells, perhaps because of his commitment to social change. "He is a materialist from sheer goodness of heart, taking upon his shoulders the work that ought to have been discharged by Government officials, and in the plethora of his ideas and facts scarcely having leisure to realise, or forgetting to think important, the crudity and coarseness of his human beings" ("Modern Fiction," CR 152). Character suffers in Wells because he has bigger projects—the contrivance of utopias, for which he transforms Mrs Brown rather than look at her, and the grandiose *Outline of History,* for which he finds an audience in Lucy Swithin of Woolf's *Between the Acts.* (It was a work that Rebecca West thought wasteful of his talents.) In her review of Wells's novel *Joan and Peter,* Woolf describes her reaction as a reader to his characters:

> Burdened as they are with the most pernicious or typical views of
> their decade, humped and loaded with them so that they can
> hardly waddle across the stage without coming painfully to grief.
> The conscientious reader will try to refer these burlesques to some
> such abstraction as the Anglican Church, or the vagaries of aimless
> and impulsive modernism in the eighteen-nineties; but if you are

indolent you will be inclined to give up playing your part in the game of illusion, and to trifle with idle speculations as to the idiosyncrasies of Mr Wells. (2 E 294)

According to Woolf, these idiosyncrasies include the pouring out of a Niagara of ideas to overcome irritations over defects in the social system and the promotion of personal attitudes such as his own rare systematic thinking and "a fiery passion for the rights of youth—a passion for courage, vitality, initiative, inventiveness, and all the qualities that Mr. Wells likes best" (296). In what seems to be a distinction between Wells's sense of order and a more modern one, Woolf notes with some deference, "He is not isolating one of the nerves of our existence and tracing its course separately, but he is trying to give that nerve its place in the whole system and to show us the working of the entire body of human life. That is why his book attains its enormous bulk; and that is why, with all its sketchiness and crudeness and redundancy, its vast soft, billowing mass is united by a kind of coherency and has some relation to a work of art" (295). Her vagueness about the nature of that relation allows us to think a variety of things, many of them unflattering. She is certainly not seeking the same relation, perhaps not relation to the same kind of art, though we will have to return to the ideal of "coherency." In *Three Guineas*, by quoting from his *Experiment in Autobiography*, Woolf would suggest that Wells's sense of "the entire body of human life" is short on its awareness of women's history and capacities. Woolf's creation of Lucy Swithin as a reader of Wells's *Outline of History* likewise completes something he left out of the grand scheme.

Both Virginia Woolf and Rebecca West treated Hugh Walpole as a dated writer, even though he was two years younger than Woolf. By 1918, Rebecca West had given Walpole so many negative reviews that he wrote a letter protesting his repeated "public scalping." Her immediate reply was devastatingly consistent with the reviews: "It's certainly true that I don't like your work; I think it is facile and without artistic impulse." But she took it as "the duty of a critic to point out the fallaciousness of the method and vision of a writer who was being swallowed whole by the British public, as you are" (West letter to Walpole, 16 July 1918, Texas).[4] Later West would worry that she had paid a price for such forthrightness. She feared that Walpole had used his influence to keep her from publishing in circles where he had influence, such as the TLS (*Times Literary Supplement*). When West wrote Walpole in 1928, blaming her penchant for harsh criticism on her upbringing, she may also have been rebuilding bridges burned in early days.

H. G. Wells's ideas and energy spoke to the progressive visions West brought with her to London as a teenager. West got Wells's personal attention not by praising his work but by challenging him in terms of gender. In an increasingly well known review of his novel *Marriage*, West objected to Wells's assumption that "Our Lady of Loot," the worshipped but parasitic woman, was an adequate representative of her sex. West complicated the sexual politics of her attack by assaulting Wells's virility in culinary and spinsterly metaphors: "Of course he is the old maid among novelists; even the sex obsession that lay clotted on *Ann Veronica* and *The New Machiavelli* like cold white sauce was merely old maids' mania, the reaction towards the flesh of a mind too long absorbed in airships and colloids" (YR 64).

Wells claimed to Dora Marsden that his novels were "supersaturated" with feminism, and that he regularly read the periodical she edited, the *Freewoman*, finding that "its policy even at its worst was a wholesome weekly irritant."[5] What probably appealed to Wells was the journal's ongoing critique of the institution of marriage and its open discussion of sexual matters. Seven months before the review of *Marriage*, Wells and novelist Elizabeth von Arnim reputedly made love *al fresco*, atop a copy of the *Times* containing a protest to Rebecca West's reviewing by the antisuffragist Mary Humphry Ward. Victoria Glendinning takes this as evidence that Wells and von Arnim were on West's side (Glendinning, *Rebecca West* 45–46). But already, in exposing "The Gospel of Mrs Humphry Ward" in the *Freewoman*, West denounces financial parasitism in marriage as an essential point of honor. The importance of work to women's intellectual and artistic development is the same basic issue that West would argue against in *Marriage*. But there are definitely ideas they could get together on, such as West's finding that Ward is antidemocratic and antisocialist. Ward's is the "gospel" of the prosperous clerical classes who monopolized higher education and controlled the mindset of the House of Commons, according to West. When West questions Ward's assignment of moral worth to the taboo on divorce, West joins Wells in an attack on Victorian social mores.

Rather than being put off by her review of his book, Wells used it as the pretext for a series of increasingly intimate meetings. She readily mixed conceptions of him as lover and mentor in reports to her editor at the *New Freewoman*, Dora Marsden. One letter confided, "I must say I like

Wells. He hasn't made love to me and it is fun watching his quick mind splashing about in the infinite" (West letter to Marsden, n.d., Princeton). Wells went through a cautious phase, whether distracted by von Arnim or worried about repeating his costly history of extramarital procreativity. Drafts of a letter to Wells suggest that West was despondent about their break, though still eager to dramatize her despondency: "I refuse to be cheated out of my deathbed scene."[6] She complains in metaphor that she has had to conciliate him "by hacking at my love for you, cutting it down to the little thing that was the most you wanted." In her estimation, what he wanted was "a world of people falling over each other like puppies, people to quarrel and play with, people who rage and ache instead of people who burn. . . . I can't conceive of a person who runs about lighting bonfires and yet nourishes a dislike of flame" (West draft of letter to Wells, n.d., Yale).

In *H. G. Wells in Love,* Wells offers a sketchy concept of the "Lover-Shadow" that is suggestive of his sexual imaginary. It makes an "other" of the female and the physical. In one explanation of the "Lover-Shadow," Wells enacts an internal heterosexual drama where socialist ideas penetrate, like sperm or a penis, and he keeps the Lover-Shadow in an inferior position: "My innate self conceit and the rapid envelopment and penetration of my egotism by socialistic and politically creative ideas was too powerful ever to admit the thought of subordinating my *persona* to the Lover-Shadow" (56).

To recuperate from the shock of Wells's denial, West traveled to Spain with her mother, who had been understandably anxious about the Wells relationship. The protagonist of one of her Spanish stories, "At Valladolid," has attempted suicide. The young woman of "Trees of Gold" burns with an intensity akin to the Spanish landscape, responding particularly to the beauty of trees whose lichenous growth "gnawed inwards as it glowed outwards" (573). In travel writing, West discovered an important release from British pressures, as well as a genre that would serve her through the 1960s.

Having read with "unquenchable amazement" her description of a Spanish dancer, titled "Nana," in the July 1913 number, Wells wrote, "You are working gorgeously again. Please resume being friends." He considered himself "amiable and self denying . . . to refuse to let you waste your flare-up—one only burns well once—on my cinders" (Wells letter to West, [1913], Yale).[7] With some glow to his own coals yet, Wells began a barrage of cards, appreciating and critiquing her *Clarion* articles, calling one "the most beautiful love letter" (Wells letter to West, [1913], Yale). West apparently did not respond to one suggestion that would have put her into the role of amanuensis. H. G offered, "I've got a heap of stuff of sorts that wants editing, cutting and breaking down into a book. I've no time to do it. You could. Is such a job beneath your dignity?" (Wells letter to West, 18 Oct. 1913, Yale). It apparently was. But this seeking after assistance may have given West the idea that she too might organize help to serve her work. During the decade of her intimate relationship with H. G. Wells, West was established with his agent, the omnipresent modernist facilitator, James Pinker. Throughout her lifetime she would employ literary secretaries rather than become one.

Soon after Wells's death in 1946, West tried to sum up their relationship in a letter to one of her closest female friends, the novelist and biographer Emanie Arling.[8] "Dear H. G., he was a devil, he ruined my life, he starved me, he was an inexhaustible source of love and friendship to me for thirty five years, we should never have met, I was the one person he cared to see to the end, I feel desolate because he is gone" (West letter to Arling, 13 Aug. 1946, Yale). For West to state that Wells had ruined her life does disservice to the scope of that life, though it is consistent with her love of dramatic statement.[9] Just as inadequate is Anthony Burgess's quip, made in 1985, that West's "association with Wells was as close as she got to real greatness."[10]

By 1928, in an essay titled "Uncle Bennett," West was treating Wells alongside other Edwardian literary men that Woolf had grouped together in "Mr Bennett and Mrs Brown" and "Modern Fiction." She had taken on a light, parodic manner. They were the "uncles," the "Big Four": H. G. Wells, George Bernard Shaw, John Galsworthy, and Arnold Bennett, who "hung about the houses of our minds" in youth (199). "Uncle Wells arrived always a little out of breath, with his arms full of parcels, sometimes rather carelessly tied, but always bursting with all manner of attractive gifts that ranged from the little pot of sweet jelly that is 'Mr. Polly,' to the complete meccano set for the mind that is in The First Men in the Moon" (SN 199). The description of Wells was very like one written the same year by Freda Kirschwey, editor of the Nation. She says to Wells, "You offered us all the world in tempting cans with lovely labels: Socialism, Free Love, Marriage, Education, World Organization, and H. G Wells's Patented Feminism—Very perishable" (308).

George Bernard Shaw was more than willing to be West's mentor. As noted in the previous chapter, there was a family tradition that West's father had debated Shaw with some success. She compared her father's wit to Shaw's (*FM* 176). West took up with the Fabians soon after she arrived in London, sharing this interest with a suffragist friend, Mary Gawthorpe, and her sister Lettie. She attended the Fabian Summer School and lectured on feminism, though she did not find her audience particularly responsive (Scott interview). Max Beerbohm assumed that Shaw was West's literary model. He drew a grossly inaccurate, Shavian drawing of West, represented as a swelling, cross-dressed, stern figure with a bun in 1916. Two years later he sent it to Shaw, along with remarks on his supposed influence: "I had marvelled much at her skill at catching your tone of mind and the hang of your sentences. Very wonderful it all seemed to me, and not quite sufferable—rather a monstrous birth." The Shavian qualities he offers in summary are "cool, frank, breezy, trenchant, vain, swift, stern, frivolous, incorruptible, kind, accurate" (Figure 9 in *YR*, following 198). Shaw took up the comparison, in a statement that still appears on her bookjackets: "Rebecca West could handle a pen as brilliantly as ever I could and much more savagely" (back cover, Virago edition, *YR*).

West was relatively kind to Shaw in her "uncles" essay, and he in return sent her a picture postcard of his "most avuncular photograph" (Shaw card to West, 13 July 1913, Tulsa). West proclaimed, "He did for his age what Voltaire and Gibbon did for theirs: he popularized the use of the intellectual processes among the politically effective class." She suggests that he did it with the style of the matador, who walks with panache, and the "pride of a species" (*SN* 200). His letters regularly responded to her reviews. West seems to have detected and resented a tendency to blend advice with sexual innuendo in his letters, though she denies that she was anything more than a family pet in one account, repeatedly asserting how much she liked Mrs. Charlotte Shaw, his partner in a supposedly unconsummated marriage. Probably in response to her review of *Heartbreak House,* Shaw said that she probably hasn't experienced a separation of "concupiscence from affection" when "animal virility still functions mechanically" (Shaw letter to West, 20 Oct. 1919, Tulsa). He also writes to her on matters of libel, in a letter with unpleasant sexual innuendoes: "If you say specifically that Viola Tree is a ninny to produce plays by a commercially worthless author like Shaw, then Shaw can instantly say, 'Rebecca: be mine, or I ruin you not only by high damages, but by making every editor in London afraid to trust you with a job' " (Shaw letter to West, 14 July 1920, British Library). West told Emanie Arling in 1952 that she "fled him because I thought him a mischief-maker and awfully silly and without style in his mind" (West letter to Arling, 13 Aug. 1946, Yale). She compared him to Gladstone as a giver of advice. Damning the works of Shaw, particularly for their lack of feminist interest, was a regular item in her late interviews.

Though he gets the most attention, Arnold Bennett fares worst of all the Edwardian uncles in West's "Uncle Bennett" essay. This matches Woolf's persecution of him. His contributions to the younger generation are the most difficult for West to detect. She finally assigns him to a joyless category of Protestant thinking: "It hates the elevation of one man above another. Mr. Bennett can never work happily on a character which is not socially and personally mediocre. It wants to skip all the moments in life that are traditionally splendid and roseate in favour of the moments that are simply pieces of the general texture of life" (211–12). Bennett did not care for this work of his "niece," and used his regular column in the *Evening Standard* to say so. His article "My Brilliant but Bewildering Niece" charges her with "irresponsible silliness," an "acrobatic, disorderly mind," and the inability to work with her gifts. After a journalist from the *Standard* published West's supposed reactions to the review, "Rebecca West Hits Back," West brought a "Statement of Claim" against the paper. Her complaint was that the report was never submitted to her for verification and approval and that it was "calculated and intended and understood to mean . . . that the Plaintiff was a vindictive and silly and impertinent and ill-bred person and an unbalanced and spiteful and uneducated and incompetent writer and literary critic and of no worth or merit in her profession" ("Fairfield vs. the *Evening Standard*" 4).

She was publicly assailed. The *Standard* had published numerous letters attacking West as she was represented in the article. One writer cheered Bennett for "standing up against the arrogance and 'push and go' so characteristic of our present-day feminism, and which flourishes mainly by men's good-humoured tolerance—a masculine quality very imperfectly understood by women" (5). Austin Clarke accused her of stealing a phrase from Yeats, noting, "Uneducated feminine brains are notorious pickers-up of unconsidered trifles" (6).[11] The poet Robert Nichols advised that "although she can be very acute in a slap-dash way, she is not really at home in letters, for they are not her true medium, which is probably something much more personal—voice, eyes, hands, gesture, all the battery (which she probably despises) of a unique feminine personality, a battery that has power to make temerity acceptable, wit pass for wisdom, and the impetuosities of a gallant incompetence charming" (7).

West wrote her own explanation of the misrepresentation to Bennett, who was unperturbed in his reply. She turned antifeminist insults to profit in the court settlement.[12] Subsequently, West invited the opportunity to dispute Bennett's critical assessments. She told publisher Jonathan Cape, for example, that she would like to write on Laura Riding after she had received "a very unfair notice from that old ass Arnold Bennett" (West to Cape, 7 Mar. 1928, University of Reading).

Always timely in her publications, West produced a pamphlet, *Arnold Bennett Himself* (1931), immediately upon his death.[13] She held to her comparison of Bennett with a "first rate solicitor's clerk" (11); this excited some of the strongest criticism of her "Uncle Bennett" article. No more flattering was her presentation of him as the self-schooled provincial, got up like a piece of English empire furniture to play the role of the "perfect Londoner" (6). But she does credit him with improving the novel from the romanticism and gentility of Robert Louis Stevenson, Kipling, and the vogue of a woman writer "John Oliver Hobbes" (15). She praises him for the daring subject matter of *Whom God Hath Joined*, a novel on divorce, and marks *Old Wives Tale* as his high point. But it was the late Bennett who proved an obstacle, rather than a help, to West. What becomes clear in this study of Bennett is his power over the book market, effected through his weekly book page in the *Evening Standard*. She finds the column a "vehicle to present his personality," and suggests that the books most apt to receive his approval treat "provincial life as soberly as he had" (20). He lacked interest in aesthetics and made his immediate reactions final, dismissing such important figures as Sherwood Anderson, Jean Cocteau, and Willa Cather.

Powerful men on the model of the Edwardian uncle attracted, courted, and enervated West throughout her life. The most compelling example of this was Lord Beaverbrook—William Maxwell Aitken, whom she had met socially with Wells and wanted as his successor. Beaverbrook made his first million selling bonds and insurance in Montreal. After emigrating to Britain in 1910, he was promptly elected to Parliament. Still an effective financier, he gained control of Rolls Royce and bought a bank and a chain of cinemas. He also acquired newspapers, commanding the *Daily Express* in 1916, the *Evening Standard* in 1923, and founding the *Sunday Express*, all of which he marketed effectively. He wrote eleven books, mostly on politicians and war. His literary acquaintances were Edwardians—Wells, Bennett, and Rudyard Kipling. Beaverbrook made Bennett a regular reviewer for the *Evening Standard,* a situation West would have loved for herself in the twenties.

West's obsession with Beaverbrook did little for her writing, producing a novel she could not publish and exhausting her in the process. Although Beaverbrook destroyed most of their correspondence relating to the affair, one exception is an undated, highly imaginative story enclosed in a letter around 1925. The fantasy may have been therapeutic. The main character is "a wicked newspaper proprietor owner (Max)" who lives with two male "familiars." He is visited by four wives, one of them presumably West,[14] all with babies in tow. Max poisons the women with cocktails and has them dumped into the flowerbed. A visiting clergyman is murdered as well. But Max finds that he has been bankrupted by the wives' million-dollar insurance policies with his *Daily Express* and commits suicide in reaction. The wives and clergymen are all revived by his "pure young enemy" who has witnessed various parts of the drama. Converted to Mormonism, they all head off happily to Salt Lake City (West letter to Beaverbrook, n.d., House of Lords).

Over the years, West's letters both challenged Beaverbrook politically and kept him as an affectionate friend, publisher, and political consultant with whom she could play the insider. He was an admirer of Bonar Law, and his politics were considerably to the right of West's. However, as early as 1918, she was admiring the capacity of "Beaverbrooks" to "get the power," while liberals do not, as she stated in a letter to S. K. Ratcliffe, a radical journalist and fellow Fabian (West letter to Ratcliffe, 9 Aug. 1918, Yale). This was an important observation relevant to modernist praxis and one that would stay with her throughout her life. During World War I, as head of the Ministry of Information, Beaverbrook was a valuable contact for West and Wells as they wrote analyses of the war. West also had an in with Bonar Law, whose confidential secretary, Sara (Sally) Melville, became one of her closest friends and a steady source of political gossip.

In the twenties, West critiqued an *Evening Standard* story that denounced her friend Emma Goldman as an anarchist: "Not only is E. G. worth 6 of you (or three of me), but she is the most powerful Anti-Bolsh eyewitness I have yet encountered" (West letter to Beaverbrook, n.d., House of Lords).[15] Billed in Beaverbrook's *Evening Standard* as "the greatest journalist in our time" in the 1940s, she wrote articles on treason, spy tribunals, American politics, and postwar Europe. West's letters to

Beaverbrook worked out journalistic ethics. She consulted with him about the advisability of making personal references on a peripheral figure, in order to make a point about totalitarian government in Germany. He backed her, stating that "the duty of the historian must come before the respect and sympathy for private susceptibilities" (Beaverbrook telegram to West, 1947, House of Lords). West challenged him to cover cases concerning supposed Communist agents such as Alger Hiss more closely in his paper (West letter to Beaverbrook, 2 Apr. 1950) and expressed suspicion of his attitudes toward Communism to friends. She was on the lookout for threats to Western security. West warned him about a book by Alan Moorhead, written with the encouragement of the Minister of Supply, that she thought threatened to split American and British intelligence efforts in 1952.

Their final exchange was over a gift from him, awarding her discretion in *The Vassal Affair,* published in 1963. In writing on the spy trial of a civil servant in the British admiralty, she had been judicious in reporting the role of his newspaper. In the past, Beaverbrook had always awarded her with roses. This time he sent a case of his finest claret, one of two remaining at the end of his life. The division "one for you and one for me" was unusually egalitarian (Beaverbrook letter to West, 31 Dec. 1963, House of Lords). She replied, with typical spirit, that accepting it was the "nearest I have come to bribery and corruption during my long career, and I like it" (West letter to Beaverbrook, 4 Jan. 1964, House of Lords). Her concern with power politics stretched usual conceptions of the woman writer, to the extent that Gloria Fromm has categorized this aspect of her writing as masculine.

A crony of H. G. Wells and Joseph Conrad, Ford Madox Ford was older than most modernists, though arguably one of them. He and Violet Hunt (who gains our attention in chapter 4) brought innovative new writers to light during his brief editorship of the *English Review* (December 1908–February 1910). Ford remained eager to help new talent when he edited the *transatlantic review* from Paris (1924–25). He may have recommended Rebecca West as a reviewer, and was himself positively reviewed by her. To weave him further into this study, Ford met Djuna Barnes in Paris and published her story "Aller et Retour" in the *transatlantic review*—an issue that Ezra Pound commended for "Hem. and Djuna" (Field 106). Like Wells, however, Ford involved himself with a series of talented women long before his marriage dissolved—often with destructive effect to the women. His loves included Brigit Patmore (who also triangulated the marriage of Richard Aldington and H. D.), Stella Bowen, and Jean Rhys (whose marriage broke up as a result of her liaison with Ford).

West's opening metaphor in her "uncles" essay attempts to dismiss as a youthful phase what often became intense physical and emotional entanglements for modernist women. They are figures that "hung about" the mind in youth. While this serves a mature rhetoric of dismissal or escape, it is important to recognize the dangers of Edwardian literary men as intimates. In secondary sexual arrangements and literary assignments, Edwardian uncles too often wanted to possess the excitement and energy of younger women, who originally looked to them for direction.

The American equivalent of the British Edwardian uncle may be taken as the charlatans and bohemians of Greenwich Village, recorded for profit in the journalism of Djuna Barnes. Her sharp eye and satirical tone in reporting on them make it hard to assess whether or not Barnes was hurt by this set of men. They are not mentioned as her father was, in the reports of abuse that appear in Emily Holmes Coleman's diaries, but, with the exception of the Barney archive, there is a regrettable lack of confidential correspondence from the teens and twenties. Barnes benefited from limited tolerance of lesbian themes and bohemian lifestyles, but recent studies of the Greenwich Village milieu suggest that its politics was dominated by men.[16]

Guido Bruno published Barnes's first collection of sketches and poems, *The Book of Repulsive Women*, in 1915. One of the poems is openly lesbian in its depiction of desire and difference. Bruno's many cheap pamphlets seem to have fallen beneath the notice of censors, though they also did little to gain their authors recognition outside the Village. Nor is Bruno's interpretation of Djuna adequate to what she became. In an article written in 1919, he offered two sides to Barnes—the morbidity of her works vs. the liveliness of her persona, seen on Fifth Avenue or in the Café Lafayette: "Red cheeks. Auburn hair. Gray eyes, ever sparkling with delight and mischief. Fantastic earrings in her ears, picturesquely dressed, ever ready to live and be merry" (Barnes, *I Could Never Be Lonely* 388). This was a creature for his gaze, or her performance of gender to gain attention. Bruno saw her in his favored tradition as a new flowering of the decadent tradition. This *fin de siècle* assignment did not contain her, any more than the Shavian model or the prescriptions of Wells could chart West's course. Bruno soon turned his energies to the career of Frank Harris—one of the earliest publishers of H. G. Wells, whose mannerisms Rebecca West had savaged when she first met him in Soho.

In their negotiations with Edwardian men, Woolf, West, and Barnes all discovered aspects of male power and management that they could match or better, deriving momentum to launch themselves into professional and modernist occupations. Whatever the personal relations may have cost, they had youth and change, as well as skepticism, on the side of their writing.

3   Stretching the Scope of Suffrage

The programme of the paper consisted of the revolt of women, philosophic anarchism, and a general whip-round for ideas which would reform simultaneously life and art.

—Rebecca West of the *New Freewoman,* "Spinster to the Rescue" 578

When she gets to the 1920s in her important study of British women writers' "literature of their own," Elaine Showalter assigns Virginia Woolf and Rebecca West to an aesthetic rather than an activist tradition. In her view, modernist women retreat from the more politically engaged writing of the turn of the century. By making this assignment, Showalter accepts the reading of aesthetic modernism promulgated by the men of 1914 and their male academic followers, F. R. Leavis and the New Critics, which was sustained well into the 1980s. Her Woolf seems to be taken largely from the biography of Woolf's nephew, Quentin Bell, whose views were close to those of E. M. Forster. Stated briefly (as we return to him in chapter 9), Forster's Woolf was a poetic novelist on the threshold of being an aesthete. She was a fragile lady and a bit of a snob. Defending his vision of Woolf against later Woolf scholars, Bell sparked a lively exchange with American "lupine" critics. Jane Marcus, who reads Woolf as far more politically engaged, was the primary respondent.[1] As noted in the Introduction, recent postmodernist theories extricate some authors from the category of aesthetic high modernism, reinserting them into popular culture and politics. Women, however, seldom appear on such lists.[2] Recently, Marianne DeKoven has given modernism a positive political reading, finding that the revolutionary horizon of the early century remained in the view of modernist men and women.[3] In my account, the women's movement, as initiated by suffragettes, moves naturally into women's discussion circles and the production of magazines that broadened the perspective of suffrage; the founders took life and art as co-principles. Young women moved from rallies to writing, testing the power of the pen as an instrument of their perceptions, as well as their progressive ideas. They wrote with a female circle in mind. One aspect of their Edwardian uncles, whom we encountered in chapter 2, was that they struggled to find a place in a feminist movement that was not of their own creation.

Merry Militant Saints and Editors

At seventeen, Cicily Fairfield came to London, ending a restive adolescence in Edinburgh. She was already a published feminist activist. Her letter to the editor of the *Scotsman* endorsing women's suffrage was published in 1907. Following the example of her best friend from childhood, Flora Duncan, West went to London with hopes of pursuing a career on the stage. This was the sort of aspiration that Elizabeth Robins, Sarah Bernhardt, and Ellen Terry (who was memorably photographed by Woolf's aunt, Julia Cameron) made possible. It was a phenomenon in which Djuna Barnes shared, through writing for the Provincetown Players and the Theatre Guild. The young woman from Edinburgh remade Ibsen's suicidal character, Rebecca West, into a feminist survivor. West did not prosper on the stage, however; she lasted only three terms at the Academy of Dramatic Art. Her first real stage was the suffrage newspaper the *Freewoman* and its discussion circle.

The *Freewoman* was founded by two former members of the Women's Social and Political Union (WSPU), the militant branch of the British suffrage movement headed by Emmeline Pankhurst and her daughters Christabel and Sylvia. Dora Marsden and Mary Gawthorpe both had a wider set of concerns than the Pankhursts and sought alternate strategies to WSPU militancy and the costly martyrdom of women it exacted. Both Marsden and Gawthorpe had distinct interests and styles, which had repercussions in the paper.

West's own involvement with the WSPU goes back to her Edinburgh days, when she sold copies of its paper, *Votes for Women,* attended suffrage rallies, and experienced a baton charge in the city streets. She reported on suffrage events in letters to her sister Lettie, who shared her interests in suffrage and Fabian socialism. One of the most dramatic, written in December 1909, records a march against the Foreign Secretary, Sir Edward Gray, at the Leith Gaiety meeting, ending in the bloody police baton charge. West celebrates the heroics of Miss Hudson, who managed to hold the purple, white, and green suffrage flag above her head while being carried off to prison by the police. In the day's contest, Hudson was repeatedly arrested by the police only to be abducted by the crowd; West records the police beating this brave woman repeatedly about the face and even in the windpipe. West's own efforts to discourage votes for the Liberals, who had failed to support suffrage, are reported in another letter of the same period:

> On Thursday I stood outside the pool at Forsyth Rd. and shouted "Keep the Liberal out!" I turned three votes on the doorstep, anyway. But the Liberal women are ghastly! They stood on the other side of the gate and shouted insults at us the whole time. I had five large Liberal ladies bearing down on me calling me a hooligan and a "silly fool" and other pretty names. One Liberal man tried to shake me and hurt me, much to their delight, but the police man settled all that. However one Suffragette, Mrs Brown of New Castle, was knocked down and trampled on by a member of the Woman's Liberal Federation. They tried to make me stop shouting "Keep the Liberal out" but of course it was no good. I kept on from 10 till 8!

In the same letter West tells Lettie that "Christabel and Lovey Mary [Gawthorpe] were at their very best" in a rally at Harrowgate (West letters to Letitia Fairfield, n.d.).

Gawthorpe regularly toured the north of England, including her native Yorkshire. She had favored West with a summons to visit the platform at one of West's first rallies (Glendinning, *Rebecca West* 31).[4] Writing about Gawthorpe in *Time and Tide* in the twenties, West retained her affectionate name, "Lovey Mary," and called her "a merry militant saint" ("The 'Freewoman' " 574). The phenomenon of the suffragist lecture platform is recorded through male eyes in West's 1922 novel, *The Judge.* There is no real equivalent to Gawthorpe in the group depicted there, though Emmeline and Christabel Pankhurst are mimicked—Christabel in a negative, histrionic part.[5] The young enthusiast, West, is evoked by Ellen Melville, whose features also preserve some of the charm she found in Gawthorpe and Marsden.

Mary Gawthorpe's background included work as a schoolteacher, leadership and writing for early Labour Party and Fabian groups around Leeds, and participation in violent demonstrations for the WSPU. Gawthorpe's autobiography, *Up Hill to Holloway,* is informative about women in education, the labor movement, and the suffrage movement to 1906, when she was imprisoned for taking a leading role in a suffrage demonstration in the lobby of the House of Commons. Gawthorpe compares her experience in a student teacher job to that of H. G. Wells, as described

Plate 6. Mary Gawthorpe.

From Gawthorpe, *Up Hill to Holloway.*

in his *Experiment in Autobiography,* and credits him for helping to develop the science curriculum studied by teachers in training, during his years at South Kensington (88, 141).

The *Clarion,* a radical socialist journal that West would write for in the 1910s, was for Gawthorpe in her youth "a sort of nation-wide club on a non-dues paying basis which united readers everywhere in an atmosphere of camaraderie" (175). She took on the women's page of a local weekly, the *Labour News,* and began making speeches for the labor movement. She knew A. R. Orage (later editor of the *New Age* and a force in modernism) through membership in the Leeds Art Club. Another acquaintance was Edward Carpenter, who had settled in Millthorpe to pursue a socialist, communal lifestyle that included vegetarianism and overt homosexuality. Her positive accounts of Orage and Carpenter are tempered by her record of their attempts at seduction. It is significant that Gawthorpe quotes from the "Object of the Leeds Arts Club," which was "to affirm the mutual dependance of art and ideas. The separation of beauty from use, or use from beauty, proves in the long run disastrous to both" (194). Gawthorpe's ill health, resulting from rough handling by the police and the rigors of imprisonment, are standard in suffrage accounts of her, including those of Sylvia Pankhurst and Rebecca West.

Gawthorpe's editing experience included work on *Votes for Women,* conducted with the guidance of Emmeline Pethwick Lawrence. In 1911, Dora Marsden convinced her to help in planning the *Freewoman.* Gawthorpe contributed to its original funding from money given her by the WSPU to look after her health. She acted as a consultant, advising that the Fabians might be good allies, and bringing young talent such as West to Marsden's attention. Marsden pressured her into briefly assuming a co-editorship, and used her fame as a suffrage martyr for early publicity. Gawthorpe was anxious about Marsden's bitterness toward the WSPU, which she did not share. Always in loving tones, Gawthorpe repeatedly resisted Marsden, until finally she made a severe break in March 1912 (see Garner 72). West's thinking remained closer to Gawthorpe's movement-based, socialist feminism than Marsden's blend of anarchism, individualism, abstract spiritual philosophy, and hard line on the WSPU. It may be Gawthorpe's influence that made the Fabian, utopian H. G. Wells such an attractive figure to the young West.

West's account of Marsden includes her WSPU credentials, with the important element of martyrdom—that she had been to prison, had hunger struck, and had been forcibly fed ("Spinster to the Rescue" 577). Mars-

Plate 7. Dora Marsden under arrest
outside University of Manchester, 1909.

From E. Sylvia Pankhurst, *The Suffragette.*

den's courageousness was all the more remarkable to West because Marsden was fragile and petite, "a perfectly proportioned fairy" ("The 'Freewoman' " 574). To West, it was emblematic of her ethereal nature that Marsden used to embroider white upon white (Scott interview). Sylvia Pankhurst had called Marsden an "angel" and used her petite stature to dramatic effect in her denunciations of harsh police interventions in suffrage demonstrations. She clearly came across to young West as charismatic: "She was brilliant in mind and saintly in character and . . . exquisitely lovely" ("Spinster to the Rescue" 577).[6] West's reaction is one of enchantment, and perhaps even physical attraction. This was an angel decidedly different from the domestic one idealized by members of the older generation and attacked, memorably with an ink bottle, in Woolf's "Professions for Women."

Like West, Marsden came from the provinces and grew up in a family that had been deserted by its father. West's account identifies her as "a graduate of Manchester University," a significant resource for Marsden as a women's leader. While it lacked the status of Oxbridge, this education was comparable to what H. G. Wells and D. H. Lawrence had pursued, and it had similar results in drawing women out of provincial and impoverished circumstances. Carol Barash argues for the importance of Marsden's educational community, actually at the Department of Women at Owen College, Manchester (an earlier arrangement than Manchester University). It was an environment in which women engaged in sports, debating, and community service, ensuring other women a respect for the equality of female intellect. She worked for wider recognition. Marsden and two other graduates, clad in their academic gowns, interrupted exercises at Manchester University to claim equal degrees for women. This event is recorded alongside her suffrage protests in Sylvia Pankhurst's history of suffrage, suggesting the breadth of Pankhurst's feminism as well. After her college days, when it came to establishing her paper, Marsden could hook into a network of women educated as teachers (Barash 37–38). Two others on the staff were Grace Jardine, Marsden's most constant companion apart from her devoted mother, and another Manchester graduate, Rona Robinson, enthusiastically described by West as "a glorious red-haired bachelor of science, who had been in and out of gaol for the cause" ("The 'Freewoman' " 575).[7]

West's remarks on women's education favored the Manchester model of institutions where women enjoyed a comparable curriculum to men's. As her identification of Robinson suggests, West was particularly keen on women's learning the sciences. This had been the goal of the heroine of her unfinished, posthumously published novel, *Adela.* West denigrated the domestic, submissive training she had received as part of the curriculum at George Watson's Ladies' College, the working women's school she attended in Edinburgh. Her dismissal of domestic tasks as comparable to "rat-poison" irritated more domestically oriented readers, but West held her ground in this continuing debate, insisting that domestic labor was "suitable for those with the intelligence of rabbits" and seeking ways to organize it as a "trade process" (YR 38–42). She was stimulated by a community of educated and committed women.

Marsden began her paper with an important vision of a more broadly cultural and philosophical feminism than that offered by the Pankhursts and the WSPU, with their tighter focus on suffrage. She had tried to bring her ideas to another suffrage periodical, the *Vote.* This was published by the less militant, Labor-affiliated Women's Freedom League, led by Charlotte Despard. However, the controversial subjects that interested Marsden and her desire for autonomy brought rejection. Marsden introduced discussion of sexuality, women's dependency in marriage, and motherhood made compulsory by culture, all of which interested West. Marsden had dramatic appeal, and a self-assurance that helped shape West's own style.

The *Freewoman* and its successor the *New Freewoman* attracted people with overlapping designs for cultural change, including various interpreters of Nietzsche, socialists who wrote simultaneously for A. R. Orage's *New Age,* anarchists, spiritualists, and male modernists. Though stronger on suffrage issues, the *New Freewoman* offered a blend of radical politics and religion comparable to the *Little Review*—one of Djuna Barnes's first important publishing homes. Like *Little Review* editor Margaret Anderson, Marsden encouraged debate between contributors and readers. Both Marsden and Anderson pointed out their own disagreements with contributors at the ends of articles. There were regular exchanges with readers in Marsden's "Notes and Letters" column. The task of responding often fell to West.

The *Freewoman* succumbed to problems of economic support and to a boycott by the newspaper industry. Much of its original support had come from the radical publisher and poet Charles Grenville, another Edwardian uncle type who was eventually imprisoned for bigamy and fraud—one of two financial scandals West retold with relish (see "The 'Freewoman' " 575–76). The paper had to look to its readership for support, which it got from many influential figures, including H. G. Wells and a host of women writers and artists—May Sinclair, Amy Lowell, Dorothy Shakespear (later the wife of Ezra Pound), Brigit Patmore, H. D., Katherine Mansfield, Charlotte Perkins Gilman, Dorothy Richardson, and Charlotte Payne-Townshend (the wife of George Bernard Shaw, to whom West was partial, even in old age).

The real savior, however, was Harriet Shaw Weaver. She was attracted to the paper by its outspoken denunciation of unearned incomes and so brought hers to it. She would later contribute to the economic and personal support of both Dora Marsden and James Joyce, having been deeply impressed by *A Portrait of the Artist as a Young Man* as it appeared in the *Egoist*. The *Freewoman* was also harmed by a boycott by the newspaper distributor W. H. Smith, which announced, "The nature of certain articles which have been appearing lately are such as to render the paper unsuitable to be exposed on the bookstalls for general sale." Marsden identified their real objection as the mixing of the sexual question with economics (*Freewoman*, 5 Sept. 1912; Hanscombe and Smyers 167; Garner 77). This the *Freewoman* did incessantly, with Rebecca West as one of the chief practitioners of the blend.

West to the Rescue

West became a presence at the "Freewoman Circle," where she and the "glorious" Robinson remarked on a churchlike atmosphere (West letter to Marsden, n.d., Princeton).[8] Her initiation to publication was in a typical genre for young women—the book review. As she would report in "Professions for Women," Woolf began with the same task in 1904, with a submission to the women's section of a paper for the clergy, the *Guardian*. But West clearly did not write with an angel over her shoulder. Brash reviews and outspoken opinions, begun at the *Freewoman*, won her the attention of the antisuffragist Mary Humphry Ward, Edwardian uncles Wells and Shaw, the transitional modernist Ford Madox Ford, and the modernists D. H. Lawrence and Virginia Woolf. Despite her youth, West worked to extricate the *Freewoman* from its financial crisis, gaining valuable lessons on the economics of publishing. On one front, she approached the anarchist publisher Fifield (Garner 98); on another, she suggested a capitalist scheme, the Freewoman Publishing Company, based on a large number of small shareholders who would build up £5,000 in capital.

West's correspondence with Marsden can serve to represent female collaboration in the making of modernism. West's letters exude admiration, disclose personal confidences, present ideas on publishing strategy, and build West's sense of her own content and style. West wrote in tribute, "You wonderful person—you not only write those wonderful front pages, but you inspire other people to write wonderfully" (West letter to Marsden, [June 1912], Princeton). West shared intimate concerns about her mother, her developing relationships with men, and new career opportunities with other papers such as the *Daily Herald,* where she politicized the women's page. She was trying out elements of writing that would serve her later. For example, she amuses Marsden with extended personal anecdotes and plays with rules of gender in creating her critical persona. Preparing to combat an antifeminist, she claimed a "chivalrous reluctance, feeling that a steam engine ought not to crush a butterfly" (West letter to Marsden, n.d., Princeton).

West is remarkably forthcoming to Marsden about her interest in, and subsequent difficulties with, H. G. Wells. In the earliest reports Wells's attitudes toward Marsden and company are stated with amused exaggeration: "He considers us the noblest work of God," and of Marsden more specifically, he "expiated at length . . . on your sweetness and brilliance" (West letter to Marsden, n.d., Princeton). On the evidence of Wells's letters to Marsden, Carol Barash has suspected him of attempting yet another seduction with Marsden (47). West was more receptive to his attentions, as recorded in chapter 2. When he temporarily cooled the relationship in mid-1913, Marsden was slow to catch on, and continued to use West to pry contributions out of Wells. At this point, West wrote bluntly that she had not seen him in months and had "no desire to dig up the corpse" (West to Marsden, [June 1913], Princeton). She was able to promise material from Ford Madox Ford instead.

West had mixed success in trying to affect the nature and survival of the *New Freewoman.* Marsden made her an assistant editor in 1913 and accepted her suggestion that the periodical should have more of a literary side. West may have had a blend of experimental form and Marsden-style philosophical ideas in mind: "A literary side would be a bribe to the more frivolous minded in London and I don't see why a movement towards freedom of expression should not be associated with and inspired by your gospel" (West letter to Marsden, n.d., Princeton). West mentions female recruitment problems to Marsden: "Where are the women who can write?" (West to Marsden, [Spring 1913], Princeton). West turned to

Ezra Pound to help overcome the paucity of submissions—a tale told more thoroughly in chapter 5. The suggestion that the title of the journal should be changed from the *New Freewoman* was male-inspired, and part of the scenario that led to West's departure. Still, West's sense of humor came through in discussing one alternative. West advised against *Free Era* because "You couldn't possibly say it when you were drunk, could you?" (West letter to Marsden, n.d., Princeton). She tried to ease Marsden into more communicative, less pugilistic prose, particularly as aimed at the WSPU: "Can't we stop attacking the WSPU? The poor dears are weak at metaphysics but they are doing their best to revolt" (West letter to Marsden, [June 1913], Princeton).

West was not limited to the *New Freewoman* as a forum for her feminist thinking. She could afford to be more radical and more in sympathy with the WSPU in articles written for the *Clarion*, an organization which also figured in Mary Gawthorpe's work, as noted above. In that more radical vein is West's cry that forced feeding was state-approved murder, and her emotional memorial to Emily Davison, the suffragette who sacrificed herself to the movement by throwing herself in front of the king's horse at the Derby: "Twenty-five years ago London was sick with fear because one such maniac crept through the dark alleys of Whitechapel mutilating and murdering unfortunate women. . . . But today Jack the Ripper works free-handed from the honourable places of government. . . . And for his victims he no longer seeks the shameful women of mean streets. To him, before the dull eyes of the unprotesting world, fall the finest women of the land" (YR 160, 178–83). Her line on the "shameful women of the mean streets" cloys, for all its drama, if read as her own assessment. I think it is meant as a parody of the view held by those who dismissed the crimes as remote from their experience; "unfortunate women," above, is closer to her view.

West retained a strong belief in the methods of political movements and socialist cooperation in the face of Marsden's increasing advocacy of individualism. In a letter to the editor signed Rachel East, West tried to convince Marsden of the impracticality of a scheme for agricultural individualism, reasserting the value of social cooperation and pointing to the remaining possibility of specialization, based on individual talents.

West was not happy with some of her colleagues at the paper. She did not admire the drama and art criticism of Huntly Carter or the writing of Barbara Low. She complained that Low had spread gossip that reached West's mother, suggesting that West was involved with a male member of the staff who was later accused of embezzlement. Sexuality, both of persons working on the journal and as explored in its pages, was a covert issue. West thought Marsden had been duped into accepting a bogus lesbian article, though she apparently would have had no objection to a genuine one. She took credit for saving the paper from Havelock Ellis's "insane wife, Edith, who according to West was in love with Gawthorpe's old friend, Edward Carpenter, whom West would remember years later as 'a homosexual religious maniac' " (West letter to Lidderdale, 29 Jan. 1967, Tulsa). Havelock Ellis was one of the world's pioneering theorists of homosexuality, basing his findings on lesbianism partially upon Edith. Bisexuality, as expressed in the workplace by Edith Ellis, may have complicated West's reception of lesbian material. It is interesting that West faults Carpenter for religious mania and not for his gestures of sexual liberation, though he seems to have pursued a number of commitments, including vegetarianism, with extreme earnestness. West's accounts of troubles at the *New Freewoman* develop her interest in diagnosing the health of cultural institutions, and the reporting on scandal and crime that became a staple of her journalism. They also betray an unsettled attitude toward lesbianism and homosexuality. She regards them as risky subjects in a publication, however fervent her endorsement of freedom from censorship. West's attitudes toward lesbianism would be further tested in reviews, and in the legal arena in 1928, as we shall see in chapter 12.

A Contest of Egoists

West had helped to draft the policy statement for the *New Freewoman* when it was seeking startup funds. It declared that "editorially, it will endeavour to lay bare the individualist basis of all that is most significant in modern movements including feminism. It will continue *The Freewoman*'s policy of ignoring in its discussion all existing tabus in the realms of morality and religion" (Lidderdale 58). In late 1913, in announcing that her journal would henceforward be called the *Egoist*, Marsden moved to a position that no longer stressed or even cited feminism, in title or policy. She reprinted a portion of a letter "by a group of contributors, to whose generous support the paper has owed much from its start":

> We the undersigned men of letters who are grateful to you for establishing an organ in which men and women of intelligence can

express themselves without regard to the public, venture to suggest to you that the present title of the paper causes it to be confounded with organs devoted solely to the advocacy of an unimportant reform in an obsolete political institution.

Allen Upward, Ezra Pound, Huntly Carter, Reginald W. Kauffmann, and Richard Aldington were the signers. The finishing anarchistic flourish dismisses the suffrage movement as ill directed toward democratic politics. Bruce Clarke has argued that the paper was more anarchistic than feminist from the start, that Marsden was pursuing her own inclinations with the new designation, the *Egoist,* and maintained a forceful correspondence with Pound.[9] But Marsden's own remarks suggest that she sees fatigue in old forms, and calls for a change in the role of the paper as regards feminism. She declares that the time for retorts to "hominism" is over. "The feminist argument was an overture many times repeated to a composition voicing the great works of women. The controversialists are now tired, and the spectators can reasonably expect to have something of the main composition. What women—awakened, emancipated, roused, what-not—what they *can* do, it is open for them to do" (*New Freewoman* 244). Rachel Blau DuPlessis finds an abiding lesson for feminists in suggesting that Marsden was too early convinced that she had entered a postfeminist era, and that nothing was lost in obliterating "woman" for a "neutral title," the *Egoist.* As DuPlessis notes, we have come to see "ego" as a social formation, though perhaps it is asking too much to expect Marsden to see it that way (*Pink Guitar* 44–45). Ego was burdened with the gender asymmetry of the early twentieth century. Its dubious qualities would become one of the topics of Woolf's *A Room of One's Own.*

West, on the other hand, was convinced throughout her life of the need for a continuing feminist movement. She felt that the *Freewoman* had provided a "keystone of the modern Feminist movement" by smashing the romantic ideas of womanhood: "It had to be admitted that women were vexed human beings who suffered intensely from male-adaptation to life, and that they were tortured and dangerous if they were not allowed to adapt themselves to life" ("The 'Freewoman' " 576). In parting she wished the *Egoist* good luck, saying of a recent number that she liked the James Joyce story "very much," but regretted that there was "far too little" of Marsden (West letter to Marsden, [1914], Princeton). She returned the check for her year's wages, sent by the ever-generous Harriet Shaw Weaver.

In 1918, when reviewing West's novel *The Return of the Soldier* for the *Egoist,* Marsden could claim with accuracy and pride that the *Freewoman* connection was probably the most important factor in West's early grounding as an author in London. But she still saw West rather patronizingly, as an author in search of identity and an authentic form. Though possessed of "brilliant gifts," she had "not yet found herself and her true form." Some critics might say she never did, or that settling into a single form would have denied readers her unceasing striving and variation in form. Marsden was not prophetic when she stated: "She is not a debater; she is not a fighter; her spirits do not rise at the prospect of a scrap" (*Egoist,* 1 Oct. 1918). Both women had the difficult task of deciding how, what, and when to fight. Marsden presented West with lessons on just how difficult that would be. West's penchant for philosophy and her capacity for feminine essentialism are represented in far more extreme form in Marsden's *The Definition of a Godhead,* a work that qualifies for the field of feminist spirituality in that it hypothesizes a Great Almighty Mother Space. In her retrospective articles, West makes it clear that she felt that the mainspring of this brilliant mind had been broken by 1914.

Time and Tide Wait for Modernist Women

West found a partial substitute for the *New Freewoman* in *Time and Tide,* a weekly journal founded by Lady Rhondda in 1920 that also claimed Virginia Woolf as a contributor and Djuna Barnes as a subscriber. Interestingly, Barnes's subscription came at the suggestion of T. S. Eliot, himself an occasional contributor of notes.[10] Among its ex-suffragette contributors was Elizabeth Robins. Vera Brittain and Winifred Holtby, author of one of the first books on Woolf, were a part of the *Time and Tide* circle and well acquainted with West. The goal of the journal was to give an independent political voice to women, consolidating the gain of partial suffrage granted to British women thirty and over in 1918. The closely allied "Six Point Group" sought legislative gains for unwed mothers, battered children, teachers, and civil servants.

West wrote one of the supplemental goals statements that appeared regularly in the journal. Hers was "Equal Pay for Men and Women Teachers," which appeared in 1923. With disarming common sense, she disputed "the argument that men teachers ought to be paid more highly than women teachers who do the same work because they have families to support." She pointed out that this was "a curious defence for a system which pays exactly the same salary to the bachelor, the childless widower, the father of one and the father of seven, and then cuts it sharply when it comes to the spinster who is keeping her father and mother and the widow who is keeping seven children" (Spender, ed. 55). West declared that "teaching, like all the arts, must spring from a condition of excess" (56). This is a view very much in agreement with *A Room of One's Own*, given its attention to the need for £500 a year and a room. West also has no haughty view of the arts, as she classifies teaching as one of them. West's discussion includes a theory of sex antagonism: "Man, baffled and fatigued by his struggle to establish and perpetuate human life in the universe, becomes afraid of judging his progress by the standard of approach to absolute good. He prefers a relative standard. He wants to feel that however badly he is doing someone else is doing worse. As the only person with whom man can compare himself is woman, it is desirable that she should do worse" (58). Her essay quickly expands to analogies in other fields—such as male putdowns of women's cookery columns, when in fact they have improved the national diet; it is a subject to which she brings the elaborate personal anecdote, which was becoming a staple of her journalism.

Time and Tide is one of the places where Woolf and West intersect. Woolf had met Lady Rhondda in 1921 and from that time onward occasionally attended her parties. *Time and Tide* published Woolf's "The Sunset and the Fish," celebrating an underwater world opened at the new aquarium in 1928, and the study of a modern queen, "Monarch." Of greater feminist significance were two installments of *A Room of One's Own* published in the journal. These complement West's earlier supplement on education. Woolf's now-celebrated work gave women the responsibility of improving on what is known about women writers, along with a revised model for methods of research and lecturing. Woolf's description of women, serving as magnifying mirrors for men, and Professor Von X demeaning them, supports West's notion that men must construct inferiors to gain a sense of self-worth. As Dale Spender has noted, *Time and Tide* provided valuable resources for Woolf's later project, *Three Guineas* (50–51).

I have used Rebecca West to challenge the standard story that modernism advanced by suppressing the spirit of the suffrage movement, focused in the *New Freewoman*. In lesser ways, Woolf and Barnes reinforce the account.

Woolf's Real Envelopes

Like Rebecca West, Virginia Woolf wrote some of her earliest criticism in defiance of the founder of the Woman's Anti-suffragist League, Mrs. Humphry Ward. She submitted a savage review to the *Speaker* in 1906, only to learn that someone had preempted her. The act of defiance is doubled when we consider that Woolf's mother had supported one of Ward's antisuffrage petitions. Woolf was certainly aware of the Artists' Suffrage League. Her Bloomsbury friend Duncan Grant received an award from this group for the best suffrage poster of 1909. In 1910, influenced by the politics of her tutor in German and Greek, Janet Case, Woolf offered to do volunteer work for the suffrage cause. Case consulted Margaret Llewelyn Davies and Rosalind Nash in order to offer her a choice of tasks. Woolf finally opted for the simple task of addressing envelopes for the Adult Suffrage League (1 Bell 161). Here she handled real envelopes instead of elastic, semitransparent forms of the literary imagination. Although she sometimes mocked their manners, Woolf was fascinated by women more militant than she—a group that includes Rebecca West and Dame Ethel Smyth, composer of the WSPU anthem as well as modern operas. Woolf defended both women in letters to Ottoline Morrell and Vita Sackville-West. In a 1921 review of one of the volumes of Smyth's memoirs, written before they met, Woolf says Smyth "looks the militant, working, professional woman—the woman who had shocked the country by jumping fences both of the field and of the drawing room, had written operas, was commonly called 'quite mad,' and had friends among the Empresses and the charwomen." Woolf feels "inclined to risk a theory that the prominent artistic figures of that time were racy, slangy, outspoken men and women; very patriotic, very combative, and very warm-hearted: differing in all these respects, not necessarily for the worse, from those who now occupy the stage" (3 *E* 298). She learned to love Smyth, trusting her with confidences and sharing her thoughts on art with her into their final years.

Jane Harrison, the Cambridge classical scholar and social anthropologist, haunts the pages of *A Room of One's Own* right after her death in 1928: "And then on the terrace, as if popping out to breathe the air, to glance at the garden, came a bent figure, formidable yet humble, with her great forehead and her shabby dress—could it be the famous scholar, could it be J—— H——herself? (*Room* 17). Her scholarly interests included the cultural shaping of Greek religion and suggested that the worship of the Great Goddess was older than observations for male deities. Her theories found their way into the modernisms of Lawrence, Eliot, and Pound, as well as Woolf, H. D., and perhaps even Djuna Barnes, as I shall suggest in volume 2. Harrison was considered eminent by the turn of the century. Virginia Woolf reported hearing her "make proclamation" as she sat at dusk in a Cambridge college garden in 1912 (1 L 498). In 1913, Harrison published a feminist claim to women's equal humanity: *Homo Sum, Being a Letter to an Anti-Suffragist from an Anthropologist.* She had led a suffragist procession around London at age seventy-two. Woolf went to visit her in her final days, and maintained a friendship with the poet and novelist Hope Mirrlees, her companion.[11]

Harrison was just one of a number of women of Woolf's acquaintance whose associations with Cambridge helped her think out women's difficult access to education. Pernel Strachey, the principal of Newnham College and one of Lytton's sisters, was another. As Woolf's hostess when she visited Cambridge to give the lecture version of *A Room of One's Own* in 1928, she goes down in fiction as Mary Seton. However weak Lytton Strachey may have been on feminist causes, his female relatives were not. He reported to Virginia that his whole family was off at a suffrage meeting one day in early 1909. Ray Strachey, his sister-in-law, published *The Cause: A Brief History of the Women's Movement* in 1928.

Woolf's 1919 novel, *Night and Day,* reiterates the struggles of the *New Freewoman.* The society for woman's suffrage office, where Mary Datchet works, is directed by an "insignificant" man who dislikes having women find fault with him, and is presided over by a scatterbrained philanthropist. These characters could change places with several of the people on the staff of the *New Freewoman* who proved frustrating to West. Woolf deploys a heterosexual couple to plan books that will effect broad political reforms, even in the vicinity of the Strand. This would seem to endorse Marsden's elimination of the special category of women from her paper. But Ralph Denham and Katherine Hilbery still respect the solitary suffragette organizer, Mary Datchet, who is left working into the night, by her own light. As Mary works on correspondence in the suffrage office, she has a vision of a new web. She feels that "she was the center ganglion of a very fine network of nerves which fell over England, and one of these days, when she touched the heart of the system, would begin feeling and rushing together and emitting their splendid blaze of revolutionary fireworks" (81).

Though *Night and Day* is usually considered one of Woolf's least exploratory works from the standpoint of form, it is different in emphasis from the work of the suffragist author Elizabeth Robins, whose stories Woolf reviewed. Woolf assigns to a world of the past Robins's stories of "very old English houses, men who explored the Yukon for gold, suffrage raids, and butlers, and haunted houses." She finds that "misled largely by her strong dramatic sense, [Robins] has backed certain human qualities which dropped out of the race and neglected others which are still running" (3 *E* 228). Woolf's remarks do not necessarily dismiss or silence suffrage; they are attuned to new historical conditions, to the changes in human nature signaled in "Mr Bennett and Mrs Brown," and to new audiences. Life can no longer be told as a dramatic tale of martyrdom and adventure, as Sylvia Pankhurst would make of Dora Marsden or Emily Davies. The suffragist had sat down to contemplate the system, and to write long into the night. For this, Woolf had another model, Margaret Llewelyn Davies, who merged the ideal of suffrage into the work of the Women's Cooperative Guild.

Barnes as Cynical Cub Reporter

Djuna Barnes's experience of suffrage began with her grandmother Zadel, whose role at the 1888 International Council of Women Convention and acquaintance with Elizabeth Cady Stanton have already been noted. To support herself in New York, Barnes began publishing journalism and sketches at a fierce rate for papers such as the *Brooklyn Daily Eagle*. Barnes had to find sensational subjects to sell her work. Her portfolio included a staged rescue by firefighters, an in-cage interview with a young female gorilla, and a report, published in 1914, on the experience of being forcibly fed. With this article, Barnes had hit upon the most flagrant form of physical abuse used against hunger-striking British suffragettes. It had fueled WSPU propaganda and prompted Rebecca West to dig up analogies to Jack the Ripper. Barnes's empathy with WSPU martyrs in her article was clear: "If I, playacting, felt my being burning with revolt at this brutal usurpation of my functions, how they who actually suffered the ordeal in its acutest horror must have flamed at the violation of the sanctuaries of their spirits." She had "a vision of a hundred women in grim prison hospitals, bound and shrouded on tables just like this, held in the rough grip of callous warders while white-robed doctors thrust rubber tubing into the delicate interstices of their nostrils and forced into their helpless bodies the crude fuel to sustain the life they longed to sacrifice" (NY 178). Male authorities on a range of subjects, from apes to medicine, are treated to the same satire by Barnes as they are in the better-known writings of Woolf.

Still Barnes reported suffrage events skeptically, aiming her satire just as willingly at earnest suffrage leaders and followers. For the sake of a story, she attended a two-week course on suffrage organized by Carrie Chapman Catt. Barnes opens with a playful observation on high-mind-edness: "Among seventy or eighty students there are bound to be some high-minded formulas for life. In fact, the thresholds to some minds are so high that one has to learn to hurdle to get into their rooms of thought. High-mindedness is necessary if in two short weeks you are handed the country" (NY 65). Barnes records Catt's more down-to-earth advice to speakers unleashed on the city—most of it pertaining to clothing and elocution. Despite her possession of a "little silver hammer with which she proclaims golden silence," Catt is unsure of what to expect from the sessions, and leaves the reporter in a severe case of doubt ("Seventy Trained Suffragists Turned Loose on City").[12] Barnes was already making use of gaps to tell her stories.

There is far less doubt in a 1918 interview Barnes conducts with Mrs. Ellen O'Grady, Fifth Deputy Police Commissioner. This article suggests that Barnes's feminism centered on strong women and their means of survival, rather than the struggle for the vote. The same preference is visible in her early plays of the era, "To the Dogs" and "The Dove." Mrs. O'Grady was a survivor—an immigrant woman, widowed with five children, who discovered the civil service as a source of employment and used her office to prevent young women from getting into trouble. Probably the fact that this policewoman writes poetry on the side qualifies O'Grady for Barnes's journalism of curiosities. Barnes strategically quotes from O'Grady's verses, but not for their own merits. The verses express common religious and patriotic feelings, as did some of Zadel's writing. Barnes quotes O'Grady as an interviewing strategy. This brings her subject out of her business world and into "home-like" topics. Barnes also tries to move the interview into the subjects of crime and death that interest her. O'Grady is wise to this, and in a recurrent pattern for Barnes's interviews, the interviewee is allowed to take over the interview to this effect: "You're a funny girl. . . . You love crime and now you adore death—I see you have the artist's soul" (NY 310). The practical O'Grady brings the artist back to a politics of life. Officer O'Grady has "great faith in" women, particularly in those who have borne children. She thinks of "hundreds of things they can do besides vote" and dignifies housework as "their master art." She extrapolates: "The state, the world, the entire administration and public life—what is it if not housekeeping on an immense scale?" (314). Mrs. O'Grady would have young women learn a trade and gain an education of the heart. Though her domestic metaphors evoke an earlier phase of new womanhood, the project for the heart was one that would occupy Barnes in her most serious future writing projects. O'Grady serves finally as a mother mentor.

Thus we find Woolf, West, and Barnes provided with a senior set of women actively pursuing women's issues, including suffrage, but not limiting themselves to a concern for the vote. They had emerged empowered from educational institutions that offered them curricula originally developed for men. They formed their own circles and societies, selecting young women for professional mentorship, and bridging social divides. These political mentors entered journalistic enterprises, repudiating arrangements and philosophies that inhibited women while they declared their own fields of interest. They have been given a chapter of their own in this study, but are not entirely distinguishable from the women who concern us next, shading more into literary occupations.

4 Midwives of Modernism

Masterpieces are not single and solitary births.

—Woolf, *Room* 68

Virginia Woolf's *A Room of One's Own,* begun with lectures presented at women's colleges and largely written in 1928, has provided my epigraph to this chapter. It goes on to assert, in the context of seeking accomplished women writers, that "masterpieces . . . are the outcome of many years of thinking in common, of thinking by the body of the people, so that the experience is behind the single voice" (68–69). Woolf would make the point that her imaginary contemporary writer, Mary Carmichael, had many models in various disciplines: "Jane Harrison's books on Greek archaeology; Vernon Lee's books on aesthetics; Gertrude Bell's books on Persia" (83).[1] Many of the women I am calling the midwives of modernism were active in literary circles and as writers well before 1914, the date when male modernists have been identified as coming of age. They set the scene not just for the men of modernism but in more complex ways for Woolf, West, and Barnes. To some extent they offered a buffer with the Edwardian uncles, whose gendered relations posed a more complicated problem for the women than the men of modernism. These women contributed their own writing and experience, as well as literary connections and hospitality, toward "thinking in common." Once women are introduced back into the modernist field, their paths repeatedly cross one another, veer off from the male-centered stories, and prepare our understanding of what I am calling the women of 1928.

Lodging Les Jeunes

South Lodge, the London home of novelist, biographer, and suffragist Violet Hunt, was a meeting place where experienced authors such as Henry James, Thomas Hardy, May Sinclair, Ford Madox Ford, Arnold Bennett, and H. G. Wells could meet younger people ("les jeunes" as Hunt and Ford called them): Ezra Pound, H. D., Richard Aldington, Wyndham

Plate 8. Violet Hunt, Rebecca West,
baby Anthony West, and Ford Madox Ford.

Cornell University Library.

Lewis, D. H. Lawrence, Brigit Patmore, G. B. (Gladys) Stern, and Rebecca West. Hunt also counted Radclyffe Hall, author of that critical work of 1928 *The Well of Loneliness,* among her admirers. Hunt claimed that, as a reader for Ford Madox Ford's *English Review,* she called the poetry of D. H. Lawrence to his attention (Hunt 257). She was also "instrumental in procuring" Rebecca West's "Indissoluble Matrimony" for Wyndham Lewis's journal, BLAST. Hunt interpreted this short story differently and more humorously than most, explaining in her memoirs that it is misread as a "tragic experiment" and better understood as a "good spoof" (216). Violet Hunt has survived chiefly in personal anecdotes, while her reading of modernism and the merits of her own writing have been largely ignored.

Hunt's novels generally treated the sexual politics of women's relationships, openly discussing sexual frustrations and frigidity. Another woman of the transitional generation, May Sinclair, wrote a review summarizing Hunt's work through 1921, overturning Hunt's reputation for "hard yet superficial cleverness." Sinclair credits her instead with sincere and uncompromising psychological realism. She hails Hunt's mastery with the *demi-vierge* type and the grim, uncanny, northern qualities of *Tales of the Uneasy,* some of which first appeared in the *English Review.* Hunt's biography of Elizabeth Siddal, *The Wife of Rossetti,* could draw upon personal acquaintance, as she was the daughter of pre-Raphaelite painter Alfred William Hunt.[2] It set a precedent for looking away from the male center of artistic movements.

Hunt invited Rebecca West to South Lodge for tea after West wrote a review of Ford's *The New Humpty Dumpty* "that laid us waste and made us friends for life," as Hunt recalls (203). West's memoirs and letters recall Hunt with appreciation and affection. West's description of Hunt as a literary midwife influenced my selection of the title of this chapter. After the birth of Anthony, Hunt was one of West's few literary contacts. The two women could commiserate about problems in their relationships with Ford, who was Hunt's partner from 1910 to 1918, and Wells, who had briefly been Hunt's lover as well. Out of the process could emerge confidence in their own common sense. West remained loyal when Hunt's memoirs of the period, *The Flurried Years,*[3] infuriated Ford and many of his male acquaintances. Reminiscing about Hunt with her novelist friend G. B. Stern, West declared her "real memory of affection for dear Ophelia," the Ophelia referring to Hunt's solitude late in life (West letter to Stern, 1942, Tulsa).[4] When Hunt died, G. B. Stern had a quip for West:

"She's gone to join Ford who was expecting Brigit Patmore instead" (Stern letter to West, n.d., Tulsa).

Something of the atmosphere of South Lodge can be detected from the following report of West to Sylvia Lynd—an important personal and literary confidante for West in the early years and a professional contact as the wife of journalist Robert Lynd.[5] Ford had "explained to me elaborately the imperfection of 'The Return of the Soldier' compared to any of his works—a statement with which I profoundly agreed but which oughtn't to be made" (West letter to Lynd, 28 Aug. 1918, Tulsa). West did, in fact, review Ford's *The Good Soldier* very positively. But her letter goes on to make a parlor game of his self-flattery. She plans to repeat the performance with Hugh Walpole, comparing his work unfavorably to hers, and assumes that he'll do the same with someone else. While West's ego withstood Ford's comparison, Walpole's did not, as we have seen in his complaints about her published scalpings of his work.

Hunt has left fine descriptions of West, both in her late teens and in her early thirties, suggesting that she was charmed by her but concerned about what might await a brilliant woman writer. West had come to them at South Lodge in a pink dress, with a "large, wide-brimmed country-girlish straw hat that hid her splendid liquid eyes . . . quite superiorly, ostentatiously, young—the ineffable schoolgirl!" (203–204). Hunt compared the Rebecca of 1926 to George Sand, in both appearance and intellect: "Though guileless, she was discreet: though frank, withdrawn. Deep as the sea yet adorably frivolous. A good gossip but no mischief-maker. Devilish well informed and yet *très femme*—and that also is very like George Sand. Like George Sand she needs a Dr. Pagellop; a De Musset would be too trying for her. Sex, in which Tom, Dick and Harry participate and indiscriminately suffer from, should not be allowed to flog our geniuses" (205). Woolf wrote a mixed review of Hunt's *The Flurried Years*—in which this report occurs. For one thing, Hunt "runs the word [genius] to death." A "novelist's book," this memoir treated situations imaginatively, leaving much unexplained. Its great success for Woolf was in its Edwardian male portraits, and especially the "unofficial side" of Henry James (4 E 340–41).

May Sinclair, one of Hunt's closest friends, deserves to be much better known as a maker and connector of modernism. It was she who introduced Pound to Ford, providing him access to the *English Review*. When Virginia Woolf expressed her suspicion that T. S. Eliot did not know her works, he protested that he probably knew them better than the novels of

Bennett, Galsworthy, and even May Sinclair—suggesting her eminence in the twenties (Eliot letter to Woolf, 2 June 1927, Berg). Sinclair was one of many women writers solicited for the *Little Review* by Jane Heap.

Sinclair proved adept at practicing and detecting in others' work the new formal and psychological aspects of modernism that would prove an important focus for Woolf, West, and Barnes. The psychological was a focus far less acknowledged by the "men of 1914." Sinclair was just as devoted to discussing newness in women writers as she was helpful in spreading the doctrines of Pound, or identifying the aesthetic merit of direct realism in Eliot's early poems.[6] Her attention to women writers is helpful today as a means of recovery. We have noted her fresh analysis of Hunt's novels and stories. It was Sinclair who clarified the qualities of Dorothy Richardson using the term "stream of consciousness," connecting psychological theory to modernism.[7] Virginia Woolf took notes on this essay in the notebook used to write "Modern Fiction," and though Richardson did not appear in the final essay, Sinclair's discussion of her psychological qualities influenced it.[8] Sinclair also detected the maturing of H. D. beyond the imagist poet of 1911, seen as the creation of Pound and toward new mythic forms. H. D.'s launching out from heterosexual male modernism has been confirmed in recent feminist criticism.[9] Her use of writing to resolve the findings of psychoanalysis, which came somewhat at Freud's suggestion, also fits the way that Woolf, West, and Barnes coped with troubling childhood situations.

Sinclair's own writing sets important content for feminist modernism. In the pamphlet *Feminism,* published by the Women Writers' Suffrage League, she counters the arguments of Sir Almroth Wright, finding them unscientific in their sampling of women, and biased by prejudices of the times. Sinclair challenges his assignment of hysteria, neurasthenia, and physiological emergencies to women exclusively and finds many healthy accompaniments to women's activism and intellectuality—the exuberance of the unleashed brain, enthusiastic humanity, and solidarity akin to the relations of the working class. She worries about new patterns in which employed women might exploit other women, and she denounces militancy without condemning women who have been driven to it. Sinclair's rational use of examples from both sexes to overcome biased views of women would prove basic to West's socialist/feminist essays as well. Her tempered resistance to suffragette militancy was shared by West, as we saw in the previous chapter.

Sinclair's novel *Mary Olivier* was published in the *Little Review* simultaneously with the middle chapters of Joyce's *Ulysses*. Its subject is important for women working out strategies as writers. Sinclair studies the stifling of a gifted female intellect by her Victorian mother's assumptions about the primacy of sons and the duties of daughters. Rebecca West suggests that in *Mary Olivier* Sinclair showed Richardson "what could be done with her own method" of "secondary stream of consciousness" ("Notes on Novels" 50). We enter the mind of this character only to experience her complicity in self-denial. Yet Mary also exerts a power of mind that connects to a tradition of female spiritual mysticism, introduced by Madam Blavatsky and perpetuated by W. B. Yeats, George Gurdjieff, and a host of modernist women—H. D., Dora Marsden, Rosamund Lehmann, and, to some extent, the three women I am most concerned with.

Rebecca West predicted that her friend G. B. Stern would be "the Miss Sinclair of her generation," identifying both of them as writers of "women's books." West also suggested that, for all her sophistication, Stern lacked Sinclair's "cold calm" and "serenity": "There is about Miss Sinclair's talent something large and primitive; she is in essentials the woman who has through all the ages been wife and mother of men, and consequently she can take violent events calmly" (50–51). The serene woman of an earlier generation is re-created in reviews by a number of modernist women, including Dorothy Richardson ("Women and the Future"). The serenity of Sinclair escaped West, who also would not have seen herself as a writer of "women's books." Both women may have been shaping a feminine foundation to fall back upon, as they ventured into literary territories they intended to share with men while developing their own sense of identity.

There was awkwardness in the personal meetings of West with Sinclair, who seemed to have a "sealed air," typical of "distinguished women with degrees and things," that shut her off from West (West letter to Ford, n.d., Yale). When Sinclair told West and Stern the story of an "author's death" (C. T. Kerry had collapsed on a table, upsetting a bottle of ink that had splashed all over his face), she was horrified to find her audience lost in hilarity. Rebecca thought it the "most macabre, insanely funny thing I have ever heard" (quoted in Rollyson). In another, perhaps more spirited meeting, Sinclair regaled West and Stern with tales of a well-known woman writer of the day, Charlotte Mew. Sinclair's topic was a new one for West at the time—Mew's lesbian pursuits. Sinclair supposedly jumped over a bed and raced about a room to escape Mew's attentions.[10] The episode provides one of many examples of West's distancing of herself from lesbian and gay identifications. Virginia Woolf considered meeting Charlotte Mew part of her professional initiation, as she told Vita Sackville-West in 1924. Woolf uses Thomas Hardy's phrase for Mew, "the greatest living poetess," which gives a sense of her prominence, but also perhaps of Woolf's working free from literary uncles who would pronounce on greatness, providing the woman poet with a diminutive, gender-marked suffix. Woolf did think enough of Mew to purchase *The Farmer's Bride* in 1920. Charlotte Mew has regained respect in recent feminist criticism for her contribution to a lesbian aesthetic—now accepted as a defining component of female modernism.[11]

Bloomsbury Resources

In the circles inhabited by Virginia Woolf, I turn first to a Victorian Aunt of Modernism, Caroline Emilia Stephen. In mature life a Quaker convert and mystic who thrived in a chaste, solitary life, Miss Stephen had spent her early years attending to aging parents and their family ideals. As her contribution to modernism, she left her niece the financial legacy of £500 a year celebrated in *A Room of One's Own*. This "spinster" may also have spun important lines of escape from the dysfunctional family described in chapter 1. She offered a philosophy of inner vision and confidence in silence that may have served Woolf's writing of the liberating *To the Lighthouse* and the inward, group meditation *The Waves* (see Marcus, "The Niece of a Nun," in *Virginia Woolf and the Languages of Patriarchy* 115–35). In her Cambridge house, which Woolf compared to a "cathedral close," Caroline Stephen helped restore Virginia from the mental breakdown that followed her father's death in 1904. Major credit for this restoration goes to Violet Dickinson, who saw Woolf's first reviews and essays into print in a church publication, the *Guardian,* and was Woolf's most important correspondent around 1905, when she was becoming an active reviewer and essayist, and even undertaking a teaching assignment at Morley College.

Elizabeth Robins, who had come to England from the U.S. in 1889, made friends with the Stephen family when Woolf was still a child. She became famous acting in the roles of Ibsen's heroines, particularly Hedda Gabler, and as a writer she had one best-seller, *The Magnetic North* (1898).

Robins founded both the Actresses' Franchise League and the Women Writers' Suffrage League, and in the twenties wrote regularly for *Time and Tide,* and thus she fits equally well in chapter 3 of this study. At *Time and Tide* she would have known another former actress of Ibsen, Rebecca West, as well as Vera Brittain and Winifred Holtby. Robins's experience in American theater has resonance with that of Djuna Barnes two decades later. Robins was a successful producer, manager, playwright, and realistic novelist, able to assert herself against the Edwardian might of George Bernard Shaw. Although a generation older than most modernists, she was writing into the 1950s and often addressed problems of interest to feminism in her plays and novels, including women's sexual passion in *Alan's Wife* (1893), conversion to the WSPU in *The Convert* (1907), and pacifism in *Ancilla's Share* (1924)—a work Jane Marcus has compared to Virginia Woolf's *Three Guineas.* At the time of Woolf's death, her physician, Octavia Wilberforce, was Robins's partner; Robins had taken interest in Woolf's fragile health. Robins was the subject of a series of Virginia Woolf's book reviews, starting with a 1905 appreciation of *The Dark Lantern,* published in the *Guardian.* By 1920, Woolf's reviewing hints at a complicated scenario of generational and stylistic difference, as noted in the previous chapter. The invocation of a historical watershed with Robins's generation of adventure writers was something Woolf could have learned from her own critic, Katherine Mansfield, whom we turn to shortly.

Several other women gave Woolf a sense of intellectual or artistic foundation. Julia Margaret Cameron, Woolf's great-aunt, though dead before her birth, left a heritage of female creativity in her photography and served as a stimulus for one of her lighter works, done as a family project, *Freshwater.*[12] I have already mentioned Janet Case, one of Woolf's language instructors, and the classical scholar Jane Harrison in the suffrage context. A woman rarely mentioned is Mary Sheepshanks, described as the "effective principal" of Morley College, an evening school for working-class men and women (1 Bell 105).[13] Woolf was at first highly amused by her name (which she applied teasingly to Violet Dickinson), her address (in a palace), and the nature of the initial request (1 L 171). But Sheepshanks persuaded Thoby, Vanessa, and Virginia Stephen to offer classes. Virginia Woolf's 1905 notebook suggests that she took a serious interest both in her women students and in defining the aims of education—as she would continue to do through the writing of *Three Guineas.* Woolf took her own approach, having confided to Madge Vaughan, "They begged me to give a course of lectures—which I feebly declined, and said I would rather get to know them personally than instruct them—but they are much too keen to let me off" (1 L 173). Indeed, the personal does seem to have flourished, as she reports after the first lecture on Venice: "Lots of jokes is what they like—and then they blossom out—and say they have written poetry since the age of 11!" (177). A "report" of July 1905, drafted in a notebook, goes on at some length about the students, particularly one who gave a very honest description of the mechanical nature of the writing she did for a religious paper (1 Bell 202). Woolf's pedagogy for teaching history was to "include one good 'scene' upon which I hoped to concentrate their interest" (203). As a teacher of writing, Woolf was sometimes frustrated over such things as a fifty-year-old male socialist inclined to bring "the Parasite (the Aristocrat, that is you [Violet Dickinson] and Nelly [Lady Robert Cecil]) into an essay upon Autumn" (1 L 210). She was seriously concerned about the superficiality of what she could offer, and disappointed when composition was elected by the Morley administrators because more students would take it; she preferred teaching history as the more valuable subject, even if it reached fewer students. Still, she persisted with teaching and learning from her students until 1907.

Woolf had another woman well placed in the academic world in Pernel Strachey, sister of Lytton and headmistress at Newnham College. It was she who could play hostess when Woolf visited to deliver her lecture on women and fiction, stimulating Woolf's thought on what was needed to foster female creativity. The women's supper was "nothing to stir the fancy," though it does stir her humorous comparisons: the "homely trinity" of "beef with its attendant greens and potatoes," suggestive of "women with string bags on Monday morning," followed by "prunes and custard," the former labeled as an "uncharitable vegetable . . . stringy as a miser's heart" (Room 17–18). And even if luncheon at the men's college—sole spread with "a counterpane of the whitest cream," partridges, and wine—did set off an electric light in the spine (10–11), it lacked something of the humming excitement behind conversations held before the war.

Woolf had held her own conversational evenings before the war in Bloomsbury, in a tradition that came and went with various hostesses throughout her life. One of Virginia Stephen's guests on a Thursday evening in 1909 was Ottoline Morrell—perhaps the leading hostess of British modernism. D. H. Lawrence, Aldous Huxley, and her lover, Bertrand

Russell, were Morrell's most celebrated visitors besides Woolf. Morrell uniquely serves the unity of this book, having entertained all three of the authors I am centrally concerned with at her country home, Garsington, near Oxford. West received the call in 1922, at about the time she published *The Judge*. The two women did not hit it off well, West apparently disappointed at the guest list on her particular weekend. Barnes was entertained much later, after Morrell had read *Nightwood*. Lady Ottoline enthusiastically placed Barnes's work in Aldous Huxley's hands. She also tried to promote it to reviewers and to urge a more aggressive advertising scheme at Faber through her acquaintance with T. S. Eliot, who shared tea with Barnes at Garsington. The invitations to West and Barnes were one measure of their having made it as modernist writers.

Morrell's letters to Woolf are of special interest because they tend to assess relationships among women. Woolf's friendships with Ethel Smyth, Elizabeth Bowen, and Katherine Mansfield all come up. Woolf had noted in her diary in 1925 that Morrell's "plethora of young men slightly annoys me. Really, I am not a good lioness. . . . A woman is much more warmly sympathetic" (3 *D* 30). Morrell felt that Woolf was far more successful than she in making and sustaining female friendships because of her attractiveness as a "great intellectual": "All women who think are proud to know her and look up to her." Her "prestige" makes it easier for Woolf "to know fine women" (Morrell letter to Woolf, 25 Nov. 1933, Sussex). Morrell and Woolf were both fascinated by Rebecca West, though Morrell turned against her, as if the two women were set in competition for Woolf's company. Morrell thought Woolf should not have permitted West to call her "Virginia." She recalled at that time that West's visit to Garsington had been a failure, and that she had "poured forth a stream of spite" on subjects such as religion and sex and life (Morrell letter to Woolf, 5 Dec. 1933, Sussex). Morrell "could angrily . . . bite Rebecca West's arms—That great hoyden—that great pushing vulgar woman—to elbow me out—I hate her!" (Morrell letter to Woolf, 22 Dec. 1933, Sussex). If there was a company of women associated with Woolf, Morrell wanted to be part of it. Her appreciation of *A Room of One's Own* also constructs a vision of Woolf liking and facilitating the company of women. Morrell got the impression that Woolf "goes out and has tea with each woman writer" entering "into their own rooms," and as she walks with them "they take her arm and whisper secrets . . . I can see a crowd of intimates waving to you from another world" (Morrell letter to Woolf, 15 Oct. 1932, Sussex).

Katherine Mansfield

One important intimate of this sort was Katherine Mansfield. Mansfield, who had emigrated from New Zealand to London, published *In a German Pension* in 1911. This collection of stories probed the dynamics of power in sexual relations, and was among her most openly feminist works.[14] She wrote rather severe but decisive reviews of many female modernists, including Sinclair, Richardson, and Woolf. These appeared in *Athenaeum,* the journal edited by her husband, John Middleton Murry, whose alliances with Eliot, Lawrence, and the Woolfs are developed further in chapters 7, 9, and 12. Mansfield expressed her admiration of Woolf's *The Voyage Out* and her desire "to make [her] acquaintance more than anyone else's" to Lytton Strachey, whom she met at one of Ottoline Morrell's literary weekends in 1916. Strachey gave a brief account of Mansfield's writing: "She wrote some rather—in fact distinctly—bright storyettes in a wretched little thing called the Signature, which you may have seen, under the name of Matilda Berry." With his emphasis on smallness, "storyettes," Strachey treated Mansfield somewhat as Eliot would in *After Strange Gods.* Eliot found that Mansfield "handled perfectly the *minimum* material—it is what I believe would be called feminine" (38). In a letter to Virginia Woolf, Strachey found her "very amusing and sufficiently mysterious," but labeled her person and intellect as vulgar: "She has an ugly impassive mask of a face—cut in wood, with brown hair and brown eyes very far apart; and a sharp and slightly vulgarly-fanciful intellect sitting behind it" (Woolf and Strachey 81).[15] Responding to Strachey, Woolf was aware of Mansfield's interest in her: "Katherine Mansfield has dogged my steps for three years—I'm always on the point of meeting her, or of reading her stories, and I have never managed either" (82).

Despite this unenthusiastic prelude, which I think was conditioned by its audience, Mansfield became one of Virginia Woolf's most important literary contacts by 1917. She envied Mansfield as much as James Joyce as a model of what she was trying to do. On visits together, Woolf and Mansfield enjoyed passionate discussions on writing, snatched while Murry and Leonard Woolf were otherwise occupied. Woolf and Mansfield discussed Richardson's *Pilgrimage* with "freedom and animation" soon after Woolf's review of *The Tunnel* (1 D 257). Rebecca West also valued Mansfield's writing. West told Ottoline Morrell that she would take

Mansfield flowers when she lay ill at Fontainbleau. While undoubtedly keeping up her publishing contacts with John Middleton Murry, West expressed her admiration of Mansfield following her tragic early death from tuberculosis in 1923.

Mansfield's 1919 review of Woolf's second novel, *Night and Day,* was devastating to its author, but also instructive about Woolf's evolving sense of her self in writing. Mansfield anticipated some of the terms that Woolf would use to challenge Edwardian writers and asserted the value of Jane Austen in discussing a tradition of women writers. Mansfield began by identifying theirs as an "age of experiment" and then assigned Woolf to a very traditional craft. Her controlling metaphor for Woolf's novel is a serene, deliberate sailing ship—a "ship that was unaware of what has been happening," whose sight makes her feel "old and chill." What had been happening was World War I. Woolf would come to this historical subject in *Jacob's Room* and her successive novels. Mansfield's sense of being aged by the war would also enter Woolf's criticism. In 1920, she called upon this trope when considering the pre-1910 world evoked by Elizabeth Robins's novels, though notably this critique does not fault Robins for realistic form. Mansfield has other remarkable observations. Woolf's infusion of her personality as a writer into her work, and her control of the world of the novel prompt Mansfield to classify her as "Austen up-to-date," an admirable comparison considering Woolf's appreciation of Austen, most fully realized in *A Room of One's Own.* Mansfield reports her reading in two stages, a palimpsestic critical approach Woolf would adopt in "Phases of Fiction." For Mansfield, it is in the second stage, when the novel is complete and one looks for enduring effect, that Woolf falls short of Austen, whose minor characters hold more enduring life. This is explained by the observation that Woolf's feeling for living continually gives way to her feeling for writing. By calling Woolf's shipshape novel "aloof," Mansfield introduces the politics of class, even where she seems to be admiring accomplishment. Critics have yet to recognize how much Mansfield gave Woolf to think about, particularly in her relationship to modernism.

Woolf's sense of Mansfield's special qualities is recorded in "A Terribly Sensitive Mind," a review of Mansfield's 1914–22 journal. It was published in 1927, though like many of the works on women, it was not collected in Woolf's lifetime.[16] Woolf made her review a study of the writer's mind at work. This emphasis on process was increasingly typical of Woolf's essays. It also set aside the rivalry that could have been reignited by Murry's claim, as editor, that Mansfield was a "great" writer—a claim that elicited the ridicule of Ezra Pound. Woolf's Mansfield is a solitary being, taking her diary as "a mystical companion" (*w&w* 184). Her mind "is alone with itself; a mind which has so little thought of an audience that it will make use of a shorthand of its own now and then, or, as the mind in its loneliness tends to do, divide into two and talk to itself" (184–85). Woolf finds in this highly sensitive mind the attributes of a "born writer," and as such Mansfield overcomes the problem of fragmentation that is a constant concern in Woolf's considerations of the modern: "Everything she feels and hears and sees is not fragmentary and separate; it belongs together as writing" (184). Mansfield is credited with shaping moments to endure: "The moment itself suddenly puts on significance and she traces the outline as if to preserve it" (185). Woolf devotes the second half of her review to the search for "health in being," upon which writing is based—a united being "in contact with what I love—the earth and the wonders thereof—the sea—the sun" (186–87). Woolf notes that Mansfield's last months were spent in "spiritual brotherhood" at Fontainbleau.[17]

Woolf admitted her envy of Mansfield in her diaries, where she made similar admissions about Joyce. The emotion of envy has been used to discredit Woolf in Joyce studies and throughout Michael Holroyd's biography of Lytton Strachey.[18] Instead, we might consider how facing up to envy and its potential to recur, identifying the social sources of presumed inequities, and moving beyond this emotion could serve her developing art. The usual sense of authorial competition posited by Harold Bloom is even less fitting to West and Barnes. West tended to see all women writers as existing at a disadvantage, while Barnes became skeptical of the trendiness of the literary market, keeping to her own goals.

Mansfield's own sense of modernism made an important figure of D. H. Lawrence, though she quipped to S. S. Koteliansky that "his ideas of sex mean nothing" (Mansfield letter to S. S. Koteliansky, 17 July 1922, British Library). She also condemned Joyce and Eliot for their neglect of Chekhov, who was one of her most important models:

> I wonder if you have read Joyce and Elliot [*sic*] and those ultra-modern men? It is so strange that they should write as they do *after* Tchekov. For Tchekov has said the last word that has been said, so far, and more than that he has given us a sign of the way we should go. They not only ignore it; only think Tchekov's stories are almost as good as the "specimen cases" in Freud.

Woolf and Koteliansky collaborated in translating Dostoyevsky for the Hogarth Press, and like Mansfield, Woolf gave the Russians serious attention in crafting her idea of modernism. Dostoyevsky was also a favorite of West and Barnes. To them, this author suggested a greater reach into dark human emotion than one generally finds in Western literature.

Dorothy Richardson

Dorothy Richardson enters the experiential weave of this chapter as a figure of importance to both Woolf and West, more co-traveler than midwife, but kept always at a distance. In 1913 Richardson began the first chapter of *Pilgrimage*. Its first volume appeared in 1915, published by Duckworth, the firm headed by Virginia Woolf's half-brother Gerald. Duckworth was also the publisher that year of Woolf's first novel, *The Voyage Out*, which had been many years in progress.[19] As she explained it in her 1938 foreword to *Pilgrimage*, Richardson made a deliberate break with "the current masculine realism," offering a "feminine" equivalent that can also be seen as a replacement of Edwardian with modernist form (Scott, ed. 429). Richardson had sounded a challenge to H. G. Wells's portrayal of women in a 1906 review of *In the Days of the Comet,* anticipating Rebecca West's feminist skepticism of Wells's professed feminism by five years. Richardson found his women to be all the same "specimen," though "dressed up in different trappings" (400).

Richardson had insight into the supposed feminism of the Wellsian Edwardian generation, which she spells out in "Women and the Future," a 1924 essay that appeared in *Vanity Fair.*

> Many men, of whom Mr. Wells is the chief spokesman, read the
> history of women's past influence in public affairs as one long
> story of feminine egoism. They regard her advance with mixed feel-
> ings, and face her with a neat dilemma. Either, they say, you must
> go on being Helens and Cinderellas, or you must drop all that and
> play the game, in so far as your disabilities allow, as we play it.
> They look forward to the emergence of an army of civilized, docile
> women, following modestly behind the vanguard of males at work
> upon the business of reducing chaos to order. (Scott, ed. 412–13)

Richardson diverts attention from the man-trained women "living from the bustling surfaces of the mind; sharing the competitive partisanships of men" to her own rather essentialist idea of a "womanly woman" who is "relatively indifferent to the fashions of men, to the momentary arts, religions, philosophies, and sciences," living instead in "the deep current of eternity, an individual, self-centered" and paradoxically capable of unselfishness (413). It is the same sort of essentialism West found in May Sinclair, as noted above. In *Black Lamb and Grey Falcon,* West also theorizes a womanly woman, juxtaposing her to a masculine "lunacy" over political surfaces. Among Richardson's book reviews is one titled "The Reality of Feminism," concerning numerous recent feminist works, including *Towards a Sane Feminism* by Rebecca West's friend Wilma Meikle. Richardson appreciates Meikle's focus upon the need for women to achieve industrial organization, seeing this as a class issue that extends the range of feminism. Combining this with her own faith in womanhood, as retaining a "synthetic" quality that assures humanity, she is not threatened by the prospect of industrialized women (404).

Like West, Richardson fell into the widespread pattern of H. G. Wells's sexual adventures with women writers and social reformers. As noted in chapter 2, she miscarried his child in 1907. Wells appears in two volumes of *Pilgrimage* as Hypo Wilson. He is at the center of an adoring circle of eager young men who entertained a sense of "rightness and completeness" in *The Tunnel* (4.122). Yet he is a sexual disappointment to Miriam, who can treat him only maternally when they finally sleep together. This was decidedly not the case in West's early sexual experience with Wells. When in late middle age Richardson began sharing her memories of Wells with biographers, including West's son, Rebecca West was irritated.[20] This can be seen as an effort at privacy, for Wells and herself, or one of loyalty to Wells.

As is well known, Woolf made a theoretical connection to Richardson. She used her reviews of *Pilgrimage* to explore a concept of feminine language. The "psychological sentence of the feminine gender" was suitable to "descend to the depths and investigate the crannies" of a woman's mind (3 E 367). The reader is able to "register one after another, and one on top of another, words, cries, shouts, notes of a violin, fragments of lectures, to follow these impressions as they flicker through Miriam's mind, waking incongruously other thoughts, and plaiting incessantly the many-coloured and innumerable threads of life" (3 E 11). While impressed by Richardson's handling of consciousness, which was an important project in her own writing, Woolf was worried about the narrowing effect of a narrative that remains in just one mind.[21]

The Village and the Left Bank

Once she made her way to New York, Djuna Barnes found sustaining circles of female friends through the Theatre Guild and the Provincetown Players, both situated in Greenwich Village. She was devoted to Mary Pyne, a poet and occasional actress for the Playhouse group. Pyne is probably represented among the drawings of Barnes's early collection, *A Book*. Pyne's death of tuberculosis may have contributed to Barnes's preoccupation with dying maidens in her works (Doughty 139). Barnes developed a long-term friendship with Helen Westley, who served as the director of Barnes's plays *An Irish Triangle* and *Kurzy of the Sea* when they were performed at the Provincetown Playhouse. An actress and a founding member of the Washington Square Players and the Theatre Guild, Westley deserves to be better known in a history of the Provincetown Playhouse now dominated by Eugene O'Neill, Floyd Dell, and Hutchins Hapgood.[22] One of Barnes's most empathetic interviews, returned to in chapter 11, was conducted with Westley in 1917. It is a rare collaborative production in which Westley calls back for a second session, and they coach each other on emerging themes. A drawing of Westley definitely appeared in *A Book*. Barnes was always eager to see Westley on return trips to New York and consulted with her when she tried to help other women with their work. Another acquaintance from Greenwich Village days was Peggy Guggenheim, who would become a parsimonious but regular patron, providing Barnes with a species of salon and a retreat at Hayford Hall, Devon, in the 1930s, where she worked on *Nightwood*. At Hayford Hall, Barnes associated with Emily Holmes Coleman, whose diary and letters from Barnes helped with the reconstruction of the Barnes family situation presented in chapter 1. Coleman became an essential promoter of *Nightwood*—a story reserved for chapter 11.

The *Little Review* has already entered this chapter as publisher of May Sinclair and reading material for Virginia Woolf. Founded by Margaret Anderson in Chicago in 1914, by 1918 it was operating out of New York, with Jane Heap assuming a larger share of the editorial duties. Heap organized the all-American issue in which Barnes first appeared. This special number was designed to offset complaints of European domination, attributable to Ezra Pound's service as a foreign editor. As will be discussed in chapter 5, his move on the *Little Review* bears some comparison to his services at the *New Freewoman*, imposing special strains on female editors. Between 1918 and 1921, Barnes published eight stories, a play, and a poem in the journal. She was identified as a member of the *Little Review* group on the jacket blurb of *Ryder,* suggesting the importance of this connection in her promotion as a writer. Barnes comforted Heap when she was distressed by Margaret Anderson's brief flirtation with another woman; they may have had a brief lesbian relationship. Anderson's own accounts of Barnes are suspiciously negative: "Djuna and the *Little Review* began a friendship which might have been great had it not been that Djuna felt some fundamental distrust of our life—of our talk" (181). Anderson may have taken personally Barnes's tendency toward privacy, which caused her to suddenly shut off talk. Anderson's charge that Barnes was "not on speaking terms with her own psyche" (181) actually points toward Barnes's great interest in dialogs and psychoanalysis, which would be formalized in Nora's dialogue with Matthew O'Connor in *Nightwood.* Her work for the *Little Review* provided the core for Barnes's first commercially produced work, brazenly titled *A Book,* published in 1923. The artist and poet Mina Loy was Barnes's closest friend in the *Little Review* group—a relationship that carried over to Paris.

Another *Little Review* writer, Emma Goldman, offers an interesting weave in the set of connections made by this chapter. Though she published *The Social Significance of Modern Drama* in 1914, Goldman is better known as an advocate of anarchism, free love, and pacifism. She was founder of the anarchist journal *Mother Earth* and lectured throughout the U.S., and indeed the world. She was an influence on Margaret Anderson, who published commentaries on Goldman's anarchistic ideas, as well as the works themselves, in the *Little Review,* starting in 1914. Goldman's antidraft agitation at the outbreak of World War I won her deportation to her native Russia. Her 1917 trial was attended and minutely reported by Anderson. This occurred in the interval when Djuna Barnes was still in the U.S. The mid-twenties found Goldman lecturing on the Bolsheviks in London. Rebecca West organized a celebrity dinner for her and listened intently to her opinions of Communism. To enrich the network further, Barnes's friend Emily Holmes Coleman served as Goldman's secretary in the late twenties. Goldman's migratory presence in this study enforces both its internationalism and its political interest.

Margaret Sanger, the birth control advocate, should also be noted as a Greenwich Village figure, moving in the circles of John Reed and *The Masses* and presiding over conversations at Mabel Dodge's salon, where Barnes appeared briefly. In 1914 Sanger published *The Woman Rebel* on a monthly basis, from March through October, and in 1915 she coined the term "birth control." She fulfilled the image of the new woman to the popular press.[23] Around 1920 when he visited New York, H. G. Wells had an affair with Sanger while he was still in his relationship with Rebecca West. The contrast between Sanger and West is presented in his rather slapdash novel *The Secret Places of the Heart.* The Wellsian character meets a casual American new woman, willing to fall in love and discuss sociology at great length. He describes his mistress, the mother of his child, whose servants inevitably give her trouble; this Westian character is typically at fault when things go wrong on their occasional days together, and the American provides the male protagonist with a new sense of vitality.

In Paris, Gertrude Stein, Edith Wharton, Natalie Barney, Sylvia Beach, and Adrienne Monnier had set up literary housekeeping long before the migration, around 1920, of Pound, Joyce, and Ford Madox Ford.[24] Gertrude Stein's early production of significant modernist work is evident in the 1909 publication of *Three Lives*—work that is experimental in both form and content. The collection includes "Melanctha"—the extraordinary narrative of a black woman whose wandering disrupts masculine order, centering a racial "other." In 1914 *Tender Buttons* would offer new rhythms and imaginative metaphors of lesbian erotics. "Gertrude Stein" appeared among the notes Woolf took in preparing her essay "Modern Fiction" between two entries on the modern interest in psychology (Scott, ed. 643). Stein became a Hogarth Press author and was sketched by Djuna Barnes. Though her salon was clearly male-oriented, with her admiration of Picasso and the literary men who clustered around her, Stein made excursions in her "undertaker's car" with Sylvia Beach and Adrienne Monnier; she visited Natalie Barney's circle.

Barney's establishment at 20, rue Jacob, with its "Temple à l'Amitié" in the back garden and its gatherings of "l'Academie des Femmes," privileged intellectual women and particularly lesbians. Meetings had begun as pacifist demonstrations in 1917. Barney's admittedly class-conscious group would include Djuna Barnes during her Paris years in the twenties. It became the subject of her *Ladies Almanack,* to which we will return in chapter 12. Colette, Gertrude Stein, Edith Sitwell, Radclyffe Hall, Janet Flanner, Anna Wickham, Solita Solano, and Mina Loy all entered Barney's temple. Sappho was the presiding deity, brought into prominence in the *Penseés* of Renée Vivien. From 1927, Barney entertained the literary world on Friday evenings. These gatherings included the "men

Plate 9. Natalie Barney, "l'Amazone," 1920.

Romaine Brooks. Paris.

of 1914" who had made their way to Paris—Pound, Joyce, and charter member Ford Madox Ford. Barney's invitations for June 3, 1927, listed "Rachilde, then Ford Madox Ford will discuss American women of letters, including Djuna Barnes" (Wickes 166). Colette (one of West's favorite writers) and Gertrude Stein had featured evenings, while Mina Loy and Anna Wickham shared in the programming.

Barnes's regular interactions with Natalie Barney date back at least to 1924, when Barney was helping her find a room in Paris. Barnes was probably one of Barney's many female lovers, and Barney acquired a suggestive nickname in Barnes's salutations, "Dear Dark Horse." But their letters suggest that affections were widely spread and freely confided. One letter sends Barney regards from "the young and beautiful Thelma Wood—who lies, curled, perfumed, ready, downstairs on the couch" (Barnes to Barney, 29 Aug. 1924, Jacques Doucet). Barnes was also attracted to Barney's partner, Romaine Brooks, admiring her dark looks. Barnes asks Barney to embrace Brooks for her in one letter. She wrote a poem dedicated to Brooks (Jacques Doucet, 2 Aug. 1924) that should probably be taken as a tribute, or even a token of love. This poem, "Love and the Beast," has some of the unearthly, prophetic power of *The Book of Repulsive Women*. It comes in for further discussion in the context of Barnes's bestiary in volume 2. A contemporaneous letter says that Barnes is thinking fondly of Brooks's "medieval silhouette." It also remarks, "What a little black boy you look! (and how, being so tremendously handsome, do you find and keep solitude?)" (Barnes letter to Brooks, n.d., Jacques Doucet).

Scholars are well aware of Barnes's satirical wigging of Barney's circle in *Ladies Almanack*, which is discussed at some length in chapter 12. But Barney was capable of her own satire of Barnes, using the same heart and blood imagery that Barnes typically employed in describing intimate female relationships, as in her early play "The Dove." She sent a sheet of impressions of Barnes, based on reading *A Book*, which contains that play: "the finger tapering command of pen—and person—a pen dipped in the blood of her models," and "a pound of flesh is not the whole flesh demanded of most of them, & cut from too near her own heart not to sometimes betray the subterfuge—the transfusion!" "DB's pistol has too easy a trigger with no safety catch" (ms. with letter, 29 Oct. [1924], Jacques Doucet). Barnes requested opinions from Barney and Brooks on the play she was writing, "The Biography of Julie von Bartman." Her questions about the reception of its lesbian content anticipate the problems encountered by *The Well of Loneliness*. Barnes worries that the "young girl Gustava loves Julie in a reverent—a passionate way—and as it is *not* vulgar, and as it is not sensual—it will be twice damned" (Barnes letter to Barney, 29 Aug. 1924, Jacques Doucet).

Barney remained a faithful reporter to Barnes. In the 1960s she gossiped about Pound, maintaining a mocking attitude bound to please Barnes. Barney continued to treasure her copy of the *Ladies Almanack*, in which she carefully identified characters. She and Barnes exchanged fond recollections of their female circle. As an aging woman living alone at Patchin Place, back in Greenwich Village, Barnes remained in contact, however sporadically, with Barney, Solita Solano, Mina Loy, and Janet Flanner. Flanner, who served as a Paris correspondent to the *New Yorker* and was a friend and correspondent of Rebecca West in the 1950s, provided funds for Barnes to buy a typewriter after her return to New York. The old Paris group worried about Alice B. Toklas as she grew feeble after Gertrude Stein's death, and shared news about new friends—Marianne Moore figuring importantly in Barnes's accounts of her acquaintances in New York.

Unquestionably, then, women were present at the advent of modernism, on both sides of the Atlantic. Though not all interested in the same experimental forms or subjects, they were aware of one another's projects. They offered formal and informal reviews, letters, and conversations that developed their sense of connections and strategies, turning encounters with the women of modernism into experience. Women's writing, and writing for women, belonged in their scheme of an emerging modernism.

Part Two: *The Men of 1914*

Not wildly anti-feminist we are yet to be convinced that any woman ever invented anything in the arts.

—Ezra Pound, *New Age,* 1 Aug. 1918

I am trying . . . to go back through the masculine imaginary, to interpret the way it has reduced us to silence, to muteness, or mimicry, and I am attempting from that starting-point and at the same time, to (re)discover a possible space for the feminine imaginary.

—Luce Irigaray, *This Sex Which Is Not One* 164

The feminist philosopher and psychoanalyst Luce Irigaray explains in the above quotation her strategy for facing the dominance of masculine figures such as Sigmund Freud and Jacques Lacan in her field of study. Her statement can suggest the value of going back in this section to the male makers of modernism. We can examine the metaphorical spaces and attributes they gave to "the feminine," and note what sort of regard they had for women writers, as these "men of 1914" set up the scaffolding for their predominantly masculine literary movement. Their attitudes were selectively reinforced as later critics canonized Pound, Joyce, Eliot, and others, presenting them to the academy as the modernist movement.

Irigaray says further that she is not interested in toppling a phallocratic order and replacing it with another, "but [in] disrupting and modifying it, starting from an 'outside' that is exempt, in part, from phallocratic law" (68). This section moves "outside" of male makers of modernism by discovering their limitations in gendered relations, and consequently their limited usefulness as attachments for women writers—particularly ones who harbored feminist inclinations. It prepares us to launch out into the networks and strategies of modernist women, going outside the formative rules, and expressing gender differently. Also largely outside of phallocratic law are the unconscious and sexuality—unruly subjects that emerged as major sources of anxiety and interest in the modernist period. I focus on members of a traditionally favored group—Ezra Pound, Wyndham Lewis, T. S. Eliot, and James Joyce—identified as "the men of 1914" by Lewis.[1] I will also consider D. H. Lawrence for his more idiosyncratic modern appeal, which aroused the interest of the women writers I am pursuing. E. M. Forster, Lytton Strachey, and Roger Fry provide a means of assessing Bloomsbury's critical and creative values, which have too often been presented as identical to and supportive of Woolf's, or subjected to homophobic dismissal.

One way of going back "through the masculine imaginary, to interpret the way it has reduced us," as Irigaray bids, is to consider the modernist canon formation that has selected such "men of 1914." Well into the 1980s, the modernist era was managed for the academy by men who paid little critical regard to gender and had little interest in giving space in the canon to women, among other outsider groups. F. R. Leavis, Edmund Wilson, and the New Critics had their opportunities at canon making from the thirties through the fifties. In his *New Bearings in English Poetry* (1932), Leavis, presiding at Cambridge, identified Gerard Manley Hopkins, T. S. Eliot, and Ezra Pound as important modernist poets. Though Jane Austen and George Eliot were enrolled in his *Great Tradition,* modernist women novelists were not. Henry James and Joseph Conrad were selected immediately. In the mid-fifties he turned to what Hugh Kenner has termed his "obsession" with D. H. Lawrence. James Joyce was given secondary status. In *Scrutiny,* the influential journal he edited, Leavis eschewed anything related to Bloomsbury—a judgment sustained by his wife, Queenie Leavis, in her attacks on Virginia Woolf's *Orlando* and *Three Guineas,* which we will attend to in chapter 12. The New Critics (to whom Leavis is connected via I. A. Richards) are generally credited by feminists with establishing a male-dominated modernist canon that serves formalist models of unity, tension, irony, and paradox, ignoring personal and political considerations, including gender, class, and colonial marginalization.[2] Contemporary theory and criticism have encouraged us to seek the ideology behind the supposedly disinterested aesthetic criteria used in various phases of the modernist canonization process.

In the same era as Leavis and the New Critics, one might look at Edmund Wilson's postsymbolist school of authors, developed in *Axel's Castle* (1932), for another attempt at canonizing. His favored group included Yeats, Paul Valéry, Eliot, Marcel Proust, Joyce, Villiers de l'Isle-Adam, and one female token, Gertrude Stein. Wilson's interest in socialist and psychological theories made him a critic Rebecca West was capable of defending, even as she resisted Eliot's ideas taking over.

Richard Ellmann, one of the most prominent modernist scholars from the 1960s through the 1980s, made valuable contacts with female makers of modernism, including Harriet Shaw Weaver and Rebecca West, while writing his landmark biography, *James Joyce* (1956).[3] Ellmann's modernist canon, however, is decidedly masculine. It can be extracted from the anthology he assembled with Charles Feidelson in 1965, including as its great modernists Joyce, Eliot, D. H. Lawrence, Proust, Valéry, André Gide, Thomas Mann, Rainer Maria Rilke, and Franz Kafka. While they achieve admirable reach toward the Continent, fewer than 10 of the 953 pages in *The Modern Tradition* go to women writers, and Woolf is the only modernist among them. She is presented in a typically apolitical grouping—the section called "The Autonomy of Art."

Ezra Pound's account of modernism was recentered in the 1970s by Hugh Kenner in his highly influential work *The Pound Era*.[4] This account included Pound's charge to "make it new."[5] He proceeded through an amalgamation of early imagist manifestoes with the vorticist program of Wyndham Lewis. The twenties brought a consolidation of modernism by T. S. Eliot. This modernist genealogy still enjoys prominence.[6] Like the New Critics, Kenner performs close readings of texts for structural clues. But he has other strengths. His recontextualizing of the men of 1914 makes a productive turn toward cultural studies. Kenner connects modernists with one another, with classical tradition, and with other arts, popular culture, technical changes, and modes of publication. Pound offered Kenner good material for a return to what he embraced as "old fashioned source-hunting scholarship." So did James Joyce, and Kenner did notable detective work on both. But it was largely a male network. Kenner went to William Carlos Williams, Wyndham Lewis, and T. S. Eliot, armed with introductions supplied by Pound himself (59).

Kenner contributes to a curriculum of master works that remains difficult to modify, even after two decades of feminist effort. *Ulysses* plays an essential part in the conception of *The Waste Land,* with both contributing to the emergence of an international modernism of "certain masterpieces" (53). Kenner's internationalism is a "story of capitals," for him "the only story" with "adequate explanatory power." Citing Marshall McLuhan as his mentor, Kenner acknowledges "new environments created by new technologies: notably, the invasion of the city by the rhythms of the machine" (53).

Kenner's technological, international, monumental modernism excuses him from venerating the very American Wallace Stevens, "Virginia Woolf of Bloomsbury," and "Faulkner of Oxford" (59), though one might question his sense of the international. The study of Russian authors, interest in rural cultures, multiculturalism, and critiques of empire and international fascism—all important to the women writers featured in this book—do not factor into his internationalism. Indeed, the political and the personal, as explored through psychoanalysis, have little place in Kenner's thinking. Despite his close reading skills, Kenner does not read metaphors of modernist men, or his own, for their betrayal of attitudes toward gender. Kathryne Lindberg finds Kenner "side-stepping Pound's most radical statements that languages are irreducibly differential and metaphoric" (37). However, as we shall see in the next chapter, Poundian metaphors often partake of the architectural, classicist, scientific, technological, and military preoccupations of their age, echoed in Kenner's discourse. Lindberg directs readers to "disseminative" metaphors in Pound, suggesting that we have been forwarded a narrower version of male modernists than they offered themselves.[7]

Woolf and Bloomsbury are worse than parochial to Kenner, as he discusses them in his indictment of English modernism, *The Sinking Island* (1988). In his denunciation of Bloomsbury, Kenner echoes F. R. Leavis and follows a script from Wyndham Lewis, as we shall see in chapter 6.[8] The usually urbane and informing wit of Kenner suddenly bristles with exclamation points. Though elsewhere he writes sensibly on canonical change, Kenner seems desperate to hold his historical moment, with its focus on the more virile men of 1914. Kenner suggests that Bloomsbury was composed of a collection of shallow simpletons.[9] A fresh source of annoyance is the Virginia Woolf industry (somehow more despicable than the Joyce one), with the daily threat of yet another book on Woolf.[10] In Kenner's estimation, only one of her novels—*To the Lighthouse*—is re-readable. But he takes as its audience seminars at girls' colleges, with the portrait of Mr. Ramsay appealing particularly to girls who hate their fathers. Is this humor? Or is it the exposure of an Achilles heel of gender, a disclosure of his belatedness, or evidence of being severely out of touch with undergraduates? Kenner was recently taken to task by Diana Trilling for dismissing Rebecca West's opinion on a writer because West was "admittedly a hysteric."

Woolf is the only woman writer of the 1930s to get sustained attention in Valentine Cunningham's *British Writers of the Thirties* (1987). In noting the absence of women recently recovered by feminists, he explains, "This particular book lacks the space to do full justice to anything like all of these customarily absented authors. But at least the gap that commonly denotes their absence can be defined, they can be granted the mention and some of the respect they deserve, and their place marked on the '30s map for future reference" (27). Yet he does not define the gap, and it would be difficult to place them on the map he provides since it is ordered by the concept of the Auden generation, retained much as Kenner has clung to Pound and Lewis.[11]

Having searched into the imaginary of their academic inheritors, this section now turns to the man/agement of gender and the woman writer by the original male makers and shapers of modernism. Indeed, modernism has been made in many versions, spaced through the twentieth century. We must apprehend the "men of 1914," not just as they were presented through the 1960s, or in 1914, but as they assumed various positions of authority on through the 1930s. Thanks to archives, it is possible to go beyond a gender-conscious reading of the public, anthologized story, considering also the men's private disclosures of attitudes toward sexuality and female colleagues. Perhaps most important, my study brings into the public realm the reactions of modernist women to their treatment by these makers of the new.[12]

5 Ezra Pound: Plunging Headlong into Female Chaos

As Hugh Kenner has demonstrated, Ezra Pound makes an attractive central figure for organizing a concept of the culture and formal goals of modernism. Pound had the necessary endowments to place himself into incessant, vigorous literary movement. He was a bohemian, confident, individualist American male—a mover and entrepreneur. He pursued editors, writers, musicians, and artists who promised something new, working his way into the offices and editorial policies of periodicals (even feminist ones such as the *New Freewoman* and the *Little Review*), editing out extraneous materials in other people's poetry, and repeatedly taking on new theories, cultures, languages, economic ideas, and forms in his own writing. He wrote his theories down in directives, circulating them for present and future consumption.

Pound had a series of backers: doting parents who gave modest support; Margaret Cravens, a pianist from Indiana whose 1912 suicide may have owed something to Pound; the New York lawyer and literary collector John Quinn; and from 1914, Dorothy Shakespear Pound, vorticist artist and tolerant English wife. Her mother, Olivia, provided Pound access to his early idol and her former lover, William Butler Yeats. Dorothy Pound's toleration included adjusting to Pound's establishment of a second household with Olga Rudge and their daughter in the late 1920s.[1]

Pound arrived in London via Venice in 1908, having escaped humdrum Philadelphia suburbs and the moral indignation of Wabash College, which dismissed him as a teacher for providing a young woman temporary shelter in his rooms. Pound had and maintained literary contacts with American friends of his generation, including William Carlos Williams, whom he met while doing graduate study at the University of Pennsylvania, and H. D. (Hilda Doolittle). H. D. played Pound's "Dryad" in Pennsylvania woodlands and in his early poetry. They were engaged before his departure for Europe. Once she arrived in London in 1911, H. D.

moved in the same circles as Pound, collaborating in the origination of imagism in 1912. In that same year Pound made contact with Harriet Monroe, editor of the new *Poetry Magazine*. As noted in chapter 4, he became the foreign editor of Margaret Anderson's *Little Review* in 1917, three years after the journal was founded.

In England, Pound met first the publisher Elkin Mathews, and next the novelist May Sinclair, who helped him find his way into *les jeunes*. Through the hospitality of Violet Hunt and Ford Madox Ford, he gained publication in the *English Review*. Pound also frequented the Thursday evening gatherings of a group surrounding the philosopher T. E. Hulme at the Tour Eiffel Restaurant. Here he found support from Frank Flint and access to publication in H. R. Orage's *New Age*—a journal we first encountered via Mary Gawthorpe in chapter 3. Flint reviewed Pound's *Personae* positively in the *New Age*, and Pound's "I Gathered the Limbs of Osiris" appeared in the journal. One of the initial presentations of imagism was done by Flint for *Poetry* magazine. Pound's array of attachments and their interconnections were truly remarkable.

Starting in 1913, Pound made the *New Freewoman*, renamed the *Egoist* in 1914, his periodical base in England. Introduced there by Rebecca West, who helped publicize imagism in the journal, he became a factor in her departure, as described in chapter 3. The English poet Richard Aldington, H. D., and Eliot (who met Pound in 1914) all followed Pound to the *Egoist*. Pound also allied himself with Canadian-born Wyndham Lewis, whom he had met in 1910. Together they brought forth vorticism in 1914. Pound did less well with the Murrays at the *Athenaeum*, where he was a drama critic for a time; by 1919 Eliot was giving Pound lukewarm reviews in that journal (see Levenson 215). Eliot had become the second, and by then the prevailing, American with a directive role for modernism in England. Having exhausted the patience and resources of the English by 1920, Pound moved on to Paris, where he showed increased interest in translations and in the blend of cultures contributed to *The Cantos*. We are only beginning to appreciate the forms of ethnographic control that went into modernists' move into Oriental and African cultures, and the possibilities for analogy between this and their work with gender.[2] Another of Pound's later tendencies was his drift to the right, toward theories of Social Credit. He moved to Rapallo in late 1924, there nurturing sympathies with Mussolini and the growing powers of fascism, which culminated in his pro-Mussolini broadcasts during World War II.

Pound began with a reverence for Yeats, which has been seen by Wayne

Koestenbaum as the first of several homosocial creative bonds.[3] Yeats's volume *Responsibilities* reflects Pound's editorial insinuation of his ideas of the "new." He pushed and packaged the writing of the men who have since been securely canonized—T. S. Eliot, James Joyce, and William Carlos Williams—and was associated with others who still command the attention of literary historians, such as Lewis and Hulme. The presence of these figures in *The Cantos,* as individuals and literary influences, has been the subject of considerable scholarship.[4] Pound was published in return by Lewis, who reciprocally had his novel *Tarr* serialized in the *Egoist.* Eliot lent Pound historical importance, proclaiming in a Faber edition that "Mr. Pound is more responsible for the XXth Century revolution in poetry than is any other individual" ("Introduction," *Literary Essays of Ezra Pound* xi). Poundian quibbles with Eliot and Joyce in the twenties have provided material for male-centered genetic theories of modernism, most notably Michael Levenson's *A Genealogy of Modernism.*

Pound benefited from his early contacts with May Sinclair and Violet Hunt, whose roles in networking modernism were encountered in chapter 4. Pound-centered critical accounts give personal rather than literary treatments of them, concentrating more on his bond with Ford. Pound's accounts of taking over the enterprises of Dora Marsden of the *Egoist,* Harriet Monroe of *Poetry,* and Margaret Anderson of the *Little Review* have been only briefly disputed to date (see Longenbach, "Pound among the Women"). Pound readily fell in with the misogynistic, antilesbian attitude of his patron, John Quinn, toward Margaret Anderson and Jane Heap, whose magazine Quinn helped to finance during Pound's period as its foreign editor (1917–19). Pound suggested to Joyce that Anderson and Heap had "messed and muddled" the publication of *Ulysses* in the *Little Review,* "never to their own detriment" (*Pound/Joyce* 184–85). Anderson and Heap had been more willing than Quinn to see the supposedly "obscene" chapters of *Ulysses* published as Joyce wanted them, with Heap demonstrating considerable understanding of the controversial "Nausicaa" episode. They gladly faced court prosecution in 1921, only to be humiliated by Quinn, who acted as their attorney, keeping them silent throughout, and the judge, who felt that Anderson probably hadn't understood what she was reading in the questioned passages. To his credit, Joyce did not join in the judgments of Quinn and Pound against his female publishers.[5]

Following his introduction to the *New Freewoman* by Rebecca West, who hoped that he would be an ally in making the paper more literary,

Pound quickly set his own terms. He communicated directly with Marsden, perhaps sensing that West had her own literary plans, and a sizable will. West did feel left out of decisions that damaged the paper. Pound arranged with Marsden to have one page per issue—selected poetry in one issue, a critical article on poetry in London and France in the next. He would arrange payment for the contributors he solicited. Marsden seems to have checked him out on her criteria, which had come to emphasize individualism. He was able to declare, "I suppose I am an individualist, I suppose I believe in the arts as the most effective propaganda for the sort of individual liberty that can be developed without public inconvenience." He didn't suppose his literary page would "queer the editorial columns" and offered West as a reference: "Miss West has inspected the data of our peculiar sect, and has not been alarmed unduly" (Pound letter to Marsden, n.d., Princeton). Pound never held to the one-page limit. Using the pen name Bastien von Helmholtz, Pound did publish one patronizing article titled "Suffragettes" in the July 1914 issue of the *Egoist*.[6] But his coming did nothing to sustain the feminist side of the paper.

West was less than enthusiastic about some of Pound's finds for the journal, including the long and "appalling translation" of Remy de Gourmont's "The Horses of Diomedes," which she protested to no avail, except to alienate Pound. The work follows the longings of the hermit Diomedes for a series of disrobed women, qualifying chiefly for the masculine imaginary. De Gourmont's *The Natural Philosophy of Love* did in fact serve Pound's male genital imaginary, as we shall see in his famous preface. West's attitude toward imagism is predictive of her relation to modernist aestheticism in general. She saw a place for imagism and was willing to help present it to the world in a brief article titled "Imagisme." Writing from the Fabian summer school, West directed Marsden to "sign that introductory column to Ezra Pound's stuff by my name" (West letter to Marsden, n.d., Princeton). Her brief remarks led into the description that had been published by Flint in *Poetry*.[7] West's original lines show her discrimination among various traditions, her wit at constructing literary allegory replete with the politics of sex, and her own talent with purified, skeletal images.

> Poetry should be burned to the bone by austere fires and washed
> white with rains of affliction: the poet should love nakedness and
> the thought of the skeleton under the flesh. But because the public
> will not pay for poetry it has become the occupation of learned per-

sons, given to soft living among veiled things and unaccustomed to being sacked for talking too much. That is why from the beautiful stark bride of Blake it has become the idle hussy hung with ornament kept by Lord Tennyson, handed on to Stephen Phillips and now supported at Devonshire street by the Georgian school. (86)

She even anticipates the vorticist: "The *imagistes* want to discover the most puissant way of whirling the scattered star dust of words into a new star of passion" (86). Carol Barash suggests that West had entered into the spirit of imagism with her essay/story "Trees of Gold," published in the June 15 number of the *New Freewoman*. West also sustains the feminist passion of her youthful suffragette persona, and offers keen analysis of religious and commercial institutions in this little prose gem.

In her letters to Marsden, West mocks and resists the self-importance of the male imagists who had come their way. She did take some blows in the letters column, which may have fed her persistent sense of male persecution. In a letter to the editor, Raymond Pierpoint accused West of "cheap phrase making in which so many 'gutter journalists' excel." He questioned her appearance in the same paper as Pound, Ford, Huntly Carter, and de Gourmont (West letter to Marsden, n.d., Princeton). West was herself critical of Carter's writing, which has been summarized as "appalling dross" by Les Garner (75). She rises to new metaphors over Pierpoint's work, taking for herself a superior, maternal tone: "His aesthetic ideas run about like ill-conditioned infants in short frocks." But as "superior cow" she feels she "ought to refrain from attacking an inferior bull" (West to Marsden, n.d., Princeton). West had "a prohibition on describing one art in terms of another." While this pronouncement remains provokingly unexplained, it does suggest that the imagist term must have been uncongenial to her. She distances the objectives of the paper from Pound's movement: "We were glad to give hospitality in our pages to the exposition and examples of imagism because it seemed to us an interesting technical experiment. But the *New Freewoman* is not to be identified with its precepts" (West to Marsden, n.d., Princeton).

By late 1913, West was reporting her suspicions of a plot against the female editors of the *New Freewoman*. She suspected that Richard Aldington and others had "the sweet intention of buying us when our money runs low, getting rid of *me* and then *you*." Pound did suggest that Amy Lowell might buy the paper (Barash 43). He and a group of male allies from the *New Age* superintended the name change of the journal to the

Egoist. By 1926, West was describing Pound as "an *arrivist* American poet who intended to oust me, and his works and those of his friends continually appeared in the paper without having passed me" ("The 'Freewoman' " 576). When Jane Lidderdale was writing her biography of Harriet Shaw Weaver, another of the editors at the *Egoist,* she received the harsh though confidential assessment that Pound was "the cuckoo in the nest." He got mixed reviews on his abilities: "Ezra Pound struck me as highly intelligent and well-informed about French literature, but he was not very well-versed about contemporary English literature, about which he was learning at a rapid rate from Ford Madox Hueffer, H. D., Richard Aldington, Bridget [*sic*] Patmore, and, if I may say so, myself" (West letter to Lidderdale, 29 Jan. 1967, Tulsa). She heard in later years that he had only unkind things to say of her, blaming him for the rift that arose between her and Aldington, whom she admired. Pound assigned West to his lesser category of journalism in his correspondence with *Little Review* editor Margaret Anderson, suggesting that she got into Wyndham Lewis's BLAST only via the efforts of Ford Madox Ford: "Rebecca West is a journalist, a clever journalist, but not 'of us.' She belongs to Wells and that lot" (*Pound/The Little Review* 100).

Pound flirted routinely with literary and artistic women, including lesbians. He offered his opinions on H. D.'s first lesbian attachment, Frances Gregg, and discouraged H. D. from accompanying Gregg and her husband on their honeymoon tour. Having arranged to marry Dorothy Shakespear, Pound steered H. D. toward her alliance with Aldington and then moved in next door. His technique with women is recorded by Bryher (Winifred Ellerman), who lived with H. D. starting in 1919. Pound visited, having claimed to H. D. that he could "manage" Bryher:

> He strolled in, his velvet jacket a shade darker than his beard, and sat down on the couch. I had already privately christened him the Leopard and did not share the circle's enthusiasm for his poetry. It seemed to me then as it does today to lack originality and to consist rather of often-superb translations. In those London days he reminded me of a jester, strolling round a Crusaders' camp with an old song and the newest gossip on his lips. (*The Heart to Artemis* 190)

For conversation, Pound chose an ancient account of warfare, occasioned by the fact that a Danish chief seduced and raped the wife of Harald the Saxon. Bryher, who knew that bit of history rather well, moved the conversation on to her interest in American poets. Pound rose to the occasion, if not the subject, and put his arm around her shoulders. "It was a most uncomfortable position, an Elizabethan would have screamed or snatched up a dagger but I decided to be wary and calm." He praised her hair, and "pecked chastely at a cheek" (191). After an interval of her abstracted silent gazing at him, he gave up.

H. D.'s prose works *HERmione* and *Asphodel* fictionalize the Poundian lover as George Lownes. In *Asphodel*, a suicide very like that of Margaret Cravens occurs. H. D. implicates George/Pound but also detects a set of social processes, including scapegoating, the expectation of marriage, and the insistence on the word "kiss." The power of these words is borne out in her repetitions: "George had killed her certainly. It was Walter saying it, 'But we thought she was going to marry—George.' George must be blamed, scape-goat. He was a scape-goat. Kissing them all. Let all the sins of all the kisses be upon him. For this was a sin. Kisses that had killed Shirley" (quoted in Pound and Cravens 162–63). One senses Pound's need to make a triangle of both heterosexual and lesbian relationships. It is a pattern he repeats with the Eliots, as Wayne Koestenbaum has analyzed in detail.

During his Paris years, Pound flirted with Djuna Barnes. He invited her to a showing of George Antheil's *Ballet Mécanique* in 1925. They also shared a much-recollected dinner party with the Joyces, when Pound made the unlikely accusation that Harriet Shaw Weaver was drunk on half a glass of wine. He may have sold a few copies of Barnes's *Ladies Almanack,* as did a number of people who frequented Natalie Barney's salon. Of his attempts with Barnes he remarked in his practiced drawl, "Waall, she weren't too cuddly, I can tell you that" (Field 106–107). When Eliot published his introduction to the American edition of Barnes's *Nightwood* in 1937, Pound enclosed an unflattering limerick in a letter to him:

> There once wazza lady named Djuna,
> Who wrote rather like a baboon. Her
> Blubbery prose had no fingers or toes,
> And we wish Whale had found this out sooner.

"Whale" was Frank Morley, Eliot's close friend and assistant at Faber. Pound may have been implying that Eliot should have stuck with him instead, as friend and advisor.

Pound encouraged some women writers and artists. The best-known example is H. D.'s setup as the quintessential "imagist." Pound told a tale of the cooperative drafting of the imagist manifestoes with H. D. and Richard Aldington. This is not entirely borne out in H. D.'s account (itself an edited version), which tells of his poring over her poetry in the tearoom near the British Museum:

> "But Dryad . . . this is poetry." He slashed with a pencil. "Cut this out, shorten this line. 'Hermes of the Ways' is a good title. I'll send this to Harriet Monroe of *Poetry*. Have you a copy? Yea? Then we can send this or I'll type it when I get back. Will this do?" And he scrawled "H. D. Imagiste" at the bottom of the page. (*End to Torment* 18)

Prior to recent feminist revisiting of her archive, H. D. was not considered important for much more than the poems Pound promoted, and once he moved on to the theory of vorticism, she could be passed over as a case of arrested development. Humphrey Carpenter's biography of Pound makes a pitiful figure of H. D.—a woman defeated after the failure of a casual engagement to Pound (82). Her only contribution to his poetry was seen in the occasional Hilda figures. This view has been challenged by a flourishing of feminist scholarship on H. D., led by Susan Stanford Friedman, Rachel Blau DuPlessis, and Robert Spoo.[8] Cyrena N. Pondrom's careful tracking of the development of Pound's imagist doctrine, along with of his own shift in poetic technique, reveals a reliance on H. D. as his model.[9] In her book written to analyze her relationship with Pound, *End to Torment*, H. D. declares that she developed in another dimension from Pound, and that he "would have destroyed me and the center they call 'Air and Crystal' of my poetry" (35). She is generous about Pound and says of "at least three women: He wanted to make them, he did not want to break them, in a sense he identified himself with them and their art" (49). Ronald Bush lists Marianne Moore, Mina Loy, H. D., Iris Barry, Nancy Cunard, and Mary Barnard as women whose careers Pound helped to launch ("Ezra Pound" 354).

Pound called special attention to Moore and Loy with his 1918 review of the *Others* anthology for the *Little Review*. But in his analysis, their accomplishments are closed in by male influences and his own competitive critical agenda. Before he gets to the verses of "these girls," Pound airs several grievances about American "nationalism" in verse and the rhetorical constraints of the *North American Review*. He next reiterates and expands his own poetic categories, running through "melopoeia" and "imagism" en route to assigning Moore and Loy to a third category of "logopoeia" as pioneered by Jules Laforgue ("Others" 365–66). It is "the utterance of clever people in despair" and "a mind cry, more than a heart cry." He admires their "arid clarity" (366). Pound offers a compliment to the male editor of the collection, Alfred Kreymborg, by telling us that he has "before now seen a deal of rubbish by both" poets, but he does give Marianne Moore credit for a "prewritten . . . counterblast to my criticism in her poem 'To a Steam Roller' " (366). Margaret Anderson added her own counterblast when she republished Pound's review of Moore in the *Little Review Anthology* twenty-five years later. She insists that "INTEL-LECTUAL POETRY IS NOT POETRY," thus resisting his high opinion of Marianne Moore and, the more generally, his mental as opposed to emotional criteria for canonization (367).

Moore, whom Pound had never met, was the recipient of one of Pound's most bizarre communications in 1918. This was a letter, partly in doggerel, that defines male and female difference, and moves on to define androgynous variations for Moore and himself. His feeling about women in general is:

> The female is a chaos ,
>
> the male
>
> is a fixed point of stupidity, but only the female
> can content itself with prolonged conversation
> with but one sole other creature of its own sex and
> of its own unavoidable specie
>
> the male
>
> is more expansive
> and demands other and varied contacts ;
> hence its combattiveness (Scott, ed. 362)

Of Moore, in particular, he said:

> You , my dear correspondent ,
> are a stabalized female ,
> I am a male who has attained the chaotic fluidities (363)

Pound goes on to consider their "mutual usefulness," displaying gratuitous racist anxieties—relief that she is a redhead, not "ethiopian," which would have posed a larger gap even than gender difference (363).[10] To her "Nathaniel Hawthorne frigidities" he offers his "cult of other ancient and less prohibitive deities." At the "threshold" of her "Presbyterian stair-turn" he sets his "lechery / capable of all altitudes" (363). She considered his letter "saucy." Nevertheless, switching the subject to professional matters, Moore did tell him some things about her publishing history—a rejection from the *Atlantic Monthly* and publication in *Poetry.* She did not enter his cult in a female "disciple" role, as H. D. had. In contrast, over the years Moore became a regular correspondent with H. D., expanding and repeating in a circle of women writers the form of the letter cycle she had learned from her mother (see Brownstein 325–26). Many years later, the elderly Moore encountered the reclusive Djuna Barnes in Greenwich Village, winning her admiration and a place in Barnes's letters to the women of her Paris days.

Though Pound enjoyed moving into other people's poetry and literary theories, he was not one to be appropriated, as Amy Lowell learned when she made her entry into the publication of imagism. Rather than cede his term to her, Pound renamed her project "Amygisme." He also managed a puerile public humiliation of Lowell, which has been frequently retold.[11] Pound redesignated H. D. a "she-bard" after she contributed to Lowell's new anthology, *Some Imagist Poets* (Carpenter 253–54). Her fellow defectors Aldington and D. H. Lawrence were not comparably denigrated.

Despite his occasional support of women writers, Pound did not see them as makers of the new. This betrayal serves as the first epigraph to this section: "Not wildly anti-feminist we are yet to be convinced that any woman ever invented anything in the arts" (*New Age*, 1 Aug. 1918). One exception to this rule about women, in a category of her own, was Sappho, whose direct descriptions of pagan rituals did elicit Pound's admiration and imitation in his early study of chivalry, *The Spirit of Romance.* Pound's access to Sappho and other ancients was aided by the classicist Jane Harrison, who also figures in Virginia Woolf's sense of the Greeks (see Bush, *Genesis* 126ff.). But Sappho was safely ancient, and subject to translation; she fell into a useful category, where he emerged the creator—the maker of the classics for his generation.

One problem with constructing a view of modernism through Pound is that there were significant modernists he did not connect with. His familiarity with D. H. Lawrence was slight. He acknowledged that his work was important and helped some of his poetry toward publication, but he disliked Lawrence's treatment of physical sexuality (Carpenter 134).

Lawrence's letters to Amy Lowell suggest that he was far kinder than Pound, offering respect for her poetry.[12]

Nor does the Pound narrative of modernism touch in a very productive way upon Bloomsbury. Virginia Woolf read Pound's essay on Gaudier-Brzeska (which was principally a repetition of vorticist principles), making one distant and unenthusiastic observation about imagism and *vers libre* in a 1917 review. Behind these movements she finds "a sensibility which, whether we think it irritable or perverted or inspired, is now urging [poets] to break up the old rules and devise new ones, more arduous than the old" (2 *E* 107). Meaningful contact with Bloomsbury was virtually ruled out by Pound's closeness to Wyndham Lewis. Originally affiliated with Roger Fry's postimpressionist group, Lewis clashed over contractual arrangements in Fry's Omega Workshop, an enterprise that produced imaginative pottery and furnishings, as well as employment for artists.

Most resoundingly, Pound's virile ethos clashed with Bloomsbury. He called the group the "Bloomsbuggers." He devised stagnant, weak, and watery feminine metaphors for them (as opposed to the positive chaos he selected for flirting with Marianne Moore). In 1917, describing a possible encounter with Clive Bell, Pound quipped to his father, "There are a lot of those washed-out Fry-ites, and I cant tell one from the other. A sort of male Dorcas-society."[13] To Henry Miller he complained of the "weak-minded Woolf female" (quoted in Carpenter 244). Had T. S. Eliot met Woolf sooner, before Pound left England, there might have been some possibility of Pound's meeting her. As it was, Eliot repeatedly mentioned Pound in letters to Woolf, but I have found no evidence that she took up the discussion.

Pound's exiled view of the United States missed some exciting developments there. He could not share Bryher's interest in going to the U.S. to meet its poets. He never fully appreciated Harriet Monroe's discoveries for *Poetry*, Vachel Lindsay and Carl Sandburg. Pound knew Nancy Cunard but was not connected, as H. D. and even Rebecca West were, to the exciting developments in black literature occurring in Harlem and in the new medium of cinema. Racism entered into his literary discussions with Marianne Moore, and anti-Semitism surfaced in remarks about Gertrude Stein, whose literary experimentation he passed off as "Yiddish" (Carpenter 400).[14]

Kathryne Lindberg has drawn attention to Pound's tendency to use "borrowed metaphors . . . in place of method" (vii), and to the sexuality of those metaphors (157–61), a phenomenon also abundantly discussed by Koestenbaum, particularly in Pound's relationship to Eliot. Pound's literary advice and his aesthetic of the new are liberally strewn with metaphors valorizing male sexual anatomy and energy, comparable to the phallicism of the psychoanalytic theories of Freud and Lacan, noted in my introductory chapter. During his courtship of Dorothy Shakespear, the couple had a disagreement about creative energy. Pound's ideas are a perfect anticipation of masculine economy as it would be defined by Hélène Cixous in her well-known essay "Castration or Decapitation?" Pound wanted Dorothy to concentrate on the serious art of painting rather than the feminine art of embroidery. When she reports, "I am doing some new early Vict[orian] wool work—which is half Italian & quite pretty" (Pound and Shakespear 247), he responds, "I am not in the least sure that you ought to embroider. It kills time but it also draws off a lot of little particles of energy, that ought to be dammed up until they burst out into painting." For relaxation he suggests that she return to her painting, experimenting with shades of green. Dorothy reports (with rare sarcasm) a daily retreat to her room to work in green, but has her own sense of economy: "I think one wastes more energy doing nothing & feeling miserable about it, than in embroidery. Doesn't energy to some extent generate itself, the more its used?" (249). Pound is able to see the recreational value of violent, energetic games such as fencing because they encourage concentration and gauging an opponent. But he holds to his own concept of energy, invoking the term "vortex," which was to enter his public aesthetic a year later: "Energy depends on ones ability to make a vortex—genius *meme*" (251). He could not see that genius moves in many ways, and not always with self-concentration, or in male-defined "major" arts. In a comparable case, Lucia Joyce told me in an interview that her father James Joyce discouraged her dancing, partially on the basis that dancing was not a major art.

The tenets of imagism might seem to clear out metaphorical elaborations. Its first principle was "direct treatment of the 'thing' whether subjective or objective." Pound calls further for exact words, the sparseness of using "no word that does not contribute to the presentation" ("A Retrospect," in *Literary Essays of Ezra Pound* 3). Pound's distaste for elaboration harks back to the rationalist cautions about metaphorical ornamentation, which they associated with feminine imprecision. But Pound was not quite so new as the revolutionary manifestoes suggest. His affinity to Walter Pater's aesthetics (expressed in metaphors such as the hard gem-

Snow Scene.   Shakespeare.

Plate 10. Dorothy Shakespear (Pound), "Snow Scene."

From BLAST 2 (July 1915).

like flame) was first cited by Yeats (Christ 71–73, 99; Bush, *Genesis* 26–29). Carol Christ has argued that the scientific vocabulary of Pound's metaphors was anticipated by John Ruskin (Christ 92–93).[15] Pound's basic definition of "image" incorporates technical metaphors derived from scientific terminology (as he takes pains to explain), and a more puzzling reference to "growth":

> An "Image" is that which presents an intellectual and emotional complex in an instant of time. I use the term "complex" rather in the technical sense employed by the newer psychologists. . . . It is the presentation of such a "complex" instantaneously which gives that sense of sudden liberation; that sense of freedom from time limits and space limits; that sense of sudden growth, which we experience in the presence of the greatest works of art. (*Literary Essays of Ezra Pound* 4)

Here growth could be organic, but it is also suggestive of male sexual arousal—sudden engorgement experienced by the male voyeur, whose presence is one of the basic assumptions of Western art. Pound later evoked male genital metaphors for successful thinking and literary making. He also knew what textures he did not want, and here again he echoes the rationalists in a distaste for what could be considered feminine filler: "If you are using a symmetrical form, don't put in what you want to say and then fill up the remaining vacuums with slush" (7). He expected twentieth-century poetry to be "as much like granite as it can be. . . . I mean it will not try to seem forcible by rhetorical din, and luxurious riot. We will have fewer painted adjectives impeding the shock and stroke of it. At least for myself, I want it so, austere, direct, free from emotional slither" (12). "Shock and stroke" are both machine-like (technical) and biologically male (natural) in this metaphor. In "The Hard and Soft in French Poetry," Pound begins with an apology "for using the metaphorical terms 'hard' and 'soft' " in his essay. "By 'hardness' I mean a quality which is in poetry nearly always a virtue. . . . By softness I mean an opposite quality which is not always a fault" (*Literary Essays of Ezra Pound* 285). Joyce's *Dubliners* merited his praise as "clear hard prose . . . with such clarity of outline that he might be dealing with locomotives or with builders' specifications" (399), even in presenting subjective things. Joyce is preferable to impressionists, who are "a rosy, floribund bore" (400), because he has made a "rigorous selection" to the "exclusion of all unnecessary detail" (401). Congratulating Eliot on the completion of "The

Waste Land," Pound wrote, "May your erection never grow less" (Eliot, 1 *Letters of T. S. Eliot* 505).

In his postscript to Remy de Gourmont's *The Natural Philosophy of Love*, Pound offered a spermatazoic model for the brain itself, relating it to image-making potential: "The brain itself is, in origin and development, only a sort of great clot of genital fluid held in suspense or reserved. . . . This . . . would explain the enormous content of the brain as a maker or presenter of images." The system leaves "woman as the accumulation of hereditary aptitudes . . . but to man, given what we have of history, the 'invention,' the new gestures . . . merely because in him occurs the new up-jut, the new bathing of the cerebral tissues in the residuum, in *la mousse* of the life sap" (150). As a parallel, he points to "the symbolism of phallic regions, man really the phallus or spermatozoide charging, head-on, the female chaos. . . . Even oneself has felt it, driving any new idea into the great passive vulva of London"—in effect a masculine model for his arrival on the London literary scene.[16] It is fitting that the bust of Pound by the vorticist sculptor he championed, Gaudier-Brzeska, resembles a phallus. The sculptor meant it to have "virile . . . significance," and Pound commented on its phallic qualities (Carpenter 233).

Another interesting metaphor is Pound's title for a collection of essays published in 1911–12—*As I Gathered the Limbs of Osiris*. The works Pound gathered and translated and commented on were Anglo-Saxon and medieval texts. The critical element gathered in the myth was the phallus, but Pound takes for himself the role of the goddess, who becomes a mother to make Osiris live again in his son.

Pound's friend Hulme lent to modernist men a macho image. He supposedly hoisted Lewis and hung him upside down on an iron fence. Hulme boasted of using brass knuckles to control women. A much-repeated anecdote celebrates a twenty-minute assignation in "the steel staircase of the emergency exit at Piccadilly Tube Station," which he complained about to a group of men he had left in the café as "the most uncomfortable place in which he had ever copulated" (David Garnett, quoted in Carpenter 115, who is quoting from Norman). Cherished and handed down, first by modernist men and later by their critics, this discourse belongs alongside locker-room pranks and vulgarities. Hulme's classicist model of the modern followed a similar line of descent, deliberately setting itself against a feminine, romantic tradition. A properly classical modern poem is "dry and hard," as opposed to a "damp" or "sloppy" romantic production. Hulme, through his reading of the German aesthetician Wilhelm Worringer, also promoted abstract, geometric, life-alien primitive art—a preference visible in the sculptures of Jacob Epstein and Gaudier-Brzeska and the painting of Lewis. Hulme celebrated the machine as organized energy. He subscribed to a religious belief in original sin and human limitation. His masculine metaphors of the modern are consistent with those of Pound, particularly around 1914. But like Gaudier-Brzeska, he died in the war that broke in upon the men of 1914—a loss that allowed Wyndham Lewis to look back nostalgically on a lost world of closely bonded men. No one did more for those bonds than Pound.

6 Wyndham Lewis: Above the Line of Messy Femininity

Ezra Pound gave credit to Wyndham Lewis for vorticism, the idea that replaced imagism as the essence of the "new" in 1914. Unlike imagism, vorticism had no female co-founder—no H. D. Pound found it preferable to share the leadership of a new movement with Lewis rather than remain in a year-old movement that had to be shared with Amy Lowell. A novelist and painter, a proponent of the virtues of space over those of time, and a blaster of the past, Lewis was founder of the Rebel Arts Center and of the vorticist journal *BLAST*, published in 1914–15. In his break with Roger Fry's Omega group in 1913, Lewis had embraced a masculine image for the group of painters who surrounded him, in contrast to Fry's group: "This family party of strayed and Dissenting Aesthetes . . . were compelled to call in as much modern talent as they could find, to do the rough and masculine work without which they knew their efforts would not rise above the level of a pleasant tea-party, or command more attention" (*Letters of Wyndham Lewis* 49).[1] Lewis's paintings, and those of male cohorts such as Frederick Etchells and C. R. W. Nevinson, are integral to understanding the vortex. Works such as "Timon of Athens," published in the first number of *BLAST*, help clarify vorticism (see Plate 11). Lewis deploys in space linear or technologically produced objects such as girders, gears, and guns, so as to suggest dynamic lines of force and energy. An object resembling an upside-down child's top appeared on the title page of the *BLAST* "Manifesto," recurring several times within the number. Vorticism as a movement implied that there was a group of artists on the scene who were capable of superior creative energies, suggested in a spinning top or a whirlpool so energized as to have watertight qualities.

Rather than give a formal definition, the first number of *BLAST* gives a barrage of blasted and blessed items, starting with England and its climate, denounced in homophobic terms, "DISMAL SYMBOL, SET round our bodies, of effeminate lout within" (11). These fragments are arranged in differently sized but always bold type, ranging from a one-word item

Plate 11. Wyndham Lewis, "Timon of Athens."

From *BLAST* 1 (29 June 1914).

on a list to a short, authoritative declaration. Lewis was for a time impressed by F. T. Marinetti's futurist doctrines of violence and the worship of machinery, but dissociated himself from futurist "automobilism" in BLAST; the ultimate insult was to call the futurists "impressionists," a blast that also worked out Lewis's antipathy to Roger Fry. The journal advances a "predatory" attitude and a new "chemistry" of abstraction. The whirlpool, originally a figure in water, serves as a formal image for vorticism, but it is carefully managed so as to avoid laxness, representation of nature, or even the most typical behavior of liquids. The vortex achieves a maximum point of energy at a central still point; it makes swift movements, has "polished sides" and "water tight compartments" ("Our Vortex," BLAST 1, 147). Vorticist artists, like Nietzsche's superman, are individualists and masters, not slaves of commotion. They are indifferent to the past and the future as "sentimental" constructions and despise and ignore an "impure Present." They are also superior to nature, which is given a subservient, sexual, female construction: "The Past and Future are the prostitutes Nature has provided. . . . Art is periodic escapes from this Brothel" (148). Vortex "plunges to the heart of the Present" (147). With its calm, its controlled, self-contained, geometric shape, and its energetic force and repeated, plunging movement, Vortex promised triumph over the troubling impurities and voids, which elsewhere Lewis would associate with nature and the feminine. One of the "Blesses" of the second number of BLAST was to "The scaffolding around the Albert Memorial" (93).[2]

The form of the feminine is blasted repeatedly, wherever it occurs in BLAST, especially where exhibited by men. Women are not necessarily blasted. Numerous individual women are blessed. Suffragettes are commended for their energy: "YOU AND ARTISTS ARE THE ONLY THINGS (YOU DON'T MIND BEING CALLED THINGS) LEFT IN ENGLAND WITH A LITTLE LIFE IN THEM" (151). But this comes rather late in Lewis's page-and-a-half-length "word of advice." Up to that point he makes uninformed and insulting overgeneralizations. The advice, titled "To Suffragettes," implicates a diverse group in a particular form of militancy that might lead to the destruction of artworks. It further assumes that suffragettes would not understand art and could not be artists. The characterization did not fit one suffragette in Lewis's own experience, Rebecca West.

IN DESTRUCTION, AS IN OTHER THINGS,
stick to what you understand.

Pronounced from aesthetic high ground, it implies that the votes suffragettes seek are not valued by vorticists.

In his work on Lewis, *Fables of Aggression,* Fredric Jameson passes over problematics of gender and the surviving, reactionary elitism of a "great" male artist and intellect. Jameson recognizes misogyny but excuses it. It is a "misogyny so extreme" that it is not "personal" (20). He also claims that Lewis's "derogation of the feminine" takes place without a celebration of the masculine, and so is not phallocentric (97). His apologies also dismiss Lewis's flirtation with the Nazis as "brief." In Jameson's view, Lewis's form of modernism, which is quite distinct from Joyce's, operates in a dialogical model of the novel (35), in a variant of expressionism. This undermines the "stable substances of Aristotelian science with their fixed and describable properties released into post-Einsteinian relational fields."[3] I do think it appropriate to see Lewis as far closer to a postmodern, deconstructionist, fragmented, demystifying sensibility than, for example, Eliot.[4] Yet Lewis's binaries always favor the masculine pole, and his art always proceeds from it. What Jameson takes as a populist textuality comes from a "stylistic cooption of the machine" (81) and a rejection of nature and all of its associations with the feminine. Lewis's relentless pursuit of notoriety as the "enemy" prevented the formation of a productive modernist circuit for his considerable energies.

Wyndham Lewis, like Ezra Pound and T. E. Hulme, contributes to modernist myths of masculinity. His capacity for sexual liberation and irresponsible paternity is legendary. Jeffrey Meyers has asserted in his biography that "Lewis enjoyed manly intellectual camaraderie as an antidote to what he felt were degrading, yet necessary, relations with women, whom he considered less intelligent than men and resented for their power to awaken and exploit his passions" (70). Lewis's long-suffering mother reared two children born in 1911 and 1913 to Lewis and Olive Johnson, though he paid no attention to them after he returned from World War I. He also fathered two children by Iris Barry, who lived with him from 1918 to 1921. One of the legends goes that, returning from the hospital with a newborn infant, Barry had to wait outside their flat while Lewis and Nancy Cunard completed their lovemaking.[5] Lewis enjoyed the patronage of Kate Lechmere, as well as the Cunard inheritance. Also intimately associated with Lewis were Beatrice Hastings, co-editor of the

New Age, and Mary Borden Turner, painter, novelist, heiress, and director of a military hospital during World War I.

Lewis's 1918 novel *Tarr* provides an opportunity to examine a masculine aesthetic of modernism through its title character. *Tarr* was well known to the avant-garde of its era, having been serialized in the *Egoist* in 1918; it was positively remarked on by Pound, T. S. Eliot, and Rebecca West.[6] The work's similarities to James Joyce's *A Portrait of the Artist as a Young Man,* which preceded it in the *Egoist,* bear notice. Tarr is an artist who regularly uses gender in metaphors of creativity. Like Pound, Lewis's character finds it necessary to conserve artistic energies for great things. Tarr's view of artistic economy is shared at length in an imbalanced dialogue with another young man on the Paris scene, Hobson, who is designed as a satire on Clive Bell.

> The artist is he in whom this emotionality normally absorbed by sex is so strong that it claims a newer and more exclusive field of deployment.=Its first creation is *the Artist* himself, a new sort of person; the creative man. . . .
>
> The tendency of my work . . . is that of an invariable severity. Apart from its being good or bad, its character is ascetic rather than sensuous, and divorced from immediate life. There is no slop of sex in *that.* But there is no severity left over for the work of the cruder senses either. (*Tarr* 12–13)

Male aesthetic dialogues dominated by Stephen Dedalus also punctuate Joyce's *A Portrait.* This is particularly true during Stephen's ascetic phase, entered after he rejects his experience of prostitutes. At the close of *A Portrait,* Stephen regulates his emotional attitude toward E. C., the young woman (reduced to her initials) who has been his primary romantic focus: "turned off that valve at once and opened the spiritual-heroic refrigerating apparatus, invented and patented in all countries by Dante Alighieri" (*A Portrait* 252). Tarr and Stephen conceive of God and mythic heroes as male. Assisted by Aristotle and Nietzsche, they place the female at the bottom of their conceptual hierarchies, with mud, vegetative material, and animals. Here is Tarr's scheme:

> Woman and the sexual sphere seemed to him to be an average from which everything came: from it everything rose, or attempted to rise. There was no mysterious opposition extending up to Heaven, and dividing Heavenly beings into Gods and Goddesses. There was only one God, and he was a man.=A woman was a lower form of

life. Everything was female to begin with. A jellyish diffuseness spread itself and gaped on the beds and in the bas-fonds of everything. Above a certain level of life sex disappeared, just as in highly organized sensualism sex vanishes. And, on the other hand, everything beneath that line was female . . . he enumerated acquaintances evidently below the absolute line and who displayed a lack of energy, permanently mesmeric state, and almost purely emotional reactions. He knew that everything on the superior side of that line was not purged of jellyfish attributes. (*Tarr* 334)

Tarr's jellyfish is comparable to an "octopus" metaphor used by Pound to describe feminine chaos in *Canto* XXIX.[7] Tarr fails in his isolation from women. He feels "captured" by the love he has aroused in Bertha, a bourgeois, sentimental female he gives the nickname "Pumpkin," sinking her to the level of a large fruit:

To give up another person's love is a mild suicide; like a very bad inoculation is compared to the full disease. His tenderness to Bertha was due to her having purloined some part of himself and covered herself superficially with it as a shield. Her skin at least was Tarr. She had captured a bit of him, and held it as a hostage. She was rapidly transforming herself, too, into a slavish dependency. She worked with all the hypocrisy of a great instinct. (61)

Another statement clarifies the artist's dangerous relation to women, as associates to nature: "Surrender to a woman was suicide for an artist.= Nature, who never forgives an artist, would never allow *her* to forgive" (219). Tarr is attracted to a second, more independent, powerfully constructed woman, Anastasya, whose intellect invites even aesthetic discussions. He must adjust his sexual engagement accordingly:

"What a big brute!" Tarr thought.=She would be just as good as Bertha to kiss. And you get a respectable human being into the bargain!"=He was not intimately convinced that she would be as satisfactory. Let us see how it would be; he considered. This larger machine of repressed, moping senses, did attract. To take it to pieces, bit by bit, and penetrate to its intimacy, might give a similar pleasure to undressing Bertha! (218)

If woman advances to the level of the machine, at least she can be dismantled, just as the more vegetative Bertha could be peeled. But Tarr is still worried. The artist seems to grow from imperfection, which Anastasya would not provide:

> He had always been skeptical about perfection. Did she and he need each other? His steadfast ideas of the flower surrounded by dung were challenged. She might be a monotonous abstraction, and if accepted, impoverish his life.= . . . Irritants were useful though not beautiful.=He reached back doubtfully toward his bourgeois. But he was revolted as he touched that mess, with this clean and solid object beneath his eyes.

By moving "above the line" of messy femininity, Anastasya brings into question the abstract, machined or "made" perfection that Tarr had labored to construct in himself, and reasserts an artist's need for difference, typically assigned to feminine/natural images.

Probably the most extraordinary moment in *Tarr* is a vorticist rape scene. The artist in this instance is not Tarr but Kreisler, whose art is dismissed by Tarr as the product of average male sexual economy "embedded in sex, in fighting, in affairs" (320), as opposed to Tarr's aloof, compartmentalized aesthetic. Woman—in this case Bertha, rebounding from Tarr's desertion—is the victim of inferior art. Lewis adjusts the point of view so that we experience the whirlpool off-center, in a violent, chaotic juxtaposition of images that denies connections in time, personal identity, or male responsibility:

> She saw side by side and unconnected, the silent figure drawing her and the other one full of blindness and violence. Then there were two other figures, one getting up from the chair, yawning, and the present lazy one at the window—four in all, that she could not bring together somehow, each in a complete compartment of its own. It would be impossible to make the present lazy one at the window interest itself in these others. A loathsome, senseless event, of no meaning, naturally to that figure there. (195)

The "moral" of the rape incident is "driven in" by Bertha's German concept of fate: She feels that her own "silly and vulgar mush, was the cause of all this" (196). If we accept her view (and Lewis distances himself from it), woman is to blame for male violence and bad male art. She figures herself as trivial, base "mush." The fragmented Kreisler eventually self-destructs, carrying other victims with him. The German identification of Kreisler and Bertha cannot be overlooked in a novel of 1918; war is brought on by bad tendencies in art and feminine mush, destroying the possibilities of the creative male artist of 1914.

Rebecca West had surprisingly positive connections with Wyndham Lewis and was always able to detect good material in his work, despite finding ways that he had gone wrong, notably over gender. West found him different from more widely appreciated modernists, requiring intelligence for analysis: "Only important people can see his importance, James Joyce can be appreciated with small talent" (West letter to M. Bernard Lafourcade, Tulsa). West examined his flaws, as she did Joyce's, with a sense of self-confidence, working this into her study of the problems of Western civilization. Lewis probably appealed to her own youthful rebelliousness and to her privileging of heterosexuality. Lewis and West met in 1912 through the circle of *les jeunes* presided over by Violet Hunt and Ford Madox Ford. West recalls that Lewis used to sit "silent but beautiful" with her at dinner. He described her as "a dark young maenad then, who burst through the dining-room door (for she was late) like a thunderbolt" (*Rude Assignment* 122).

Urged by Hunt, Lewis published West's short story "Indissoluble Matrimony" in the first number of *BLAST*.[8] The story was a good fit for vorticism, though it introduced several feminist twists to the male-inspired figuration. The Nietzschean superman, so evident in Lewis's writing, is played by a strong and sensual, maternally identified, socialist heroine, Evadne. She cannot be contained in a jerrybuilt suburb, or her husband George's conventional ideas of marriage and femininity. She seeks instead to bathe in the pool where she used to swim with her mother, since deceased—a woman whose coloring "was a little darker than the conventions permit" (*YR* 270). Creating her own image of the vortex, West provides a dramatic whirlpool scene, representative of the couple's sexual antipathy. But both partners survive the cataclysm, the husband denied self-satisfying violence and martyrdom. Gilbert and Gubar consider him an ideal representative of the anxious and feeble no-man later visible in figures such as Eliot's Prufrock.[9] But the phenomenon extends to his work. George's firm had been reduced to "hysteria" over the legal requirements of an old woman—a client who disgusted George when he took on the case. George had approached the intimate relations of marriage as a sickening physical taint—an attitude not far removed from Tarr's. Evadne is essentially maternal in her final, untroubled sleep, embracing and annulling her husband's efforts to drown her, and to deny or confine her powers.

In reviewing *Tarr,* West points out ways that it is important to its time. She compares it to the work of Dostoyevsky, who was considered a great influence on modernists by Woolf and Barnes as well. Like the Russian, Lewis's work is "too inquisitive about the soul, and . . . it contains one figure of vast moral significance" (67). West is critical of Lewis's handling of women. She turns to his preface, which restates Tarr's position that sex should not imperil his creative will and pronounces this view "lop-sided." She finds Anastasya, the strong woman who fascinates Tarr, unconvincing. She is a "Kitsch Cleopatra from Dresden." West finally invokes the politics of war. She compares Lewis's treatments of Germans to "the baffled feeling with which Europe has watched Germany for the last four years" (68). It was a topic that clearly interested her. As we shall see in volume 2, she sustained this political interest through the onset of World War II.

Demonstrating her penchant for psychological analysis, West analyzed Lewis as a case of irrational human behavior, unable to make "a comprehensible whole" of his "artistic and polemical selves." This analysis anticipates Fredric Jameson's presentation of Lewis in terms of a "field of forces within a scaffolding of the agon" (*Fables of Aggression* 38–49). But she sees him finally in terms of a destructive binary. According to West, Lewis was interested in primitive things. He had a love/hate relationship to gorilla types and became less beautiful, more pugilistic and gorilla-like himself over time (West letter to Lafourcade, Tulsa).

In a 1929 article concerned mainly with Lewis's *Paleface,* West describes an author whose work is "full of good things yet is spoiled by a fault," which she falls just short of calling racism. We might connect the "fault" to the reactionary politics of Pound and Eliot, and also learn from her remarks about West's views of Western civilization, including the preservation of traditions. In her analysis, West considers the current "admiration for the Negro . . . a movement toward death" in which "the Western man . . . has turned his back on the civilisation he himself has made, and has gone to bend the knee at altars of gods whose other names are chaos and disorder" ("On Making Due Allowance for Distortion" 624). She argues for the constructive nature of black "propagandist" novels, likening them to suffragist novels. West appreciates the muscular advantages of dance derived from Africa, and the "hold on experience" achieved in Negro spirituals, particularly as sung by Paul Robeson, whom she knew personally. She suggests that, whereas "white civilisation is built up on the power to guard tradition against assaults," blacks have their own conservation of traditions, even though "they have the power to do this merrily and with all the appearance of . . . being open to every assault" (624). As suggested in the dark skin of the mother in "Indissoluble Matrimony," West did not regard the black as other. West herself, on several occasions, claims Berber blood, through her mother's line, and recalls having remarkably dark skin as a child. Like H. D., though more superficially, she ventured into the Harlem Renaissance and liked what she found.

West offers the further critique of Lewis that he has failed to adjust his style to history. Whereas an attitude of pugnacity was appropriate to clear-thinking people before World War I, "when there was a damned compact majority who was pretending that all was going very well with the world," it was not productive in Lewis's *The Enemy* or in 1929, "when the majority is not compact, but distraught, when they are pretending that the world is going so ill that all is over with" (625). West had a remarkable ability to move on with history. This remark sustains my argument that the women of modernism had come into a sense of their own strength by the late twenties, by which time many of the male modernists were feeling a loss of vitality.

West and Lewis were apparently still on good terms in 1932, when he did a sketch of her that suggests both muscular power and pensiveness (see Plate 12).[10] West is shown with her left hand clasping her neck, triangular brows, her eyes looking to her right, her mouth and chin set, some strands of her short dark hair slightly out of place. It is more alive and less mannered than Lewis's famous portrait of Edith Sitwell. Vera Brittain singled it out for praise when she attended a Lewis exhibition in 1932 (*Diary* 93). West also appears positively portrayed as Stella Salt, a "great feminist authoress" found "having coffee with her admirers" in Lewis's *roman à clef, The Roaring Queen* (1936).

> Stella was a big old girl, very determined looking, with an easy platform manner and a beefy swing of arm. She was a somewhat greying golden blonde, with an amusing feline face, who in her time had hungerstruck with the best and trumpeted slogans of democratic revolt and red feminine revolution. (122)

Stella attacks Lewis's Arnold Bennett character (as West did the real Bennett) and is seen in contrast to a snobbish, self-aggrandizing Virginia Woolf character, Rhoda Hyman. Lewis would call West "the ablest reviewer in contemporary England" (Meyers 31).

Lewis chose Virginia Woolf, on the other hand, as an emblem of bad

Plate 12. Wyndham Lewis sketch of Rebecca West.

National Portrait Gallery.

female art. In *Men without Art* (published 1929), Lewis debases Woolf through word play, taking this feminist "cow by the horns" (170). He is the brave and overpowering master, she the cow pretending to masculine or phallic horns. Of course, cows do grow horns and are generally easier to subdue than a bull—observations that undermine the metaphor. Jane Marcus has credited Woolf with her own metaphoric toppling, in a phrase dropped in a letter—"Taking the bull by the udders" (*Virginia Woolf and the Languages of Patriarchy* 137). Lewis does not condemn all women to the clearly undesirable Woolfian realm, nor does he admit all male writers to his masculine art. He is happy to assign Lytton Strachey to the same class as Woolf. "Is it necessary for us . . . to point out how many women are far more grenadiers or cave-men than they are little balls of fluff . . . that a veneer of habit, and a little bit of hair on chin and chest, is about all that fundamentally separates one sex from the other?" (*Men without Art* 159). To the cow metaphor of authorship he adds more physical traits—"pallid" vs. "robust," and a slap at the domestic realm and women's literary tradition in a reference to the "salon." The work demonstrates "a bogus sort of 'time' to take the place of the real 'time'—to bring into being an imaginary 'time' small and pale enough to accommodate their not very robust talents," on a "salon scale." We are "invited . . . to install ourselves in a very dim Venusberg indeed: but Venus has become an introverted matriarch, brooding over a subterraneous 'stream of consciousness'—a feminine phenomenon after all—and we are a pretty sorry set of knights too" (167). As evidence of her powers of feminine corruption, Lewis paraphrases Woolf's review of Joyce's *Ulysses,* which she characterizes as "a little good stuff by fits and starts, a sketch or a fragment" (164). In his more masculine evaluation, *Ulysses* is a "masterpiece" (166) and a "robustly complete" work (167), not to be confused with Woolf's "salon pieces," the sort of "half-work in short 'pale' and 'dishevelled' of a crippled interregnum" (167). It is remarkable that Hugh Kenner continued to speak of Woolf in these terms of corruption and feminization of literature in the late 1980s, as noted in the introduction to this section. Lewis did sense in Joyce a certain relaxing of the masculine. Joyce handled time badly, and had an "internal method." Lewis regretted that it "robbed Joyce's work as a whole of linear properties—contour and definition in fact":

> In contrast to the jelly-fish that floats in the center of the subterranean stream of the "dark" Unconscious, I much prefer, for my part,

the shield of the tortoise, or the rigid stylistic articulations of the grasshopper. ("Satire and Fiction" 47)

In *Finnegans Wake*, Joyce assigned Lewis and himself to animal roles in a pair of fables, "The Mookse and the Gripes" and "The Ondt and the Gracehoper," mocking Lewis's arguments.

Woolf planned her reaction to *Men without Art*. The assault by Lewis coincided painfully with the death of Roger Fry (an arch enemy to Lewis, but a family intimate to Woolf). She felt the need for a strategy to battle depression and maintain her own productivity. "What I shall do is craftily to gather the nature of the indictment from talk & reviews: &, in a year perhaps, when my book is out, I shall read it. Already I am feeling the calm that always comes to me with abuse: my back is against the wall: I am writing for the sake of writing: &c. & then there is the queer disreputable pleasure in being abused—in being a figure, in being a martyr. & so on" (4 D 251). Her "disreputable" helps to mark the strange divisions of emotion occasioned by the persecuting male. One strange last piece in the Lewis/Woolf relationship is the homemade New Year's card Lewis sent to another Bloomsbury figure, Edward Garnett, in 1930.[11] Pasted in the upper-right-hand corner was a picture of Virginia Woolf (*Letters of Wyndham Lewis,* plate 12). Ironically, or perhaps ahead of his time, Lewis was circulating Woolf as a popular commodity.

Djuna Barnes discussed Lewis with Peter Negoe and Emily Holmes Coleman. She could have heard something of him from Natalie Barney, who had supported Lewis's Rebel Arts Centre. Reacting to his critical work, Barnes considered him "damned good about Eliot, Pound and Joyce" and about himself in war. But though she conceded to Negoe that he had written some "astonishingly Goya-like passages," she considered him "essentially crude and brutal" (Barnes letter to Coleman, 30 Nov. 1937, Delaware).

In his biography of Lewis, Jeffrey Meyers suggests that Lewis never recovered the sense of vitality he had before the outbreak of World War I:

> The war that began in August 1914 demolished the vital and promising world of prewar Europe, and the very machinery that had recently been grouped by the Vorticists blasted out of existence the greatest art movement that had ever appeared in modern England. The "Men of 1914"—Lewis, Pound, Eliot, Joyce—belonged to a confident future that failed to materialize. (68)

7   T. S. Eliot: Playing Possum

T. S. Eliot has the most secure connections to Woolf, West, and Barnes of all the male modernists addressed in this study. Yet his professional focus was decidedly not upon the women of modernism, nor have his complex responses to gender and sexual orientation been sufficiently analyzed.

In writing about the London literary scene to Isabella Stuart Gardner, Eliot described "my friends Ezra Pound and Wyndham Lewis" as "the ablest literary men in London" (*Letters of T. S. Eliot* 251). Eliot arrived there about five years after Pound. Their 1914 meeting, he pronounced, "changed my life" (xvii). Eliot benefited from Pound's literary sponsorship, which led to early publications and his position as contributing editor to the *Egoist*. Pound even intervened with Eliot's father, explaining in a long letter the literary necessity of Eliot's remaining in London, when the elder Eliot wished to summon his son home. The letter was timed to precede the announcement that Eliot had just married an Englishwoman (Vivien Haigh-Leigh)—another reason for remaining. The most famous Eliot/Pound literary collaboration is Pound's editorial work on *The Waste Land,* which was dedicated to him. Pound's reaction to Eliot's final product is as notable for its gendered metaphors as for Pound's humility over his own work: "Complimenti, you bitch. I am wracked by the seven jealousies, and cogitating an excuse for always exuding my deformative secretions in my own stuff, and never getting an outline." He continues into the homoerotic poem "Sage Homme":

> These are the Poems of Eliot
> By the Uranian Muse begot;
> A Man their Mother was,
> A Muse their Sire

To readers who wonder how the "printed Infancies" came forth "from Nuptials thus doubly difficult," Pound claims the surgeon's role in "the caesarean Operation." This metaphor cedes the maternal function to a technical performance by the male editor (*Letters of T. S. Eliot* 498). Later Pound discloses how he typically wastes his sperm: "His foaming and abundant cream / has coated his world" (quoted in full by Koestenbaum

121). Writing on the "homosocial collaboration" of Pound with Eliot in *The Waste Land,* Wayne Koestenbaum, I think rightly, suggests that Pound's ejaculations normally are masturbatory, but that the seminal references make some claim to fatherhood in the case of *The Waste Land.* It is a careful combination of bawdiness, deference, and self-importance. Koestenbaum's book, titled *Double Talk,* is highly conscious of sexual metaphors used in the discourse of male collaborations. "Bluntly" summarized, "Men who collaborate engage in a metaphorical sexual intercourse, and . . . the text they balance between them is alternately a child of their sexual union, and a shared woman" (3).[1]

With Pound, Eliot occasionally tried on lusty language to match his recipient's. He signs off in one letter, "O student of the Kama-Sutra . . . grow fat and libidinous" (539), and closes another even more directly, "Good fucking, brother" (550). With his male audience (Conrad Aiken, Pound, Lewis, and Joyce), Eliot shared verses worthy of a sexually obsessed schoolboy; his had racist coloration, as in this sample:

> Now while Columbo and his men
> Were drinking ice cream soda
> In burst King Bolo's big black queen
> That famous old breech l(oader)
> Just then they rang the bell for lunch
> And served up—Fried Hyenas;
> And Columbo said "Will you take tail?
> Or just a bit of p(enis)?" (42)

Eliot follows this with a parody of critical analysis of such texts via a German academic (Dr. Hans Frigger) who has restored "bracketed passages" and detected (but not understood) a *double-entendre* in the last two lines. Not thrown off the critical task by Eliot's defenses, our own criticism might turn to the overlay of sexual, racial, imperial, and animal tropes in his next Swiftian scene. It is full of reversals, where a pornographic "big black queen" bursts in upon men prepared to consume male animal genitalia. Eliot never got much encouragement for these verses, even from Lewis, who declined to print "words ending in -Uck, -Unt, and -Ugger" in BLAST (*Letters of Wyndham Lewis* 67). But they do suggest recurrent themes of male self-mutilation and anxious sexuality, produced for a private male set, and kept until recently from an academic public.

Despite his private verses, Eliot fit in better than either Pound or Lewis with the established London scene. His Harvard connections provided a meeting with Bertrand Russell, who took a paternal interest in him. Russell even extended his help to the Eliots' marital difficulties. Russell's situation at the heart of Lady Ottoline Morrell's circle was noted in chapter 4. He introduced Eliot at Garsington, where Morrell drew him into the company of Katherine Mansfield, John Middleton Murry, and figures associated with Bloomsbury—Clive Bell, Mary Hutchinson, Lytton Strachey, Aldous Huxley, and most notably Leonard and Virginia Woolf, whom he met in November 1918. It was his own observation that he got on better with the group who wrote for Murry's *Athenaeum* than Pound did. Eliot's Bloomsbury alliance summoned forth Lewis's misogyny along with his prejudices against the rival group in letters to Sydney Schiff. He was "afraid that [Eliot's] Bloomsbury cultural groove, combined with the wife obsession," would inhibit his writing. Lewis congratulated himself upon not living with a woman (Lewis letter to Schiff, 2 May 1922, British Library). He was still on the theme several months later: "Eliot I feel is desperately too much under the poor and ridiculous uterine influence, and is in any case too fundamentally at house with Bloomsburies, to extend himself beyond himself" (Lewis to Schiff, 3 Oct. 1922, British Library). Lewis was, however, very supportive of Eliot as he turned to editing his own journal.

Editions of Eliot's *Prufrock and Other Poems* and *The Waste Land* were published by the Woolfs' Hogarth Press. He became a reviewer for the TLS in 1919 and was supported by Lady Rothmere in launching the successful journal the *Criterion* in 1922. For a decade, Eliot held on to the secure routine and income of a position at Lloyd's Bank, despite separate efforts of Pound and Bloomsbury figures to remove him from his double grind. In 1925, Eliot finally moved on to a comparably businesslike venture in publishing at Faber and Gwyer (later Faber and Faber), an institution where he could shape culture and yet be sheltered from personal intrusions. This was less true of smaller publishing ventures such as the Woolfs' Hogarth Press. Faber provided another male set, which proved particularly useful for insulation, when Eliot was separating from his wife in the 1930s. Eliot's biographer, Peter Ackroyd, suggests that businesslike working circumstances were a way of satisfying the expectations of Eliot's father. While he disappointed his family by not entering academic life at an institution such as Harvard, and he favored residence in London over Oxford, Eliot did manage better relations with ivy-towered institutions than any of the other "men of 1914." Cambridge honored him with the Clarke Lectures in 1926. He was able to return to Harvard in 1932 (and in the removal to escape his troubled marriage); the University of Virginia sponsored the set of conservative lectures that became *After Strange Gods* in 1933, preparing the way for the agrarian embrace of Eliot by the New Critics.

While studying briefly at the Sorbonne in 1910, Eliot met a man who, like many men of Bloomsbury, would have presented a contrast to the virile, crusading tradition of Pound, Lewis, and Hulme. Jean Verenal, a medical student later killed in the First World War, writes a reminiscence appropriate to a lover. Verenal describes gliding through a springtime landscape of translucent leaves in a boat, and then observing a more controlled explosion of spring along the "artificial lines" of the avenues of Saint Cloud. He was moved to write Eliot about this landscape because it suggested him—a landscape they had "senti ensemble" or "felt together" (*Letters of T. S. Eliot* 33). Verenal would not have been totally attuned to the Pound-Lewis spirit, as he expresses distaste for "writers and artists who create new schools every six months, and . . . the weakness which makes them band together to fight. The mischance of violence and lack of strength is not a good omen and we suffer from the fact that art is not on a par with our sensibilities." He closes with hope for Eliot's literary "germinating" (34). Perhaps Eliot lost in the war, or in cultural attitudes toward men's love for one another, a man with an emotional landscape matched to the sort of serenity he usually associated with nurturing females, and referred to as lost in the Thames imagery of *The Waste Land*. We have insufficient evidence of an attitude not taken.

Eliot's correspondence with Conrad Aiken, his friend from Harvard days, includes some of the bawdy verses he shared with Pound and numerous expressions of misogyny, but on the whole it is more revealing of insecurities, disclosing more serious attempts to explore his sexuality through writing. Eliot shared with Aiken a set of poems on martyred saints he had been working on in Germany in mid-1914, before going to Oxford. Apparently concerned about both attitude and form, he asks Aiken whether he finds them "morbid, forced?" A contextual remark that has not been particularly attended to in previous studies of these troubled verses is Eliot's statement "there's nothing homosexual about this—rather an important difference perhaps—but no one ever painted a female Sebastian, did they?" (44). In his love of the martyred young male, did Eliot sense a forbidden love? Was he admitting to a constrained tradition in art? In the first stanza, the speaker aligns himself with St. Sebastian, in conditional tenses ("I would come"; "I would flog") performing his own martyrdom until his blood stands in a pool. The next action is "to follow" an undefined being "toward your bed." The drama would seem to end when by morning "I should be dead . . . between your breasts." Interestingly, though there are feminine attributes of breasts and braids, and the second being is largely passive and centered in bed, the feminine pronoun is never used—only "You," as appropriate to a dialogue. The second stanza would make a murderer of the "I" figure, who, in the process of positioning "your" head for strangulation, caresses the curve of the ear, a unique physical detail he will remember "when all the world shall melt in the sun / Melt or freeze." The deed is explained as mutual love and destruction: "You would love me because I should have strangled you / And because of my infamy. / And I should love you the more because I had mangled you" (47). The encounter is shifted to heterosexual interaction, but in its avoidance of pronouns maintains homosexual dimensions, and is clearly masochistic. This is also an early attempt to write on a Christian theme for Eliot. It demonstrates the influence of monuments of art that obsessively ritualize torture and male martyrdom. In Eliot's text, killing and loving are entwined in glory and unclearly defined along gender lines.[2] Djuna Barnes, whose work interested Eliot, would face similar struggles in writing love scenes with complex sexualities.[3]

Managing a Dependency upon Women

Emily Hale, whom Lyndall Gordon describes as Eliot's "first love" (9), was a talented actress and producer. Though her family ruled out a professional career in the theater, she took these abilities into a career of teaching and school administration. Eliot fell in love with her around 1912, but left her behind (as Pound did H. D.) when he went to Europe in 1914. He did not fully renounce the relationship, however. Their correspondence was restarted in 1927, and the relationship flourished in visits exchanged in the mid-1930s. Lyndall Gordon couples the renewal of their affection with Eliot's conversion to Anglo-Catholicism, casting Hale in the role of Eliot's confessor, and the inspiration for the visionary moments evoked in "Burnt Norton" (*Eliot's New Life* 3, 45–48). But to Hale's surprise, when he was freed by his wife's death in 1947, Eliot did not marry her.[4] Also rejected was Mary Trevelyan, his British partner in Anglican devotion and in social intercourse for nearly twenty years, beginning in 1938. She evoked what Gordon has called his "informal" mask (196), but not his love, as Hale did. Access to Eliot's letters to Hale is denied, by Eliot's direction, until 2019, whereas Eliot destroyed letters he received from her.[5] In seeking privacy, Eliot's solution was biased by gender—a persistent problem that makes it difficult to recover the female side of these relationships.

A significant letter from Eliot to Aiken, written in December 1914, has survived. It betrays a lingering attraction to Hale (Aiken had just delivered roses to her for Eliot), nervousness over the prospect of becoming a professor (he was in Oxford on a Harvard graduate fellowship), and "nervous sexual attacks" experienced in London. According to his analysis, "University people . . . are the same everywhere, with pregnant wives, sprawling children, many books, and hideous pictures on the walls." His alternative suggestion: "Come let us desert our wives and fly to a land where there are no Medici prints, nothing but concubinage and conversation." He also acknowledges his need for women, as did Lewis. The nature of that "need" wavers unclearly between social and sexual functions and anxiety about wanting to "dispose of" sexual initiation:

> I am very dependent upon women (I mean female society); and feel the deprivation at Oxford—one reason why I should not care to remain longer—but there the exercise and routine, the deprivation takes the form of numbness only; while in the city it is more lively and acute. One walks about the street with one's desires, and one's refinement rises up like a wall whenever opportunity approaches. I should be better off, I sometimes think, if I had disposed of my virginity and shyness several years ago: and indeed I still think sometimes that it would be well to do so before marriage. (1 *Letters of T. S. Eliot* 75)

It is to be suspected that both his reserve with women on the street (most likely he refers to prostitutes) and his virginity persisted into marriage. Eliot's need to cope with his own emotions and his sexuality is clear in the nervous illness that accompanied his first decade as a writer, which was doubled and reflected by Vivien Eliot, whom he married in never fully explained haste in June 1915.[6]

Though letters by Vivien Eliot have been published in the first volume of Eliot letters, edited by Valerie Eliot, none of these are to Eliot. Vivien sometimes describes his sensitivity and ill health to others. She takes over for him in literary dealings at times when he is ill, or when her frank intervention is of use. But her letters also betray the nervous flow of questions and distrust of circumstances that characterized her social intercourse, and probably her married life as well. In the letters of T. S. and

Vivien Eliot, there is no hint of sexual vitality in either partner. Ackroyd encourages us to think that Vivien's irregular menstruation may have contributed to their sexual disaster. But Eliot's letters also betray a morbid love of physical symptoms, both his and hers. He readily takes on her body text, reporting symptoms to correspondents such as Ottoline Morrell, Violet and Sydney Schiff, and Virginia Woolf; Woolf and Morrell sometimes wished they had been spared. Tom and Vivien Eliot were comparably fragile in temperament, it seems. Koestenbaum appropriately attaches his poem "Hysteria" to their conditions (115). But while her condition led to solitude at home, desertion, and finally institutionalization, Eliot's role of male responsibility pulled him from the state of nervous distraction. His role may also have encouraged a retreat behind walls of civility and monuments of authority, including the church. This contributed further to the frustration of women such as Hale and Trevelyan, as well as the devoted John Hayward.[7]

In daily life, Eliot operated on a low energy level, particularly when compared to men of the "vortex." Vivien Eliot's stories refer repeatedly to energy as an essential quality. She writes in "Letters of the Moment—I," "The whole question of the success of the artist lies in how much energy he has to start with" (221). In "The Dansant," her female protagonist tries to improve her partner's dancing technique with the admonition, "You've got no energy, that's what's the matter with you. *Dance* I say" (78).[8] Eliot's sartorial formality along British lines outdid the natives, who observed this theatrical facade (sometimes topped off with ghastly tinted face powder) and joked about it among themselves. Woolf attributed a four-piece suit to him, and Ottoline Morrell called him the "undertaker." Pound's name for him was "Old Possum," which gets at a lot of Eliot—his American origins, his early admission to middle age, and his ability to play dead as an evasive or self-protective maneuver. Eliot adopted the name himself, using it even in his correspondence with Virginia Woolf, and in the original title of his work for children, *Old Possum's Book of Practical Cats.* Eliot, his heroes, and his persona in Vivien Eliot's stories all fit the "noman" category offered by Gilbert and Gubar, but it is important to see his playing possum or hysteric as an empowering strategy, commanding support from a long line of caretakers.

Vivien Eliot had creative potential in writing, music, and dance, and seems to have contributed to Eliot's career path, as well as his depiction of neurasthenic women in poetry. She may have given him one excuse (which Pound was happy to encourage) to renounce a trajectory that would have led back to a professorship in the United States. Eliot was capable of taking a liberal feminist attitude on her behalf. During the war years, he protested the ways that married women, and particularly British women married to Americans, were at a disadvantage in gaining employment (1 *Letters of T. S. Eliot* 207). He asked Virginia Woolf to encourage her writing. In 1928, Woolf expressed thanks to both "Mr. and Mrs. T. S. Eliot" in the preface to *Orlando.*

Vivien Eliot's unpublished diaries and drafts of stories in the Bodleian Museum provide a gloss on Eliot's own writings, particularly where they deal with the encounter of the sexes or comment on modernist enterprises, including book reviews and periodicals. These writings have proved perplexing to scholars; they are fragmentary, with mixed handwritings that may include Eliot's own (Ackroyd). Preparatory to *The Waste Land,* Eliot collaborated with Vivien in assembling a portfolio of poetic fragments, many of them inspired by fertility myths contained in James Frazer's *The Golden Bough.* This had as a working title "He Do the Police in Different Voices."[9] This project and Vivien's marginal reactions to early drafts of *The Waste Land* have received little notice.

Vivien Eliot's contributions to the *Criterion* were written under the pseudonym "Feiron Morris," or "F. M." They belong in the same genre as Djuna Barnes's stories written under the name Lydia Steptoe and Rebecca West's stories of dancers (see *The Only Poet*). In two stories, Vivien Eliot's bored female character takes the resonant mythical name "Sibylla" and seeks amusement in social dancing. Particularly interesting for their resonances with T. S. are several drafts of an essay titled "Letters of the Moment—II." They parody Eliot's interests in Fraser, and even lift phrases from "The Love Song of J. Alfred Prufrock"—a project Eliot seems to have collaborated in, as her workbooks have some of these passages in his hand. The female correspondent, writing to "Volumnia," speaks of a seventeenth-century revivalism where "the poor dear Mermaid Society" thinks of reviving old plays; one title may be "Green Goddess." Pope, Prufrock, and a sense of daily tedium emerge in the lines "sniffling Chloe, with the toast and tea / Drags back the curtains to disclose the day." She replays a scene of discomfiture between the sexes in "Prufrock." At a dance in Hampstead, her persona feels "tested" by a young man who asks whether she has tickets to *The Pirates of Penzance.* She replies "faintly, painfully aware of all that was involved," that she is bored by Gilbert and Sullivan, whereupon his display of convulsed features throws her into an analogy to a Prufrock situation. It was "as if one had said, 'settling a pillow or throwing off a shawl': No, I did not care for the *Boutique* at all, not at all." As for modernist enterprises, she mocks John Middleton Murry's book reviewing, suspecting that he wants to show that he would be a better professor of poetry at Oxford than the "insensitive Mr. Garrod." There is a comic commentary on the character of various modernist periodicals on display on her table, the most notable challenge coming from *Vogue*—the women's magazine that Woolf and West gladly conspired with:

> The pink *Dial,* the golden *Mercury,* the austere N.R.F., *les feuilles libras* so black and white, buff *Blackwood,* the lemon yellow *Adelphi;* the slim and elegant *Nation* with the modest *Statesman* cowering behind; and beneath all but shamefully in sight the gaudy covers and uncouth dimensions of *Vogue.* One turns to the *Dial* flip flip go the pages. Very dull, very dull—ah, Paul Morand, in what? a Paris letter—perhaps good—will read. Begin—clatter, clatter whiz bang, rather trying. ("Letters of the Moment—II")

In a sample Morand letter, written in the "pastiche style," the correspondent proves to be one of Proust's hangers-on, forced by his death to proclaim Cocteau a genius! Vivien Eliot is a lost satirist of modernism.

The subjects of the emotions, the feminine, and the disorder of sexuality recur in Eliot's writing and make him a more confused figure than we found in the gender-blind critical accounts offered through the 1960s, or in more recent accounts that cite only his most violent texts on women. When it comes to questions of gender analysis, there are several Eliots. Sandra Gilbert and Susan Gubar supply a list of texts in which Eliot displays murderous impulses toward women, most of these acknowledged in Ackroyd's biography, though he couches the pattern in Eliot's more general enthusiasm for thrillers. An Eliotic hero, "Eeldrop" (*Little Review* 1917), has murdered his mistress. Eliot was fascinated by the wife-murderer Dr. Crippen and came to a party powdered and costumed as him. The hero of *The Family Reunion* is presumably the murderer of his wife. Eliot may have modeled *Sweeney Agonistes* on Sweeney Todd, the "demon barber of Fleet Street." Eliot's hero tries to lure a young woman into "missionary stew" and discusses the need to "do a girl in" (Gilbert and Gubar 37; Ackroyd 52, 81, 184, 246). The cannibal concoction suggests additional racial anxiety.

But Eliot could also be entwined in images of nature, in his associations with loved ones, such as Jean Verenal, and women who cared for him. As one of the two epigraphs to the first volume of Eliot's letters,

Valerie Eliot chose a reminiscence by Eliot's sister, Ada, born nineteen years before him. It describes a shared rhythmic babble, suggestive of the semiotic language associated with the mother in French feminist theory: "When you were a tiny boy, learning to talk, you used to sound the rhythm of sentences without shaping words—the ups and downs of the thing you were trying to say. I used to answer you in kind, saying nothing yet conversed with you as we sat side by side on the stairs" (xxxi). Mother and sister speak again in *Ash Wednesday:*

> Sister, mother
> And spirit of the river, spirit of the sea,
> Suffer me not to be separated

> And let my cry come unto Thee

"The Love Song of J. Alfred Prufrock" (1910–11) presents a failure of heterosexual desire, told in metaphors that isolate the human from natural images. Prufrock imagines himself categorized by society women at tea, "formulated, sprawling on a pin." It is a reversal of gender, given that the scientific collector and designator of categories is more typically male. One response is to dismember the women into ugly parts in the imagination, and the other is to flee to an essentially maternal, or visionary, seascape. But in the seascape he lacks belief and the power to connect.

> I have heard the mermaids singing, each to each.
> I do not think that they will sing to me.

So all he does, until too late, is linger

> . . . in the chambers of the sea
> By sea-girls wreathed with seaweed red and brown
> Till human voices wake us, and we drown.

In *The Waste Land,* with the exception of the vision of the hyacinth girl,[10] there is a further decline of love. Lovemaking for a typist and clerk has become so mechanical as to be appropriately set between a taxi engine throbbing and the playing of a gramophone record. On the Thames, where the lovers Elizabeth and Leicester once were rowed in a boat with a stern like "a gilded shell," making a "brisk swell" to both shores, "carried downstream" to the "peal of bells," now a woman recounts her undoing, at various stages downriver:

"Highbury bore me. Richmond and Kew
Undid me. By Richmond I raised my knees
Supine on the floor of a narrow canoe."

Her lover "promised 'a new start.' I made no comment / What should I resent?" The Thames meets the sea near Margate, the resort T. S. and Vivien visited just before he went to the clinic in Lausanne, where he re-wrote *The Waste Land*. The final version betrays a total inability to connect.

"On Margate Sands.
I can connect
Nothing with nothing." (Ll. 300–303)

In one of her last independent sojourns before she was institutional-ized, Vivien Eliot returned to the banks of the Isis River in Oxford, where Eliot had apparently gone punting with her in the days preceding their marriage. "Letters of the Moment—II" ends in a pastoral description of a "you" who could be Eliot:

The country air, the wind tearing the hair and reddening the face
as you push push push against it trampling across the marshes.
Your scarf blows out like a flying jib behind you. Boots wet with
splashing through salt water pools, you slip and slide over the rank
grass, the seaweed slime. The sky is clean and scrubbed, reflected in
the blue pools, then cloudy. A shower stings you, you shudder; all
horrible, I hate it, vile cold beastly, get home. Then the sun comes
out to laugh at you, warms you. You smile and swing your stick,
call to the dog, and push on towards the sea.

Her 1919 diary is most positive when it describes her holidays at Bosham, sometimes sailing with "Tom" or having a picnic with friends, among whom Mary Hutchinson (usually identified as Clive Bell's mistress) proved most congenial (14 June; 6, 9 July, Bodleian Library).[11] Seaside holi-days temporarily restored both her health and Eliot's, who once told Syd-ney Schiff, "One becomes dependent . . . on sea or mountains, which give some sense of security in which one relaxes" (1 *Letters of T. S. Eliot* 485).

Like Pound, Eliot was somewhat supportive of the writing of many contemporary women. His list includes Vivien, his mother, Charlotte C. Eliot (who painted and wrote poetry directed toward finding a celestial paradise), May Sinclair (who helped establish him, as she had Pound, in

London), Mary Hutchinson (a close friend to both Eliots and to Bloomsbury, via intimacy with Clive Bell), Marianne Moore, and two writers central to this study—Virginia Woolf and Djuna Barnes. Eliot's letters to talented women have creative appeal and sometimes search the emotions, suggesting a continuing need for caring women. A playful personality emerges for his cousin and confidante Eleanor Hinkley, who studied at Radcliffe College and with George Barker and introduced Eliot to Emily Hale. Eliot illustrates these letters and constructs a drama for the cinema, starring Effie. Eliot explores the nature of relationships in letters to Mary Hutchinson and Brigit Patmore. Briefly stated, his letters to Virginia Woolf take up the problem of forming an attitude toward tradition; he plays the role of humble self-doubt in comparing his letter-writing skills to hers. Letters to Djuna Barnes encourage her current writing projects, sharing the burden of Puritan heritage and a love of privacy. We will return to both of these sets of letters.

Still, when it came to constructing an enduring modernist canon, Eliot left women off his most select lists. Summarizing his achievements at the *Criterion,* he was "proud" to have introduced Proust's work to English readers, and "proud" of having published Lawrence, Lewis, Joyce, Pound, Auden, Spender, and MacNeice ("Preface" v). When Eliot did promote women, he often discredited them by the categories he chose for them.

For a set of lectures on "The Makers of 19th Century Ideas," given at a time of economic need in 1917, Eliot did "work up" George Eliot and the Brontës, modestly expanding the canon that had been offered in his education. He reports to his mother, "I found *Jane Eyre* and *Wuthering Heights* amazingly good stuff, but I cannot endure George Eliot" (1 *Letters of T. S. Eliot* 219). He was aware of having a primarily female audience for these talks, and had some ambivalence about the "extraordinarily learned" quality of some of the old ladies in attendance—though their expertise is reduced by his assignment of it to the category of "the private life of the worthies . . . which I have never bothered my head about" (219).

Eliot was bombastic and strident in writing to Pound about the American trends in mass education he observed in the 1930s. Most of these related to female audiences. He remarked that "the function of the university is not to turn out Culcher and Civic Pageants," and bemoaned the existence of subjects such as "How to Appreciate the Hundred Best Paintings, the Maiden Aunt and the Social Worker. Something might be said (at another time) about the Evil Influence of Virginity on American Civilisation" (96). Eliot enjoyed mimicking Pound's epistolary style (including category and misspelling "culture," though Pound did so with a "K"). He did not go along with Pound's anti-Semitic letters.

Eliot had been restive about working for female editors and with female colleagues at the *Egoist*. He remarked to Pound, "I struggle to keep the writing as much as possible in Male hands, as I distrust the Feminine in literature, and also, once a woman has had anything printed in your paper, it is very difficult to make her see why you should not print everything she sends in" (204). He changes the insults slightly while displaying his own mastery to one of those female contributors, Mary Hutchinson. His choice of articles and pronouns for *Egoist* editor Harriet Shaw Weaver suggests somewhat less than human regard. Explaining the delay in publishing Hutchinson's work, he writes: "The Weaver found that she did not have room, and printed a rather bad story instead"; and "I will ask Weaver to send you the proofs, but it usually demurs—however I shall insist" (208).[12]

Although he had married a literary woman himself, Eliot was particularly disparaging of H. D. and Katherine Mansfield. It is tempting to read homosocial desire in the configuration of his relationship to their husbands, Richard Aldington and John Middleton Murry. On the eve of his departure for Lausanne in November 1921, where he would rewrite *The Waste Land*, Eliot gave Richard Aldington his negative opinion of H. D.'s poetry, stating, "Our correspondence would be irreparably injured if I did not deliver my opinions." He steers Aldington away from Miss Weaver as a publisher of a critical book, and toward a larger firm such as Cape or Collins. He also tries to secure a better opinion of his own poetry from Aldington. The verdict on H. D. is particularly interesting because it ends on his own sexual prudery, clothed in the elaborate term "Prudentianism," a category to which he unpredictably assigns James Joyce:[13]

> I did not conceal from you that I think you overrate H. D.'s poetry. I do find it fatiguingly monotonous and lacking in the element of surprise. I mean that this last book is inferiour to her earlier work; that many words should be expunged and many phrases amended; that the Hellenism lacks vitality; and also morally, I find a neurotic carnality which I dislike. (I imagine you dislike equally the Prudentianism of myself and Mr. Joyce, and expect you to abhor the poem on which I have been working and which I am taking away with me!) (1 *Letters of T. S. Eliot* 488)

T. S. Eliot: Playing Possum 125

Eliot also disparaged John Middleton Murry's opinion (expressed to Ottoline Morrell) that Katherine Mansfield "was the only living writer of English prose." Writing to Pound in 1920, Eliot described Katherine Mansfield as "a dangerous WOMAN" whose presence made Murry difficult to deal with (389). He assigned Mansfield and Murry to the category of "sentimentalists." His denunciation of Murry's criticism to Sydney Schiff as "dictated by emotion" (422) sustains this judgment. Eliot may have dreaded a sense of his similarity to his own wife—both of them plagued by nerves and sexual dysfunction. As he laid plans for the *Criterion,* Eliot opined to Pound that "there are only half a dozen men of letters (and no women) worth printing" (593). Eliot told his brother, "There is very little contemporary writing that affords me any satisfaction whatever; there is certainly no contemporary novelist except D. H. Lawrence and of course Joyce in his way, whom I care to read" (617). This was not exactly the story he gave Virginia Woolf, as he defended himself from her feeling of being undervalued by him as a writer.

By 1928, the year in which modernist women were clearly coming into their own, Eliot had taken refuge in another institution, the High Anglican Church, which provided a sense of order envied by the unbelieving Djuna Barnes and questioned by Woolf during a session with Eliot that lasted some hours. The religious structure provided a "carapace" against Vivien's increasingly chaotic behavior (Ackroyd 169), and religion became an important standard for ministering to the condition of the world. In speaking on "Religion and Literature" in the mid-1930s, Eliot used Woolf as a negative example of modern moral attitudes (see Ackroyd 207).

The composition of the lectures that constituted *After Strange Gods* coincided with Eliot's desertion of Vivien, and he later repudiated them as the work of a "sick" period in his life. There are troubling xenophobic, racist, anti-Semitic attitudes used to justify a formula of homogeneous, sealed-off cultural and religious security; these were disregarded by the fellow travelers and new critics who set Eliot in academic eminence.[14] Still, it is possible to see this work as the "reformulation" of "Tradition and the Individual Talent" it proclaims itself to be. Among the subjects treated there is the "heresy" he detected in prominent modernists.

Eliot's test of good literature is that it display "orthodox" sensibility (as opposed to amoral individualism) and that there be a sense of tradition. He sets out to test three texts by these criteria: "The Dead" by James Joyce, "The Shadow in the Rose Garden" by D. H. Lawrence, and "Bliss" by Katherine Mansfield (an interesting inclusion, considering his distaste for the living Mansfield). Joyce is commended for his fidelity to orthodoxy and culture; Lawrence is taken as "an almost perfect example of the heretic" (*After Strange Gods* 41). By the time he makes these judgments, Eliot has forgotten Mansfield, whose story was passed over rapidly at the start of the discussion as a work with "negligible" moral implication; the author "has handled perfectly the *minimum* material—it is what I believe would be called feminine" (38). It is notable that T. S. Eliot's laudatory review of Marianne Moore's *Poems and Marriage,* published in *The Dial,* gives "one final 'magnificent' compliment: Miss Moore's poetry is 'feminine' as Christina Rosetti's, one never forgets that it is written by a woman; but with both one never thinks of this particularly as anything but a positive virtue" ("Review of Marianne Moore's *Poems and Marriage,*" Scott, ed. 149).[15] It is of equal interest in the study of gender in modernism that, in concluding *After Strange Gods,* Eliot returns to Lawrence, criticizing him for a number of failings. Eliot emphasizes Lawrence's "sexual morbidity" as the least considered (63), and as evidence that Lawrence was "a very sick man indeed" (66).

Rather than blast existing things, or bless new ones, Eliot set them in order, though we are becoming increasingly aware of the discomfiting sense of sexual disorder that motivated such constructions, and the ready dismissals made possible by his ordering categories.[16] Ackroyd detects this impulse in Eliot's 1916 Ph.D. thesis on F. H. Bradley. In reaction to Bradley's "finite centres" which in their "mad and strange" nature and "partial and fragmentary" form are all we can know of lived truth, Eliot "postulates 'degrees of truth' which help to create an objective world in which 'the cruder and vaguer, or more limited, is somehow contained and explained in the wider and more precise.' The purpose is to reach beyond the miasma of private experience and construct a world, or rather an interpretation of the world 'as comprehensive and coherent as be possible' " (69–70). The basic structure of the literary order is contained in Eliot's thoroughly canonized essay "Tradition and the Individual Talent," published in the *Egoist* in 1919. The poet must write "not merely with his own generation in his bones but with a feeling that the whole of the literature of his country has a simultaneous existence and composes a simultaneous order." Tradition changes because "the existing monuments form an ideal order among themselves, which is modified by the introduction of the new (the really new) work of art among them" (*Selected Prose* 38). He gives warning that personal emotion and new emotions do not work to produce new art. While this construct may have empowered Eliot, who embraced a rich heritage of literary ancestors from Dante to the meta-physical poets and on through Henry James, it lacks the universality that has been claimed for it. Eliot's invalidation of "personal" emotion under-mines a potential focus of the isolated writer. His skepticism over "new" emotion denies validity to the artist who writes of experience that has not been taken up adequately in literary monuments—women's experience and homosocial desire, for example.[17] Finally, Eliot's theoretical image of literary "monuments" and his living role as the great modernist created awe and a fear of exclusion in any but the most self-assured newcomer; it still discourages hope for rethinking on the canon.

Connections to Woolf, West, and Barnes

Eliot had significant professional and affectionate personal relation-ships with both Virginia Woolf and Djuna Barnes. Furthermore, he was the subject of Rebecca West's assessments of the criticism and publishing of her day. The Woolf and Barnes relationships confirm Eliot's emotional reliance on sympathetic women, testing his attitude toward publishing them. Woolf met Eliot in late 1918, when he was still finding his way in London literary circles, and before the advent of *The Waste Land*. The Barnes relationship originated much later, in the mid-1930s, when he was an established figure in criticism and publishing.

When Eliot met the Woolfs, he was a promising young poet. His work had appeared in *Poetry* magazine, and his editing career had begun at the *Egoist*. The Woolfs had set up their Hogarth Press in 1917, and considered a collection of his poetry a good prospect. He responded to Virginia Woolf's note inviting him to bring by a few of his poems in November 1918. A volume was agreed upon, so that *Prufrock and Other Poems* ap-peared in May 1919. In a letter to his brother, Eliot describes publication by the Woolfs and the resulting reviews as a boost to his career, referring to the Woolfs as "my friends" (1 *Letters of T. S. Eliot* 309). There was some intrigue over negative opinions of Woolf's writing which Eliot may have expressed previous to meeting her. Some remarks were circulated and perhaps distorted by Mary Hutchinson, Clive Bell, and others. Vivien Eliot expressed anxiety that publication of the volume of poems would be stopped by Virginia in revenge; Vivien made her own unpleasant plans for Virginia. His wife's letters revert back to T. S.'s older alliance with the "men of 1914": Joyce is better out of these conditions. Vivien suggests that it was because of such literary intrigues that "Pound was ruined" and became "a laughing stock. . . . Only a person of coarse fibre, a Wyndham Lewis, *can* stick it and remain undamaged" (ibid. 288–89). The worry came to nothing, though for Eleanor Hinkley's benefit, Eliot made an amusing account of the envies and distortions of various characters in this drama, each assigned a letter (Woolf was B). Eliot compared dealings with Bloomsbury to a psychological fencing match, presenting himself as anxious but ready to play in this game of wits (ibid. 304). Once they had become his publisher, the Woolfs saw Eliot regularly, in both their London and Monk's House residences. Woolf and Eliot both intimidated and amused each other, as their letters and her diary reveal. They cautiously engaged each other's affections. Woolf has a deserved reputation for teasing in her conversations, and for mocking descriptions of her encounters with people—both of which emerged in her dealings with Eliot.

Their exchanges over literature offer one of the best means we have to reconstruct the nature of the modernist enterprise. Woolf deliberately shaped the subjects of their conversations and carefully chose her submissions to the *Criterion*. She constantly compared her ideas of the modern and her way of expressing them to Eliot's, trying to decide how much they had in common. The comparisons were complicated by the fact that sometimes the "we" that Woolf associated with was she and Leonard as publishers, or as a man and woman comfortable with one another; sometimes it was Bloomsbury, or the group of people who might meet at Ottoline Morrell's; sometimes it was an antipatriarchal outsiders' society, where Eliot and much of Bloomsbury could not be accommodated. Eliot also changed, from the advocate of hard and high modernism, affiliated closely with Pound, to the Anglo-Catholic of 1928 and, slightly later, the antidemocratic and indeed protofascist advocate of the 1930s. It was Eliot's consolidated view of modernism which held strong appeal in academic circles, and particularly with the socially conservative, aesthetically focused New Critics. To some extent, Virginia Woolf anticipates more recent feminist and postmodernist discussions of what Eliotic modernism was trying to close out, and why this worked through the 1950s.[18]

After their first meeting, Woolf was aware of Eliot's attachments to "the men of 1914," his recourse to an "organized framework of poetic belief," and his wish, by writing with extreme care, to make "this new poetry flower on the stem of the oldest" (1 D 218–9). This was a synthesis of Pound's modernist directives and canon and an anticipation of Eliot's "Tradition and the Individual Talent," first published in the *Egoist* in September 1919. In a letter to Eliot, Woolf attributed the Eliot part of an anonymous review of his poems printed in June 1919 in *Athenaeum* to Leonard, though probably the ideas were shared. The review senses from Eliot's "newness and strangeness" that he is " 'trying for something' . . . which has grown out of and developed beyond all the poems of all the dead poets" (3 E 56). The reviewer uses the term "evolved," with the comment "one drops instinctively into the scientific terminology," and credits him for the "subtle juxtaposition" of words and ideas.

Eliot's overnight visit to Monk's House in September 1920 was a test of the growing relationship. Clearly, Woolf was moved by his proximity: "Eliot is separated only by the floor from me" (2 D 67). This reads somewhat like young Clarissa Dalloway's emotions at having Sally Seton under the same roof in *Mrs. Dalloway,* though Woolf proclaims immediately, "Nothing in mans or womans shape is any longer capable of upsetting me," and she distances him: "He is decidedly of the generation beneath us—I daresay superior—younger, though." The next day, labeling him "dominant and subversive," she would consider him "a consistent specimen of his type, which is opposed to ours." Woolf carefully maintained her sense of self as artist, despite neglect in his discussions of literature: "I kept myself from being submerged, though feeling the waters rise once or twice. I mean by this that he completely neglected my claims to be a writer, & had I been meek, I suppose I should have gone under—felt him & his views dominant & subversive" (2 D 67).[19]

In their discussions, Woolf posed challenges of form. She charged that he willfully concealed transitions. He responded that the facts should not be diluted, and should be felt without explanation. To her probe about psychological writing, he announced that "his turn is for caricature," a change since "Prufrock," at which time he had been developing in the manner of Henry James. He was now a writer of externals. But he very much admired Joyce as a writer of internals, and left Woolf with a thorough sketch of *Ulysses* and its author (2 D 67–68). This troubled her more than she at first admitted. A week after Eliot's visit, she recorded the famous misgiving, "I reflected how what I'm doing is probably being better done by Mr. Joyce." *Jacob's Room* was placed under doubt and came to a stop (2 D 68–69). Eliot's letters immediately after the visit say nothing of her. They reflect back on his August visit with Wyndham Lewis, and his first meetings with Joyce (1 *Letters of T. S. Eliot* 408–409).

Eliot gave the Woolfs a performance of *The Waste Land* shortly before it was published. It created a "strong emotion" in her: "He sang it & chanted it rhythmed it. It has great beauty & force of phrase: symmetry;

& tensity." Again, there was the question of transitions, but the acknowledgment that what he did worked: "What connects it together, I am not so sure" (2 *D* 178). When, as editor of the *Criterion*, Eliot began publishing Virginia Woolf, she sent him essays that sustained her exploration of form in modern criticism as well as poetry and fiction.[20] The most important of these was "Character in Fiction," published in July 1924. It has become famous under another name, "Mr Bennett and Mrs Brown."[21] In the portion of her essay where she takes up Eliot, Woolf is highly complimentary to his verses, as he acknowledged in a letter. He pronounced her comments on him "excessive for what I know my own work to be." He credited her with "a most important piece of historical criticism," her point about the moderns being that in the "absence of masters" there is the "necessity . . . of building one's own house before one can start the business of living" (Eliot letter to Woolf, 22 May 1924, Berg).

What Eliot did not acknowledge was that Woolf was dramatizing a very different critical style from his. Anticipating the fantasy flights of *A Room of One's Own,* Woolf created a persona of the critic who takes risks and places herself in awkward positions, shared with the reader. This reader/critic shares the labors necessary to negotiate the modernist "obscurity" of T. S. Eliot's poetic form: "As I sun myself upon the intense and ravishing beauty of one of his lines, and reflect that I must make a dizzy and dangerous leap to the next, and so on from line to line, like an acrobat flying precariously from bar to bar, I cry out, I confess, for the old decorums, and envy the indolence of my ancestors who, instead of spinning madly through mid-air, dreamt quietly in the shade with a book" (3 *E* 435). Reading Eliot is very like spinning a web for transportation among sparse though beautiful supports. The physical body of the reader is made as awkward and at risk as it might be in a dream. While she is up to the challenge, Woolf also leaves the impression that she is more caring of her readers than Eliot; she would show comparable concern for readers in her reactions to Joyce.

Woolf had discussed the difference between the moderns and the classic romantic writer Keats in a private conversation with Eliot as they went to the theater by cab in 1921: " 'We're not as good as Keats' I said. 'Yes we are' he replied. 'No: we dont write classics straight off as magnanimous people do.' 'We're trying something harder' he said. 'Anyhow our work is streaked with badness' I said. 'Compared with theirs, mine is futile. Negligible. One goes on because of an illusion.' He told me that I talked like that without meaning it. Yet I do mean it" (2 *D* 103–104). She continued the theme in her essay for the *Criterion*. Woolf locates a feeble and fragmentary Mrs Brown in the work of Eliot, Joyce, and Lytton Strachey, and waits with patience and anticipation for her realization by the moderns. "We must reconcile ourselves to a season of failures and fragments. We must reflect that where so much strength is spent on finding a way of telling the truth the truth itself is bound to reach us in rather an exhausted and chaotic condition. Ulysses, Queen Victoria, Mr Prufrock—to give Mrs Brown some of the names she has made famous lately—is a little pale and dishevelled by the time her rescuers reach her. And it is the sound of their axes that we hear—a vigorous and stimulating sound in my ears" (3 E 343). Uncharacteristically, Eliot's letter admitted to an unfinished quality in his writing: "Everything I have done consists simply of tentative sketches and rough experiments" (22 May 1924). In her essay "How It Strikes a Contemporary," Woolf distances herself from critics' assessment "that it is an age incapable of sustained effort, littered with fragments, and not seriously to be compared with the age that went before," conscious that "we do not believe a word we are saying" (CR 241).

Woolf was disappointed when Eliot failed to show enthusiasm for her essay "On Being Ill," which was published in the *New Criterion* in January 1926. Though she and Leonard had considered the essay among her best, Eliot's postcard, calling it merely "characteristic," gave her formal doubts. She suddenly found "wordiness and feebleness." As in his inadvertent interruption of *Jacob's Room,* Eliot indirectly cast doubt upon her writing in general, such that she wondered whether she actually had a theme, or might only get lost in her mother and father, writing *To the Lighthouse* (3 D 49). "On Being Ill" was a deliberate departure from TLS style, as were other efforts of this period, among them "Conrad: A Conversation" and her lives of the obscure, including her sketch of the entomologist Eleanor Omerod. Part of the purpose of "On Being Ill" was to discover a language of the body, which in comparison to the mind was neglected in literature. The essay sustained topics that Woolf was investigating on her own, and furthered discussions with Eliot. Woolf was beginning work on an extended critical study, "Phases of Fiction," at this time. Her interest in different phases of the mind would become a major subject and organizing principle of that difficult-to-manage work. It was a principle that argued against set canons and attended to the process of reading. In "On Being Ill," Woolf described reading while under the effects of influenza—a condition well known to Eliot, whose discussion of both his illness and those of his wife were common matter in his letters. She found that "in illness with the police off duty, we creep beneath some obscure poem by Mallarme or Donne, some phrase in Latin or Greek, and the words give out their scent and distil their flavour" (200). Thus the essay furthered her effort, begun in conversation, to make Eliot plunge into the unconscious: "When the lights of health go down, the undiscovered countries that are then disclosed, what wastes and deserts of the soul . . . what precipices and lawns sprinkled with bright flowers" (2 CE 193). A very bright underworld, quite different from the feminine swamp suggested by his colleague Lewis!

Eliot's conduct of business repeatedly brought the Woolfs up short, partially because they were trying to free him up for writing. Woolf tried to secure him the literary editorship of the *Nation,* and to set up a literary fund so that he might cease work at Lloyds Bank, both of which he rejected. He was hard to help: "He elaborates & complicates, makes one feel that he dreads life as a cat dreads water. But if I hint so much he is all claws. Now, considering my activity on his behalf no doubt I have some of the vile & patronizing feelings of the benefactor. It's American, L. says; that & neurotic" (2 D 238). Eliot managed to find a more congenial solution than patronage when he moved to the publishing house of Faber and Gwyer while still editing the *Criterion.* Having sent Eliot a letter to the effect that Hogarth should reprint their 1923 edition of *The Waste Land,* Woolf is shocked that Faber has seized the opportunity. Eliot offered her palliations:

> Tom has treated us scurvily, much in the manner that he has treated the Hutchinsons. On Monday I get a letter that fawns & flatters, implores me to write for his new 41y; & proposes to discuss press matters as soon as we get back; on Thursday we read in the Lit Supt. that his new firm is publishing Waste Land & his other poems—a fact which he dared not confess, but sought to palliate by flattering me. (3 D 41)

He tried to point out that the usual list at Faber posed no competition to Hogarth Press, citing listings on nursing and Indian education, but in fact it became a very literary press indeed. The subject of what he was publishing did not come up with any regularity. One notable exception was Eliot's suggestion that Woolf should read Djuna Barnes's *Nightwood.* Though this urging fell far short of his campaign for *Ulysses,* Eliot did call it "a remarkable book" (6 L 96) when it was published by Faber in 1936.

Their letters suggest that Eliot and Woolf had an affectionate relationship, that he depended on her to hear his troubles, but that he withheld as well. Virginia decided in 1921, "One could probably become very intimate with Eliot because of our damned self conscious susceptibility: but I plunge more than he does: perhaps I could learn him to be a frog" (2 *D* 104). Although he certainly went through agonies with his marriage, Eliot also received a great deal of sympathy over it, with the Woolfs giving their share. Virginia was reading symptoms of Vivien Eliot's lack of ease with them from their first visit. The symptoms may have been exacerbated by Eliot's presentation of the challenge to the wits afforded by this company. But Woolf read nervousness in Vivien's relation to Eliot, as contrasted to the ease of the Woolfs' relationship. In 1925, when Eliot shared with them his attendance on his wife's psychological struggles, Woolf felt her sense of human worth touched—"his liking for us, affection, trust in Leonard, & being so much at his ease in some subconscious way he said, not in conversation, with me, all making me lay my arm on his shoulder; not a very passionate caress, but the best I can do" (3 *D* 15). She was put off when he started writing in great detail about Vivien's symptoms. At his request, Woolf wrote to encourage Vivien's writing. She apparently shared a piece on the "Cam River," perhaps a version of *A Room of One's Own*. By 1930, Vivien showed extreme nervousness and suspicion of harm during a visit, "biting, wriggling, raving, scratching, unwholesome, powdered, insane, yet sane to the point of insanity." The way Virginia saw it, Eliot had a "bag of ferrets . . . round his neck" (3 *D* 331). The Woolfs inferred from Vivien's inability to locate Eliot on his return from Harvard in 1933 that he had deserted the marriage. Their first response was to offer her help. The Woolfs thought of establishing a fund, and Leonard offered to be her executor. Virginia gratified Vivien by talking with her when they met at the theater where one of Eliot's plays was being produced. Vivien had hung out there, hoping for a glimpse of her husband.

Virginia was critical in her reception of Eliot's first letter after the split: "Tom is all artifice & quips & querks" (4 *D* 174). But when they finally did meet, after hours of talk, she was spellbound. She wrote in her diary instead of composing her novel. The Eliot she had just met was in command, back on course toward his mastery of the modern:

> He is 10 years younger: hard, spry, a glorified boy scout in shorts & yellow shirt. He is enjoying himself very much. He is tight & shiny as a wood louse (I am not writing for publication). But there is well water in him, cold & pure. Yes I like talking to Tom. But his wing sweeps curved and scimitar like round to the centre himself. He's settling in with some severity to be a great man.

Later in the entry, after the suggestion that Eliot was pleased that his mother had lived to see him a "great man," Woolf hit upon a peculiar African metaphor she would use in *The Waves*: "What a queer naive vanity all this is! But of course, when you are thrown like an assegai into the hide of the world—this may be a definition of genius—there you stick; & Tom sticks. To shut out, to concentrate—that is perhaps—perhaps—one of the necessary conditions." Part of what he shut out, she implies in the middle of the entry, is her own writing. He does seem to be moving some priorities—preferring letter writing to *Times* leader writing, and saying that he no longer "felt so sure of a science of criticism." But, though she hopes to "talk out to Tom about writing," she has "always the reservation—I can't talk about 'my writing'; so that talk about his writing palls[?]" (4 D 178–79).

Eliot typically humbled himself to Woolf in his letters. His favorite persona was the "Prince of Bores," who planned visits of less than twenty hours, so as not to tax his hosts. On one occasion he thought the visit could be extended if he were sent off to the curate and the divine service for a time on Sunday (Eliot letter to Woolf, 7 Apr. 1924, Berg). Like Roger Fry, he bowed to her skill as a letter writer, citing his "inability to satisfy the standards of correspondence which are set by even a post-card from yourself" (28 Dec. 1939, Berg). He strove to amuse her with comic verses. A beer song for New Year's Eve was a takeoff on *The Waste Land*: I won your heart at Harlem / At Bronx you murmured Yes" (dated "Twelfth Night," Jan. 1935). This particular letter she considered "affected," deciding cynically that she "must put [it] away, as it will be so valuable. Did he think that when he was writing it?" (4 D 273). More suited to her was his thank you poem on "the bread and butter letter," which has class identification as well as egregious rhymes:

> But Mrs Woolf could not rejoice
> In anything that's so bourgeois
> So what can poor Old Possum do,
> Who's upper-middle through and through?
>
> . . .
>
> Whoever gives him their approval—
> He hopes that Mrs Woolf'll (23 July 1937, Berg)

His most inventive rhyme paired "tetrahedral" with "Southwark Cathedral" (3 Feb. 1939, Berg). Eliot's Old Possum persona was suited to Woolf, who had played "goat" to her family as a child, and "mandrill" to Leonard's "mongoose." Besides the effort to teach him to dive like a frog, she never took on an animal identification with Eliot. Though he may have thought of his letters being saved, Eliot flattered her with the notion that she was his posterity. He foresaw that "some passing reference in journals and correspondence of Mrs. Woolf" might "lead to the inference he was author of a considerable body of writings, some with limited popularity" (12 Oct. 1939, Berg). It is impossible not to be touched by this same letter's arrangement to have tea in wartime: "on a chair without a leg, and from a cup without a handle," or by his last message, written only days before her suicide, which conveyed "the undying affection of OP" (19 Mar. 1941, Berg). After one particularly relaxed evening in 1935, she proclaimed of "Tom," "He is a dear old fellow: one of 'us': odd: I felt I liked him as I liked Lytton & Roger—with intimacy in spite of God" (4 D 324). This "us" seems the Leonard and Virginia us, interested in the gossip of publishing and the careers of younger men. The "I" moved him in with the Bloomsbury types most scorned by the other men of 1914.

Woolf had a number of conversations with Eliot on the subject of religion, beginning in 1928, when he became an Anglo-Catholic. This she expressed with comic shock to her sister Vanessa, reporting a two-hour conversation (3 L 457). With the publication of *After Strange Gods* in 1934, there had been a group discussion, led by Maynard Keynes, in which Woolf pressed him for a definition of belief in God. But Woolf reports in her diary, "He sheered off" (4 D 208). Woolf's essays demonstrate little sympathy for Eliot's antidemocratic thinking, or his privileged and aloof relation to tradition. In 1917, Woolf criticized the American essayist Henry Dwight Sedgwick for excluding literature from the democratic impulse: "The men of genius and learning are to constitute a priesthood, held in special reverence; and the intellectual traditions of generations of educated men should be taught by them as a special cult. . . . Was there ever a plan better calculated to freeze literature at the root than this one?" (2 E 81). In 1927 ("The Narrow Bridge of Art") Woolf regretted that twentieth-century poetry "has remained aloof in the possession of her priests" (223), as she looked to prose as the democratic art.

Anticipating Irigaray in her decentering project, Woolf eventually developed a distancing, double vision of Eliot, amid a set of modern male writers—Herbert Read, George Santayana, and H. G. Wells. She reduced them to little boys building sand castles that she as "the sea" could "demolish": "I mean, as I am not engrossed in the labour of making this intricate word structure I also see the man who makes it. I should say it is only world proof not weather proof." She develops a strategy as she reads their work: "the idea of women discovering, like the 19th century rationalists, agnostics, that man is no longer god. My position, ceasing to accept the religion, is quite unlike Read's, Wells', Tom's or Santayana's. It is essential to remain outside; & realise my own beliefs: or rather not to accept theirs" (5 D 340). A month later, in December 1940, Woolf fit praise of Eliot into a scheme in which she asserted her own being and trajectory, outside patriarchy: "The idea came to me that why I dislike, & like, so many things idiosyncratically now, is because of my growing detachment from the hierarchy, the patriarchy. When Desmond praises East Coker, & I am jealous, I walk over the marsh saying, I am I; & must follow that furrow, not copy another. That is the only justification for my writing & living" (347).

What Virginia Woolf might have hoped for from Eliot would have been recognition, on a par with the male modernists. With the exception of generous comments on *Jacob's Room*,[22] which must have been welcome after her Eliot/*Ulysses* agonies, Woolf heard more praise for her letters than her novels. While at Harvard, Eliot left the Woolf lectures to his assistant, he told her, though he did the Joyce himself.

When asked for a memorial, Eliot sidestepped critical comment, claiming that except in conversation, he was not interested in criticizing contemporary writers. Besides, "when an author of unquestionable importance has received due tribute, and is not in the slightest danger of being overlooked or belittled, there is no compulsion to criticize: what chiefly matters is that his writing should be read" (Eliot in Noble, ed. 145). How might the canon of 1940–65 have been affected if he had done so? Eliot proposed to do something for her memory that she had failed to do in her biography of Roger Fry—an odd way of offering a tribute in a criticism. He offered the ineffable feeling of something lost in her death. In saying that he wished to avoid giving "a false impression of 'accidental advantages,' " some of which "may have helped to smooth the path to fame," he introduces a discrediting notion that might not otherwise have occurred to Woolf's readers. Eliot places Woolf at the center of the literary life of London. At the same time, in tortured syntax, and without using the term "Bloomsbury," he points to its discrediting: "I am well aware that the literary-social importance which Virginia Woolf enjoyed had its nucleus in a society which those people whose ideas about it were vague— vague even in connection with the topography of London—were wont, not always disinterestedly perhaps, to deride" (148). Perhaps this only reiterates his need for women's society, expressed to Aiken in 1914. His final act is to deny her a place among the moderns. Hers was "Victorian upper middle-class culture," and his memorial to her is finally only a dating and a distancing of her.

When Djuna Barnes met T. S. Eliot, he had just given her one of the most important breaks in her career—the acceptance of *Nightwood* by Faber.[23] Theirs was neither as early nor as even a relationship as that between Woolf and Eliot. The complex tale of the publishing of *Nightwood* does not begin with Eliot, and its early episodes, including the literary agency of Emily Holmes Coleman, belong in the next section on "The Women of 1928." As her informal and highly unconventional literary agent, Coleman informed Barnes of her elaborate strategies with Eliot. She approached the "deeply cautious" Eliot through Edwin Muir, whom he trusted, supplying extracts to gain his interest. When they failed to do so, she wrote a "dynamite" letter, tempered with advice from Peter Negoe, who "took out a couple of sentences which he said resembled a religious orator in Hyde Park and which he said would not impress Eliot; who is known to be cold and cautious, loathing mess." One Coleman letter "put down every weakness I knew in the book, to disarm him, finishing up with 'Yet I think you will agree with me that it contains as extraordinary writing as has been done in our time; that the human truths revealed in it (the light it sheds on the relation of good to evil, *in this life*) make it a document that absolutely must be published.' " Coleman suspected from Eliot's criticism (which, unlike Rebecca West, she admired) that he would be "really interested in the fascinating philosophical inklings one gets from almost every page of it." Coleman felt that she had to get around the fact that "like everyone else he has gotten ossified in a way and it needed some dynamite to wake him up." Coleman sees it as a disadvantage to Barnes that, for Eliot, "form and order have become the most important things on earth. But he is a poet, too. The fact that he is moved by your book shows that the poet in him is not dead" (Coleman letter to Barnes, 26 Jan. 1936, Maryland).

Eliot began immediately to suggest what should come out of *Nightwood,* though even the text he read had already been cut and rearranged by Coleman, in accordance with her sense of its best focus, and what Eliot might not like.[24] Eliot's letter expressing interest in the manuscript advises "*strongly* the omission of the last chapter, which is not only superfluous, but really an anticlimax.[25] The Doctor is so central a character, and so vital, that I think the book ends superbly with his last remarks" (Eliot letter to Coleman, 20 Jan. 1936, quoted in Coleman letter to Barnes,

26 Jan. 1936, Maryland). Muir and Eliot's crony Frank Morley suggested other cuts. Barnes reported that "Anatomy of Night" had encountered resistance, and that she was "taking out a few 'shits' " which was all right, to get it printed (Barnes letter to Coleman, 14 May 1936, Delaware).

In his introduction to the American edition, Eliot reviews his early reading of the text, which had emphasized the importance of the Doctor to the expense of other characters, making the opening seem slow and the final chapter superfluous. But while he advocates appreciating all parts of the novel, including Nora and Robin as characters, the bulk of his attention still goes to the Doctor. He discourages reading the work as a psychopathic or philosophical study, suggesting that it be taken as poetry, or drama in the Elizabethan tradition. He plays around cultural constructions of perversity, as Puritan or socially produced, but rests his case in general humanity. Sexuality is never broached as a topic. Eliot's essay shows some debt to Coleman's original presentation of the manuscript. It addresses the slowness of the early chapters to a first reader, and bases the importance of the work on its relevance to "profound human truths" and suffering, as Coleman had in her correspondence (Coleman letter to Barnes, 27 Aug. 1935, Maryland). Yet Coleman was the bolder critic when it came to assessing its sexual content, particularly concerning female passion, and in pushing Barnes to bring unconscious depths to words and conversations (Coleman to Barnes, 27 Aug. 1935). Eliot also leaves the Jewish and homosexual contents of *Nightwood* untouched. Barnes had already protested Clifton Fadiman's reading of *Nightwood* for avoiding issues of difference in Jewish history. Barnes also continued to have insights about homosexuals—one of which she wished she had put into *Nightwood:* "No matter how nice they always like themselves far better than they can you, they are a divided people therefore a wedded people, wedded to the other half that walks in them with the step of the bride" (Barnes letter to Coleman, 22 Sept. 1936, Delaware). The feelings of exclusion and the attempt to empathize with internal divisions of the invert, expressing them in marital terms, are difficult to interpret. While this account of homosexuality verges on homophobia, Barnes may have been offering consolation to Coleman for her frustrating pursuits of homosexuals, often shared in her letters.

Eliot's introduction to *Nightwood* pleased both Barnes and Coleman, though not Barnes's patron and supporter Peggy Guggenheim, who passed on a reaction that it was "condescending." Barnes challenged this, saying that the charge was typically made of "anyone who feels their own worth, though writing of another," and that if anything, Eliot had been "a little over humble in tone" (Barnes letter to Coleman, 30 Dec. 1936, Delaware). Guggenheim's own complaint was that Eliot "gave Emily no credit" and "acted as if *he* discovered the book" (Guggenheim letter to Barnes, 1 Nov. 1937, Delaware).[26] In 1945, Barnes tried to find out more about Coleman's activities on her behalf from Eliot. Though he tried to dispel any notion that Coleman had claimed undue importance as an editor, his report was demeaning: "She practically forced the book down my throat, I admit I didnt appreciate it at first; and as for editing it, well Morley and I cut out a lot ourselves, and all to the good, I say. It was one of those rare books within which cutting out a lot of stuff perfectly good in itself actually improved the whole." Eliot suggested that Barnes might not like the fact that Coleman was "parasitic" on Barnes (Eliot letter to Barnes, 23 July 1945, Maryland). Barnes gave Coleman an interesting consolation in 1937 when she complained of problems with Eliot at the *Criterion*: "To a man like *that,* who as far as I can see, wants nothing personal in his life (and that would mean any just ordinary person) the thought of someone like you naturally probably gave him fits. He does not become an Englishman and an Anglo-Catholic for nothing" (Barnes letter to Coleman, 2 Mar. 1937, Delaware).

Barnes was at first delighted to be presented to the world by Eliot. Yet her feelings that things could have been better were occasionally shared with her female correspondents. She noted to Coleman that Morley was limiting the circulation of the *Nightwood* introduction, with a wary eye toward Eliot's future reputation: "A preface to a work of permanence so soon begins to date, and it would not be fair to have him smiled at if the reasons for the book's importance to our generation should look a little odd to a future generation" (Barnes letter to Coleman, 1 Dec. 1936, Delaware). Following the publication of *Nightwood,* Barnes was invited to Garsington by Ottoline Morrell, who quickly concerned herself with getting good reviews for the work. In her letters to Morrell, Barnes is eager to see Eliot at Garsington, but she also welcomes help from Morrell, who might be able to convince Eliot to run more advertising and obtain influential reviews (Barnes to Morrell, 24 Nov. 1936, Texas). Barnes passes on the explanation she had received from Faber that both the pricing and the limited advertising relate to the publishing house's fears of censorship from the home office—a problem we will return to in discussing the history-making lesbian novel of 1928, *The Well of Loneliness.* Barnes thought the introduction by Eliot backfired on Americans: "The two countries are always jealous of each other, or whatever it can be called, and the Americans always writhe under a feeling (correct) that the English are better, snobby and poisonous" (Barnes letter to Coleman, 3 May 1937, Delaware).

However mild her doubts about Eliot's introduction to *Nightwood,* she was greatly dissatisfied with a blurb he wrote for *The Antiphon.* In both cases, Eliot had made a point of narrowing her potential audience. Her criticism of the *Nightwood* effort was couched in appreciation of its being "so thoroughly well done, so British, so somber." But Barnes "could have done without the line to the effect that it had nothing to offer those of easy optimism" (Barnes letter to Coleman, 22 Sept. 1936, Delaware). Eliot's blurb for *The Antiphon* (which was not used) began with a pat on the back to Faber for taking on a book that "no other publishing house on either side of the Atlantic . . . would not have rejected out of hand." Barnes wondered why he needed such speculation, and would have gone directly to its recognition "as a classic of its period." She picked out other items of discouragement—Eliot's sampling of reactions of the "people of conventional manners" and "conventional taste" who found *Nightwood* shocking or "tedious and incomprehensible," and could be expected to find *The Antiphon* worse. She wondered at his phrase "Never has so much genius been combined with so little talent," and did not care to have *The Antiphon* compared to the "grimmer and grislier masterpieces of Jacobean tragedy"—grim and grisly having "lost their meaning to the penny dreadful." She still cherished the closing words of the *Nightwood* introduction, where Eliot prepared the reader to find "the great achievement of a style, the beauty of phrasing, the brilliance of wit and characterization, and a quality of horror and doom" which he compared to Elizabethan tragedy (Barnes letter to Eliot, 9 Jan. 1957, Maryland; blurb by T. S. Eliot, Maryland). Barnes ends her critique of the blurb with a witty metaphor, integrating garments and stitchery, as she had in her earliest writing, and probably intending a pun on "crewel": "I cannot recall seeing a 'blurb' . . . so tailored to a jacket that so resembles a shroud; and with such fine crewel work of approval and displeasure." Reminiscing with Natalie Barney in 1963, she claimed only the "early approval of T. S. Eliot" (Barnes letter to Barney, 31 May 1963, Maryland).

Barnes and Eliot saw each other occasionally in England and in the U.S. after her permanent return to New York in 1939. In 1937, she reported that he looked jittery at tea at Ottoline Morrell's, but ran after her to ask how her work was progressing. She was struck by the sadness of his poetry, identifying "dry" as his favorite word. She found a line from "Gerontion" applicable to the introduction, which she still cherished: "Unnatural vices / are fathered by our heroism." She did not understand why people were "so bitter" about his conversion to Anglo-Catholicism: "He's been defeated in his heart and life from the beginning as far as I can see, and going into the Anglo-Catholic church is not startling at all, he was headed for it" (Barnes to Coleman, 20 Feb. 1938, Delaware). He offered encouragement on new projects, including a work based on her eccentric Dadaist friend Elsa, Baroness Von Freytag-Loringhoven, which never saw publication (Eliot letter to Barnes, 28 Jan. 1938, Maryland). He tried unsuccessfully to get Gide to write an introduction to the French translation of *Nightwood*.

Barnes's female network fed her occasional gossip. She heard from Solita Solano that "Eliot loves Jane Heap and takes her to his club," where she is "the only woman among 40 men" (Barnes letter to Coleman, 22 Aug. 1936, Delaware). Heap was reported further to be going around saying that T. S. Eliot "wasn't nearly so crazy about [*Nightwood*] as he said he was" (Barnes to Coleman, 23 Nov. 1936, Delaware). But by 1938 Barnes was getting rollicking communications from Eliot, who was probably diverting himself from his failures to make enough of his relationship with Emily Hale. They shared their heavy drinking: "I shan't have had more than three double Booths, I don't expect, before I meet you." He signed himself off as "faithful and affectionate" (Eliot letter to Barnes, 22 Dec. 1938, Maryland). Eliot was left with the impression that he was "being rather affectionate" after a party at Helen and Georgio Joyce's in 1951 (Eliot letter to Barnes, 19 Feb. 1951, Maryland). During the late 1940s and early 1950s, when Eliot was also relying on Mary Trevelyan, Barnes and Eliot helped one another out—Eliot keeping up Barnes's magazine subscriptions in England and paying the rent on her furniture storage, and Barnes sending him food packets, including Kools cigarettes, which she thought would be good for his throat. He worried, in turn, that she might not be eating well enough. He recommended her for a Guggenheim Fellowship that she did not receive. There were some comparable elements in their natures—nervousness in social situations and over travel, where they could help each other out. Eliot advised her to ask for more money for a submission to *Mademoiselle* magazine, and joked that the title of the magazine "sounds pornographic."

Eliot's letters of the sixties took pains to describe the merits of his new wife, Valerie, and I suspect that she adversely affected the tenor of some of these. Unlike his relationship to Mary Trevelyan, the Barnes friendship continued after his marriage. One letter suggested that Djuna leave her letters from Eliot to Valerie, "the most trustworthy of all the people whom I trust" (Barnes sold them to the University of Maryland). Another corrected Barnes's misspelling of his "darling" Valerie's name (Eliot to Barnes, 4 May 1961, 30 Sept. 1964, Maryland). Barnes was hurt by this "sour little note" and, unrebuffed corrected his impression of each aspect of her brief letter. Eliot told her that he displayed her picture in his office, where it joined W. B. Yeats, Virginia Woolf, and Groucho Marx (4 May 1961). In his last communication, Eliot assured her that he was recovering from an operation, and expressed concern about her health and her ongoing writing. Barnes gave Peggy Guggenheim a positive account of Mrs. Eliot, which may have betrayed her own sense of need in old age: "There is no doubt that his wife was absolutely darling to him and made his decline, which might have been lonely and frightful, as gentle as could be" (Barnes letter to Guggenheim, Maryland). She and Valerie enjoyed sharing negative comments about the Ph.D. industry (Barnes letter to Valerie Eliot, 17 Nov. 1968, Maryland).

Barnes continued to discuss Eliot with her former lover Peter Hoare. When the facsimile of *The Waste Land* was published in the early seventies, Barnes expressed interest in the omitted portions, which suggested that Eliot had "an absolute disgust of women." She expected that "the attempt to keep Eliot's life muffled up will break down in due course" (Barnes letter to Hoare, 14 Dec. 1971, Maryland). It was Pound, she felt, who got Eliot to take out the questionable female passages of *The Waste Land* (21 June 1974, Maryland). Her suspicions have been confirmed.[27] One final reaction to Eliot comes in the notes, scribbled in aged handwriting, on letters that relate to Eliot's final editing role for *The Antiphon.* They insist that Eliot and Muir were wrong about their suggestions for cutting, sometimes recording their own admissions of this; the cuts fell heaviest upon the violent male figures. The relationship with Eliot was bittersweet at best, more denying than affirming of her authority with her own texts.

Rebecca West would have preferred to do away with Eliot's whole formulation of tradition. Starting in the late twenties, she was wary of his increasing influence in English critical circles. Unlike Woolf and Barnes, West had only chance encounters with Eliot, and she was not impressed by his personality. In an interview with Jane Marcus, she suggested that Eliot got her fired from the *Bookman.* I suspect a dramatic rewrite of much more subtle influences. West's work for this respected New York periodical began with essays on Shaw and Joyce in 1928, included her appreciative assessments of Lawrence and Woolf, and ended in 1930 with her

"Last London Letter," a resignation based on the *Bookman's* apparent alliance with the questionable "humanistic" judgments of T. S. Eliot. West in effect raises the contemporary issue of political correctness. She does not like the company her articles have been keeping, when Edmund Wilson can be found lacking in correctness for his proclamation that "it is no longer possible for a first-rate mind to accept the supernatural basis of religion" (514). She feels that, unlike the humanists, Wilson shows "a high standard of dialectical conduct." Her Hegelian terminology reminds us of his situation on the political left. Reared on Eliot's sense of tradition, gifted new writers will be "eaten up by a sense of inferiority," she fears. They will be encouraged to "convert this sense of inferiority into a sense of superiority, not by performance, but by subscription to a very easily held faith. One will then have a world of T. S. Eliots who have not achieved *The Waste Land,* who are utterly sterile and utterly complacent" (520).

While West was prepared to concede that Eliot wrote "true and splendid poetry," her 1932 review of Eliot's *Selected Essays* proclaims that "the years this American author has spent in England have inflicted damage on our literature from which it will probably not recover for a generation" (Scott, ed. 558). Her history states that when Eliot arrived in England at the start of World War I, "criticism was at its low ebb, when—perhaps because politics exercised such a compelling force on many able minds— it was purely arbitrary and impressionist" (588). He had a defined position, and spoke with authority. People did not stop to recognize that humanist formulae that made sense in educating Midwesterners were ill suited to an older culture that needed no new emphasis on tradition.[28] What his criticism lacks, in her mind, is the ability to "establish where authority truly lies, or to hand on tradition by continuing it in vital creation" (589). In resigning from the *Bookman,* she hoped to draw attention back to the moderns she valued most—Proust, Joyce, Woolf, Lawrence, and Huxley. In an essay called "Tradition in Criticism," West encouraged a subjective form of criticism that "takes almost the likeness and habits of imaginative work." She notes parenthetically that "Mr. Eliot would disapprove, and I would not" (194). West's various affronts to Eliot were a bold political move. In her old age West complained of a "fixed" literary market, and noted that she could well have used the support of an Eliot (Scott interview). She had to feel that it was not a good idea to disparage the "men of 1914"—a lesson reinforced with Joyce.

8 James Joyce:
Halting Female Pens
with *Ulysses*

The same narrative that exalts the "men of 1914" also halts at the remark-able year of 1922, when T. S. Eliot's *The Waste Land* and James Joyce's *Ulysses* both appeared, setting the standard for difficult, experimental po-etry and prose. While Lewis and Eliot built hard surfaces and monumen-tal defenses against feminine influences, Joyce and D. H. Lawrence at-tempted to master and move into them. This only complicates the problem of their relationship to feminists of both the modernist and the postmodern eras. Joyce was more an exemplum of modernism than one of its movers or makers. He was erected as a monument. He can be looked to for modernist theory, however. The concept of the "epiphany," not published until 1944 in *Stephen Hero,* has taken its place harmoniously beside modernist concepts of the image. The aesthetic of *A Portrait of the Artist as a Young Man,* derived from Aristotle and Aquinas, has served an austere, classicist view of modernism, while Joyce's undercutting of Stephen Dedalus in *Ulysses* and *Finnegans Wake* has been considered far less—one exception being feminists working within Joyce studies.[1] While there were critics ready at an early date to idealize Molly Bloom as an earth mother (see Scott, *Joyce and Feminism* 156–61), it has taken the cur-rent wave of feminist theory to chart the currents and limits of his semi-otic metaphors. More than any other modernist, James Joyce posed crea-tive and critical challenges to Woolf, West, and Barnes. While they had been encouraged by his supporters to hold him in awe, they all eventually turned Joyce to their own purposes. Going beyond *Ulysses* was a basic re-quirement for the women of 1928.

Joyce was aware of all three women writers. He knew Barnes personally while she was in Paris during the 1920s. He played a mentoring role that is exceptional, compared to his relationships to other women. Joyce hoped at one time to have *Ulysses* published by the Woolfs. Conflicting versions of its reception by them have occupied scholars ever since Harriet Shaw

Weaver brought it to the Woolfs' attention. Joyce became keenly aware of Rebecca West when "The Strange Necessity," with its irreverent dismissal of his poetry and its fault-finding even in *Ulysses,* was read to him.[2] By 1928, Joyce was not keeping up with the writings of his contemporaries, except where they wrote on him. He was aware, for example, of Wyndham Lewis's attack on him as a "time man" in his 1927 work, *Time and Western Man.* Except for a letter to Harriet Shaw Weaver and satirical asides toward West in *Finnegans Wake,* Joyce left no written reactions to the works of Woolf, West, and Barnes. Ironically, while women writers have been attacked for their critiques of Joyce, even in their private diaries and correspondence, his neglect of their writing has been virtually unquestioned. The reassessment of Joyce made possible by the convergence of Woolf, West, and Barnes on the man, his writings, and his critical reception, provided the original impulse for this book. This chapter is brief only because it builds upon my earlier studies of Joyce, which I have not wished to repeat.[3]

Joyce came to Woolf's attention primarily through the avid promotion of T. S. Eliot. Joyce's classicism and the priestly relation toward literature assumed by Stephen Dedalus were congenial to Eliot. They represented to him an ordered and acceptable version of modernism. Unlike a "scaffolding . . . of no interest in the completed structure," the mythic structure offered a way of "controlling, of ordering, of giving a shape and a significance to the immense panorama of futility and anarchy which is contemporary history," as Eliot stated in "*Ulysses,* Order and Myth" (681). Woolf set about reading *Ulysses* for its "method." She found, however, other qualities that impressed her more, particularly ones that penetrated the mind.

Method had become an issue with Woolf because it was so much emphasized in her critical age. Joyce was being glorified for his form and method. In a related set of observations, Woolf contended with method in assessing Percy Lubbock's 1921 study *The Craft of Fiction.* She discussed her distaste for Lubbock's formal priorities with Katherine Mansfield, E. M. Forster, and Lytton Strachey, and complained of his effect on her to Janet Case: "Every idea has gone under water. They were swarming last week, when I wanted to write a story" (2 L 531). Woolf's published reactions came with the essay "On Re-reading Novels," published in the TLS (July 1922). "Whenever Mr Lubbock talks of form it is as if something were interposed between us and book," the "presence of an alien substance which requires to be visualized imposing itself upon the emotions"

(3 E 340). Woolf's own criticism is so reliant upon visual similes and metaphors that her objection seems at first spurious. But the difference lies in the primacy of Lubbock's sense of "form."

Woolf calls for greater regard for the reading process, at the same time expressing her habitual distrust of the facility of images that characterizes her own writing:

> Here we have Mr Lubbock telling us that the book itself is equivalent to its form, and seeking with admirable subtlety and lucidity to trace out those methods by which novelists build up the final and enduring structure of their books. The very patness with which the image comes to the pen makes us suspect that it fits a little loosely. And in these circumstances it is best to shake oneself free from images and start afresh to read and set down impressions. (339)

For Woolf the " 'book itself' is not form which you see, but the emotion which you feel, and the more intense the writer's feeling the more exact without slip or chink its expression in words" (341). Lubbock's attention to method, which she compares to the x-ray, dissolves all but the bone, and misses the process of production and the connection to audience. She admits, however, that this method has some use. Lubbock "draws our attention to the solid and enduring thing to which we can hold fast when we attack a novel for the second time" (341).

Woolf's resistance to formal emphasis is, I believe, one way that she situated herself as a female critic and writer. Woolf finds that women had never benefited from available formal rules. She suggests in *A Room of One's Own* that women writing prose at the beginning of the nineteenth century had the wrong formal precedent—"a man's sentence . . . unsuited for a woman's use." This form rendered Charlotte Brontë clumsy, and it elicited atrocities from George Eliot (*Room* 79–80). Both fame and form contributed to Milton's bogey, making it difficult for women to write poetry even into the twentieth century. *A Room of One's Own,* of course, has memorable ways of dismissing the professorial bogey: a congregation of Oxbridge academics, heaving about like "giant crabs and crayfish. . . . soon to be obsolete if left to fight for existence on the pavement of the strand" (8), or the fictitious composite Professor von X, shown jabbing pen to paper to kill off woman as one would "a noxious insect" (31).

Woolf's reading notebook for *Ulysses* provides an ideal view of Woolf in the process of reading for the first time. She copes with her own bogey of form, writing, "Perhaps it's unfair to consider the method so much—doesn't it limit one a great deal?" ("Modern Novels [Joyce]," in Scott, ed. 642). She has "the quite unjust sense that he's doing it on purpose to show off" (643). A few pages farther on, she detects "queerness" of form, but admonishes herself in the margin, "Unfair to approach Joyce by way of his 'method' " which "is on the surface startling" (645). The final version of the essay, "Modern Fiction," reiterates, "In any case it is a mistake to stand outside examining methods. Any method is right, every method is right, that expresses what we wish to express, if we are writers; that brings us closer to the novelist's intention if we are readers." Joyce's method "has the merit of bringing us closer to what we are prepared to call life itself" (CR 156). One of the critical tools Woolf is developing in her scrutiny of Joyce is a sense of positioning; "outside" here is the position of the critic absorbed with formal aspects of works.

Searching for larger significance, Woolf uses Joyce to explore what is important to modern readers. "Our object is not to improve." Moderns go backward; she thinks of *Tristram Shandy,* and of "the desire to be more psychological—get more things into fiction." "Gertrude Stein," listed next, seems part of the new emphasis. Then again, "The interest is psychology" ("Modern Novels" notebook, in Scott, ed. 643), an observation that survives in the final essay; "the point of interest [for the Georgian writers], lies very likely in the dark places of psychology" (CR 156).

Admitting that all methods have their limits, Woolf regrets that Joyce misses a lot of life in his focus on thought processes and the "indecent" contents of the unconscious. "Is it due to the method that we feel neither jovial nor magnanimous, but centered in a self which, in spite of its tremor of susceptibility, never embraces or creates what is outside itself or beyond?" ("Modern Fiction," CR 156). And "the worst of Joyce &c. is their egotism—no generosity or comprehensiveness. Also seems to be written for a set in a back street. . . . Indifference to public opinion—desire to shock—need of dwelling so much on indecency" ("Modern Novels" notebook, in Scott, ed. 643). Identification of "a set in a back street" as Joyce's audience may be intended by Woolf as a call for broad appeal, though this sort of comment has laid her open to accusations of social superiority by the class-conscious Leavisite generation. Another insight is that Joyce's writing is dissective: "thought made phonetic—taken to bits." Joyce aims to "extract the marrow" (ibid.). This is quite similar to her carefully considered reaction to the critical methods of Percy Lubbock, who seemed too dissective and obsessed with form. Yet "marrow" has the merit of being the deep and living part of the bone. She credits Joyce with reaching mental depths in "Modern Fiction": "The scene in the cemetery . . . with its brilliancy, its sordidity, its incoherence, its sudden lightning flashes of significance, does undoubtedly come so close to the quick of the mind that, on a first reading at any rate, it is difficult not to acclaim a masterpiece" (CR 155). Woolf's qualifiers are many; it is only a brief scene, but it is an achievement in the field that most interests her.

Woolf wrote Joyce into a view of modernism that is fragmented and momentary in its brilliance. It was not a unique assignment; she took it herself, and placed Lawrence there too. She had tried to share this troubled vision of modernism with Eliot, as noted in the previous chapter. In "How It Strikes a Contemporary," *Ulysses* is summarized as "a memorable catastrophe—immense in daring, terrific in disaster" (CR 240). Again in "Character in Fiction," published by T. S. Eliot in the *Criterion* in 1924, Woolf cites the "memorable catastrophe" of *Ulysses* as part and parcel of an emerging pattern of modernism that denies unified masterpieces.[4] She remains critical of indecency as a formal element in Joyce's style, but she accounts for this as part of the fragmenting process of modernism. Indecency serves the project of breaking out of the metaphorical confines of the Edwardian house:

> Mr Joyce's indecency in *Ulysses* seems to me the conscious and calculated indecency of a desperate man who feels that in order to breathe he must break the windows. At moments when the window is broken, he is magnificent. But what a waste of energy! And after all, how dull indecency is, when it is not the overflowing of a superabundant energy or savagery, but the determined and public-spirited act of a man who needs fresh air! (3 E 434)

It is the "enormous stress on the fabric of things," the overfurnished house and idealistically encumbered characters of Edwardian form that Joyce and a varying list of "Georgians" were smashing.[5] She praises the moment of the smash, but feels the exertion may not be for the best of reasons. Joyce is "conscious and calculated" with his insertion of indecency, a deliberateness comparable to Wells's insertions of social ideas, which she found damaging to the elder writer's achievement of life in his writing. Woolf holds up the possibility of a "savagery" that is less conscious and more abundant in energy, showing an attraction to the primitive that was shared by Roger Fry and Picasso. That the breakage is a "public spirited act by a man who needs fresh air" makes Joyce both a hero of society and its ill-housed victim. Public-spirited window break-ing evokes memory of the suffragettes' assaults on the windows of public buildings, both in London and in Joyce's Dublin, where Joyce was ac-quainted with Hanna Sheehy-Skeffington, a leading suffragette. We have noted Woolf's assessment of Elizabeth Robins's stories of suffragette raids as dated. Joyce's window smashing is done from the inside out, how-ever. The consciousness of the act reconfirms Joyce's self-centered, egotis-tical smallness. He has not a whole house, but only a "bright yet narrow room, confined and shut in, rather than enlarged and set free," as Woolf suggests in "Modern Fiction" (CR 156).

It should be noted that "indecency" is not taboo with Woolf, but it is suspect if done for shocking effect. In "The Patron and the Crocus," Woolf suggests that the various presses and publics that constitute the patron of the twentieth century "must be immune from shock. The pa-tron must distinguish infallibly between the little clod of manure which sticks to the crocus of necessity, and that which is plastered to it out of bravado. He must be a judge, too, of those social influences which inevi-tably play so large a part in modern literature, and able to say which ma-tures and fortifies, which inhibits and makes sterile" (CR 214). Woolf's modernism also allows for contact with "social influences." Her sur-roundings at home and her social reading of Harriet Shaw Weaver inflect her description of the submission of *Ulysses* to the Hogarth Press:

> I remember Miss Weaver, in wool gloves, bringing *Ulysses* in type-script to our teatable at Hogarth House. . . . Would we devote our lives to printing it? The indecent pages looked so incongruous: she was spinsterly, buttoned up. And the pages reeled with indecency. I put them in the drawer of the inlaid cabinet. (5 D 353)

To some extent, Woolf is enjoying a study in contrasts here, between the indecent pages and Weaver (or even Woolf, who was comparable in slim figure to Weaver). It was a manuscript to be handled with wool gloves, certainly not displayed on the "teatable," and put away in the "inlaid cabi-net," a tasteful and decent piece of furniture. Miss Weaver was the sort to devote her life to Joyce—though actually she had a series of interests, in-cluding the work of Dora Marsden, which she brought to Joyce's atten-tion. One account of Woolf's refusal cites the number of pages, not their indecency, as what prevented publication at the Hogarth Press. Although the Woolfs would consistently protest censorship of literature, they were rightfully wary of the problems that might come their way with this text.

Regrettably, when Leonard Woolf selected from the diaries of Virginia Woolf for their first publication in a single volume, he favored two of her most negative reactions to Joyce, with lasting effect on critics.

Rebecca West's handling of Joyce in "The Strange Necessity" bears comparison to Woolf's jesting about Joyce in her diary, and to Woolf's playful attitude toward male monuments in her own extended, experimental essay, *A Room of One's Own*. These two works of 1928–29 have young, intellectual female personas, who sort through their feelings and integrate trivial happenings of their day as cultural evidence applicable to literary production and reception. That Joyce had "The Strange Necessity" read to him and reacted to it in several ways, enriches its value to this study. West's persona in the essay immediately distances herself from Sylvia Beach, who like Harriet Weaver had a reputation for devotion to Joyce. Having purchased one of Joyce's least notable works, *Pomes Penyeach*, at Beach's bookshop, West's character notes, in double deflation, that the work is sold "not exactly pretentiously, indeed with a matter-of-fact briskness, yet with a sense of there being something on hand different from an ordinary commercial transaction: as they sell pious whatnots in a cathedral porch" (sn 13). A typical difference between West's character and Woolf as reader is that West offers a brash and absolute judgment, whereas Woolf is tentative, pending a second reading. West's persona immediately pronounces the first of the *Pomes Penyeach* "exceedingly bad," comparing it to the "sole poetic production" of one Helen Wills, which she guesses appeared in *Vanity Fair*. To connect the high, much published and pushed modernist with a woman who has placed one thing in a popular magazine aimed largely at a female audience, is a shocking ploy. West may seem to participate in standard putdowns on women's writing and markets, though she contributed to comparable periodicals. She may remind us of Joyce's parodic ventures into women's journalism in the "Nausicaa" episode of *Ulysses*, now mischievously redrawing the lines of textual comparison. The protagonist of "The Strange Necessity" is delighted because Joyce's tasteless and sentimental words betray something about the man—an understanding of maker, as well as artifact, that also describes Woolf's eventual position on modernist men.

West's reaction to *Ulysses*, like Woolf's, praises certain passages, but denies that it works as a masterful unit. Both accuse him of using shock tactics. Her first extended analogy in the piece compares the impact of Joyce's sentimentality to the French game of *boules*. The "sentimental artist . . . is playing a game, he is moving certain objects according to certain rules in front of spectators. Those objects one may take as the isolated units of his material which he has passed through his imagination by an unfortunately discontinuous process. He sees that one of those objects occupies a certain position on the ground, and knows that he will score a point if he can remove it to another position; he therefore sends another of these objects rolling along to displace it. *Shock* [*sic*] . . . one hears that ugly sound" (17). The shock resonates in modern literature, according to West, particularly among writers who, "having a streak of Puritan optimism," expect to be rewarded for having observed "some revolutionary austerity regarding the superficialities of writing" (18). Defined in this way, sentimentality is something committed in Pound's editing austerities and his advocacy of imagism. West finds that both Gerty MacDowell and Stephen Dedalus suffer from the shock of sentimentality. In Gerty's case, "her erotic reverie is built up with as much noisy sense of meeting a special occasion as a grand-stand for a royal procession, in order that we may be confounded by the fact of her lameness" (20). Stephen is "transparently a hero," with "eyelashes an inch long. . . . He rolls his eyes, he wobbles on his base with suffering, like a Guido Reni" (20–21).

In Stephen's academic debates, West finds "the constant ingredients in almost every novel in which an Oxford or Cambridge graduate looks back on the Oxford or Cambridge undergraduate that he was five minutes previously and reverently commemorates the chrysalis" (22). It is the sort of novel that West congratulated Sylvia Lynd for *not* writing (see chapter 11). Joyce does have better material, "to which his imaginative experience of it has given absolutely just values—like the exquisitely pathetic picture of the visions of a sweet and ordered life that sometimes come to the squalid Dublin Jew Leopold Bloom, which is evoked in the question-and-answer part of the book" (22–23). She further celebrates Molly Bloom and the stories from *Dubliners* that partake of Joyce's classical training, "A Painful Case" and "The Dead."

West challenges the much-valued classical scaffolding of *Ulysses*, labeling it boldly as literary "incompetence" and mocking those who are taken in. She jests that recognition of the parallel incidents and characters "plunges Mr. Joyce's devotees into profound ecstasies from which they never recover sufficiently to ask what the devil is the purpose that is served by these analogies" (28). The Classical parallel suggests to her "that a pedantic accuracy about the letter and an insensitivity about the spirit can lead him wildly astray." Joyce's mistake, she feels, is to try to impose the Greek frame on an essentially Manichaean theme, quite alien to the Greek. While West is pursuing one of her most obsessive themes in finding the Manichaean in Joyce, it is useful to question how good the Greek fit actually is, whether devotees such as Eliot and Richard Aldington should have found solace in it, and why William Carlos Williams should have been moved to an all-out attack on West, particularly by this remark.

West's own structure for *Ulysses* is simplified to paired figures of the father, mother, and son: Simon Dedalus, supplanted by Leopold Bloom as father; May Dedalus and the far more realized Molly Bloom as mother; and Rudy Bloom and Stephen as sons, one killed, the other stifled by what his fathers have made of Dublin. It takes some stretch of the imagination to see Bloom as the father who slays his son (West admits this, and acknowledges Bloom's care of Stephen), or Molly as "the Universal Mother, that which conceives, which cherishes any life that is given to it, without care for anything but its physical fate" (40). But her centering *Ulysses* in family struggle has lasting psychological and cultural importance. It touches the depths of gender and sexuality, rather than the Classical surface design of the text, anticipating the murderous family dynamics of *Finnegans Wake* and postmodern readings of Joyce. Her utopian feminism comes through in the statement, "Personally I would prefer man to draw a better design, even if it was drawn but once and was not repeated like the pattern on a wall-paper" (50). West searches for a way out of the scaffolding.

Another consistent theme for West is that all people have a right to art and beauty rather than squalor. She attaches "squalor," rather shockingly, both to Leopold Bloom and to Joyce in his Dublin milieu. It is a mistake, I think, to dismiss West as anti-Semitic or aesthetically aloof for these attributions.[6] Her scheme makes a carnivalesque character of Bloom the court jester, pulling life back down to its marshy places, reducing language to gibberish. His Jewishness is a return to a "dark and massive materialistic religion" (42). In that "something true is said about man" through Bloom, West finds him "one of the greatest creations of all time" (43). But contrasted to Notre Dame, Bloom is a facade with holes, progressively leaning towers, and no nave to form the body of his structure (44). West's analogies are more ponderous and demanding than Woolf's. But she constructs a falling architecture of male modernism, in striking similarity to Woolf's. Later in the essay, she also portrays Joyce in metaphors too painfully true to his physical condition (including near-blindness) to rest well with her later readers. She imagines mixed elements of his mind "furnished like a room in a Westland Row tenement in which there are a bedstead and a broken chair, on which there sits a great scholar and genius who falls over the bedstead whenever he gets up" (56). I suspect as well the influence of Charlie Chaplin, whom West met in the mid-1920s. The account also has affinity to Woolf's contemporaneous description of the helpless scholars in bath chairs who congregate outside King's College Chapel in *A Room of One's Own.*

This Westland Row description occurs in the latter half of the essay, which becomes increasingly variable in its focus, starting at page fifty. At this point we become aware of the narrator's variety of activity, which combines the pedestrian with the exalted. She discloses that she has been working out her opinions of Joyce as she selected a dress, visited a milliner's shop, and went on to lunch in a golden room on Ile de St. Louis. Joyce's is not the only art she has considered. She has viewed Pruna panels of nudes plunging into depths, thought of a Goya print suggested by her dress, and viewed a painting by Ingres. She has thought appreciatively of Proust, and pondered lessons about the human cortex to be learned from Pavlov's famous research with salivating dogs. She is more faithful to the mind's movements from intellectual to practical things than traditional critics, even modernist ones.

West comes to recognize two pleasures: art and the development of the cortex, both enabling an understanding of the universe. The "interweaving rhythms of Leopold Bloom and Stephen Dedalus and Marion Bloom make beauty, beauty of the sort whose recognition is an experience as real as the most intense personal experiences we can have, which gives a sense of reassurance, of exultant confidence in the universe, which no personal experience can give" (50). In the latter sense, a bad poem by Joyce pleases, in that it throws light "on a certain system of relations, on the nexus of forces which is Mr. James Joyce" (69). This terminology appropriates from Nietzsche and the vorticism of Lewis, though her sense of cortical development seems compatible to my notion of spinning a web among existing supports. She has come to value Joyce not for his scaffolding but for the self-confirming web she makes of him within culture.

When Joyce had heard only the first fifty pages of "The Strange Necessity," he took it well. Writing to Harriet Shaw Weaver, Joyce felt that *Pomes Penyeach* had "the intended effect of blowing up some bogey bogus personality, and that she was quite delighted with the explosion." He wonders whether he might have escaped Wyndham Lewis's attack on *Ulysses* if Lewis had also read the poems (Joyce, *Selected Letters* 337). Joyce too would blow up bogey bogus postures of the young male artist he had once been, in a series of portrayals that culminates in a review of the Dedalus/ Joyce career in *Finnegans Wake*. The second portion of the essay seems not to have gone so well with Joyce. Padraic Colum recollected that Joyce was "irritated profoundly" by the essay. "That his critic had her illumination while about to buy some bonnets was a thing that seemed to leave a particularly bitter sting."[7] Joyce worked "West" and "Rebecca," sometimes associated with hats, into the word scheme of *Finnegans Wake*. Joyce's biographer, Richard Ellmann, thought the essay was "mocked" in *Finnegans Wake* (605). I think Joyce took West into the self-mocking spirit of that work. Joyce imports the early morning odyssey of West's persona through Paris streets, where while thinking of Joyce's poem, her eye "lit upon a dove that was bridging the tall houses by its flight" (*SN* 13): "Look in the slag scuttle and you'll see the sailspread over the singing, and what do you want trippings for when you're Paris inspire your hat?" (*Finnegans Wake* 453.23–25). West had praised Molly Bloom as a great mother figure "who lies in a bed yeasty with her warmth and sweat, and sends forth in a fountain from her strong, idealess mind thoughts of generation and recollection of sunshine" (*SN* 14). In *Finnegans Wake* she becomes one of the incarnations of Anna Livia Plurabelle, another woman on the move, who travels "robecca or worse" (203.4–5). On ALP's journey from the hills, West is "wist": "And whitside did they droop their glows in their florry, aback to wist of affront to sea?" (204.24–25). Glossed with "The Strange Necessity" in mind, the "affront" was to Joyce, seen alternately as the mythic father, the sea god Mannanan, and the "cold mad feary father" to whom ALP makes a fond return at the end of *Finnegans Wake* (628.2). But "affront to sea" is also fantasy, the sort of flight or "florry" into imaginative asides that West was capable of, even in the criticism Joyce heard. She discusses "fantasy" vs. reality extensively in the midpart of her essay. "Whitside" reads well as West's turning of her wit to Joyce. As "wist" West shares the passage with a card game. As noted above, West's favored analogy, used to describe Joyce's sentimentality, was another game—*boules*.[8]

William Carlos Williams served up a humorless rebuttal to West in the collection edited by Samuel Beckett, *Our Exagmination round His Factification for Incamination of Work in Progress*—an episode ably reviewed by Austin Briggs. The essay, like others in the volume, may have been coached by Joyce, though Williams reported feeling "ill" and "infuriated" the moment he read West's piece, and had begun an article before Beach approached him for the Beckett volume (Williams letter to Sylvia Beach,

Princeton, quoted by Briggs).[9] In response to one of West's major points, Williams argues that the Greek frame in *Ulysses* is useful for contrast. He condemns West for her supposed "descent into" psychological analysis. His attempt to assign her to a dated and provincial category of English criticism set a precedent for Hugh Kenner's later work on modernism, in which Williams assisted. Williams is interesting in his defense of Joyce, as Joyce stoops low to play the fool. But he also comes across as a chauvinistic American male. He uses the essay to call for a liberation of American from British criticism, and perhaps responding to West's fingering of aesthetic Puritanism, he dismisses her sensibility as that of a "scared protestant female"—a singly inadequate label for this devotee of St. Augustine. He cannot follow her "mixing of categories" and fails to appreciate the highly experimental nature of the very criticism he is reading.[10]

Beckett also gave space to West's critique in his essay for *Our Exagmination*. His admonition, which Briggs calls a "cheap shot," plays upon her references to Pavlov's salivating dogs: "One feels that she might very well wear her bib at all her intellectual banquets, or alternatively, assert a more noteworthy control over her salivary glands than is possible for Monsieur Pavlo's [*sic*] unfortunate dogs" (13). With this comment, Beckett joins West's earliest male detractors, issuing instructions on her manners in relation to great men. The focus on saliva assigns her to the semiotics of disgusting feminine ooze also favored by Wyndham Lewis, as noted in chapter 6. There is an ironic postscript to this bashing of West. In the 1933 trial of *Ulysses* that cleared the way for its publication in the U.S., defense attorney Morris Ernst published quotations from "The Strange Necessity" in order to argue its value as literature (Moscato and LeBlanc, eds.).

"The Strange Necessity" places West in Paris at a time when Djuna Barnes and Joyce himself were living there. Barnes had already written about the artistic and cultural attractions of Paris, so evident in West's "The Strange Necessity," in an article that went on to speak of her first meetings with Joyce. "Vagaries Malicieux," published in the *Double Dealer* in 1922, approached Paris via a satire on human nature:

> No man dares have a fixed opinion on life, love or literature until he has been to Paris, for there is always someone at his elbow to hiss: "Have you visited the Louvre? Have you reacted to Giotto? Have you run your hand over the furniture of the fifteenth cen-

tury? Seen the spot where Marie Antoinette became most haughty? No? Well then, my dear friend, keep in your place." (249)

The list reads like West's itinerary. But having exposed Parisian one-up-manship, Barnes shows herself falling for it: "And so it was that I, also, came to Europe" (ibid.).

Barnes could be grouped with Sylvia Beach and Harriet Shaw Weaver as one of Joyce's devoted circle of women, regarded cynically by West. She was published in *transition,* where there appeared many segments of Joyce's "Work in Progress," as well as analyses of his works prepared under his supervision by devotees. *Transition* editor Eugene Jolas set her (like Joyce) in the tradition of "the revolution of the word": "Instead of choosing the desiccated language matter of her contemporaries, Miss Barnes gives us what at first sight seems an archaic style, but which is merely the resuscitation of a highly charged word mechanism that succeeds in electrifying us" (326). Robert McAlmon recalled an evening when Djuna Barnes and Mina Loy "were very adoring toward Joyce, the master" (McAlmon and Boyle 128). Barnes admits to the impact of Joyce upon her group. Recollecting Paris in a 1941 article, "Lament for the Left Bank," she recalls with some self-mocking that, with *Ulysses,* "Stein's star, Cocteau's moon, had set" and "expatriate pens stood still. . . . They wept in joy and copied in despair," taking the blue book of *Ulysses* home as a souvenir ("Lament" 138). In "James Joyce," an informative, fairly straight-forward article centered on Joyce that she wrote for *Vanity Fair* in 1922, Barnes begins with a tribute to the "singing quality of Joyce's words." He was formerly a singer, and "because no voice can hold out over the brutalities of life without breaking—he turned to quill and paper, for so he could arrange, in the necessary silence, the abundant inadequacies of life, as a laying out of jewels—jewels with a will to decay" (65). Like West, Barnes recognized the sordid aspects of Joyce's experience, but his talent is in their "laying out." Joyce's metaphorical jewels escape cultural materialism in their mortal "will to decay." Decay was as important a consideration to Barnes as Manichaeanism was to West.

Barnes makes it clear in these articles that she did not go seeking Joyce. Echoing the wanderings of Robin Vote in *Nightwood,* she went instead seeking the oldest church in Paris, Saint Germain des Près. From there she proceeded across the street to the café Deux Magots, where Joyce approached her. Joyce sought Barnes because she could provide information

Plate 13. Djuna Barnes pen and ink sketch of James Joyce.
Papers of Djuna Barnes, Special Collections,
University of Maryland at College Park Libraries.

on the suppression of the *Little Review* for publishing chapters of *Ulysses*. Possibly he wanted a different version from that offered by the misogynist lawyer John Quinn—a view enhanced by Ezra Pound, as we have seen in chapter 5.

Barnes was an expert interviewer by 1922 and quickly sensed what not to do with Joyce. He was "the Grand Inquisitor come to judge himself. To ask him a question was to receive a cold, terrible gaze. Joyce alone could question Joyce" ("Lament" 148). Or as she put it more strategically in her *Vanity Fair* article, "Because one may not ask him questions one must know him" ("James Joyce" 65). Instead of questioning, she observed Joyce minutely, providing the most remarkable physical descriptions of the man that I have encountered. His most characteristic pose, "that of the head; turned farther away than disgust and not so far as death" (ibid.); "A quiet man, this Joyce, with the back head of an African idol, long and flat. The back head of a man who had done away with the vulgar necessity of brain room" ("Vagaries" 252). Her admiration for the hand-embroidered vest he had inherited from his father and grandfather elicited a bit of history. Though questionable, it suggested a Joycean fabrication of gentility: "Made by the hand of my grandmother for the first hunt of the season" ("James Joyce" 65). Barnes dutifully recorded his frequently shared opinions of Yeats, Moore, Synge, Strindberg, Irish politics, and Freud. She got bored with Joyce's favorite talk of the Greeks, allowing her mind to wander. But whereas West had found incongruity in Joyce's Greek framework, Barnes saw its divergence. She noted that Joyce makes his Greeks " 'naughty boys,' and leaves them shaking hands, across the gulf, with Rabelais" (253).

In the article for *Vanity Fair*, Barnes quotes Nora Joyce (whom she came to know and like) on "the great fanaticism is on him," referring to his valise full of notes and his preoccupation with the book of saints, all channeled into *Finnegans Wake*. Barnes notes that Nora's brogue was "a little more defiant than Joyce's which is tamed by preoccupation" ("James Joyce" 104). Barnes is aware of Joyce's famed memory, but qualified that it functioned with "the slow dragging quality of an inland mist" ("Vagaries" 153). She seems to have sensed that her *Vanity Fair* readers would be interested in Joyce's attitude toward women, which she recorded with cynicism: "About women he seems a bit disinterested. Were I vain I should say he is afraid of them, but I am certain he is only a little skeptical of their existence" ("James Joyce" 65). From actual observation, Barnes set

Joyce in the same sort of room that West would imagine for him: "He was living, though seldom seen, in great poverty in the rue de l'Université."

Barnes provides one indication that Joyce served as a literary advisor. The advice (contained in a long story about an eccentric baroness he had met) included the admonition not to write of outlandish characters, as that was the task of journalists ("Vagaries" 253). Perhaps Joyce was aware of Barnes's most striking interviews and participatory journalism, or of her friendship with the eccentric Elsa, Baroness Von Freytag-Loringhoven. Barnes embarked on a work based on the baroness after *Nightwood,* acknowledging to Emily Coleman that to write on Elsa violated Joyce's admonition to avoid the "uncommon" (Barnes letter to Coleman, 30 Nov. 1935, Delaware). *Transition* carried Barnes's half-page tribute to the baroness, written just after her suicide, in an issue that also carried Joyce's "Work in Progress." Joyce also regaled Barnes with a story that mixed animal and procreative themes, Ovid's *Fasti.* We will return to its possible influence on her own fabulations in volume 2. Joyce connected with Barnes's own fascination with monologues, in the process showing his use of the form to reveal psychological depths in *Ulysses:* "All great talkers . . . have spoken in the language of Sterne, Swift or the Restoration." Of *Ulysses,* "They are all there, the great talkers . . . them and the things they forgot. In *Ulysses* I have recorded, simultaneously, what a man says, sees, thinks, and what such seeing, thinking, saying does, to what you Freudians call the subconscious" ("James Joyce" 65). Barnes did not think of herself as a Freudian, but recorded the remark without comment.

Some of Barnes's discussions with Joyce suggest that they connected on favorite themes as well. She recalled, "It has been my pleasure to talk to him many times during my four months in Paris. We have talked of rivers and of religion, of the instinctive genius of the church which chose, for the singing of its hymns, the voice without 'overtones'—the voice of the eunuch" (ibid.). "We talked of death, of rats, of horses, the sea; languages, climates and offerings" (104). Barnes sees Joyce in the mold of Stephen Dedalus, who had "not even one friend," vowed not to serve "that which I no longer believe," but to "express myself as freely as I can and as wholly as I can," and to use the strategy of "silence, exile, and cunning." These were to prove her strategies as well. When she took up her pen again, after encountering *Ulysses,* Barnes showed the same absorption in church rituals, appropriating them for art. She pushed the revelations of the solitary voice to the margins of sexuality and eccentricity where Joyce scarcely ventured.

Wyndham Lewis and William Carlos Williams attempted to place Joyce out of range even of the criticism of Woolf and West. Yet our recovery of their reactions to Joyce is an invaluable help in reinterpreting modernism. Eliot's scaffolding yields to West's sense of a web in which Joyce himself is tangled. Eliot's structuring classicism becomes Rabelaisian when experienced by Barnes, or mere skeleton to the cultural and emotional marrow sought by Woolf. All three modernist women connect to Joyce's interest in psychology and find his physical conditions, including their Irish origins, remarkable and relevant to his writing.

In the Introduction, I noted some aspects of the more recent feminist response of Sandra Gilbert and Susan Gubar to Joyce. Though suspicious of Joyce's charm with language, they engage in comparable word play to topple him from eminence, including the positive readings given him by "Derridaughters." Gilbert and Gubar have collected evidence of misogyny in statements by Joycean characters, though in doing so they often strip statements of contextual irony and an implied critique of patriarchy. They have suspected Joyce of entering feminine language in order to reassert priestly male control (*patrius sermo*), citing as evidence the "Oxen of the Sun" chapter of *Ulysses*.[11] Gilbert and Gubar have cast Joyce in a scenario of sexual anxiety and war between the sexes. But the women of modernism were in touch with a different Joyce. They produced admirable, original interpretations before, or in spite of, formalist guides. It may have been Joyce's agents, rather than his work, that were briefly daunting—seeming to sentence them to oblivion. Ultimately, Joyce prompted Woolf, West, and Barnes to write their own way into modernism, as we are coming to appreciate it, as a disruptive exercise.

9 Lawrence, Forster, and Bloomsbury: Male Modernist Others

In his harsh critique of rational, scientific, mechanized modern Western culture, D. H. Lawrence departs from the "men of 1914," as we have been encouraged to know them. He looks below the belt, and back to a pagan, preindustrial world for life-sustaining forces. In "Surgery for the Novel," Lawrence was critical of technically experimental modernists (James Joyce, Dorothy Richardson, and Marcel Proust), whom he described as "listening at great length to the death rattle in their own throats." His origins as the son of a coal miner and a schoolteacher place him in a decidedly different position on the social scale from Pound, Lewis, Eliot, and even Joyce.

Lawrence's female connections, as demonstrated in biography and letters, are of great literary and artistic interest. Himself a banned writer for *The Rainbow*, Lawrence was not in a position to help others into print. Yet he communicated supportively with women, holding on to relationships which he seems to have needed to ground his own work. It is widely agreed that Lawrence wanted, and needed, to see things through women's eyes, and that he frequently rewrote their texts to achieve his own. The list of his female witness/collaborators includes his early love, Jessie Chambers, whose notes and commentary were helpful (some would argue critical) to the development of *Sons and Lovers;*[1] Helen Corke, whose diaries Lawrence worked over for *The Trespasser;* Mollie Skinner, whose Australian narrative was the foundation of *The Boy in the Bush;* and of course his wife, Frieda Lawrence, whom Martin Green has elevated to the status of co-writer of certain works.

Lawrence became a topic in women's autobiographical writing, including its exploration of issues of gender. Jessie Chambers, Catherine Carswell, Dorothy Brett, Mabel Dodge Luhan, and Frieda Lawrence left idiosyncratic accounts of his magnetic personality, as well as his demands. H. D.'s *Bid Me to Live* was self-healing retrospective writing, encouraged when she underwent analysis with Sigmund Freud and needed to understand her relation to male modernists. In it, H. D. re-viewed and worked out of the critical force of Lawrence, the failure of her marriage to Richard Aldington, and her experience of World War I. Rico, her Lawrence figure, "could write elaborately on the woman mood, describing women to their marrow in his writing; but if she turned round, wrote the Orpheus part of her Orpheus-Eurydice sequence, he snapped back, 'Stick to the woman-consciousness, it is the intuitive woman-mood that matters' " (62). Despite Lawrence's condemnation of the death rattle in other modernists, H. D. did not see Rico as a life force: "But Frederico, for all his acceptance of her verses, had shouted his man-is-man, woman-is-woman at her; his shrill peacock-cry sounded a love-cry, death-cry for their generation" (136). She observed that "there was also the woman, not only the great mother-goddess that he worshipped, but the woman gifted as the man, with the same, with other problems" (136).

In a famous letter written to Katherine Mansfield in late 1918, Lawrence explores human relationships, implicating Mansfield, her husband, John Middleton Murry (who later analyzed Lawrence in homosexual terms in *Son of Woman*), Frieda Lawrence, and himself, as well as the dynamics of *Women in Love*. In sending Mansfield a book by Carl Jung, he warns her about male obsessiveness with an incestual return to the womb of the Magna Mater. Lawrence fears that Murry staged this return with Mansfield, and that he has done the same with Frieda, and is now "struggling with all my might to get out." He reports grimly, "It is awfully hard, once the sex relation has gone this way, to recover. If we don't recover, we die." It is interesting that, in writing to Mansfield, the male is presented as the agent of his own destruction. Lawrence reverts to a hierarchical power structure of the genders late in this letter: "Woman must yield some sort of precedence to man and he must take precedence." Lawrence does report that this formula has been pronounced "antediluvian" by Frieda. His phrase "some sort of precedence" leaves some room for selection. The same crucial letter expresses an ideal of friendship, described first as "a pledging of men to each other inviolably" but expanded also to "friendship between men and women, and between women and women, sworn, pledged, eternal, as eternal as the marriage bond, and as deep." He has neither "met" nor "formed" such a relationship, but may in fact be seeking it in these very letters (2 *Letters of D. H. Lawrence* 301–302).[2] Mansfield's 1922 letters to S. S. Koteliansky admire Lawrence as "a living man" (*Letters of Katherine Mansfield* 477). She uses *Aaron's Rod* as a pretext to criticize (in quite un-feminist terms) "half-female, frightened writers-of-today" that "remind me of the greenfly in the roses—they are a kind of blight" (482). Though Lawrence would seem to offer the unblighted leaf, Mansfield goes on to say, "I do not go all the way with Lawrence. His ideas of sex mean nothing to me" (483).

The constitution and site of the feminine and the relation of women to men figure in virtually everything Lawrence wrote. Hilary Simpson offers an admirably concise and accurate survey of the historical contexts of Lawrence's interest in sexuality and women in culture, as well as a chronological survey of his changing attitude on the subject in his fiction and essays. *Sons and Lovers* makes an early probe into the topic of maternity. It has been argued that Lawrence, like his hero Paul Morel, is able to advance beyond an Oedipal relation to the mother and try on different modes of sexual alliance with women. In his personal life, the alliance with Frieda fulfilled adult sexuality, according to biographer Harry T. Moore (62). *The Rainbow* offers Lawrence's most affirmative views of matriarchy and of young women's development. It thinks back through the mothers of Ursula Brangwen and moves forward with her growing sense of autonomy.

The negative cultural response to the sexual themes of *The Rainbow*, seen in its seizure by British authorities and delayed publication in the U.S., combined with the personal disruptions, destruction, and gender-specific social upheavals of World War I, made Lawrence a reactionary in regard to women and the feminine, according to Simpson. *Women in Love* is a transitional text. Sandra Gilbert and Susan Gubar have pointed to its sexual violence—the voluptuous violence of Hermione's assault on Birkin with a ball of lapis lazuli, the deadly embrace Diana gives the doctor who would be her rescuer, and Gerald's attempt to strangle Gudrun, interrupted by the no-man Loerke (38–40). The cultural necessity becomes male assertion of power; all else, disaster. Despite his fine visions of lovers in "an equilibrium, a pure balance of two single beings:—as the stars balance each other" (139) and the fights he gets from her, submission lurks behind Birkin's demands of Ursula, and she fades as a vigorous character after their marriage. His sense of the existence of something beyond heterosexual love puts him in a different league from her, and it is difficult not to see his as a privileged viewpoint at the close of the novel. The duality of male assertion vs. female submission is again clearly evident in the attempt at male mastery of March by Grenfel in *The Fox*, a work in which gender tensions are heightened with parallel animal symbols.

Lawrence's *Fantasia of the Unconscious* insists that, although men and women may play each other's roles in our historical period, a child is born either wholly male or wholly female (131–32). What is natural in the male is the volition, action, utterance; it is polarized from the female's sympathetic center of feeling and emotion. A consequence to the woman writer that echoes the later theory of Jacques Lacan is that "women, when they speak or write, utter not one single word that men have not taught them" (137–38). The Lawrence of this text finds the dynamics of power "superior" to sexual dynamics with woman, and power is religious in nature and male-defined: "The desire of the human male to build a world: not 'to build a world for you dear'; but to build out of his own soul and his own belief and his own effort something wonderful" (60). But has the religious soul really driven beyond the woman? In works of what has been called his "leadership phase" (*The Fox, Fantasia, Aaron's Rod, Kangaroo, The Plumed Serpent*), Judith Ruderman finds an unresolved pre-Oedipal perception of the mother, focusing on dyads of mother-child dependency and the perception of the mother as a wild animal who would devour her child (10–13).

In *Lady Chatterley's Lover*, his final novel, published in the notable year of 1928, Lawrence gives central importance to vital sexuality and "tenderness" (235, 260–61). Both the lowborn gamekeeper, Oliver Mellors, and the socially privileged Lady Chatterley are remade as successful lovers. Though she is capable of self-containment and independent action, Constance is contrasted both physically and mentally to the flat-chested, "smart," "cocksure" modern woman (18). Constance's aristocratic husband, Clifford, has been unmanned by war. He emerges as a mechanical, cerebral captain of the modern mining industry. This industry is devouring the sensual spaces of nearby Wragby wood. Clifford at first depletes Constance's energies with his demands for personal attendance, but in her absence replaces Constance with a Magna Mater figure, his nurse Mrs. Boulton. Lawrence makes his gamekeeper both a guardian of nature and a political spokesman whose views on lesbians and cocksure women are pronouncedly unsympathetic.

The phallus may be Lawrence's ultimate character. In his defense of his novel, "A Propos of *Lady Chatterley's Lover*," Lawrence speaks of "the blood of man and the blood of woman" as "two eternally different streams . . . that encircle the whole of life, and in marriage the circle is complete, and in sex the two rivers touch and renew one another, without ever commingling or confusing." But the phallus is special. "The phallus is a column of blood that fills the valley of blood of a woman" (507). In looking at the future of England, he says that "if England is to be regenerated . . . then it will be by the arising of a new blood-contact, a new touch, and a new marriage. It will be a phallic rather than a sexual regeneration. For the phallus is only the great old symbol of godly vitality in a man, and of immediate contact" (508). Like Ursula before her, Constance bows down to male loins, worshipping at Oliver's renewed, "cocksure" penis (196).

Lawrence's late essays "Matriarchy" and "Cocksure Women and Hensure Men" are more playful renditions of these themes. Lawrence works with distinct categories and spheres, offering a troubling evolution in the history of gender relations. In "Matriarchy" he embraces (however bemusedly) the conservative orientation of John Knox, complete with his horror of a "monstrous regiment of women." Lawrence assigns animal metaphors as women exchange the place and voice of the hen with that of the cock in "Cocksure Women," or descend like a plague of locusts upon the postwar job market in "Matriarchy." Woman no longer operates in a personal, one-on-one relationship, but engulfs with vast numbers. Her legs come in sixes, as serves both the insect metaphor and the theme of engulfment, but suggests monstrous fusion as well.[3] Women are commodified and impersonalized as body parts, as grotesque here as the women's vaguely threatening bare arms in T. S. Eliot's "The Love Song of J. Alfred Prufrock." Lawrence concedes names, clans, and domestic spaces to women, trivializes the male connection to procreation and the domestic realm, and moves men at puberty to the grand and primitive social system of the tribe and the transcendent spiritual function of religion.

Rebecca West helped to establish the reputation of D. H. Lawrence in the U.S. through her laudatory reviews in American publications. She had met him in a hotel outside Florence, and walked with him through the countryside. This meeting provided the centerpiece for her personal "Elegy," written upon Lawrence's death. West appreciated Lawrence's ability to make such landscapes a symbol for the state of his soul, a literary project that she preferred to naturalistic fiction, and that she had begun to attempt early with works such as "Trees of Gold." She admitted to being "entranced" by him, and compared his travels by cheap trains to destinations where he had no preordained purpose to "the journeys that mystics of a certain type have always found necessary" (*Essential Rebecca West* 389). Lawrence appreciated her ability to write scathing reviews, and she preserved an appreciative letter from him, framed on her wall, alongside one from Virginia Woolf. Here was a woman he could admit to his tribe. He wrote, "I always like you when you are on the war path," and that she was "a real good squaw for scalps" and shouldn't be downhearted: "There are such a lot of scalps ripe for taking. . . . The battle is here below and it's too soon for us to look on from the heavenly balconies. So I am once more spitting on my hands—so no doubt are you. Then a war whoop. . . . I hope you are renewing your energy like the eagle" (Lawrence letter to West, 15 Apr. 1929, Tulsa). The letter also encouraged her to write an article on him for *This Quarter*, which she did not manage at that very pressing time in her own career.

Despite the obvious empathy between the two, West was still capable of irreverence toward Lawrence, and of turning his writing to her own uses. Her "Elegy" turns to dark themes that interest her, such as the "death of the soul" and "the will to die" vs. the "will to live." She regrets that he lacked the symbolic vocabulary of theology, and thus reverted to "clumsy creation of images" in presenting Gerald Critch's death in the mountains in *Women in Love*. She questions the "base" sexual vocabulary of *Lady Chatterley's Lover*, though she accounts for it in mystic terms, as an offering to be transmuted in his approach to creation (*Essential Rebecca West* 394). *Aaron's Rod* struck her as "silly," its sense of the relation between men and women too "pugilistic and exhausting" (see Rollyson).

West wrote a practical, comic response to an article by Lawrence on men's lost virility, "Good Boy Husbands" (1929), which belongs in the same era as "Matriarchy" and "Cocksure Women and Hensure Men." She takes off from Lawrence's remark "It may be that men nowadays are all grown-up babies . . . because they were delivered over in their tenderest years, poor little devils, to absolute petticoat rule; mothers first, then schoolmistresses" ("Reply to Good Boy Husbands" 584). What Lawrence should do with "this extraordinary remark is to tie it up in a brown paper parcel and drop it over London Bridge at midnight and deny all knowledge of it, if the Thames Conservancy people ask questions" (584). She then explores questions that interest her, such as why it is that men do not take care of small children—a probe that ranges from fantasizing men leaving "the field of Agincourt so that they could go home and mind their babies," to an assessment of the low pay scale that makes schoolmistressing a female profession. She also assures him that spinster schoolmistresses (she adds the spinster), because of their lack of experience with men, are most apt to trust in the "ideal of virility" (585). In her conclusion, West deploys her own essentialism. While women as wives and mothers have remained in contact with primitive instincts, men have been put into conflict with their primitive selves. While much of the time they pursue "beauty, or justice, or wisdom as fearlessly as if it were the wild boar in the jungle," sometimes they "kick and scream" instead—one example of this being "gratuitous attacks on women" (587). But this is only one of Lawrence's moods, to West, who is pleased to find in his published letters the balance of serenity and good sense (591).

Woolf's experience of Lawrence was more limited than West's, partially because she resisted reading him. This resistance had something to do with attending to her own work without being distracted by contemporaries such as Lawrence "doing the same thing on another railway line: one resents their distracting one, flashing past, the wrong way." But it also involved the way he was presented to her. Woolf told Ethel Smyth that John Middleton Murry, "that bald necked blood dripping vulture, kept me off Lawrence with his obscene objurgations" (4 L 315). She states in "How It Strikes a Contemporary" that Lawrence offered "moments of greatness, but hours of something very different" (CR 240), admitting, however, that this was based on limited reading. Woolf reviewed one of Lawrence's least-noted novels, *The Lost Girl,* with disappointment in 1920. Where she had expected a modernist, she found a writer akin to Arnold Bennett, supplying a work which could be read for story and facts. The qualities she had expected are a better index of her general interest in Lawrence, and are consistent with attitudes toward the body expressed in "Professions for Women": "We conceived him to be a writer, with an extraordinary sense of the physical world, of the colour and texture and shape of things, for whom the body was alive and the problem of the body insistent, and important. It was plain that sex had for him a meaning which it was disquieting to think that we, too, might have to explore" (3 E 271). She got the most pleasure from *Sons and Lovers,* read after Lawrence's death, and was by then prepared to call him a genius. While writing *The Waves,* Woolf was inspired by thoughts of Lawrence to write as he did for the sake of writing.

Though she never met him, Woolf saw Lawrence twice, first in her beloved St. Ives, and later in a train station in Rome. It may be some sign of reverence that she and Leonard visited his grave in Vence. Aldous Huxley, S. S. Koteliansky, and Ottoline Morrell knew both Woolf and Lawrence well, and discussed him with Woolf. Morrell shared details of Lawrence's late letters, in which he attempted to overcome the rupture that had resulted from her unflattering likeness as Hermione in *Women in Love*. In summarizing, Woolf doubts that the letters are good for Morrell:

> But his letters are wildly phallic and philosophical; and mad, and I dont see much point in renewing that. All germs are devils which attack us because we lower our selfishness, and women can only live in the imaginations of men, and Ottoline once lived in his, and so on—what dammed but conceited nonsense it all is; but it seems he is dying, and is I suppose a genius and so on. (3 *L*508)

Woolf deplored incidents of his censorship, and was appalled by the hypocrisy of the press at the time of his death (4 *L* 14–15, 48, 167). She identified his masculinism, indirectly, in an exchange over *A Room of One's Own* with Desmond MacCarthy. Sensing that MacCarthy had detected Lawrence in "Mr A" (who protests the equality of one sex by asserting the superiority of his), she says, "He was not in my upper mind; but no doubt was in the lower" (4 *L* 130 and n). There were other Lawrentian qualities that seemed more troubling. His letters induced claustrophobia; she resisted his need to preach and to put people and things into a system, which he reiterated monotonously. *The Man Who Died*, his last work, offered "something sham. Making himself into a God, I suppose" (4 *D* 28). Woolf had little use for gods, sham or otherwise, as her debates with Eliot had proved.

Bloomsbury

Bloomsbury has been characterized as a snobbish and trivial world apart in accounts fed through the "men of 1914," as suggested already in chapters 5 through 7. It is inhabited by buggers, in Pound's account. It is a uterine underworld and arty family salon, according to Lewis. Eliot entered Bloomsbury with sharpened wits and caution about gossip and the play of jealousy among its inhabitants. Hugh Kenner takes cheap shots at Bloomsbury manhood, as in a summary of the diverse sexual alliances of Duncan Grant that verges on homophobia (*Sinking Island* 161). Feminist critics have demonstrated ways that the Bloomsbury association devalued Virginia Woolf, noting that men such as E. M. Forster and Lytton Strachey had homosocial relations that excluded her, even as they were marginalized by a more virile modernist ethos.[4] Woolf cautioned in *Three Guineas*, "Inevitably we look upon societies as conspiracies that sink the private brother, whom many of us have reason to respect, and inflate in his stead a monstrous male, loud of voice, hard of fist" (3 G 105). Thoby Stephen is generally credited with inaugurating Bloomsbury Thursday Evenings. Even at the start, Virginia Woolf exerted power as a listener, and from her listening gained valuable material for later appropriation. Duncan Grant recalls that Virginia and Vanessa sat silently and fiercely. If Virginia talked at all, it was privately, to the person next to her, though with her teachers of Latin and Greek, Miss Pater and Janet Case, "she was more open and less reserved" (Noble, ed. 27–30). For a starter, this demeanor violates Mrs. Ramsay's Victorian expectation, expressed in *To the Lighthouse,* that young women must be charming, keep the conversation going, and offer sympathy and encouragement to the men. As time went by, she turned to parody and refutation of the men present. The "Memoir Club" of 1920 was where she came out about her childhood experience of incest.

In the category of refutation, we should record Woolf's responses to Desmond MacCarthy. As "Affable Hawk" MacCarthy made Bloomsbury's most public attack on women's abilities as writers. His eruption over the "arrant feminism" of Rebecca West served as a motif of male anger in *A Room of One's Own.*[5] This forms one of West's connections to Bloomsbury, and it is notable that there were vast differences between the female and the male connection. Woolf's most direct and public answers to MacCarthy came in a series of articles (see 2 D 325). Woolf's late essay "The Leaning Tower" offers another cultural analysis of MacCarthy, as it situates the male critic in an elevated position of material and cultural privilege. In the tower figure, Woolf simultaneously evokes the architecture of Oxbridge and the prewar assumptions of Desmond MacCarthy's generation of critics. "He sits upon a tower raised above the rest of us; a tower built first on his parents' station, then on his parents' gold. It is a tower of the utmost importance; it decides his angle of vision; it affects his power of communication" (169).

As early as 1905, Woolf had declared the limits of that view in a sarcastic record of the critical pronouncements of Oxbridge men, "The Effect of Oxbridge on Young Men" (see Monk's House Papers/A13). These observations come from an era when she was experiencing her own frustrations trying to teach working-class women history at Morley College. Woolf's second novel, *Night and Day,* evokes the early Bloomsbury evenings in the creation of the "society for the free discussion of everything." It also pokes fun at the male speaker. William Rodney nervously offers a paper on "the Elizabethan use of metaphor . . . with plenty of quotations from the classics" (49). In that Rodney is "scrupulously well dressed, and a pearl in the center of his tie," he is suggestive of Eliot's "Prufrock," who made semiotic assertions with the simple pin in his tie. As noted in chapter 7, Eliot's careful dress was one of Woolf's favorite topics for epistolary mockery (52). On the basis of his awkward appearance and manners, Jane Marcus has identified Lytton Strachey as Woolf's model for Rodney (*Virginia Woolf and Languages* 33).

Strachey has become synonymous with the most aloof and affected manners and subject matters of Bloomsbury. When she wrote him, Woolf accommodated to these qualities, though some teasing emerged from both parties to the correspondence. Thus when she complained of the strictures placed on her reviewing by the editor of the *Cornhill Magazine,* Strachey pretended to think she was making them up. Virginia's report of Cambridge on a May visit shortly before her marriage in 1912 uses Strachey's lethargy and ventures into gross physicality to condemn the very institutions he was privileged to enjoy. This includes the "apostles," the secret, elite society of which both he and Leonard were members: "The ap-s-les are so unreal, and their loves are so unreal, and yet I suppose it's all going on still—swarming in the sun—and perhaps not as bad as I imagine. But when I think of it, I vomit—that's all—a green vomit, which gets into the ink and blisters the paper" (Woolf and Strachey 48). Reporting on the war-wounded Josiah Wedgwood's appearance before the 1917 Club, she writes of her discovery that "*virility*" was the secret of his fascination: "(perhaps to lose one's parts sends the semen to the surface—it seemed to splash and sparkle like phosphorescent cod's roe from every glance)—Marjorie [Strachey] all a tremble at one corner, and Miss Dudley immensely receptive at the other—I thought him a random untrustworthy mongrel, utterly incontinent" (2 L 206). She titillates him with a homoerotic description: "The naked boys run like snipe along the beach, balancing their buttocks in the pellucid air" (2 L 5). In 1914, a year plagued by mental illness, she seems to have read Strachey's essays and even typed for him, as a form of therapy. Her letters mention the problem of seeming too eager to review friends' books at TLS, and he gracefully backs off a request that she ask to review *Eminent Victorians.*

Strachey was encouraging about her writing, even where it offered mild satire of Stracheyesque characters. In February 1916, he reported reading *The Voyage Out* with "breathless pleasure." His aesthetic judgments identify categories of wit and solidity that we will encounter again in Forster, though as she notes, Strachey had a better impression than Forster of her rendering of character. Strachey is surprised at finding not only the "expected wit and exquisiteness," but more amazingly "such a wonderful solidity as well! Something Tolstoyan . . . especially that last account of the illness," and also "the people were *not* mere satirical silhouettes, but solid too, with other sides to them: Shakespeare wouldn't have been ashamed of some of them." He did look in vain for the "cohesion of a dominating idea" (73), and in her response, she discusses the difficulty of presenting both detail and controlled conception, offering the "tumult of life" as the intended conception. Strachey prophesied that *Jacob's Room* would be "immortal" because of its formal excellence, akin to poetry, and economic in narrative. He recalled specific scenes, left whirling about him, and not surprisingly identified his own point of view with Bonamy. This he opposed to a romanticism he detected as closer to her, and a potential danger (Woolf and Strachey 144). Strachey dedicated his 1921 work, *Queen Victoria,* to "V. W." In 1928—the year I shall focus upon for female modernism—he published *Elizabeth and Essex,* a work in Woolf's favorite historical period. Woolf was well aware of its superior sales in comparison to her own *Orlando.* But she was not awed by its literary achievement. As early as 1908, she told Clive Bell that Strachey's "verbal felicities" were evasive, whereas the "true poet would have committed himself" (1 L 344). When she heard from Strachey that Bell compared his poetry to Catullus, she asserted her own art: "Where are my works then? I shall have to alter my standard for judging Clive's praise" (Woolf to Vanessa Bell, 1 L 366). Woolf may have been expressing her suspicion that Bloomsbury men placed only one another in serious literary company.

Clive Bell probably enjoyed an undue influence on Woolf when she was the young Virginia Stephen, shifting about for direction. His 1908 letters to her can be viewed only as love letters. At one point he banned Lytton Strachey from his home, jealous of his intimacy with Virginia and Vanessa (1 L 449n). He also told Walter Lamb discouraging things about Virginia's personality, perhaps to put him off of a proposal (Woolf to Vanessa Bell, 1 L 471). His opinions on the technical merits of her works were frequently reinforcing. In 1917, he found "The Mark on the Wall" to be "infinitely subtle and profound and exciting," admiring her word choice and phrasing as "exquisite." He pronounced that, compared to Woolf's rendition of "what goes on in your head," Mr. James Joyce made "a damned silly mess" (Clive Bell letter to Woolf, 19 July 1917, Sussex). *Or-*

lando received technical praise; this time she compared favorably to Proust in her treatment of time, and "came hard on the Wellses and Bennetts" by her quiet assumption that the artist's mind conditions everything. But this letter contained a political warning against stepping out of the mind, in effect. He found "moments when the poet gives place to a lady with a grudge" (C. Bell letter to Woolf, 15 Oct. 1928, Sussex). Not surprisingly, Bell pronounced *Three Guineas* "her least admirable production" (Noble, ed. 89). Bell denied her a political stance.

Roger Fry received the exceptional honor of having Virginia Woolf write his biography—a taxing task, done at the request of his devoted and demanding sister, Margery. *Roger Fry* leaves evidence of numerous forms of attachment.[6] Fry was a more consistent and constructive colleague than Bell or Strachey, and a formalist of a different stripe from Eliot or Lubbock. According to Woolf, "Fry insists over and over again [the critic] must lay himself open to all kinds of impressions and experiences: to science, to music, to poetry, and must never be afraid to revise a view which experience has altered" (*Roger Fry* 101). Though he was as old as many of the writers I am classifying with the Edwardians, Fry clearly set the pretexts for modernism. He was capable of moving on to new areas of aesthetic interest as he did in 1910 with the postimpressionist exhibition—one of Woolf's indicators that "on or about December 1910 human character changed" (3 *E* 421). As a translator of Mallarmé, and thus an artist keenly aware of language, he valued her literary judgments.

In letters to Woolf, Fry comes across as an alert and open reader of her novels, eager to report the effect of form. His letters are less pontifical than Bell's, usually without the competitive spirit of her brother-in-law. When Woolf confides her jealousy of Katherine Mansfield to Fry, he considers the confession a "splendid idea" and predicts a cure by the time that she is his age (2 *Letters of Roger Fry* 486). Fry praises *To the Lighthouse* for being "the most intensely human thing" she has done. He is not troubled by simultaneity and going backward and forward in time in the work, as this leads to the "enrichment of each moment of consciousness" (Fry letter to Woolf, 17 May 1927, Sussex). Simultaneity was a form that interested him. His query about a symbolic reading of the lighthouse will be addressed in volume 2. Fry "yielded" to the "physical delight of [*Orlando*] . . . laughing and crying with different feeling all the time." It was as if she had got "spirit free—revolving and scintillating in space and eternity uncontrolled" with "inherent motion" (Fry letter to Woolf, 3 Dec. 1928, Sussex). In effect, he credited her with achieving the vortex idolized by

Wyndham Lewis, in her case energy and eternity, without the mastery and control sought by that self-proclaimed enemy of Fry and Woolf alike.

Fry plays up to Woolf's presumed superiority as a letter writer, as did T. S. Eliot, suggesting that for him to write to Woolf was rather like Sargent offering to exchange works with Velazquez (2 *Letters of Roger Fry* 659). He writes character sketches and appends little drawings of scenes from his travels, often accompanied with pessimistic commentary on the state of intellect in England and elsewhere. In her biography, Woolf would mention in particular his dread of the herd instinct—a concern aired in her last novel, *Between the Acts* (202). Writing the biography in 1939, Woolf also finds quotations in Fry's *Vision and Design* to support a communal view of art that she was moving toward in her final works: "The greatest art has always been communal, the expression—in highly individualized ways no doubt—of communal aspirations and ideals" (*Roger Fry* 150). Fry's experiences of "pure delight" in burgeoning nature are identical to those of her characters and her autobiographical self, as we shall see in turning to "A Sketch of the Past" in volume 2. She quotes him reporting childhood rapture: "I conceived that nothing could be more exciting than to see the flower suddenly burst its green case and unfold its immense cup of red" (*Roger Fry* 256). In summing up his character, she finds many Frys, just as in her mock biography she finds many Orlandos. She traces a mind in which pure delight is followed by the operations of reason, and where the analytic process of making a picture "halts before the ultimate concrete reality of a work of art" and "must leave untouched a greater part of its objective" (258). Strachey's death in 1932 and Fry's in 1934 thinned the sympathetic ranks of Bloomsbury.

E. M. Forster, the most successful of the Bloomsbury novelists and critics besides Woolf, remained a rival. Like Strachey and Hugh Walpole, whose opinions also concerned her, he belongs in the ranks of the Bloomsbury homosexual establishment. Woolf's diaries are full of concern for the opinion of Forster, whatever her latest project. His opinion of *Three Guineas* matched Bell's in its negativity; he called it "the worst of her books" (Noble, ed. 239). His determination to keep women—and specifically Woolf, when her name first came up—off the London Library Committee rankled with her for life. This despite the fact that he later did offer her the position, which she refused. It went down as the "London Library Syndrome" in one of her last diary entries, as she battled depression. Woolf and Forster did occasionally share projects, such as the joint letter they penned at the time of the trial of the lesbian novel *The*

Well of Loneliness—which we return to in chapter 12. Woolf's summary article on "The Novels of E. M. Forster" makes it clear that she finds his work more comparable to Ibsen's than to modernists'. Her evaluation of *Aspects of Fiction* upset Forster.[7] But for a complex sense of the Forster-Woolf connection, I shall go back in time.

On December 9, 1910, Forster gave a talk titled "The Feminine Note in Literature" to the Friday Society, a Bloomsbury gathering convened by Vanessa Bell.[8] Forster recalls that the subject the previous week had been John Stuart Mill's *The Subjection of Women,* suggesting that the group had some interest in the status of women, which he was sustaining in his contribution. His diary includes entries made before and after the lecture, and notes that "Miss Stephen [Virginia] liked it . . . which pleases me" (ms., King's College, Cambridge).

Forster's opening is coy. Like Eliot as he prepared the early lectures noted in chapter 7, Forster recognized a predominantly female audience: "We are going to talk about women, and very fortunately, more of them are in the room." He discloses feelings of self-consciousness, inspired by a concern for what women might say about men. Forster wants to avoid two attitudes for the paper: "It would like not to be chivalrous. And it would like not to be insulting." His ideas about the drawbacks of chivalry have cultural significance:

> Chivalry entails a reaction. When gentlemen have been handing ladies up and down steps all day, they will naturally retire to what they term their "den" in the evening, and scarify the fair sex to the accompaniment of whiskeys & cigars. And conversely, the ladies who have been being handed up & down the steps will naturally have a boudoir and they will naturally all retire to it and have a quiet talk about those men.

He regrets that in this system, "they must go back to their real homes—she to the boudoir, he to the den—never to breathe the common air that is at once honesty and literature" (ms. 91–92, Kings College). It is notable that Forster did not want to carry the notion of "common air" too far, however, or he might have been more willing to share the space of the London Library Committee. The proposal to revise "chivalry" conforms with Eve Sedgwick's identification of a new chivalry in the homosexual discourse of J. A. Symonds, co-author (with Havelock Ellis) of *Sexual Inversion* (Sedgwick 206–209).

The body of the paper offers two categories of women writers, set in a metaphorical literary landscape with Parnassan heights and categorical gulfs. The implication is that the second class is a progression out of the first, since "nearly every authoress, except Miss Austen, hastened to leap the gulf" between the two classes. According to his description, "the first class is light, naive, amusing, illogical, full of flashes of insight interspersed with unfairness and stupidity; full of details that are often photographed from life with consummate skill; full of crude and intermittent idealism; in a word it has all the qualities that women are popularly supposed to have. *Evelina* is an early example of this class in fiction; the modern examples are innumerable." The "illogical" is further explained as a quality shared by all humans, but "man owing to 10,000 years of public life, have become diabolically skillful" at concealing it. Forster also sneers at the imagined attribution of the illogical to women in male discussions, conducted in the den, and acknowledges the role of male prejudice in their literary criticism: "That women should be good over details and have no general grasp, suits so well with a man's notion of the universe. 'Run away; photograph your own emotions and experiences; you can do that so well. Leave me, the artist, to synthesize and climb the heights' " (Forster 112–13).

The second class is small but it contains names as great and as diverse as George Sand, Charlotte Brontë, George Eliot, and Charlotte Young. "It is full of qualities that women are popularly supposed not to have: solidity; and the literature of the future will probably spring from it" (107–108). Forster qualifies his admiration for this latter class of writers: "It is not surprising that a great outburst of moral enthusiasm should rise among the successful competitors. When we resent the instructive tones of Miss Charlotte Young or Mrs. Humphry Ward, we must remember that this literature is still new. It has struggled for expression for thousands of years, and it cannot be expected to win aesthetic mastery at once, and to tell us of the good only through the beautiful. It is solid, that is something—occasionally stodgy, but always solid and offers a firm beacon for the future" (117–18). Forster holds up Thomas Hardy and Arnold Bennett as examples of authors who have seen beauty of space and time, respectively, while women authors have at best seen these "spasmodically."

In addition to recording the literary woman's broad jump into solidity, Forster has one more version of the "feminine note," which is probably the most significant. This relates gender to relationship—an emphasis of Bloomsbury usually connected to the philosophy of G. E. Moore. "Men love an unembodied ideal. Women embody their ideal in some human being" and are preoccupied with "relative worthiness" (130–33). This view would seem to be prophetic of Forster's own focus on character in his criticism, and of two of his most memorable women characters, Mrs. Wilcox and Mrs. Moore. Mrs. Wilcox gauges worthiness in her choice of Margaret Schlagel as her heir in his 1910 novel, *Howard's End,* and in *A Passage to India,* Mrs. Moore locates the qualities she resonates with across the cultural divide, in Aziz.

There is much in Forster's manuscript that looks forward to Woolf's *A Room of One's Own,* including the positive valuation placed upon Jane Austen and Emily Brontë, and the sense that it takes hundreds of years to build a women's tradition in writing. He praises the skill at miniatures that T. S. Eliot was to label as "feminine" in his dismissal of Mansfield's fiction, noted in chapter 7. At this early date, Forster is still taking Edwardian male writers as a measure of the solidity that could be achieved by women. He values massive continuity rather than spasmodic brilliance. Forster does seem to have a positive anticipation of what women may bring to the future of the novel—one of those women finely attuned to aesthetics, a member of his audience.

Interestingly, Virginia Stephen had written a review in 1905 of a book that bore a similar title to Forster's talk—Leonard Courtney's *The Feminine Note in Fiction.* Woolf expected from his title that Courtney would tell us what is "essentially feminine and why" in the writing of women, but finds that he offers only tentative suggestions—an approach sustained by Forster. One of Courtney's suggestions, "a passion for detail which conflicts with the proper artistic proportion of their work," is readily refuted by Woolf with the examples of Austen and Sappho (1 E 16). Woolf would seem to endorse the value of "artistic proportion" at this point, but a "widening of intelligence" and a "sterner view of literature" can be acquired through education, giving woman the ability to create a "permanent artistic shape" where at present she has "blurted out her message somewhat formlessly" (16). Woman's formless "blurting out her message" in 1905 bears some comparison to the modernists' "smash and splinters" of which she complained a decade later. Woolf anticipates a gradual putting on of form for women writers of both types. She does not allow Courtney to get away with the statement that "more and more novels are written by women for women, which is the cause, he declares, that the novel as work of art is disappearing." She admits to the probability of the first part of his declaration, and offers a feminist explanation: "Women having found their voices have something to say which is naturally of supreme interest and meaning to women." The second part is more doubt-ful, and she turns the subject toward a bid for women's education in the subjects she had most desired for her own development, Greek and Latin classics. Already Woolf was collecting the egregious declarations of men, whose parts would become more fully dramatized in *A Room of One's Own* and *Three Guineas*.

Like T. S. Eliot, Forster left a memoir of Virginia Woolf that sets her in a questionable position. Forster dispels Arnold Bennett's "legend of the Invalid Lady of Bloomsbury" and praises her poetic skills, anointing *Mrs. Dalloway, To the Lighthouse,* and *The Waves* as her triumphs. But, echoing Bennett, Forster ultimately calls her a failure in what he valued most, the creation of enduring characters. He only partially spares her the title of aesthete. Forster makes a privileged and well-financed lady of her, de-tached from the judgments of critics and the literary market, scornful of journalism, and a snob. He calls her feminism of *Orlando* and *Three Guineas* an out-of-date holdover from suffrage days, no longer needed by the thirties (Noble, ed. 226–42).

If Woolf, West, and Barnes agreed on the importance of any modern male writers, we would have to cite ones outside their own Anglo/Ameri-can traditions—Proust and Dostoyevsky. The Irishman turned Continen-tal, Joyce, also qualifies with all three, as discussed in chapter 8. Among the early moderns, Proust was the most successful. He appeals to Woolf as a psychological writer, with characters "made of a different substance. Thoughts, dreams, knowledge are part of them." Woolf uses the meta-phors of elastic netting and watery access, suggested in the Introduction, to describe his achievement. He is most unlike Pound, in that he does not direct the reader.

> The mind of Proust lies open with the sympathy of a poet and the detachment of a scientist to everything that it has the power to feel. Direction or emphasis, to be told that is right, to be nudged and bidden to attend to that, would fall like a shadow on this pro-found luminosity and cut off some section of it from our view. The common stuff of the book is made up of this deep reservoir of perception. It is from these depths that his characters rise, like waves forming, then break and sink again into the moving sea of thought and comment and analysis which gave them birth. (*Gran-ite and Rainbow* 125)

Proust's "frequent passages of elaborate metaphor" seem to Woolf to "spring out of the rock of thought like fountains of sweet water and serve as translations from one language into another" (139). They also are compatible with her own reliance on metaphor to negotiate language, as will be discussed in volume 2.

Dostoyevsky was also universally valued as a writer of the soul in the solemn register of the Russians. He was a much more fundamental figure to Barnes than Freud and Jung: "I believe Freud, Jung, and the rest are of little importance because they now have a canned and labeled precept for every action, having, as it were, commercialized the findings of the intuitive artists, like Dostoyevski" (Barnes letter to Coleman, 10 Jan. 1936, Delaware). Correspondingly, Woolf discusses Dostoyevsky within the category of psychologists in "Phases of Fiction." Having the Russian tendency to explore the "labyrinth of the soul," he also probes deeply into the same sort of mental pool where she found Proust in attendance. She compares his writing to "the little bits of cork which mark a circle upon the top of the waves while the net drags the floor of the sea and encloses stranger monsters than have ever been brought to the light of day before" (84). Dostoyevsky also has an unusual capacity to track the mind in process:

> From the crowd of objects pressing upon our attention we select now this one, now that one, weaving them inconsequently into our thought; the associations of a word perhaps make another loop in the line, from which we spring back again to a different section of our main thought and the whole process seems both inevitable and perfectly lucid. But if we try to construct our mental processes later, we find that the links between one thought and another are submerged. The chain has sunk out of sight and only the leading points emerge to mark the course. Alone among writers Dostoevsky has the power of reconstructing those most swift and complicated states of mind, of rethinking the whole train of thought in all its speed, now as it flashes into light, now as it lapses into darkness. (2 E 85)

Clearly the men of modernism, from Pound through Forster, did not have a framework that could include or contain Woolf, West, and Barnes. These women of modernism were already making selective use of the "men of 1914," running astray of their declared structures and intents, and discovering ways that men had been shaped to disadvantage by literary culture. The next section looks to alternate resources offered in a contemporary female network that was complexly linked to the Edwardian and modernist men we have been examining, encompassing the horizon of suffrage, and the women who had prepared the delivery of their modernism.

Part Three: *The Women of 1928*

Exploratory beauty, turning dark jungle into a safe habitation for the spirit, is here as it is in the work of the greatest of those who in the past used verse for their medium.

—Rebecca West, "High Fountain of Genius," on Virginia Woolf's *Orlando*

On or about October 11, 1928, the character of the woman writer changed. My dating is even more overdetermined than Virginia Woolf's, when she declared in "Character and Fiction" that "on or about December 1910 human character changed" (3 *E* 421).[1] The time I have chosen is the "present moment" of Woolf's novel *Orlando,* its date of publication set with playful self-referentiality within the text (298). And an extraordinary text it is—a parodic biography concerning a sequentially male and female poet who survives three hundred years of cultural experience. As shown in the epigraph, written that same month, *Orlando* was hailed by a well-known critic of the time, Rebecca West, as a beautiful exploration of the human spirit. The dark jungle made habitable by Woolf might be taken as centuries-old, male-dominated literary traditions, or the dark places of psychology that Woolf had identified as an important subject in "Modern Fiction." We will learn from Djuna Barnes's texts of this same year that she was performing comparable explorations, leading toward her best-known work, *Nightwood*—its very title suggestive of exploring a dark jungle. This section presents many reasons, besides *Orlando,* for selecting 1928 in order to examine not the triumph of a single aspect or identity of the woman writer but an active, exploratory period, when it was clear that women writers were developing a new sense of the literary world and setting their own objectives, largely through what they could learn from one another. Lest we consider their endeavors safe, we should recall that this was the heyday of the lost woman aviator Amelia Earhart, her image promoted by her lover and publisher, G. P. Putnam, who in 1928 was taking on new challenges in flying.

"The men of 1914" have provided a scaffolding for a favored view of modernism. We revisited this structure in Part Two, reading its pervasive politics of gender, including aspects of female suppression and exclusion, written in masculinist metaphors. We have met the women of 1928 as the acquaintances and critics of these supposed definers of modernist novelty, learning which ideas and forms Woolf, West, and Barnes found worthy of attaching to, and which they questioned or rejected. Indeed, their literary criticism had hit stride by 1928—a date frequently attached to their boldest pronouncements on male modernists, cited in the previous section. T. S. Eliot's conservative declaration of his Anglo-Catholicism, classicism, and royalist politics came in 1928. Their level of independence is seen in the comments all three women made on this avowal—Barnes finding Puritanism a basic expression of his nature, Woolf taxing him with hours of discussion on religion, and West declaring that his ideas of tradition had set back British criticism by a generation (Scott, ed. 558).

Woolf, West, and Barnes now claim our sustained attention as they make attachments and arrangements not generally cited for modernists, and undertake projects to suit their own personal and political interests. Thus we launch out again, moving toward the complexities of a richly varied modernism of 1928. The most notable new attachments of Woolf, West, and Barnes are to female literary colleagues. Historic issues such as censorship and lesbian identification gain their interest and response. They begin to think of themselves as professionals, profitably venturing into journalism and radio, and thinking across the professions to women who do other forms of work and must cope with public celebrity. Woolf, West, and Barnes develop their own metaphors for the modern and a distinct sexual imaginary. They challenge and redirect notions of feminine "charm." The women of 1928 develop political awareness inflected by gender. As noted in the previous section, escaping the law of their fathers, they rewrite Freud and Nietzsche. They look ahead into history, registering alarm at nascent Nazi attitudes building toward World War II—a development which will be studied in the final chapter of volume 2.

Nineteen twenty-eight was a remarkable year for issues of gender: women in Britain finally got the vote on equal terms with men, and much of the literary world battled the censorship of Radclyffe Hall's lesbian novel, *The Well of Loneliness.* Anticipating censorship, D. H. Lawrence had decided not to put his new book, *Lady Chatterley's Lover,* on the market in England. It did make its way into Woolf's *Orlando* via a directive gamekeeper (o 268) and into Barnes's *Ryder* with Lady Bridesleep, the sexually active bride of an elderly cripple (*Ryder* 274). Skirting the censors, Virginia Woolf, Rebecca West, and Djuna Barnes all made creative departures, of feminist intent, in their publications and writing in progress. These works included Woolf's transhistorical, transgeneric, and transsexual *Orlando* and the lectures on women and fiction that became *A Room of One's Own.* West produced a formally experimental, iconoclastic collection of critical essays, *The Strange Necessity,* and turned to *Har-*

riet Hume: A London Fantasy, a work comparable to *Orlando*, exploring politics through an uncanny feminine musician (published 1929). Barnes offered a sprightly, self-mocking lesbian group sketch, *Ladies Almanack*, and an autobiographical family history named for its obsessively progenitive father, *Ryder*. The fiction of Woolf, West, and Barnes took on the qualities of poetry, as West notes in the epigraph, as well as drama, travel writing,[2] and, in Barnes's case, even an almanac. They borrowed from art and music (all of them being partial to opera) and freely parodied literary styles of the past and traditional genres.

Woolf, West, and Barnes were succeeding as professional writers, having gained access to publication on both sides of the Atlantic, and a smattering of recognition. In a rare acceptance of a literary tribute (taken perhaps as the gesture of a women's society), Woolf received the *Femina Vie Heureuse* prize—though she mocked such ceremonies in *Orlando* (312).[3]

By 1928, women publishers were issuing women's works in numbers, alongside the most noted writers of the period. Having become Joyce's patron and publisher, Harriet Shaw Weaver made a comparable investment in West's mentor, Dora Marsden, whose exploration in feminist spiritual philosophy, *The Definition of a Godhead*, appeared in 1928. Two other publishers of Joyce, Margaret Anderson and Jane Heap at the *Little Review*, gave Djuna Barnes's short stories prominence and solicited work from her for *The Little Review Anthology*. Heap's management of the paper made significant additions to the set of writers brought to it by Ezra Pound; the founding of the journal had preceded his collaboration by several years. By 1928, the list of the Hogarth Press, owned by Virginia and Leonard Woolf, included Katherine Mansfield, Vita Sackville-West (one of its best-sellers), Jane Harrison, Julia Cameron (with an introduction by Virginia), Elizabeth Robins, Mary Hutchinson, Nancy Cunard, Hope Mirrlees, Rose Macaulay, Vernon Lee, Gertrude Stein, and Edith Sitwell. Virginia Woolf would solicit Rebecca West's *A Letter to a Grandfather* for a series of imaginary letters in 1933.

Women's journalism flourished and was generously paid, particularly in the United States, in this year before the stock market crash. West succeeded best here, commanding regular columns in several newspapers and journals, including the *Bookman*, the *Herald Tribune Books*, the *New York American* (one of the Hearst Papers, it paid her $6,000 for columns written in 1932),[4] and the *New Republic* (also an outlet for Woolf). Woolf had become one of the enviable (though unsigned) reviewers for TLS in 1905, and even in 1992 was the only woman among twelve authors included in John Gross's *The Modern Movement: A TLS Companion.* The *Dial, Forum,* the *Saturday Review of Literature,* and the *New York Evening Post* published essays and stories by Woolf from time to time. Barnes had cut her teeth working for the popular press in New York at papers such as the Brooklyn *Daily Eagle* and the *New York Morning Telegraph.* Her arrival in expatriate Paris around 1920 had been partially financed by a commissioned article for *McCall's.* The well-paying women's magazines claimed all three writers. In Britain, *Vogue* published West, Woolf, and Vita Sackville-West, among others, and another Conde Nast publication, *Vanity Fair,* brought the work of Barnes to a comparable women's audience in the United States. The potential conflict of the professional designation "journalist" with the exalted literary label of "modernist" will be the subject of further discussion in chapter 11. All three writers bridged these categories. Woolf and West entered radio as well.

Thus the women of 1928 had crossed the "cultural divide" focused upon in Andreas Huyssen's postmodern reconsideration of their era. I hope that this section diversifies and enriches the current readings of this divide, in terms of audience as well as political activism. In recent discussions of women's writing by Celeste Schenck, Rita Felski, Suzanne Clark, and Ann Ardis, a new division has been struck between experimental women writers, seen as operating along the lines of the men of 1914, and women neglected by genre, due to their assignment to realist or sentimentalist traditions.[5] I should like to suggest that we have not yet fully explored the full diversity of experiment, or exploration, entered into by Woolf, West, and Barnes, and that they cannot readily be closed in, or out of, the better-known circle of modernists.

10 Arranging Marriages, Partners, and Spaces

The normative family structure that evaded Woolf, West, and Barnes in their childhood years was also remote from their adult lives. The attitudes that made them successful writers, compounded by their denial of traditional domestic expectations for women, affected the living arrangements they sought or managed by 1928. The daily arrangements of work and life for Woolf, West, and Barnes were as various as their backgrounds and personalities. Still, taken together, these reflected the pressures faced by women writers in this era, their perceived domestic needs, and the structures and resources available to them.

In all cases, marriage had been an expectation or goal of their original families. We have noted that Barnes was mated to a much older family relation at sixteen. This was only a preliminary to a number of brief relationships with individuals of both sexes, and one sustained lesbian alliance with Thelma Wood. The relationship was in the process of dissolving by 1928. In the 1930s, Barnes told Emily Holmes Coleman that she would have liked to settle down with a man. She did live for a time with Charles Henri Ford, one of several bisexual men in her life.

Though the younger group of Stephen children eschewed the high-society courtship customs of their Duckworth relations, the three surviving siblings married into a congenial Cambridge set. Vanessa agreed to marry Clive Bell, one of her brother's Cambridge friends, soon after Thoby Stephen's tragic death from typhoid in 1906. It is difficult to rule out some form of consolation, perhaps for both Vanessa and Clive, in the match. Woolf was courted by a succession of Thoby's friends, one of her offers (quickly withdrawn) coming from Lytton Strachey, despite his homosexuality. Nor would such a match have been unusual in her circle. Vanessa Bell and Vita Sackville-West were partnered with homosexuals—Vanessa in a long-term relationship with Duncan Grant which resulted in their daughter Angelica, and Sackville-West in her marriage to Harold Nicolson, a match that produced two sons.

Rebecca West developed cultural theories, reminiscent of the marriage plots of Austen and Brontë novels, to explain the marital misfortunes of women in her family. The Fairfields' fall from fortune ended their women's eligibility to the landed gentry. Nor were they desirable brides to Edinburgh merchants and professionals, who sought more advantageous financial mergers. West tells one such marriage story in the opening pages of her 1922 novel, *The Judge,* basing it upon her mother's experience. At the age of twenty-one, West was transformed from new woman to the mistress of H. G. Wells, abiding monogamously with him for a decade. By the late 1920s she was a highly publicized career woman, looking for a restful retreat in marriage.

Woolf's Home Enterprise

Woolf's Bloomsbury Group is generally dated from the move of the Stephen children from Hyde Park Gate to Gordon Place, in Bloomsbury, following Leslie Stephen's death in 1904. Woolf's much older, sexually abusive half-brother, George Duckworth, married that same year, becoming only "an occasional diversion for the intellect" ("Reminiscences" 58). Thoby Stephen is credited with starting Thursday evening gatherings in Bloomsbury. These survived his death and Vanessa's 1907 marriage. Virginia and her younger brother Adrian set up housekeeping at 29 Fitzroy Square, where the evenings were resumed. There were several schemes for these gatherings. A correspondence among imaginary, assigned characters circulated in 1909. Virginia Stephen briefly became Eleanor Hadyng to Lytton Strachey's Vane Hatherley, presumably with comic results. Vanessa Bell ran a Friday Club that looked more to the arts. Novelist Molly MacCarthy's Memoir Club, begun in 1920, was supposedly designed to give her husband, the TLS critic Desmond MacCarthy, expressive opportunities.[1] But it probably served women in the circle best. Woolf began to tell the story of her childhood sexual abuse to this group.

Virginia Stephen, chaperoned in Victorian style by her aunt Kate Stephen, had been introduced to Thoby's Cambridge friends at tea during May Week in 1903. The group included Leonard Woolf and Lytton Strachey. Fredric Spotts, editor of Leonard's letters, suggests that at this time "Virginia, Vanessa and Thoby Stephen must have had an irresistible charm and physical attraction. To meet them was evidently to be captivated by them, individually and almost interchangeably" (155). Leonard Woolf described his rather unfocused love for Thoby, Vanessa, and Virginia in his correspondence with Strachey, written from Ceylon.

Leonard's confidences were prompted by Clive Bell's expression of love, apparently for Vanessa, though Woolf thought that he was originally attracted to Virginia: "You think that Bell is really wildly in love with her? The curious part is that I was too after they came up that May term to Cambridge, & still more curious that there is a mirage of it still left. She is so superbly like the Goth [Thoby]. I used to wonder whether he was in love with the Goth because he was in love with her & I was in love with her, because with the Goth" (*Letters of Leonard Woolf* 98). In a 1967 interview, Leonard Woolf recollected Virginia and Vanessa as a pair: "Virginia and Vanessa were amazingly beautiful in white dresses and quite enormous hats. They had a great effect upon anyone who saw them at the time." He also found them frightening: "They were frightfully—well I wouldn't say contemptuous—but critical of anything that wasn't up to the standard of the Stephens." What he had in mind, both in 1903 and in 1967 when he was interviewed, was her patriarchy—the set of people "who provided all the rulers of India and the empire and all the judges," and of course Sir Leslie Stephen (Noble, ed. 248–49). Thus Virginia and Vanessa Stephen were attached in the Cambridge imagination to their patriarchal past, and to "the Goth," their brother Thoby.

In 1913 Virginia Woolf married, not from romance or passion but with good prospects of affection, continued access to her siblings, and opportunities to write. Leonard Woolf was an insider as a Cambridge Apostle and a friend of her brothers; he was an outsider as a Jew. He not only shared Virginia's literary pursuits but developed a fresh scaffolding for their production. Leonard carefully regulated her time so as to ward off the recurrent manic-depressive illness that had blighted the first years of their marriage, including the focal year for male modernists, 1914. He consulted frequently with Vanessa about Virginia's health and even the couple's sexual difficulties, making Virginia somewhat the construction of her sister. Virginia had looked forward to having children, and so Leonard has been criticized for ruling this out—a judgment reached after consultation with Vanessa and the family doctors (see Showalter, *A Literature of Their Own* 270–81). Woolf became an entertaining and indulgent aunt, particularly to Vanessa's children, Julian, Quentin, and Angelica. On the subject of children, Woolf decided by 1927:

> I scarcely want children of my own now. This insatiable desire to
> write something before I die, this ravaging sense of the shortness
> & feverishness of life, make me cling, like a man on a rock, to my

one anchor. I don't like the physicalness of having children of one's own. . . . I can dramatize myself as parent, it is true. And perhaps I have killed the feeling instinctively; as perhaps nature does. (3 D 167)

Marriage to Leonard Woolf permitted access to the sort of female affection that had sustained Virginia through her parents' deaths. She could continue her intimacy with her sister and the compensatory children. Vanessa provided a model of multiple attachment, keeping the good will of Clive while moving on in her affections to Roger Fry and Duncan Grant. Woolf's own marriage could accommodate her most serious female passion with Vita Sackville-West, though other women—notably Dame Ethel Smyth—were not equally welcomed by Leonard.

An important common endeavor of the Woolfs was the Hogarth Press, named for the home they lived in when it was founded in 1917. The enterprise was flourishing by 1928. It provided a liberating mode for the production of all of Woolf's novels after *Night and Day.* The press can also be seen as a domestic enterprise. Virginia's early labors included assembling type in the dining room and stitching bindings—work deemed therapeutic. Hogarth granted her rare independence as a writer, which she had assessed in 1925, as she turned down a commission from Herbert Fisher, "knowing I can write a book, a better book, a book off my own bat, for the Press if I wish! To think of being battened down in the hold of University dons fairly makes my blood run cold. Yet I'm the only woman in England free to write what I like. The others must be thinking of series & editors" (3 D 43). Woolf did make strategic cuts in her own writing. In several cases, the changes showed deference to her heterosexual living arrangement. She muted feminist and lesbian topics in works such as *Mrs. Dalloway* and *Orlando,* but never at the direct insistence of an editor. Leonard read her works on the verge of their publication; though she hung on his opinion and undoubtedly had it in mind all along, Woolf was never forced into the massive cuts demanded of Djuna Barnes, first by commercial publishers Boni and Liveright, and later by T. S. Eliot and his staff at Faber. Like West and Barnes, she benefited from income derived from publishing and republishing pieces in the United States, at generous periodical prices, though she did not need to travel there.

Loving the city and feeling that her writing was stimulated by it, Woolf was delighted by the couple's move to 52 Tavistock Square, Bloomsbury, in 1924, after years in quieter Richmond. By 1928 she divided her time between Bloomsbury and rural Sussex. The Woolfs purchased Monk's House, near Lewes, in 1919. Virginia and Vanessa had started the pattern of maintaining a village retreat by renting Firle and then Asham House in 1910. While at Monk's House, Virginia was within bicycling distance of Vanessa, who had settled at Charleston Farm in 1916, with Virginia's encouragement. Woolf's decor partook of the domestic arts produced by Vanessa Bell and Duncan Grant for Roger Fry's Omega Workshop. Gardening at Monk's House was an important recreation for Leonard, whose pruning and planting are often remarked on by Virginia, the last time being her final diary entry. She sometimes put her hand to weeding, regularly made preserves, and gave gifts of plants and cuttings. Virginia wrote in a little shed beyond the garden, which they called her "lodge." Income from novels such as *Mrs. Dalloway, To the Lighthouse,* and *Orlando* permitted improvements at Monk's House—first the practical addition of a water closet, and in 1929 the construction of a bedroom of her own, with its sole entrance on the outside. Mobility was provided by the Woolfs' motorcar, an item Woolf would mention as a goal for the revenues of the aspiring writer in "Professions for Women." In this vehicle they ventured periodically to France (particularly Cassis) and Germany.

Emotionally, 1928 was a tumultuous year for Virginia Woolf as she explored the means of sustaining her affection for Vita Sackville-West, which had begun in 1925. Considering the potential rivalry for Virginia's love, Leonard Woolf did surprisingly well with Vita. She seems to have passed his primary test of keeping Virginia well, as posed in a letter Leonard wrote as Virginia started a visit with Vita at Long Barn in 1925:

> Dear Vita,
>   I enclose Virginia & hope she will behave. The only thing I ask is that you will be adamant in sending her off to bed not 1 minute later than 11 P.M. She ought not to talk for too long a stretch at a time. (*Letters of Leonard Woolf* 228)

By 1928, Sackville-West had taken at least two additional lesbian lovers, the newest being Hilda Matheson of the BBC. *Orlando* was a unique demonstration of Woolf's affection and her tenacity. Her prose celebrated the spiritual and especially the physical qualities that she found attractive in Sackville-West.

Woolf escaped the calm routine encouraged by Leonard to entertain at dinner and at tea. At one such occasion, which we return to in the next chapter, Woolf brought together Ethel Smyth and Rebecca West. Balanced variations of company and quiet, city and country living, and deep and light writing tasks were Woolf's successful arrangement in the late twenties—one sadly lost by the time of her suicide in 1941.

West as Mistress, Mother, Writer

In an event that darkened her life and dominated her literary reputation, West gave birth out of wedlock to Anthony West, the son of H. G. Wells, in 1914. Wells pursued a series of new women. The list to date included his second wife, Catherine (Jane) Wells, Dorothy Richardson, Violet Hunt, Elizabeth VonArnim, Margaret Sanger, Amber Reeves, and Moura Budberg. Like West, Richardson and Reeves both conceived his children, though he was not allied to them as a consequence. Richardson miscarried, and Reeves was quietly married off to another man. Jane Wells (as he had renamed her) had borne him two sons and by 1914 was cast as his helpmeet, while he pursued other women for sexual and intellectual satisfaction. Jane was ever the efficient secretary and literary hostess—a role West would have ill served even if the position were vacated, though her skepticism of Jane Wells was deep and abiding. Jane Wells died in 1928, five years after West and Wells parted.

During their courtship, West and Wells had developed defiant fantasy personas as large predatory cats, befitting their critical attitudes as writers. Wells frequently illustrated his letters to West with "pikshas" of the two breeds of cats in different enterprises. One from 1914 depicts a relatively realistic jaguar in a tree "lying in wait for Rebecca," who appears an innocent girl below, reading a book as she approaches the tree limb (in Ray, ed. 44; see Plate 15).[2] He writes that his love for her is related to her panther quality. As large cats, they hunted separately, pouncing on all that was in need of reform in society, and sharing their common enterprise in their private retreats: "You have written me the most beautiful love letter in the Clarion to say that you are happy. And that you are a panther.—I hunt alone. Of course we hunt alone, dear panther, and come padding back to the lair with the blood of dogs round our mouths, dogs we amuse ourselves killing" (Wells letter to West, n.d. [1913?], Yale). His surviving letters also suggest that they had vigorous and mutually pleasing sexual experiences.

As mistress to Wells and mother to Anthony, West was alienated from her own mother, denied access to important female friends, and forced to develop a marginal mode of family and literary life. At various times,

Plate 14. H. G. Wells sketch of egotistical cats.

West Collection,

Beinecke Library, Yale University.

Wells objected to her sister Lettie, who, unlike their mother, continued to visit often.[3] He was also irritated by Wilma Meikle. A friend from suffragette days and author of *Towards a Sane Feminism,* Meikle was West's companion at her house in Alderton in 1915 and 1916. Wells eventually told West to get rid of her. The tone and message of Wells's letters changed with Anthony's birth. He addressed her as "Dear Little Mother" and conditioned her to a new role, as his relief from hard labor. He declared to West his need for a "healthy woman handy to steady nerves and leave mind free." In speaking of their physical intimacy, he slid into the role of her creator, "bone of my bone, flesh of my flesh, and my making" (Wells letter to West, Autumn 1914, Yale). His letters sent a barrage of ideas about what was best for the couple, the mother, and the baby. It was for the moment neglected that she too had ideas on great social movements. Having argued for the dignity of intellectual labor, West could not have rested easily in this arrangement. She was for the moment his dependent, if not quite the parasitic woman she had constantly denounced in the *Clarion.*

As parents, both Wells and West took on false family identities, pretending to be the uncle and aunt of their offspring. Anthony called his mother "Panther." Suggesting that he would be safer from World War I bombings, West placed Anthony into a Montessori boarding school before he turned four. The troubled liaison between West and Wells, sustained through many strategic addresses, calculated intervals of togetherness, rivalries, and recuperative travels, lasted ten years. West at times suggested that she sustained the relationship as long as she did in order to provide Anthony with financial security. Wells was jealous whenever he suspected rivals. Sinclair Lewis and Compton Mackenzie both posed threats, at least in his imagination.[4] He resisted the breakup, which came in its final form in 1923. The couple continued to squabble over decisions regarding Anthony. Their son was a lifelong torment to West, a central problem being that he never felt that he had achieved adequate affiliation with his father. When a small boy, he wrote to "Dear Mr Wells (or should I say dear father)," telling him that his mother was well equipped to handle his future: "You only came to see me to get Panther when I was small." He closed with the declaration, "God how I loathe you" (Anthony West letter to Wells, n.d., Yale).

West was living independently in 1928. In 1919 she had moved to a stylish flat at 36 Queen's Gate Terrace, Kensington—the part of London where she would locate her 1929 novel, *Harriet Hume.* Starting at about the time of her break with Wells, West undertook frequent travel to both France ("The Strange Necessity" of 1928 is situated in Paris) and the United States. In summer, she and Anthony regularly vacationed on the Riviera, sometimes sharing their accommodations with her set of professional women friends and her secretary, June Head—one in a line of cherished female assistants. The author Gladys (G. B.) Stern had succeeded Meikle as West's companion around 1916, and remained one of her closest friends. Stern usually went by the masculine name "Peter" or "Tynx," presumably provided by West. West's first major venture to the United States had come with a lecture tour in 1923. This new initiative articulated her final break with Wells. Thereafter, she typically went to the U.S. for a month or more in spring and fall, giving lectures and building and maintaining American literary ties, while her sisters looked in on Anthony at school. She regularly saw the theater critic and editor Alexander Woollcott, and confided in the novelist Fannie Hurst. Both Hurst's Jewishness and her capacity for entertaining captivated West, who enjoyed her contacts with celebrities. As they went about to clubs and fine stores, West observed entertainers and beautiful people with an eye toward fiction she could sell in the U.S.

At parties in London, on the Riviera, and in her American travels, West was casting about for a lasting relationship with a man. She had been denied this with Wells and with their mutual friend Lord Beaverbrook. West's Christmas 1923 assignation with Beaverbrook in New York not only failed to produce a hoped-for alliance but cast doubt on her future prospects with men. In 1925 she had a brief, happy fling in London with the young John Gunther, whose political journalism later rivaled her own. A lack of privacy did little to aid her romantic efforts.

Perhaps because she was associated with the beautiful theatrical people and dancers who inhabited her short fiction, West was pursued by the American press as a celebrity, the emblem of the independent, accomplished woman. She was rumored to be attached to a variety of men, including Charlie Chaplin, publisher George Doran, and *Vanity Fair* illustrator Ralph Barton. Her letters to Fannie Hurst may have been designed to alternately feed and stifle the rumor mills. She complained, for example, that a New York City boat tour was spoiled by reporters: "It gave me time to be crawled over—to be eaten alive by ship reporters, one of whom asked me pointblank if my going to England had anything to do with the fact that George Doran was over there! My God what am I to do?" (West letter to Hurst, Texas). Once her fame could have proven fatal. A letter to

Lettie from New York reported a terrifying experience with a man representing a film company. She had invited two representatives of his firm to her hotel room in order to discuss a filmscript patterned on her story "The Magician of Pell Street." After making his formal departure, the man returned alone, chased her around the room, and attempted to strangle her. He explained that he had become obsessed with her photograph and accused her of rendering him impotent. This incident fed West's theory that she caused impotence in men, already shared with Fannie Hurst at the time of her disappointing episode with Beaverbrook. West entered psychoanalysis in 1927, partly to cope with her troubled relationships with men.

Anthony remained a source of concern. In 1928 he was attending boarding school, though not particularly happily. He was diagnosed (wrongly, it turns out) with tuberculosis—a worry West shared with Virginia Woolf during one of their visits that year. In accounts of his adolescence, Anthony claims that his mother turned against him after the final rupture with Wells, and since then "she has minded to do me what hurt she could, and . . . remained set in that determination as long as there was breath in her body to sustain her malice" ("Mother and Son"). West's contemporary letters on his behalf effectively refute this. She opened up possibilities for him through Lord Beaverbrook at the *Evening Standard* and through Charles Curran, Emily Hahn, and Harold Ross at the *New Yorker*. But she was suspicious and defensive, particularly in relation to Anthony's efforts at defining himself to the public.

After his father's death, Anthony started a biography of Wells, but the project got shelved by a variety of complications, some implicating his mother. Anthony planned to work on the biography after a move to the U.S., but this became impossible when he was not permitted to take Wells's uncatalogued papers—the Wells family having been alerted to his imminent departure by Rebecca. Though she would seem to have caused difficulty in this way, West did assist the biographical effort in other ways.[5] She favored a political and literary work, not a personal one, claiming that this had been Wells's wish, concurred in by the estate. Rebecca was also protecting her own personal life, having wearied of public interest in her alliance with Wells.[6] The personal story was not for sale, even by their son, even to better his career prospects. She objected to a paragraph written for *Time* magazine in 1947, sensationalizing the alliance of the new woman and the superman amid conditions of freedom that led to Anthony's birth. Anthony West's autobiographical novel of an illegitimate child, *Heritage,* was published in 1955. Rebecca is readily recognized in the mother, an actress called Naomi Savage, as is her husband, Henry Andrews, in the colonel Naomi marries. When she wrote Beaverbrook about the difficulties she anticipated from this work, he tried to reassure West that she would not be identified with any of the characters by Canadian and American readers. One can infer from Beaverbrook's consolations that *Heritage* could indeed do West harm with British readers.[7]

West's late correspondence is burdened with her versions of the Anthony story—pages of explanations of her actions and Wells's. Her accounts of "Tony" are not so entirely negative as he suspected, though they do identify periods of instability.[8] She had him psychoanalyzed by Hans Sachs. The war of their wills was waged over access to documents, and through selective accounts.[9] West called Anthony's 1982 interview with the *New York Times* "a characteristic production." She denied his charge that she asked Wells not to leave any income to Anthony after his death, and supposed the article would do her harm. Her only consolation was "I shall be dead soon" (West letter to Hahn, 20 Apr. 1982, Tulsa). So was he, of prostate cancer, only two years after his mother. West had been concerned about his cancer, prying Emily Hahn for reports on his surgery and prospects for recovery. She had depended on mutual friends for reports on her grandchildren Edmund and Caroline, Anthony's children with his first wife Kitty, in between rare visits. Her estrangement from Anthony over his divorce and later marriage to Lily West separated her almost entirely from their children, Adam and Sophie, who grew up primarily in the U.S. She did, however, help pay for the older children's educations, and visited with Sophie when she was studying in England. Her granddaughters were included in her will. But her primary beneficiary and literary executor was neither son nor grandchildren, but her sister Winnie's son, Norman Macleod. With the exception of Norman, West's childless sister Lettie was generally more successful as an aunt and a great-aunt.[10] West admitted to a friend, still in the feline language shared with Wells, that she was not good with "cubs." In a late interview, she offered the opinion that the world does not forgive a bad mother.

In 1929 West met Henry Andrews, an international banking consultant and connoisseur of the arts, at a party given by Vera Brittain, her colleague at *Time and Tide.* Their 1930 marriage was probably more a reaction to the tumult of being a celebrated single woman in the late twenties than an act of passion and sole commitment. Writing to her old friend S. K. Ratcliffe, she said 1928 and 1929 had been "bad years" and that the wedding could be taken "as a sign of gratitude to Henry for what his feeling for me during the last year has done to build me up" (West letter to Ratcliffe, Oct. 1930, Yale). In a typically suggestive telegram to Alexander Woollcott, she provided the marriage date, while addressing him as a "second husband."

West's life became more settled after her marriage and the acquisition in 1940 of a much-loved country home, Ibstone House, in Berkshire. This set up the same sort of country/city diversity that helped Woolf in pursuit of her career and mental well-being. West was the better manager of their demanding property, gardens, and dairy herd. Like Woolf, she participated in village events and wrote about them. Ibstone House may have allowed her to play curator of the big house, a role lost a generation ago by her Anglo-Irish patriarchy.

Andrews's best side seems to have been his art-historical knowledge. He traveled with West in Yugoslavia, becoming fictionalized as a wise husband in her 1941 work, *Black Lamb and Grey Falcon*. Henry was an upsetting addition to the adolescence of Anthony West. His efforts to intervene in Anthony's disputes with his mother, though appreciated by her, failed to create much understanding. Andrews took a common interest in helping the Yugoslavian refugees of Hitler's aggression, many of whom stayed briefly at Ibstone House. His worst trait was a withdrawal from sexual relations, which West says occurred after five years. Like Wells, he had a penchant for philandering. West rose to the challenge in 1946, when she had a brief affair with Francis Biddle while she was in Nuremberg reporting on the postwar Nazi trials. Biddle's withdrawal from the relationship merely reconfirmed to her the problems of conducting intimate relationships with married men, however. West kept up appearances at home. She looked after Andrews in his final, invalid years, summarizing him as an "inconvenient husband" for a woman writer.

West lacked a press of her own, and after her break with Wells, despite an allowance given for Anthony, she had to depend upon writing commissions. In 1928, with the assistance of agents in Britain and the U.S., she was doing very well in securing them, combining her efforts with those of her agents. In her letters, West put herself on familiar terms with numerous publishers, editors, and reviewers who could be expected to have an impact on her literary production. She developed a style that inserted familiar and domestic references into business correspondence. She could be personally mischievous and worldly wise by turns. She wrote as an intimate to Beaverbrook, Jonathan Cape, theater critic Alexander Woollcott, and many others. Her correspondence with novelist Sylvia Lynd had the advantage of putting her in touch with Robert Lynd, then an influential critic and literary editor of the *Daily News*.

An important strategy of her agents in marketing Rebecca West was to win her regular columns in large-circulation journals and newspapers. West was signed up for a weekly review at the *Daily Telegraph* and in late life was a regular with the *Sunday Telegraph*. When the BBC came along with offers in 1928, West responded to topics on order. In the U.S. she became a regular contributor of reviews to the *Herald Tribune*, and of political essays to the *New Yorker*. Doran handled her highly profitable series, "I Said to Me," in one of the Hearst papers, the *New York American*.

While censorship for indecency was a concern for authors such as Joyce, Lawrence, Barnes, and Hall, West had to worry more about libel suits. In 1928 she benefited from one suit and avoided another, both related to Lord Beaverbrook, in his capacity as editor as well as disappointing lover. West claimed successfully that his paper, the *Evening Standard*, had misrepresented and published without permission an interview with her concerning her assessment of Arnold Bennett, their regular reviewer. She argued that, given his reputation and power, this was damaging to her. West was unable to complete her novel *Sunflower*, fearing that Beaverbrook would sue her for a work which reflects his part in their failed affair. She took the advice of G. B. Stern to let her novel wait "until our loved one has left for a better land," and it actually waited for her death (Stern letter to West, n.d., Tulsa). In 1929, with *Harriet Hume*, West would transform sexual conflict between man and woman, politics and art, into a probing of gendered binaries. This time the female protagonist was modeled on another of Beaverbrook's flirtations, the pianist Harriet Cohen, also a close friend of West (Glendinning, *Rebecca West* 92).

West looked back on the late twenties as an overworked time. Shortly before her psychoanalysis in 1927, she remarked upon the number of her female colleagues who had sustained breakdowns—a list that included Stern. Though she had episodes of poor health throughout her life, West used it as a particular excuse for the shabby appearance noted in a 1928 letter Virginia Woolf wrote to her sister Vanessa, which West eventually read in Woolf's published letters (Noble, ed.). Eating and dressing well were basic rights claimed for women in West's early journalism. She was determined not to be found lacking in these assets.

Arranging Marriages, Partners, and Spaces 199

Barnes as Mother to Solitude

Djuna Barnes's year with Percy Faulkner, apparently in his territory of Bridgeport, Connecticut, is a blank in all the biographies and archival resources I have searched. Barnes had cast him off by the time she appeared as a journalist, artist, poet, and playwright in Greenwich Village around 1911. There she lived for a number of years with Courtenay Lemon, whom she casually referred to as her "husband." Like her, he was involved with the Theatre Guild, serving as a reviewer for their magazine; his politics are standardly stated as "libertarian." Their break was also casual, by her account. Barnes was annoyed that he did not approve of her pendulous earrings.

As noted in chapter 4, her most important Greenwich Village connections were to the Provincetown Players and the *Little Review*. Her friends there included Mina Loy, Helen Westley, Jane Heap, Elsa, Baroness Von Freytag-Loringhoven, and Peggy Guggenheim. Barnes left New York for Paris on assignment for *McCall's* around 1920. She quickly adopted Paris as her preferred setting, taking Natalie Barney and her lover Romaine Brooks as intimates and occasional advisors on her work.[11] Sylvia Beach and James Joyce were acquaintances. After sharing hotels with other American expatriates on the Left Bank, Barnes bought an apartment that she cherished at 9, rue St. Romain late in 1927. She did "everything but whoring" to support it (Barnes letter to Barney, 30 Jan. 1929, Jacques Doucet).

By the late 1920s, like Rebecca West, Barnes had become migratory. She devised the plan of nine months in Paris, where she could do her own work, and three months in New York, where as Barney had advised she must go to make money (Barnes letter to Barney, 15 Feb. 1929, Jacques Doucet). She reported with great self-satisfaction doing eight articles and eight other pieces in short order, and lining up two articles at *Vanity Fair* on the 1929 trip. Important work for the *Theatre Guild Magazine* dates from this period as well.[12]

Literary agency was a problem for Barnes that she never fully resolved. When she returned to New York in 1926, she began negotiating with Horace Liveright for the publication of her first novel, *Ryder*. Liveright had status as an avant-garde publisher, his list including *The Waste Land* and a 1923 collection of Barnes's stories, plays, and drawings, titled with daring simplicity *A Book*. The former publication gave Liveright an option on *Ryder,* which he published in censored form, much to Barnes's indignation. Barnes complained to Barney, "They want *all* the charming impossibilities removed—the drawings cleared of chamberpots—the things generally gelded! I have refused and hope to get the contract broken in this way." The remarks are interesting for their gendered metaphors. In commenting on the lost virility of the text, Barnes gives it a virginal status and assumes her favorite, maternal pose: "I feel like a mother with a virgin girl and this poor child in a compromising position" (Barnes letter to Barney, [21 Dec. 1926], Jacques Doucet). Her gesture of defiance to the censorship of sexual and excretory functions was to mark every omission with an asterisk and insert a foreword on censorship in America; the asterisks, but not the foreword, remained in a 1956 reissue. Barnes was also outraged by Liveright's minuscule advertising, and their underestimate of the number of copies that would be sold. It was briefly a best-seller, but the pessimistic publisher broke up the type, preventing a second printing. Barnes never contracted a professional agent, unlike the more business-like West. In representing Thelma Wood, Mina Loy, and Natalie Barney during her visits to New York in the late twenties, she had begun a practice of exchanged female agency, which would be sustained on Barnes's behalf by Emily Holmes Coleman when it came to placing *Nightwood* in 1936. By 1928, Barnes was writing *New Yorker* editor Katherine Angell regularly for advice on placing her stories.

Barnes could not neglect her mother, now divorced and living in New York, though it was a trying relationship, weighted with maternal opinions about the corruptions of Paris and her friends there—particularly Thelma. New York was not congenial: "One cannot possibly maintain any masculine vanity in a place that is monstrous—careless and hurried." It brought out her "Puritan condition"—the "flaw in my soul—a general will to guilt, and a propensity for taking on sins" (Barnes letter to Barney, n.d. [1926?], Jacques Doucet). Sexual harassment was part of Barnes's experience, as shown in her notes on interviews conducted in the 1920s. She speaks of one of her most important employers, from a financial standpoint—*Vanity Fair* editor Frank Crowninshield:

> He tried to see my garters the first time I went in to sell him a picture. When he failed, he asked me out to lunch. When lunch had been ordered . . . he leaned forward and said in his impersonal and impudent way: "Now tell me *all about* your dear little life." (Ms., "Fragments and Reviews," Maryland)

In 1928 Djuna Barnes was living most of the year in Paris with the American silverpoint artist Thelma Wood. Her novel of 1928, *Ryder,* is dedicated "to T. W." By this time she had little hope of stability in the relationship. Barnes's mother wrote with concern that Barnes was giving too much away to her lover. Thelma wandered at night, reportedly seeking other women, and, like Barnes, drank to excess. "I'm not a lesbian; I just loved Thelma" has become one of Barnes's most quoted statements (Field 101, 153; Lanser 165; Doughty 149). Barnes said this as an extremely private, elderly woman and in a context of not wishing to be appropriated commercially by lesbian booksellers.[13] This attitude may contradict recent definitions of a "lesbian continuum" and the post-Stonewall politics of gay and lesbian identification. Yet it also resists the acceptance of sexual categories, favoring a more detailed account of individual difference. I suspect that Barnes was no more in favor of being termed basically heterosexual, the category selected by her biographer, Andrew Field (153).

The liaison with Wood may have been made unduly prominent by its central position in her best-known work, *Nightwood.* It was preceded by others with women, both in the Village and in Paris. Mary Pyne, Jane Heap, Natalie Barney, and Romaine Brooks all seem to have been her intimates. Mina Loy and Solita Solano were close friends during the Paris years, Loy sharing the same apartment building. One interesting aspect of Barnes's partnering with women and bisexual men is that she cast herself in the familial role of mother, acknowledging the politics of a maternal desire for control.

Barnes mulls over relationships with men at great length with Emily Holmes Coleman, in letters dominated and perhaps influenced by Coleman's own pursuits of men. Coleman's list included Dylan Thomas and one of Barnes's own lovers, Silas Glossop. Barnes's male liaisons, besides Lemon and Glossop, include Putzi Hanfstaengl, Peter Negoe, Scudder Middleton, and Charles Henri Ford. Hanfstaengl became an associate of Hitler in the 1930s, and through this contact Barnes tried to set up an interview with the Führer (who proved too expensive).[14] Ford was the youthful founder and editor of *Blues: A Magazine of New Rhythm,* a little magazine published in 1929–30.

Barnes's alliance with Ford in the early 1930s suggests the importance of viewing her in other relationships besides the celebrated one with Wood. Barnes was well known as an avant-garde writer by 1931, when Ford moved into her Paris apartment. She needed care after an appendectomy, and he needed a place to stay. They visited Munich, Vienna, and Budapest together later that year and again shared her apartment through

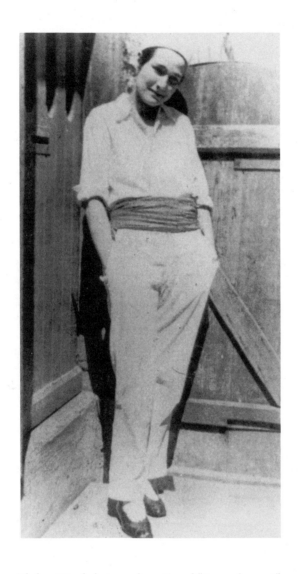

Plate 15. Thelma Wood photograph captioned "Remember me?" 1929–30.
Papers of Djuna Barnes, Special Collections,
University of Maryland at College Park Libraries.

much of 1932. In 1933 she joined Ford in Tangier, sharing a rat-infested house originally secured by Ford's *Blues* collaborator, Paul Bowles. She was working on *Nightwood* and Ford served as her typist. Based on this encounter with the text, he later boasted to Edith Sitwell that Barnes was a "better writer than Virginia Woolf." He reports that Sitwell's response was to draw herself up and announce, "She's my best friend and she's coming here this afternoon" (Barnes letter to Coleman, 1 Nov. 1937, Delaware). Ford said that he would have liked to have a child with Barnes. Instead he accompanied her back from Tangier to Paris, where she sought the abortion of a child conceived with painter Jean Oberle.

Barnes's recently published autobiographical story, "Behind the Heart," evokes the waning of this relationship, as Ford turned to a homosexual alliance with the painter Pavlic Tchelitchew and Barnes assumed the role of a maternal advisor. She was never quite content with the qualities of his heart and expressed skepticism in his youthful enthusiasm for Marxism. In "Behind the Heart" a woman who has "known life for almost 40 years" is cared for after an operation by a southern boy of scarcely twenty, who has only recently come into experiencing life. His closeness to her emerges in the similarity of their eyes, "as kinspeople," and in his dream "that I was you" when suddenly he had her legs and bracelets. Sensing that she loves him "with a love from the back of the heart, alien and strange," he too is an unusual lover, who displays cannibalizing and incestuous tendencies.[15] He gives her a kiss, "his mouth on her mouth, softly, swiftly, with one forward movement of the tongue, like an animal who is eager and yet afraid of new grass." He would dance with her as he does with his sister. As he departs to join his male lover, he comforts her with an odd, ritually posed embrace, "his hands on her shoulders, forearms against her breast." This is the beginning of solitude. While relationships that would seem to define Barnes as a bisexual are significant, it may be just as important to see her as a profoundly solitary being. While she started her life in an insular family arrangement, she ended as a recluse, living in a one-room Greenwich Village efficiency. Dedicated people looked in on her, but her chief companion seems to have been her own copy of the OED.

Women's Spaces

In their works, as in their daily lives, Woolf, West, and Barnes renewed metaphors and rites suggestive of a serene and/or separate feminine world. They took refuge in imaginary or real gardens, pairing with other women writers. As demonstrated by the abundant contacts I have made between the men and women of modernism, I resist the tendency to situate women writers exclusively in a space, set, or style of their own, to assign them a garden, even if they played with such tropes themselves. The garden as a women's world is an attractive structuring myth, to which modernist women, particularly lesbians, and their feminist critics have contributed.[16] Barney re-created a temple to Sappho in her back garden, and Woolf wrote in her lodge beyond the garden at Monk's House. In restoring Woolf to her close relations with women—her sister Vanessa Bell, Violet Dickinson, and Vita Sackville-West—Ellen Hawkes can call upon Woolf's own phrase, the "magical garden of women." Woolf imagined a utopian garden space in her fantasy work "Friendship's Gallery," written for Dickinson. As noted in chapter 4, she was one of a series of women who restored Virginia Stephen from abuse and mental illness, introducing her to publishing via the women's pages of the *Guardian*. In "Friendship's Gallery," Woolf also locates her friend and herself within the tradition of the goddess. Elizabeth Abel identifies a return to the mother in the garden world of Bourton, a space reduced in the final draft of *Mrs. Dalloway*, but still the setting for a memorable kiss. Woolf chooses the garden of a women's college for the introduction of Jane Harrison's phantom form in *A Room of One's Own*, magically transforming the season. Woolf's lover Vita Sackville-West was a consummate gardener, first at Long Barn, where Woolf had her first intimate visits, and then at Sissinghurst Castle. On one visit recorded in the *Diary*, she came to Woolf bearing "a whole tree of blue lupines" (3 D 28).[17] The farming year became the subject of her award-winning poem "The Land," which is embedded in *Orlando*. Being together in the garden created by Vanessa and Virginia at Asham, while their husbands strolled apart, was a source of pleasure to Woolf and Katherine Mansfield. There they discussed Woolf's progress on *Kew Gardens*, later reviewed glowingly by Mansfield. Mansfield's letters offered descriptions of orchid cups in her own garden; Woolf sent her columbines. Elizabeth Bowen focused her memories of pleasurable visits with Virginia in the garden and acknowledged gifts taken from it. This sets one of Woolf's last important literary relationships in the garden. Bowen's letters preserve a mental image of Woolf shredding red currants and recall the cyclamen, arum lilies, and embroidery at Monk's House (Bowen letter to Woolf, 18 Feb. 1941, Sussex). The eroticism of Woolf's letters to this whole set of women is centered upon the floral metaphors, so important to the development of Clarissa Dalloway's lesbian affection for Sally Seton.

The garden was just as constructive a space to Rebecca West, who planted window boxes in Kensington and had an ambitious garden at Ibstone House, where she learned to milk the cows and planted untold numbers of bulbs. As we shall see in volume 2, the garden is very important to the narrative fantasy of her novel *Harriet Hume.* As in *A Room of One's Own,* when Harrison's phantom is introduced, a surreal transformation of seasons occurs in a ghostly section of this work. In the meditative introduction to her laudatory review of *A Room of One's Own,* West tells a long gardening anecdote. She defies the recommendations of the nurseryman for her window boxes, willing to have her preferred stocks and fuscia crushed and scattered but fragrant in the wind. West portrays Woolf as similarly fragile but able to stand up to the wind. Both women have feminine knowledge of the seasonal cycle that will allow them to endure what turns out to be adverse masculine winds. West found the garden at Monk's House (which she identifies as Leonard's creation) the ideal setting for Virginia Woolf and a resource for her creativity. With a typical preference for life over death, she wonders how Woolf could have walked out of that garden to her suicide.[18]

Nevertheless, women writers could spend but brief time in their gardens and make only limited use of essentialist metaphors of woman in nature. As Woolf reveals with ominous force in *The Waves,* gardeners are often male and may keep out the curious, exemplified by Bernard and Susan as they approach Elvedon. The woman writing in Elvedon and the children nearing it might benefit from sharing this space, just as the narrator of *A Room of One's Own* might have sustained her thoughts had she not been chased from the college lawn by a beadle. Nor do gardens belong exclusively to women. Leonard Woolf was the family's main gardener. J. R. Hammond has suggested that H. G. Wells's writing, which frequently hosts secret gardens, could have been a source for the many gardens in West's work (243).

Djuna Barnes attaches no sentiment to gardens, as will become abundantly clear in volume 2. She takes us to cultivated fields, demonstrating that what is culled there is often a young woman. Her women characters in both *Ryder* and *Nightwood* tend to flee to the woods and accrue a scent of dead vegetation, in distinct contrast to West, with her constant focus upon life. *Ryder* offers more of a father than a mother nature (see Scott, "The Look in the Throat"). Instead of investing herself in gardens, Barnes attempted to created an interior living space expressive of her relationship with her lover Thelma Wood. Indeed, domestic furnishings and spaces are generally more expressive of women than gardens in her work. The furnishings of her Paris apartment are mentioned in Barnes's correspondence, from the time that she described purchases and plans to Natalie Barney through the years of World War II, when she paid for its storage in London from across the Atlantic, using T. S. Eliot as her local agent. In *Nightwood*, where Nora and Robin share accommodations, there is a comparable inventory and "every object in the garden, every item in the house . . . attested to their mutual love, the combining of their humours. There were circus chairs, wooden horses bought from a ring of an old merry-go-round, venetian chandeliers from the flea Fair, stage-drops from Munich, cherubim from Vienna, ecclesiastical hangings from Rome, a spinet from England, and a miscellaneous collection of music boxes from many countries; such was the museum of their encounter" (55–56). I treat the artificial garden of potted plants that provides a bower for Robin Vote of *Nightwood* in volume 2.

In *Nightwood*, the character closest to Barnes, Nora, dreams of another room, her grandmother's, with its "expansive, decaying splendour." It is full of belongings—"Portraits of her great-uncle Llewellyn, who died in the Civil War, faded pale carpets, curtains that resembled columns from their time in stillness—a plume and an inkwell—the ink faded into the quill." Nora finds herself looking down from it "as if from a scaffold," and though she summons Robin to come up, she knows this is "taboo" and the more she calls, the farther away Robin gets (62). The more she thinks about it, the more Nora realizes that the dream room is false, "opposite to any known room her grandmother had ever moved or lived in." It is "bereft as the nest of a bird which will not return." However false and empty, the idea of grandmotherly architecture "rebuilt her everlasting and continuous, flowing away in a long gown of soft folds and chin laces" and brought another more troubling version of her grandmother "for some unknown reason . . . dressed as a man . . . her arms spread saying with a leer of love, 'My little sweetheart!' " Nora takes from the dream experience new insight into her relationship, not just with her grandmother, who is " 'drawn upon' as a prehistoric ruin is drawn upon," but also with Robin, as she is "disfigured and eternalized by the hieroglyphics of sleep and pain" (63).[19]

Women writers such as Woolf, West, and Barnes seem to have put one another into the living spaces of their books for many reasons. This was a gesture of affection and a fantasy supplement to real life. Furthermore, these contrived spaces allowed them to plot greater accessibility to one another, and to achieve an understanding of the challenges posed to happiness in the lives of creative women of their era. Though they had entered the public sphere, they still required private peace and restorative affection.

11 Becoming Professionals

> Our nearest equivalent in charm was, perhaps a group of factory chimneys
> in a northern draw or an assembly of Fords at a parking place.
>   —West, "Notes on the Effect of Women Writers" 70

The "Hillary Clinton complex" of the 1992 presidential election shows
that there is still strong resistance to highly competent professional
women. D. H. Lawrence's protestations to the "monstrous regiment of
women" entering the job market in his era were only half in jest. Embracing the term "professional" in 1928 was daunting, even to women who
took experimental leaps in their writing. By producing work for the public, they relinquished the genteel pretensions of "ladies" generally held by
the middle-class wives and daughters of professional men. In "Professions
for Women," Virginia Woolf identifies herself as a "journalist," and thus
one of the professionals of her title.[1] But the origins of her professional
persona are harmless enough—a young girl, writing in the comfort of
home, mails off her first essay for pay and buys an exotic Persian cat with
the proceeds. By 1928, Woolf, West, and Barnes all depended upon income
for much more than cats—this despite Woolf's famed £500 a year, West's
child support from H. G. Wells, and Djuna Barnes's occasional checks
from Peggy Guggenheim. They allow us to study women as producers in
a capitalist system. "Becoming-professional" also emerges as a conceptual
persona, comparable to "becoming–woman" or "becoming–animal" as
theorized by Gilles Deleuze and Félix Guattari.

Dispensing with Charm

The title of this chapter invites punning on the word "becoming."
Such slippage occurs when gender disrupts traditionally male economic
and class systems used to constitute a professional world. Thus the process
of growth or "becoming" is diverted by the social expectation that women
should be "becoming," or display "charm," to embrace a key word for
women of their era. As young women, Woolf, West, and Barnes were all
capable of charming men. They were posed in the male memoirs we have

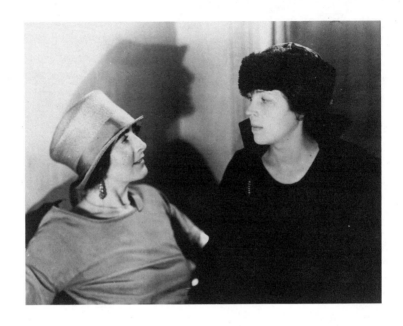

Plate 16. Mina Loy (*left*) with Djuna Barnes. Man Ray,

copyright 1995 Artists Rights Society (ARS),

New York/ADAGP/Man Ray Trust, Paris.

Sylvia Beach Collection, Princeton University Library.

encountered as "stunning subjects." I borrow the phrase from photographer Man Ray, as he used to describe Djuna Barnes and her friend Mina Loy (see Plate 16). Ray also claimed Virginia Woolf among his photographic subjects (see Plates 2 and 16). Woolf, West, and Barnes were all much-photographed objects of the gaze. As girls, Woolf and Barnes pose in fragile, antique dresses, usually in profile, or otherwise with eyes averted (see Plate 1). As young women, West and Barnes increasingly draw attention to their physical persons with striking hats and other accessories. West even sports a whip in one photo (see Scott, ed. 297).[2] In some mature poses, all three look directly back at the camera.

"Stunning" applies to both appearance and wit for these women. As recorded in earlier chapters, their critical quips could enchant H. G. Wells or T. S. Eliot, even if such remarks carried an astringent sting. Though Djuna Barnes contributed regularly to a magazine called *Charm,* she used the pseudonym Lydia Steptoe as if to step on toes. Her stories carried a satirical edge—taking issue with charm itself as a normative value for women. West left off her delicate and proper-sounding original name, Cicely Fairfield, in favor of the more forceful and exotic Rebecca West, derived from her brief encounter with the dramatic profession. Though West may have conveyed a schoolgirl impression at first to Violet Hunt, she quickly gained the reputation for critical scalping noted in chapter 2. One of her self-defining essays, written in 1914 for the *New Republic,* was titled "The Necessity of Harsh Criticism." It made the serious historical argument that nothing less was needed in a nation faced by war.

Was charm possible for the experienced woman, who by 1928 had put on years, along with her literary accomplishments? Could or should any vestige of this male-directed behavior be sustained by working women? At a P.E.N. banquet in 1929, West sensed that she and her female colleagues had disappointed Max Beerbohm's Edwardian expectations of women. She came forth with my epigraph: "Our nearest equivalent in charm was, perhaps a group of factory chimneys in a northern draw or an assembly of Fords at a parking place" ("Notes on the Effect" 70). West went on in her article to reject charm as something belonging to her mother's generation. In "Professions for Women," Woolf killed the proponent of "charm," the angel of the house, seeing this as necessary to the survival of her critical mind, particularly in engaging with male writers. She was skeptical of women who managed to turn on a certain glow in Clive Bell and Desmond MacCarthy. Woolf remarked of a set of readings and essays in December 1928, "I am surprised & a little disquieted by the remorseless severity of my mind: that it never stops reading & writing; makes me write on Geraldine Jewsbury, on Hardy, on Women—is too professional, too little any longer a dreamy amateur" (3 *D* 210). Andrew Field saw fit to name his biography *Djuna: The Formidable Miss Barnes*—suggesting that the mature modernist woman was distant rather than charming in accomplishment and manner. Sometime in the 1920s, Barnes seems to have made a deliberate alteration of her behavior. She recalled that she at first developed a "gay and silly and bright" personality that worked in her newspaper dealings, but later rejected it. She told an interviewer in 1971:

> Years ago I used to see people, I had to, I was a newspaperman, among other things. And I used to be rather the life of the party. I was rather gay and silly and bright and all that sort of stuff and wasted a lot of time. I used to be invited by people who said, "Get Djuna for dinner, she's amusing." So I stopped it. (Quoted in Field 21)

This account mixes genders, as Barnes designates herself as a "newspaperman" yet describes girlish behaviors. The same blending of gender roles occurred in her early journalism. Barnes braved a staged rescue by firemen and a re-creation of forced feeding, in both cases playing the passive female victim for the sake of a professional accomplishment. But assignments could be pushed too far. Barnes reported to Hank O'Neal that she was fired from the *Journal American* for not divulging facts she had discovered on a rape case. She had been shocked by her own invasion of the hospitalized woman's privacy (O'Neal 357).

All three women felt altered and threatened by their own fame, and were critical of the pursuit of celebrity. Woolf leaves the most negative account of other professional women, though it is always useful to bear in mind the recipient of her remarks. Her long-term partner in social satire, Vanessa, gets the most catty remarks. Woolf found Rose Macaulay, whom she met in 1928, overly concerned with reviews. Assuming her role as protective aunt, Woolf told Vanessa that she was "determined not to allow Angelica, whatever happens, to become a novelist. All this fame that writers get is obviously the devil" (3 *L* 501). Hilda Matheson, Talks Director for the BBC, offended in other ways. Woolf told Vita Sackville-West that Matheson affected her "as a strong purge, as a hair shirt, as a foggy day, as a cold in the head" (4 *L* 110). Woolf could not understand the attraction of this "drab & dreary" type of the "middle-class intellectual"

(3 D 239), though she could hardy be expected to be objective about a woman who was winning Vita's affections at the time. Woolf describes the rooms of former *Vogue* editor Dorothy Todd as "rather to her credit, workmanlike . . . and the whole atmosphere professional; no charm, except the rather excessive charm of [Madge] Garland," the fashion editor of *Vogue,* who had come "pear[l] hung & silken" (3 D 184). Garland was a long-term friend of West.

Rebecca West's decor at Portman Square, encountered at a dinner party, did not come off as well with Woolf, though her account shows an effort to comprehend West's lifestyle: "Of course its admirable in its way—impersonal, breezy, yes, go ahead, facing life, eating dinner at Savoy, meeting millionaires, women & men of the worldly" (4 D 326). Woolf's first impression of West when she met her in 1928 was that she was "a hardened old reprobate I daresay, but no fool" (3 D 184). Her account to Vanessa singles out West as "much the most interesting" of many "celebrities" met that week. Her impressions are mixed between admiration of West's energy and intelligence, and criticism of her grooming. "Hard" is a persistent word—the effect of worldly experience, where Wells is implicated. She describes West as

> hard as nails, very distrustful, and no beauty. She is a cross between a charwoman and a gipsy, but as tenacious as a terrier, with flashing eyes, very shabby, rather dirty nails, immense vitality, bad taste, suspicion of intellectuals, and great intelligence. . . . Rebecca has knocked about with all the mongrels of Europe. She talks openly of her son, who has got consumption: They say she is a hardened liar, but I rather liked her. (3 L 501)

West told me that she was hurt by these impressions, published long after Woolf's death. Despite their acquaintance, she did not consider them "twin souls." She retaliated for the comments on grooming: "Virginia and Vanessa were extremely untidy. They always looked as if they had been drawn through a hedge backwards before they went out" (Noble, ed. 110).[3]

As a Matter of Class

Woolf's impressions of West and Matheson demonstrate that female professionalism in the 1920s was entangled in class—usually a matter of subtle distinctions and discriminations of the middle class that typically produced the woman writer. We learned in chapter 1 that Woolf,

Plate 17. Elsa, Baroness Von Freytag-Loringhoven, 1920.

From *The Little Review* 7.3 (September–December 1920).

West, and Barnes were subject to the aristocratic bias of some family members: Wald Barnes with his agrarian stronghold and indisposition to work, George Duckworth with his preparations of Virginia and Vanessa for assemblies of polite society, and Charles Fairfield with his nostalgia for a lost Anglo-Irish patrimony. Though they resisted these attitudes, all three authors were attracted to aristocrats. They took pleasure in their beautiful possessions, and interest in their eccentricity, idealized as creative freedom. Woolf's fascination with aristocrats permeates her reviews of their memoirs and reports of meeting them.[4] Barnes was loyal to the highly eccentric Dadaist Elsa, Baroness Von Freytag-Loringhoven, even unto death, and sought to interview royalty. Indeed, work on the the rich and royal sold well. On the other hand, though they were not immersed in problems of the underclass, the urban literary perambulations of all three writers register empathy and respect for prostitutes, immigrants, servants, and blacks. West's early socialist essays consistently summon respect for working-class women. The title of Barnes's early collection of poetry, *The Book of Repulsive Women,* critiques all sorts of social biases, including attitudes toward lesbians and practitioners of the oldest profession.[5]

Publication of *Three Guineas* in 1938 put Woolf in touch with a large and varied set of women readers, as the collection of "fan" letters, now housed in the Sussex archive, reveals. One notable correspondent was the author Naomi Mitchison. Mitchison was curious to know about other women's reactions to *Three Guineas* and suggested some flaws in Woolf's thinking about professional women. As one of the "daughters of educated men" imagined in Woolf's work, she offered specific professional data. Her annual earnings were £300 to 400, derived from articles and work for the BBC. Realistically, this would support only two of her five children without the contributions of her husband. This was perhaps a reminder that family life could breed financial and emotional interdependencies overlooked in the abstract separatist designs of Woolf's work. Mitchison also puts in a bid for "revolutionary action," which she finds missing in Woolf's book. Mitchison suggests that one "must have contacts with ordinary life" and one "can't help doing things in connection with them" (Mitchison letter to Woolf, 1938, Sussex).

A much more negative and far-reaching critique of *Three Guineas* came from Queenie Leavis, who in 1928 had been a member of the audience at Girton that heard an early version of *A Room of One's Own.* Leavis's essay for *Scrutiny* was titled "Caterpillars of the World Unite."

While claiming that Woolf lacked contact with the motherhood and the working classes, Leavis was also arguing the superiority of her own achievements. She had three children by the noted Cambridge don F. R. Leavis, had risen from poverty to a Cambridge education, and had an enviable list of publications. Leavis argued that the feminist movement was outdated. She affiliated instead with the male-dominated academic establishment that was severely challenged by *Three Guineas.* One of Woolf's guineas had gone for training women in an experimental college—an outsider's society that endorsed female difference. Woolf thought that Leavis's harsh criticism was her reaction to a personal "snub." Woolf had not responded to Leavis's praise of the introduction Woolf wrote for Margaret Llewellyn Davies's book on the cooperative movement, *Life as We Have Known It.* Even worse, in a letter to Davies, Woolf had said that the sample essay Leavis sent her was representative of "all that is highest and dryest at Cambridge" (5 L 425).[6] *Three Guineas,* despite the trappings of academic footnotes, was far from high and dry; it was boldly connective, moving from Creon to Mussolini, and freeing women from the masculine scaffolding of war. One of its guineas went to women in the professions, who were expected to bring domestic values into their work. Leavis may have betrayed her own professional frustrations in attacks such as the one on Woolf. Though the author of academic essays (many of them concerned with women writers of the nineteenth century) and *Fiction and the Reading Public,* and though the instructor of numerous Cambridge students, Queenie Leavis was never granted a university position, nor status as an editor at *Scrutiny.*

Chloe Liked Olivia

On a very different note, depiction of the positive relationship between two women at work is heralded in *A Room of One's Own* as one of the most important achievements of the contemporary author Mary Carmichael. Woolf, West, and Barnes all entered into creative and supportive pairings and networks with professional women, beginning with the literary midwives encountered in chapter 4. The charm supposedly reserved for men could be exerted by women on one another. Female circulation of charm entered their fiction in texts such as *Orlando, Harriet Hume,* and *Ladies Almanack,* with often more than a hint of lesbian attraction. Many of the attachments of Woolf, West, and Barnes with female contemporaries have been mentioned briefly: Woolf with her sister Vanessa

Bell, Katherine Mansfield, Vita Sackville-West, Ethel Smyth, and Elizabeth Bowen; West with Sylvia Lynd, G. B. Stern, and Fannie Hurst; Barnes with Helen Westley, Thelma Wood, Natalie Barney, Jane Heap, and Emily Holmes Coleman.

There has been abundant treatment of the special relationship between the actual sisters Vanessa Bell and Virginia Woolf, whose dispositions complemented one another far better than the assertive natures of the Fairfield sisters, noted in chapter 1.[7] In her illnesses, Virginia usually received what nurture Vanessa was free to give, considering all the people who looked to her for maternal support. That Virginia occasionally cared for her sister has been largely overlooked. She was of help in crisis periods, as in 1906, when Vanessa fell ill during the family's expedition to Greece, and again when their brother Thoby died of typhoid shortly after their return home; she helped Vanessa endure the tragic death of her eldest child, Julian, who was killed during the Spanish Civil War. Virginia liked "to drop a little salt on Dolphins [Vanessa's] snout so that she may spout columns of fury into the air." Virginia salted with such subjects as her own dislike of the profound instinct of motherhood, or Vanessa's pronouncement that "the chief end of life is one's work" (3 L 366). *To the Lighthouse* was undoubtedly the closest merger of Vanessa with Virginia, though it is not the only one. Vanessa's story of a moth provided an origin for *The Waves* (3 L 372). Lily Briscoe, the very private, nonprofessional artist of *To the Lighthouse,* is certainly not constructed on the model of Vanessa or Virginia. Still, Lily derives her aesthetic considerations, some of her brush strokes, and her problems of defining the mother from both. Woolf's evocation of their parents was probably her most significant gift to her sister, whose opinion was particularly important to Virginia as a confirmation for this work. The endorsement came complete with a painter's metaphor of successful portraiture. Vanessa's letter begins with their mother, detecting the sort of evasiveness in female character that Woolf made the object of her writing in "Mr Bennett and Mrs Brown":

> You have made one feel the extraordinary beauty of her character, which must be the most difficult thing in the world to do. It was like meeting her again with oneself grown up & on equal terms & it seems to me the most astonishing feat of creation to have been able to see her in such a way—You have given father too I think as clearly, but perhaps, I may be wrong, that isnt quite so difficult. There was more to catch hold of. Still it seems you see as far as por-

trait painting goes you seem to me to be a supreme artist & it is so shattering to find oneself face to face with those two again that I can hardly consider anything else. (2 Bell 128)

Vanessa's "grown up & on equal terms" is one of the most empowering statements in her assessment, only hinting at the problems addressed in chapter 1, where we considered family (dys)functions. Virginia also gave Vanessa and her family regular entertainment as a parodist and gossip, both in personal visits and in their abundant correspondence. Virginia was Vanessa's patron, purchasing wares from the Omega Workshop, as noted in the previous chapter, and commissioning Vanessa's designs for Hogarth Press book jackets.[8] Among her more trivial gifts, but one with significance to this connective study, was a copy of Rebecca West's first novel, *The Return of the Soldier*.

Just as daunting as a discussion of Woolf's relationship with her sister is the subject of Vita Sackville-West, whose multifaceted relationship with Woolf has been dispersed through all three chapters of this section on the women of 1928. One of the original sources of the interest Woolf found in Sackville-West was her aristocratic mien—a distinct set of manners and resources that intrigued Woolf in ways that self-supporting middle-class women closer to her own background rarely did. She admired immediately Vita's manner, with "no false shyness or modesty" (2 D 216). Indeed, these are qualities of confidence she could use in her professional life. It is well to recall that Vita Sackville-West's novels became a staple for the Hogarth Press, finding popular audiences in ways that the most experimental of the Woolfs' writers did not. Vita led Virginia into new public experiences. She provided a subject for rapturous language—a topic returned to in volume 2.

Woolf served as Sackville-West's advisor on literary form. In criticizing her friend's poetry, Woolf conditioned a preference for modernist textual forms to a personal love relationship. Some of her critiques verged on the sexual, generalizing from Vita's behavior to her writing, and perhaps liberating her own attitudes toward sexual expression:

> And isn't there something obscure in you? There's something that doesn't vibrate in you: it may be purposely—you don't let it. . . . It's in your writing, too, by the bye. This thing I call central transparency—sometimes fails you there too. I will lecture you on this at Long Barn. (3 L 302)

The "lecture" at their Long Barn rendezvous hints at sexual play, which apparently was initiated in 1925. Woolf's identification of a missing element hit its mark with Sackville-West, who wrote to her husband, Harold Nicolson, "Damn the woman, she has put her finger on it" (Glendinning, *Vita* 169). During the writing of "The Land," in a practical and realistic vein, Woolf advised the inclusion of farming "facts" (3 *L* 198). With "central transparency" she meant "some sudden intensity" (3 *L* 244). She led Vita toward modernist fragmentation: "Now that you have mastered the question of technique, throw your technique into the air and let it smash on the pavement" (Glendinning, *Vita* 170). Despite its formal limitations, from the point of view of a modernist, Woolf came to know "The Land" well and quoted fondly parts of it that reminded her of Vita. When Edith Sitwell panned the work, Woolf contrasted Vita, the "traditional naturalist," with Sitwell, the "natural innovator." She consoled Sackville-West on her better sales, suggesting that this factor could have sparked Sitwell's envy (3 *L* 394). Four recently recovered letters from 1932–1939 reveal that Woolf's sexual interest and the consultations on poetry continued.

Rebecca West's criticisms of "The Land" were in line with Woolf's. West said that the work expressed "conventional emotions with literary grace" (Glendinning, *Vita* 188). As early as 1925, Woolf was trading remarks with Vita about Rebecca West, whom Vita met before Virginia did. Both appear to have appreciated her wit (3 *L* 159). Vita, like Rebecca, was active in the P.E.N. club and tried to interest Virginia in attending their meetings, though she used the prospect of sitting by H. G. Wells, rather than Rebecca West, as an enticement. In the end, West found Vita a kinder friend, though she seems to have experienced social barriers with both.

We return to Woolf's major gesture toward Sackville-West, *Orlando,* in the next chapter. By the time that Woolf was delivering her lectures on women writers to young women at Cambridge, she was regarded as a celebrity. Her status came of course from the professional success of such works as *Mrs. Dalloway* and *To the Lighthouse.* Her Cambridge heritage was also a factor. But so was Vita, who had her own fame for writing and for the scandal that accompanied her earlier relationship with Violet Trefusis.[9] In 1928, the publication of *Orlando* hinted at another relationship with Woolf. The young women of Girton were struck by the glamour of both Virginia Woolf and Vita, who accompanied her.[10]

The travel narrative was a genre in which Vita had wider experience to offer Woolf. Vita's letters from her travels of 1926 were a partial consolation for the women's separation at an early stage in their relationship. En route to Tehran, where her diplomat husband was stationed, Vita visited Egypt, Aden, India, Basra, and Baghdad. In Baghdad she stayed with the anthropologist Gertrude Bell—one of the women available as models to Mary Carmichael in *A Room of One's Own*. Providing the basis for her book *Passenger to Tehran*, Sackville-West's experience of Persia also contributed to the depiction of Orlando at his/her critical stage of gender transformation. Aphra Behn, who marks the important transition of women into professional writers in *A Room of One's Own*, was another gift of Vita to Virginia, as she seems to have discovered this older woman traveler, dramatist, and novelist first (Glendinning, *Vita* 199). We will return to radio as another professional endeavor that Woolf experienced through Vita's introduction.

In considering Woolf's contact with a wider world and with less experimental forms of modern writing, it is important to acknowledge a relationship that has received far less attention than Woolf's affair with Sackville-West. Stella Benson visited Woolf on her terrace at Rodmell in 1932, gaining her personal admiration. At that time, Benson was in London gathering awards for her novel *Tobit Transplanted*, which Woolf had read and appreciated when it came out in 1931.[11] Woolf's diary account betrays fascination with Benson's stories of the corruption and violence of the Hong Kong trade. She liked this "serious, weary, intent" woman, living a boring life (4 *D* 118). Upon her return to China, where her husband worked for the Customs Service, Benson shared confidences about her work in a series of letters to Woolf. Benson assumed an adoring and subordinate position in their correspondence. *The Waves* (she had her copy signed by Woolf) presented a contrast to her own "pre-occupation with the hard bones, living with very common people in China." This had "warped her from rarity"—a quality Woolf watched for, while Benson watched for "common things" (Benson letter to Woolf, 1 Sept. 1932, Sussex). She envied Woolf, "living in a center of books." In a remark that retains its importance in our postcolonial critical era, Benson worried about her own reputation—that she might be sold as a sort of stuntwoman, remarkable for her lack of civilization (Benson letters to Woolf, 3 Feb. and 6 June 1933, Sussex). Her description of life in China, where the male voice was constantly booming its instructions and boasts in the female ear, may have been encouraged by *A Room of One's Own*. In turn, it could have affected Woolf's depiction of colonials in *The Years*—a work often cited for its return to a more realistic mode. When she learned of

Benson's death in December 1933, Woolf felt that it was a relationship that might have gone farther, comparing it to her encounters with Mansfield. "And now, so quickly, it is gone, what might have been a friendship. Trusty & patient & very sincere—I think of her; trying to cut through, in one of those difficult evenings, to some deeper layer—certainly we could have reached it, given the chance" (4 *D* 192). Part of her sense of loss was that she had "a feeling of the protest each might make: gone with their work unfinished—each so suddenly. Stella was 41" (192).

With the elderly composer Ethel Smyth, whom she met in 1930, Woolf had relatively few aesthetic interactions. Yet Smyth's presence in Woolf's life grounded the musical qualities of *The Waves* and the militancy of *Three Guineas* (see Moore 15). Serving as Smyth's literary advisor, Woolf identified "sentimental & hysterical passages for her benefit" in her writing (4 *D* 33). In the typescript for her "Professions for Women" lecture, Woolf had cited Ethel Smyth as a different model of the professional— one more forceful than her own youthful counterpart, who found it possible to mail off essays penned at home. Smyth's type had conquered greater obstacles. Men had expected women to maintain "a home and servants." Ethel Smyth changed that. "Women like Ethel Smyth don't allow things to stand still. So they take matters into their own hands. They go off to Germany and get educated. So one day, the man came home to find that his servants had gone—they had set up for themselves and there they were, playing the piano, becoming doctors, barristers, chemists" ("Appendix," *The Pargiters* 167). Movement into the professions was a triumph for the servant class as well as the female sex.

Woolf organized a tea, at Smyth's request, so that she could meet Rebecca West. As vital, garrulous activists, the two women made a good combination. Woolf reported to Ottoline Morrell, whose own response to West had not been so positive:

> Rebecca was fascinating—ungainly, awkward, powerful, arboreal like some sloth or mandrill; but oh what a joy to grapple with her hairy arms! I mean she was very upstanding and outspoken, and we discussed religion, sex, literature and other problems, violently, in a roar, to catch Ethel's ear, for three hours. This is to corroborate my view, and in opposition to yours. (5 *L* 261)

The account is unusually physical and contentious. Discussion includes the taboo subject of sex, and West delivers her points in an "upstanding" style quite different from Woolf's. While it would hardly seem compli-

Plate 18. Dame Ethel Smyth.

Hulton Picture Company Library.

mentary to be compared to a "sloth or mandrill," Woolf had actually chosen one of the animals associated with her own imaginary being.[12]

The first meeting of Rebecca West and Virginia Woolf had occurred at a party given by former *Vogue* editor Dorothy Todd in May 1928. Thus they met on common, feminine professional turf. For years, Woolf and West had been carefully appraising each other's work and its impact upon the profession. As early as 1922, Woolf had requested that Morrell introduce them. For the introduction to this section, I chose, as an important professional conjunction, West's October 1928 review of *Orlando*. She greeted it as an "important historical event" ("High Fountain" 592). Among the accomplishments of *Orlando*, according to West, are the discovery of the *donnée* of each age visited and the demonstration, through the fantasy of changing sex and the fine perceptions of the central character, of "how far one's sex is like a pair of faulty glasses" (595–96).[13] West was pleased to discover that, though Woolf was a "skeptic" product of a "critical" age, and (unlike the young Rebecca) no believer in "progress," her "genuinely creative spirit" still flourished, while that of Aldous Huxley, among other men, had not (596). In contrast to Woolf, "Man" with "more force than sense . . . ceremonially uncovers some dead cat of dangerous myth that has been carried round the town a score of times already" (593).

Woolf responded with an appreciative letter to an ideal reader. She was pleased to find West's "mind working where mine tried to go" and expressed gratitude that West would spend the riches of her intelligence, insight, and brilliance on her (Woolf letter to West, 11 Nov. 1928, Tulsa). Woolf also defended West when Vita Sackville-West complained that *Harriet Hume* was an imitation of *Orlando*. Woolf avowed that West was at least preferable to Hugh Walpole, even if the style chosen for the work was occasionally foppish (4 L 88). Writing in her *Diary* in late 1933, after the women had exchanged numerous visits, Woolf records activity that differentiates the two women. West was speaking on married women's right to earn at a meeting where Ethel Smyth was conducting her "March of the Women."[14] She is glad to have West as "a buffeter and battler" who "has taken waves . . . and can talk any language" (4 D 189). It had become possible, and essential, to take pleasure in complementary women.

A critique is couched in West's compliments for Woolf's poetic qualities and original design in *Orlando*: Woolf constructs her designs out of "trifles"; "she knows that to insist on such laxity of subject is an excellent prophylactic against failure, since it involves the artist in no intellectual discussion, seduces him into the service of no moral propaganda" ("High

Fountain" 593). But Woolf would provide that, to West's satisfaction, in *A Room of One's Own*. West used her regular "Letter from Abroad" column for the *Bookman* to hail *A Room of One's Own* as "an uncompromising piece of feminist propaganda; I think the ablest yet written." West congratulates Woolf for bracing herself against the current intellectual wind of anti-feminism, led by a rising tide of postwar "effeminacy." Anticipating Woolf critics of the 1980s, West saw Woolf meeting her halfway on activism, and offering a more vital form of modernism than the men in the field.

There have been numerous attempts in criticism to take Rebecca West away from her early feminism and to claim that her interest in women was secondary, and thus relegated to less important work.[15] Yet West was extensively reprinted by the feminist Virago Press in the 1980s and chose as her biographer Victoria Glendinning, who is well known for her biographies of women of the modernist era, including Elizabeth Bowen (herself a late professional friend of Woolf) and Vita Sackville-West. West enthusiastically assisted the feminist critic Jane Marcus in collecting her early essays for publication—an effort that resulted in the feminist collection *The Young Rebecca*. Despite her interest in engaging the minds and affections of men, West's commitment to other women is clear. She told me that she would have liked to review more women's publications, but had to work with the books that were sent her. Even more provocatively, she entertains lesbianism as a missed option in a 1975 diary entry (Glendinning 125); indeed, much of her fiction betrays a clear appreciation of the female body.

When she wrote a profitable contract with the *New York American* for a weekly column, West pointedly reserved the right to continue her arrangement for occasional writing for *Time and Tide*, where she could fulfill a female focus. West spent what Victoria Glendinning has called the "feminine summer of 1929" on the Riviera with G. B. Stern, Pamela Frankau, and her secretary, June Head. In her letters to West, Frankau referred to her as "Darling Lady Mary" and signs "Pussinger," indicating her entrance into West's intimate feline language. West also used her connection with P.E.N. to introduce female colleagues to well-connected writers. When West and Henry Andrews moved to their country home, West became occupied with Women's Institutes, as did Virginia Woolf. West wrote a play for her local group, and instructed others on canning goods during wartime—activities that made good subjects for her American journalism, as noted in the previous chapter.

West enjoyed associations with a long list of women in the writing profession and gave some of them valuable help and reinforcement. West's support of Violet Hunt included going over her manuscripts to remove split infinitives and take out redundant commas "which I scatter, she says, on my pages as a dressmaker drops pins" (Hunt 205). West cheered Sylvia Lynd for writing a novel "which is not about how the author went to Oxford and left without, on the highest grounds, taking his degree." But she regretted it when Lynd set aside her writing for domestic demands: "I suppose that in the conscientious way of us females you have let it [her novel] get put aside because of homelessness and moving. How we literary women want wives to look after us" (West letter to Lynd, n.d., Yale). When Emma Goldman arrived in London in 1924, West set up a celebrity dinner to launch her crusade, and was exhausted by supporting her in various ways for years.[16]

West's association with G. B. Stern was one of the most sustained and significant of her life. Though little known today, Stern was a prolific author. Most successful were a series of five novels on a Jewish family, the Rakonitzes, which was adapted to the London stage as *The Matriarch* in 1929. Virginia Woolf attended a performance of the play and reviewed one novel in the series, *A Deputy Was King*, for the *New York Herald Tribune* in 1926. Both West and Woolf admired Stern's representation of Jewish family life. Woolf's remark on the fleeting fashionability of the book suggests some professional distancing. It was Stern's depiction of relationships that received West's particular admiration.

Their friendship was deeply caring. West went to Stern's aid when she suffered a mental breakdown in 1927. She expressed her disgust at Stern's being urged by her mother toward marriage with an appropriate Jewish man. Stern was able to respond with professional help to West. She provided needed advice and encouragement when West's "Uncle Bennett" essay was under attack in 1928, and could promise her own glowing review of the volume in which it appeared, *The Strange Necessity*. She countered West's pessimism with the notion that the controversy would help sell her book. Stern was known to her best friends as "Peter," suggesting at least some form of masculine identification. She used West's intimate feline nickname, "Panther," a product of West's love affair with Wells, and accepted the puckish "Tynx" for herself. One reassuring letter closes, "I'd like to state aloud that I found the Panther's conclusion *very* helpful and uplifting to a humble Tynx" (Stern letter to West, n.d., Tulsa). Perhaps sensing West's pronounced heterosexual identification, Stern carefully

Plate 19. G. B. Stern. E. O. Hoppé.

Mansell Collection.

stated her "romantic" enjoyment of a time they shared in Henley: "Don't misunderstand me: I'm not that way about you and it wouldn't be nice if I was" (Stern letter to West, n.d., Tulsa).

West met the up-and-coming political journalist Dorothy Thompson in Berlin in 1924. Thompson became an important confidante and an ideological soulmate until her death in 1961, sharing West's fascination with Eastern Europe and her pessimism over the politics of the 1940s and 1950s. Among their important shared friends was John Gunther. Both women wrote for the *New York Herald Tribune* and reacted to each other's pieces. Their correspondence develops both professional and personal concerns. West cultivated her feelings about Communism and Joseph McCarthy in letters to Thompson, who was largely of the same opinion. When they met, West was in the awkward stage of having just left Wells; she was trying to make a relationship with Beaverbrook work, and attended at least one of Thompson's parties with him. In early 1923, Wells had suspected an amorous relationship between West and Sinclair Lewis, who became Thompson's second husband in 1928. West was abroad when the wedding took place, but said, "I doubt if I could have borne to go." She was "sure . . . that all would be for the worst"—a prognosis that proved accurate (West letter to Anne Ford, 10 Sept. 1963, Harvard). The two women had comparable difficulties with their sons, both only children whom they raised largely on their own. Thompson offered advice during West's crisis over Anthony's novel *Heritage*,[17] and convinced Henry Luce to take out a paragraph concerning Anthony's birth, planned for a 1947 article in *Time* magazine. When Michael Lewis was taken to court over difficulties with a young woman, West wrote Lord Beaverbrook to ask that his press "temper the wind to the shorn lamb" (West letter to Beaverbrook, 5 Dec. 1950, House of Lords). Like West, Thompson was upset by her son's plan to divorce his first wife. West advised Thompson, from the heart, not to be upset by her grown son's hostility: "I wonder if your Mike isn't unconsciously gunning for your autobiography. Don't let him get away with it. . . . It is a feminist work we have to perform. In the past women subscribed to the legend that the mother was always wrong, and gave themselves up to the sense of guilt. We have got to refuse to go under" (West letter to Thompson, 6 Dec. 1959, Syracuse). She added, with characteristic physical humor, "Let us not beat our breasts, we will only spoil our elegant contours and do no good."[18] Peter Kurth, Thompson's biographer, notes that "with Rebecca, sometimes, [Thompson] might have been a teenager at an overnight slumber party. They exchanged recipes, dresses, effulgent praise" (389).

West's work for the *New Yorker* brought Janet Flanner and Emily Hahn as friends. Letters to and from Flanner discuss the politics among editors at the *New Yorker* and other women writers, such as Mary McCarthy.[19] Flanner offered West generous appreciation of her writing. She praised her review of Mme de Staël and gave her a sense of being needed as a psychological resource: "I have been incomparably depressed lately, and it was pride in your writing, your mind, your scholarship, your entity, that lifted me up yesterday, reading you in the country garden" (Flanner letter to West, 6 July 1959, Tulsa). Though she gave a more mixed impression of West to Natalia Murray, she did say that West's writing on South Africa was a "very great and simple piece of reporting" (*Darlinghissima* 272).

"Mickey" Hahn was a more personal friend. Hahn helped compensate for information gaps between Anthony and Rebecca, particularly where her grandchildren were concerned. Her children were of an age with Rebecca's grandchildren, and knew them as friends. In the later years, she kept West informed about professional developments. After attending a conference on women at Rutgers University in 1978, she reported that West's name had been mentioned approvingly (Hahn letter to West, 4 Oct. 1978, Tulsa). West lived just long enough to see herself taken up enthusiastically by a new generation of feminists.

As noted in the previous chapter, Djuna Barnes cast herself in a maternal role with both male and female friends, providing services that merge the personal with the professional. The most bizarre person she sponsored was the Dadaist poet Elsa, Baroness Von Freytag-Loringhoven. The baroness had started her writing career in Greenwich Village publishing with the *Little Review,* where in 1919 Jane Heap defended her art as the production of a willed state of madness.[20] She had moved on to Paris at about the same time as Barnes. In 1927, when the baroness died of gas inhalation, a possible suicide, Barnes wrote a tribute to her for the avant-garde magazine *transition,* which had also published Von Freytag-Loringhoven's poetry. As a monument, she appended the letters the baroness had written her from her native Germany, at a time when she was contemplating death. Von Freytag-Loringhoven served Barnes's own fascination with death, hers "a stupid joke that had not even the decency of maliciousness." She found this death a tragedy "because she had fought it so knowingly all the latter part of her life, rated it for what it was, feared it, and honored it, adding to it the high tempo of dread and love that set it above her, enormous and evil, by this splendid appraisal" (Barnes, "Elsa Baroness" 19).

The salon of Natalie Barney and its usefulness to Barnes were attended to in chapter 4. It is important to note that Barnes probably gave to as well as received from Barney and her partner, Romaine Brooks. She scouted out accommodations for Brooks in Cagnes and found Berthe, the maid who stayed with Barney for life. Barnes advised Barney on producing a literary series, suggesting Ford Madox Ford and Adrienne Monnier as sources for mailing lists. While in New York in 1927, she worked as Barney's informal agent, seeing the publishers Knopf and Covici on her behalf, and running errands for Barney's mother. She could confide to Barney about the increasingly difficult New York market, where she tried to find a publisher for *Nightwood* for several years in the mid-1930s. The editor at Scribner's pronounced that, in producing work such as *Nightwood*, Barnes had not kept "abreast of the times." He advised that she might still make a living as a model for cloaks (Barnes letter to Barney, 4 Apr. 1934, Jacques Doucet). Barnes's confidences were aimed at a reader who could maintain her own sense of fashion and worth.

In Paris of the twenties, Thelma Wood and Djuna Barnes were a sensation when they walked together, wearing sweeping cloaks and jaunty hats, Wood often in trousers. Wood's silverpoint drawings of deeply cupped flowers, animals, and fashion accessories such as gloves and shoes have affinity to some of Barnes's lesbian literary subjects and her own drawings, as we shall examine in detail in volume 2. In 1927, on the same New York trip that included negotiations on behalf of Barney, Barnes tried to set up an art show for Wood. Alcohol was a major factor in the failure of their relationship, which was drawing to a close by 1928. Wood was hospitalized that year. As Barnes sat with her in the hospital, she turned to a lighter form of female identification, writing much of her sketch of the Barney circle, *Ladies Almanack,* which we return to in the next chapter.

In the mid-1930s, Djuna Barnes was often the guest of Peggy Guggenheim at summer writers' retreats, staged in rural England at places such as Hayford Hall, Warblington, and Yew Tree Cottage. Among the other women writers present were Kay Boyle, Antonia White, and Emily Holmes Coleman, who all left descriptive correspondence. Coleman was already known for her autobiographical, psychological novel *Shutter of Snow* (1930), and for poetry that had appeared in *transition* magazine. From the letters circulated among these women, one senses that Coleman had an erratic, presumptuous, and sometimes frightening personality. She irritated Guggenheim and worried Barnes, who thought Emily might be capable of destroying her manuscripts. In the summers of 1932–33, as Barnes worked on drafts of *Nightwood* at Hayford Hall, Coleman was writing *Tygon,* a novel that was never published. Barnes was predictably drawn to a childbirth scene in this work, praising its power.

Coleman was openly and extravagantly admiring of *Nightwood* at a time when Barnes had despaired of its publication. She suggested in her letters that Joyce was dead in comparison to Barnes. Coleman sometimes tries to root out what she terms Barnes's "introversion," so as to free up her access to the unconscious, this leading to a proper emphasis on female love. Coleman's interpretations of *Nightwood* placed the emphasis not on the Doctor (though she knew he would appeal to Eliot) but upon the relationship of the two women, Robin and Nora, as based on Barnes's experiences with Thelma Wood. She felt that the Doctor should play a role like the fool in *King Lear* (Coleman letter to Barnes, 27 Aug. 1935, Maryland). The knowledge of "you only of all the company" which presumably one lover has of another at the "resurrection" and which is a "cashed expense," in Barnes's terms, strikes Coleman as "revealing of the mystery of sexual love in a way that *nothing else which has been written about it in the past has ever been*" (Coleman letter to Barnes, 26 Jan. 1946, Maryland). Under Coleman's direction, *Nightwood* would have been a relatively straightforward lesbian work. Modernism becomes a much more variable text when we consider the versionings of it by women helping to direct one another as writers.

Coleman's lengthy progress reports to Barnes, as she promoted *Nightwood* to T. S. Eliot, are deliberately amusing. They take credit for canny manipulation. Chapter 7 recorded her assessments of the difficulties that had to be confronted in Eliot's character, but also deep affinities with Barnes that Coleman hoped to summon forth. In her letters, Coleman makes a practical division between what she knows is good in the novel and what she knows will sell with the publishers.

As a matter of formal style, the "sentimental" was faulted by all three of the modernist women I am focusing upon, suggesting that it was a major issue among female modernists.[21] The writing of Kay Boyle, like Djuna Barnes a resident at Hayford Hall, was dismissed by Barnes and Emily Holmes Coleman as too sentimental (Barnes letter to Coleman, 30 Nov. 1935, Delaware). Barnes credited Boyle with "good spots, talent, but

Plate 20. Emily Holmes Coleman, 1935–36.

Coleman Papers, University of Delaware Library, Newark.

all gone to the sugar bowl" (Barnes letter to Coleman, 13 Feb. 1936, Delaware). That T. S. Eliot compared Barnes unfavorably to Boyle on his first reading of excerpts from *Nightwood* was discouraging both to her and to Coleman.

A Women's Market?

However skeptical they may have been of the sentimental, Woolf, West, and Barnes all wrote for an emerging "women's market," though not necessarily the market we have come to identify as such. Feminist readings of popular media in the wake of Betty Friedan's *The Feminine Mystique* suggest that, with the exception of the World War II era, women from the 1930s through the 1950s were encouraged to accept images of themselves as homemakers and sexual objects and to invest themselves in consuming goods along those lines. Friedan's research, and indeed the whole contention with mother figures of the 1950s, seems to be up for postmodern reconsideration. Historian Joanne Meyerowitz, for example, is finding more varied models of womanhood, including independent, achieving women, in the nonfiction of periodicals such as *Ladies' Home Journal, Good Housekeeping,* and *Ebony.* Dorothy Thompson, known even more than West as a political journalist, was also a contributor to the *Ladies' Home Journal. Vanity Fair* contributors in 1922 (the year of Barnes's first publication in that journal) included Ezra Pound, Hugh Walpole, Clive Bell, Aldous Huxley, Alexander Woollcott, e. e. cummings, Edna St. Vincent Millay, and Eleanor Wylie. Barnes's work usually appeared in a section called "Literary Hors d'Oeuvres," a title that suggests some need to lighten the presentation of intellectual content. There were also sections for theater, art, "The World of Ideas," poetry, and satirical sketches.

Vogue, as defended by both Woolf and West, also has a serious aspect. When in 1925 Logan Pearsall Smith questioned the ethics of "writing articles at high rates for fashion papers like *Vogue*" and suggested that "one must write only for the Litt Supplement and the Nation," Woolf reacted, "I say bunkum. Ladies' clothes and aristocrats playing golf don't affect my style; and they would do his a world of good. . . . What he wants is prestige: what I want, money" (3 *L* 154). Besides flaunting her mercenary intent, Woolf's response suggests that she isn't worried about losing prestige by crossing a cultural divide, and that she is in contact with a more diverse world than Smith, who would benefit from extending himself. Rebecca West praised *Vogue* as "the best of the fashion papers and a guide to the modern movement in the arts." On a more professional tack, she credited its editors with giving a "firmer foundation" to young writers by asking them to write "articles on intelligent subjects at fair prices" (Noble, ed. 111). Perhaps with prestige still at issue, West was pleased to find Woolf asking Todd and Garland about their professional experiences, and listening receptively to their responses at the party they both attended in 1928 (ibid.).

Woolf, West, and Barnes all embraced journalism for income, even if they sometimes set it a notch lower than fiction in their writing priorities. Woolf liked some journalistic tasks better than others. She found it a relief to reduce the time spent on book reviewing, which drops off sharply after 1928. But in 1933 she found time to write a profitable series, "The London Scene," for *Good Housekeeping.* Woolf benefited from working on a variety of projects simultaneously. She composed the lectures for *A Room of One's Own* in 1928, while keeping *The Waves* slowly developing in her mind and moving rapidly through the writing of *Orlando.* During much of that year she struggled with "Phases of Fiction," a project undertaken partially to boost a new series for the Hogarth Press. A curtailed version of this project was sold to the American *Bookman,* a journal to which West was a regular contributor. Excerpts from *A Room of One's Own* went to *Time and Tide,* also a regular site for West's work. Journalism could be restorative or diversionary when the writing of fiction hit a snag—as it did for West in 1928 with *Sunflower.*[22] G. B. Stern assured her that her essays would convince the public of her continued productivity. Barnes had a tendency to rewrite "serious" works over and over again, while she had learned as a young woman to turn out journalism with dispatch. Regular writing for *Vanity Fair, McCall's, Charm,* and the *Theatre Guild Magazine* went on simultaneously with her work on *Ryder* and *Nightwood.*

West, whose contributions to women's magazines spanned six decades and took on various genres, may be of great assistance in reconsidering sixties feminist assumptions about the women's market. Although Gloria Fromm has suggested that West "wrote fiction as a woman addressing women and nonfiction as a man speaking to men; and men were patently more important in her eyes than women" (50), I should like to suggest that she blurred the distinction between male and female audiences. West reported to Dora Marsden, with apparent delight, that she had been given license to change the usual content of a newspaper's women's page to revolutionary effect:

"The Daily Herald" has seduced me into editing the Woman's Page. They are tired of baby clothes, they say and want 'Non[?]-Gospel' talks to women. I fear this means trials for sedition, so I may not long be free. (West letter to Marsden, June 1912, Princeton)

In 1919, West was able to write about the possibilities and limits for women in culture in a supposedly political journal, the *New Republic*. One of a series of essays titled pessimistically and self-reflexively "The World's Worst Failure" describes a central character who is the product of the "system of chic." It is a theme that suggests that West too was interested in the social construction of "charm," discussed earlier in the chapter, and it provides another example of feminine interview/dialogue. The central character of the essay/story is a man-directed woman. In the wake of World War I, she no longer has her husband or her lover. Thus she has to make do for a few days with a professional woman—West's persona, who readily admits to her own flaws as she diagnoses those of her companion.[23] West provided what might seem to be women's topics to other journals with diverse audiences, including essays for the *New York American* on Stella Benson (one of Woolf's cherished correspondents, as noted above) and Ellen Terry. Storm Jameson has hailed West's wartime domestic sketches for the *New Yorker*, a journal which also published her famous trial reportage in the 1940s. Harold Snoad, editor of the *Women's Home Companion*, requested various subjects of West, including "Are You a Happy Woman?" and "Men and Women Who Matter." "The Salt of the Earth," the most popular of the stories from the collection *The Harsh Voice*, was first published in his journal, with its title shifted from her morbid original, "The Murderee." The same story was adapted for a BBC radio production. West analyzed the evolution of modern women for a variety of journals and papers around 1928–1929: the *New York Times*— "Place of Woman in Western Civilization" (selected from a speech to the Fabian Society); *Woman's Journal*—"It Used to Be Unladylike"; *Bookman*—"New Fashions in Feminine Revolt" (part of her "London Letter"); and *Royal Magazine*—"Phases of Modern Womanhood." While West's fiction recurrently delivers fashionably attired members of a wealthy international set, or melodrama as an aspect of romance, she does not inhabit the structures we have come to expect in popular women's works. *The Harsh Voice* and her novel *The Thinking Reed* (both published in the mid-thirties) offer a critique of the male industrialist from the point of view of a commodified but still thinking woman in his life. Her acknowledgment of the Depression was rare in the 1930s fiction cited as typical in women's magazines. Jonathan Cape was eager to market a second collection of West's stories, promising lavish publicity if West would continue in this vein, but readers had to wait until 1992 to get the next new collection, *The Only Poet*. *The Fountain Overflows,* which in 1956 ushered in West's late autobiographical novels, may have appealed to a large female reading audience because of its emphasis on the experience of a talented and visionary family of women, including a musician of international repute. As Victoria Glendinning has recorded, the serial rights in the *Ladies' Home Journal* netted West $35,000.

As noted toward the start of the chapter, Djuna Barnes seems to have felt that a special mask was called for in her contributing certain sorts of work to popular magazines. Works signed "Lydia Steptoe" which appeared in *Vanity Fair* and *Charm*[24] offer a youthful persona, setting her in decadent or privileged places. This scenario parodies her assumed audience while it invites it to achieve self-awareness along with the autobiographical protagonist. In the late 1940s, Barnes's witty definition of *Mademoiselle* magazine for T. S. Eliot is less respectful of a female audience: "It is the middle classes Vogue Harpers Bazaar sort of thing, strictly for the sweet young girl not over seventeen and never likely to be" (Barnes letter to Eliot, 15 Sept. 1949, Maryland). Although Barnes republished some of her periodical writing in *A Book,* she increasingly identified this work as juvenilia—a judgment that may have been influenced by Eliot, who was assembling her collected works for Faber. The works of Lydia Steptoe do award readers, as they offer spirited, performative personas, leaning out of decadence toward self-definition.[25]

The year 1928 welcomed West and Woolf to the relatively new, popular medium of radio. West's relationship with the BBC can be traced to 1927, when they asked her to take part in a "mass telepathy experiment" on the air. No acceptance is recorded.[26] A notable political topic which she broadcast to India in November 1927 was "Women as Legislators." In 1936, West brought Yugoslavia (later the subject of her massive, best-received work, *Black Lamb and Grey Falcon*) to the BBC. She was intent on sensitizing the public to a country that she feared would disappear with the advance of fascism. Her wartime talks were carefully monitored by the Foreign Office.[27] Radio welcomed fanciful topics, such as West's memorable "Biography of a Witch," broadcast in November 1929.[28] West's serious message concerns "persecuting the strange, the unlucky, and all those we do not understand" (ms., BBC Written Archive).[29]

Woolf made her first visit to the BBC with Vita Sackville-West in April 1928, when Vita made her own initial broadcast. By 1929, Vita's new love, Hilda Matheson, had become the first Talks Director for BBC, and was enlisting both Rebecca West and Virginia Woolf for programs, sometimes giving them the option of choosing their subject. Woolf consented to having parts of *Orlando* read.[30] In producing work for the radio, it was necessary to adapt to a popular audience and to accept the judgments of managers more accustomed to the aural medium. Woolf complained to T. S. Eliot that the BBC had "made me castrate" Beau Brummell, and had "at the last moment . . . condemned Dorothy Wordsworth" (4 *L* 111). Her broadcast on "Craftsmanship," delivered in 1937, has become one of Woolf most cited essays. Taking signs in the underground as its initial images, the talk was well grounded in common experience, and effectively gauged for her audience. While they were a long way from the information superhighways of today, Woolf and West did encounter new challenges with language and the media that anticipate postmodern conditions.

Formal Distinctions

By 1928, Woolf, West, and Barnes fit the modernist category of experimentalism. Furthermore, all had participated in the criticism of their unfolding literary age. A few generalizations can be made about what they considered important as literary projects. All three thought of human character as their greatest representational challenge. They were committed to probing the depths, whether of the mind (a favored territory for Woolf), the heart (a focus for Barnes), or the passion for beauty (something frequently cited by West). All studied the impact of social contexts. This follows a tradition of psychological realism identified by May Sinclair's criticism (see chapter 4), whether or not we embrace it as an aspect of feminist modernism.

Despite the cautious reactions of Woolf and Barnes to psychoanalysis,[31] all three women identified psychology as a concern of modern literature. Woolf's "Modern Fiction" draws us to the dark places of psychology. Her "Phases of Fiction" sets up "the psychologists" as the richest category for modern writers. In "The Strange Necessity," the mind of West's critical persona runs from Joyce to Pavlov. West suggested to her publisher, Jonathan Cape, that it should be marketed as "a technical, highbrow book" which was "reviewable really as a book on psychology"

(West to Cape, n.d. [1928], Reading). The interviews of Barnes's *Night-wood* have been compared to psychoanalytic sessions.

In "Hours in a Library," Woolf is not prepared to raise any author to eminence on the basis of form. She seems distressed that form proliferates rather than endures.

> We do not doubt that at the heart of this immense volubility, this flood and foam of language, this irreticence and vulgarity and triviality, there lies the heat of some great passion which only needs the accident of a brain more happily turned than the rest to issue in a shape which will last from age to age. It should be our delight to watch this turmoil, to do battle with the ideas and visions of our own time, to seize what we can use, to kill what we consider worthless, and above all to realise that we must be generous to the people who are giving shape as best they can to the ideas within them. No age of literature is so little submissive to authority as ours, so free from the dominion of the great; none seems so wayward with its gifts of reverence, or so volatile in its experiments. (2 E 59)

Chapter 4 noted Woolf's distrust of the mind behind the new sets of rules for *vers libre,* and her lack of interest in Ezra Pound when Eliot mentioned him in letters. West showed herself able to summarize and even imitate imagism, but not willing to subscribe the *New Freewoman* to its service.

Woolf is well known for the stream of consciousness of *To the Lighthouse, Mrs. Dalloway,* and *A Room of One's Own.* Likewise, West's "The Strange Necessity" uses this much-vaunted modernist technique. But Woolf, West, and Barnes explored connections and differences between people in dialogic patterns that have not received equal attention. In one experiment with critical form that she regarded as unsuccessful, Woolf offered a dialogue between two readers of Joseph Conrad. By 1923, Conrad was becoming an early modernist "classic." Her essay unsettled the singular voice of critical authority, while it suggested that Conrad's texts had ongoing life in readers and their discussions. "Mr Conrad: A Conversation" was published in *Nation & Athenaeum* and reprinted in *The Captain's Death Bed,* but did not appear in the common readers.[32] Woolf begins with a mildly cynical social positioning of a fictional female reader, Penelope Otway. Like Woolf, Penelope has been given the liberty of her father's library, a "method of education" with the advantage that it "spared his purse" (3 E 376). Her limited knowledge qualifies Penelope as an ideal conversationalist on books. That narrator tells us that more education might have stinted her enthusiasm or "diverted less fortunately into the creation of books of her own." This seems both a self-satirical joke about Woolf's books and a critique of patriarchy.

Penelope holds her dialogue with David, who has written to her about Conrad over the years. By offering one female and one male reader, Woolf tempts today's feminist reader to attach gender to their differing observations. David sees Conrad as a romantic, with "a mind of one facet." Penelope is outspoken in response: "Your gimcrack theory is a confection of cobwebs spun while you shave, chiefly with a view to saving yourself the trouble of investigating and possibly admiring, the work of a living contemporary." She is humble enough to share the "cobwebs" metaphor as a description of her own theory (opening the possibility of its serving for all theories), but she is "sure" that Conrad is coping in his works with multiple selves. His novels set the "man of words" against the type of the sea captain, who insists that "the world, the temporal world, rests on a very few simple ideas." She sums this up structurally: "The beauty of surface has always a fibre of morality within" (378). David, who is reluctant throughout to declare Conrad's works "classics," offers some final reservations about Conrad's difference from English traditions, and his lack of intimacy—this deficit owing to "the fact that there are no women in his books" (379). While the female character might have been expected to raise this objection, Woolf instead has Penelope offer a refinement: "There are the ships, the beautiful ships. . . . They are more feminine than his women, who are either mountains of marble or the dreams of a charming boy over the photograph of an actress. But surely a great novel can be made out of a man and a ship, a man and a story, a man and death and dishonour?" (379). Penelope resists David's limited conception of intimacy as dependent upon women. She distributes the feminine in a non-deterministic way. With the repetition of "man," however, she may encourage us to think about "the woman and. . . . "

Woolf records in her *Diary* that she was "slightly dashed" by the reception of this experimental review: "No one has mentioned it. I dont think R[aymond] M[ortimer] or [Francis] B[irrell] quite approved" (3 E 379n). She then has a series of reactions. The first are self-confirming and constructive: "To be dashed is always the most bracing treatment for me." It helps prepare for beginning a book, and she begins again on *The Common Reader*. Her dashing makes her say "I write to please myself." It makes her "more definite & outspoken in my style." Woolf had a comparable response to Wyndham Lewis's assault on her in *Men without Art*, as noted in chapter 6. But in the case of the "Conrad adventure," Woolf is backing off, having learned from it that "characters are to be merely views: personality must be avoided at all costs. . . . Directly you specify hair, age, &c something frivolous, or irrelevant, gets into the book." She is going to "curtail" the use of fictional character for criticism. If she is to supply characters only as "views," is she not going against the rich sense of character she demands in her fiction? Does situating views in characters of different sexes lend to the lamented distraction? An unfortunate effect of the implied disapproval of two men is that conditions of gender are suppressed, perhaps reducing the possibility that she will fulfill her own goal in this project of "answering certain questions about ourselves" (379–80). Or perhaps she was only warming up for *A Room of One's Own*. Woolf resists making the conversation a competition or a lover's quarrel, which would be the more likely outcome for Wells or Lawrence.

The conversation was to prove one of Djuna Barnes's most successful forms, particularly in *Nightwood*, where she moved from long storytelling monologs to the revealing dialogue between the equally troubled Nora Flood and the usual monologist, Dr. Matthew O'Connor. The technique could well have derived from the many interviews she conducted for her early journalism. Her article on the policewoman Mrs. O'Grady, cited in chapter 3, is highly interactive, with her subject making observations on the interviewer's preoccupations. Mary Lynn Broe has suggested that in "The Confessions of Helen Westley" Barnes deconstructs the "masculine economy of the interviewer who always reserves comment," disrupting "the power lines of the interview format" (Scott, ed. 24). The interview begins with a summons on the telephone from the interviewee. Westley arrives at the Brevoort Hotel, equipped with a secondhand book, used by both to stage their discussion: "She takes the seat before me, shaking her earrings and thrusting the book upon the table. It is Murray's *History of Greek Literature*, and she knows it looks well" (40).[33] Barnes's youthful persona, as interviewer, evokes Westley's remarks about her sense of her own beauty: "A secondhand book is like a person who has traveled; it is only when a book has been handled by several persons and has become dirty that it's fit for contemplation. . . . Ah, to be young and beautiful! Now I am beautiful and you are young; I can never again be what you are, and you in all probability will never be what I am" (40). Through the remainder of the interview, the Barnes persona paces and elicits, knowing much of the story already, and timing it so as to make the interview cooperative and suggestive. One of its most enticing parts concerns a snake, which is something to be observed at the right point in life, something that calls for being Baudelairian and Wildeish. Westley observes:

> "Well, I should advise young, aspiring women to live their lives first, to get through with their emotional training soon, and to do their thinking and reading. Then, afterward, comes the time for calm, unemotional observation—a snake—"
> "A little too early for the snake, I think."
> "No; by all means, let the snake enter here. . . . " (41)

We experience the pacing of life and the pacing of interview combined. The two women eventually break out laughing over their mutual definition of the "vampire": "She burst out laughing. 'We are a funny couple to be sitting here talking a lot of nonsense, aren't we?' " (44). But Barnes won't let her stop, moving their creation to a practical textual level, all the more poignant for a previous discussion of poverty: "I have at least three pages more to fill" (44). The dialog is one of mutual mockery, admiration performance, and empowerment in difference.

Dialogs are also critical to West's writing. This is true of *Harriet Hume,* where the same couple has dialogs throughout their lifetime; in the short stories of *The Harsh Voice,* one of them named "There Is No Conversation"; and in *Black Lamb and Grey Falcon,* in which the dialogs of a wife with her husband gradually clarify impressions of history and culture in Yugoslavia. The problem of genuine dialog troubled West, as is clear in "There Is No Conversation." It opens:

> There is no such thing as conversation. It is an illusion. There are intersecting monologues, that is all. We speak; we spread round us with sounds, with words, and emanation from ourselves. Sometimes they overlap the circles that others are spreading around themselves. Then they are affected by those other circles, to be sure, but not because of any real communication that has taken place, merely as a scarf of blue chiffon lying on a woman's dressing-table will change colour if she casts down on it a scarf of red chiffon. (63)

The Harsh Voice is full of disastrous dialogs, of various constitution. Yet it is in failure that West often identifies a structure to contend with, or a personal aspiration. The business of "There Is No Communication" is to bring two professional women into meaningful contact.

I have taken 1928 as a high point for the women of modernism. It was not only a time of varied, innovative, and profitable literary production. By 1928, Woolf, West, and Barnes were not solitary women writing in isolated sitting rooms. Looked at together, they suggest the importance of different projects from those derived from famous male modernists, and they encourage us to take a fuller inventory of where even the men sought publication. Woolf, West, and Barnes all feature women characters as participants in dialogues, and use their personas in dismantling cultural assumptions about feminine chic and charm, moving their female audience to other expectations. By identifying as female professionals, they gained experienced consultants to field their complaints and review their strategies with the literary marketplace and the critical establishment. They could appreciate and feel appreciated. Rebecca West—still an active professional into the 1980s—expressed the following, as a survivor who probably missed her company of 1928:

> If one is a woman writer there are certain things one must do—first not be too good; second, die young, what an edge Katherine Mansfield has on all of us, third, commit suicide like Virginia Woolf, to go on writing and writing well just can't be forgiven.
> (West letter to Arling, 11 Mar. 1952, Yale)

Indeed, the women of 1928 cry out not for individual commemoration but for professional connection. The final chapter of this book studies a critical issue of their day and ours that did bring Woolf, West, and Barnes together intellectually—lesbian representation.

12 Rallying round *The Well of Loneliness*

> You've got work to do—come and do it! Why, just because you are what you are, you may actually find that you've got an advantage. You may write with a curious double insight—write both men and women from a personal knowledge.
>
> —Hall, *The Well of Loneliness* 205

In 1928 the literary world, including Virginia Woolf, Rebecca West, and Djuna Barnes, focused on the obscenity trial of Radclyffe Hall's lesbian novel *The Well of Loneliness*. This event opened to discussion aspects of sexuality of central importance to feminism, making its date a watershed in cultural history. For some time, the courts in Britain and the U.S. had been occupied with obscenity cases. To avoid prosecution, editors, publishers, and even authors often suppressed vulnerable material before publication, or withdrew works that met resistance. We have already encountered Djuna Barnes's protests to Natalie Barney over having to remove chamberpots from *Ryder*. The many delays in the 1914 publication of Joyce's *Dubliners* (which has implicit homosexual content), the 1915 suppression of D. H. Lawrence's *The Rainbow* (which has a lesbian interlude), and the 1921 obscenity trial of Margaret Anderson and Jane Heap for publishing the "Nausicaa" episode of *Ulysses* in the *Little Review,* demonstrate the potential of even heterosexual, as well as lesbian and gay, subject matter to cause alarm. *Lady Chatterley's Lover,* published privately in Florence in 1928 to avoid prosecution, had its British obscenity trial in 1960, with Rebecca West serving as one of its successful defenders.

Obscenity defenses did not necessarily mean toleration of lesbianism at the start of the 1920s. One of the less explored aspects of the celebrated *Ulysses* trial is the homophobic reaction of the defense attorney, John Quinn, to the lesbianism of the *Little Review* editors. Quinn, whose picture with the "men of 1914" is often reproduced in canonical modernist studies, complained to Pound about defending these women. "I have no interest at all in defending people who are stupidly and brazenly and

Plate 21. Radclyffe Hall, 1928.

From Vera Brittain,

Radclyffe Hall: A Case of Obscenity?

Sapphoistically and pederastically and urinally, and menstrually violate [*sic*] the law, and think they are courageous. . . . The bugger and the Lesbian constantly think in terms of suits and defenses" (Quinn letter to Pound, 16 Oct. 1920, Northwestern University). James Joyce and Rebecca West were just as capable of lawsuits. But Quinn's charge has little to do with demonstrable facts. It would be fascinating to know Barnes's version of the trial, given to Joyce in Paris. Barnes's lesbian link to Jane Heap is unlikely to have been mentioned.

The Well of Loneliness was published in England by Jonathan Cape in July 1928. In August, James Douglas in his review of *The Well* in the *Sunday Express* found lesbianism an "undiscussable subject" and said that he would "rather give a healthy boy or a healthy girl a phial of prussic acid than this novel" (Brittain, *Radclyffe Hall* 16, 55). Douglas called upon the publisher to withdraw the book. An immediate consequence was that its first printing sold out. Cape submitted the novel to Home Secretary Sir William Joynson-Hicks, offering to withdraw it if he considered the book a mistake. It is notable that Cape did not clear this course of action with the book's author. This failure to consult Hall was questioned by one of the trial's closest observers, Vera Brittain, whom we have identified as one of Rebecca West's colleagues at *Time and Tide*. Brittain wrote a positive review of *The Well* for the journal, which also published a long series of letters concerning the trial as it progressed.[1] Cape was forced to withdraw the book when, predictably, Joynson-Hicks found it obscene, but Cape immediately took steps to have *The Well* published in France.

Led by E. M. Forster, a long list of writers were ready to defend *The Well of Loneliness,* first in a petition and later in court.[2] As his dealings on the subject with Virginia Woolf reveal, Forster's support was greatly complicated by his sense of power as a literary man and his own insecurities as a homosexual. Woolf's diary records his difficulties with Hall's personal defense of her work. Visiting with the Woolfs in late August, Forster reports that Hall "screamed like a herring gull, mad with egotism & vanity. Unless they say her book is good, she wont let them complain of the laws." But Woolf also records Forster's attitudes toward lesbianism, revealed during an evening of heavy drinking. He reported that Dr. Head could "convert" lesbians. Put to the test by Leonard Woolf, Forster admitted he would not want his own homosexuality converted. One reason he gave for his distaste for lesbians was disliking that "women should be independent of men" (3 *D* 193). Woolf's record is remarkably matter-of-fact when we consider that Dr. Henry Head was a neurologist consulted by the Woolfs at Roger Fry's recommendation during her 1913 illness, and further that Woolf's lesbian attraction to Vita Sackville-West was reaching a critical stage at this very time. Woolf was coping with Vita's other lesbian loves, she was composing her imaginative "biography" *Orlando,* and she would go off alone with Sackville-West for a week's holiday within the month.

Still, Virginia Woolf and Forster wrote a joint letter to the editor of the *Nation & Athenaeum* in which they playfully quibbled with authority. They inquired into the nature of the ban on a subject matter that "exists as a fact among the many other facts of life . . . recognized by science and recognizable in history," though they minimized its presence in a manner that would be challenged today. They were matter-of-fact and detached about the negative reception of lesbianism, offering a very modest estimate of its occurrence and impact: "It enters personally into very few lives, and is uninteresting or repellent to the majority."[3] Defiantly seeking a loophole while simultaneously threatening to make more work for the presumptuous judge, they ask if novelists might "mention it incidentally? Although it is forbidden as a main theme, may it be alluded to, or ascribed to subsidiary characters? Perhaps the Home Secretary will issue further orders on this point" (*Nation & Athenaeum,* 8 Sept. 1928). More ominously, they alerted readers to other themes that might be rendered taboo—birth control, suicide, and pacifism. Their serious intellectual objection was to the obstacle posed to the "free mind" which both of them considered essential in producing great literature. "The free mind has access to all the knowledge and speculation of its age." This statement and the episode in general are indications of Woolf's engagement with political controversy and the foment of ideas.

When *The Well of Loneliness* went to trial in November, Virginia and Leonard Woolf were in attendance. As Woolf records on the day of the trial, the literary people, booksellers, medical professionals, and professors who went to court willing to testify (the Woolfs included) were not allowed to make judgment on obscenity or literary merit.[4] The distinctions made between literature and obscenity, subject and treatment fascinated Woolf.[5] She decided that "in these banks runs a live stream" (3 D 207)—a statement that leaves much to interpretation. Are the "banks" the court, and the stream its handling of language? Or do taxonomies—designations such as "obscene"—shut in her "living stream"? Considering

Woolf's capacity for satirizing authority, even in Mrs. Ramsay's anticipation of little James, wigged and gowned as a judge in *To the Lighthouse,* it is interesting that Woolf does not glibly dismiss the whole exercise.

Woolf's personal contact with Radclyffe Hall was slight. They had a brief conversation concerning costs on the day she attended the trial. Woolf describes "John," as Hall preferred to be called, as "lemon yellow, tough, stringy, exacerbated." To Hall's partner, Una Troubridge, there was a stronger connection. They had last met as children at a party, their families connected by friendship through Woolf's great-aunt Julia Cameron. The Woolfs, not realizing that there was no personal defendant in the case, offered to post bail for Hall should it be necessary, according to Brittain's account (*Radclyffe Hall* 90).

During the 1920s, Hall and Troubridge also were familiar with both Rebecca West and Djuna Barnes. West and Hall were thrown together by their mounting celebrity. They met at the home of *Sunday Times* editor Leonard Rees sometime after the publication of Hall's *The Unlit Lamp* in 1924 (Dickson 112). West was the dinner guest of Hall and Troubridge at their Georgian-style house on Holland Road, participating in lively literary conversation.[6] The list of books published by Cape in 1928 also included Rebecca West's *The Strange Necessity.*

When West wrote about the trial, she argued for the value of freedom, as had Woolf and Forster, making a bit more of "discussion," while Woolf and Forster had talked about a more insular "mind." West went into far more detail in characterizing homosexuality, and both her tone of authority and her opinions are currently more vulnerable to attack. West's greater interest in preserving the institution of law is evident in a pair of essays. In "A Jixless Errand," written for *Time and Tide* in March 1929, West is more respectful of the Home Secretary than were the mischievous Woolf and Forster. West gives Joynson-Hicks (nicknamed Jix) past credit for respect shown to freedom of political and religious expression. But West faults him for placing sexual matters in a separate, less free category.

West's cultural history of homosexuality does not let homosexuals off easily. She goes back to the trial of Oscar Wilde and the martyrdom he achieved.[7] West's life-centered philosophy is consistently opposed to martyrdom. "In no time homosexuality was given a status as a form of revolt against the Philistine decrepit; and to-day we have an army of young prigs who are as self-righteous about their abnormalities as missionaries who volunteer for Africa in pious mid-Victorian novels" (284). Showing her familiarity with Freud's theories of homosexuality, West presents the viewpoint of unidentified "psychologists" that "the homosexual is not a fixed type, but a person like any other who has for some psychic reasons failed to develop past a stage, common to the immaturity of everybody, when he prefers the companionship of his own sex. He is doing nothing unthinkably abominable, and nothing heroic." But "the sooner he stops doing it the better" (284). She does not say, the better for whom. In denying the "fixed" category, West ignores the category of "sexual inversion" as an "inborn constitutional abnormality" introduced by Havelock Ellis (1) and still supported in recent studies that suggest that at least 10 percent of the population is inherently homosexual. Given the association of Ellis's lesbian wife, Edith Lees, with the *New Freewoman* and the fact that Ellis provided a preface to *The Well*, West might be expected to have encountered the "inversion" theory. Edward Carpenter may have fulfilled her own category of homosexual "prig." As noted in chapter 3, he was one of the figures she found most uncongenial at the *New Freewoman*.

West's basic argument is for access to accurate psychological and literary representations of homosexuality, so that "frank discussion" can occur. In her article she writes more to those who would suppress *The Well* than to the converted, presenting ways that censorship backfires. Suppression has produced in Radclyffe Hall "a handsome, distinguished, and estimable martyr for the female branch of the movement," and West suggests that a work that might have had a life of three months was guaranteed thirty years. West finds *The Well*'s publisher (who is her own) blameless for bringing out the book. She is clearly sympathetic with the content of the book and its plea for victims of homophobia: "It was written without the use of an indecorous word or phrase, it had the command on sympathy which belongs to a plea for the persecuted, and it was, in view of the state of ignorance regarding the real facts of homosexuality which prudery has maintained, not an unfair statement of the case" (285).

In another article addressed to her American audience, West brings up additional angles of discussion, including the character of the author and questions of literary quality. Radclyffe Hall is described as having "a kind of austere, workmanly handsomeness which makes one think of a very beautifully made sporting rifle or golf club. . . . She has all the virtues of the English aristocratic type, courage, self-restraint, steadfastness, and a very fine intelligence which . . . likes to exercise itself on eccentric material" (*Ending in Earnest* 6–7). "Eccentric" behavior is something we come to expect from an aristocrat; applied to selecting lesbian sexuality as a subject matter, "eccentric" seems reductive. A more sympathetic reading might have considered the selection bold, culturally significant, experimental, or creative. There is perhaps some room for seeing this usage of "eccentric" as decentered. The "aristocratic" label, which was appropriate to Hall's class and that of the protagonist of *The Well*, has some bearing upon the privileged status of members of the Barney circle, whose welcoming of Hall is echoed in *The Well*.

Taking on the point of view of those who signed a petition in favor of the publication of *The Well*, "which included practically every writer of standing, some of them high in academic respectability," West reports that most would have preferred to back a book of more imaginative value (*Ending in Earnest* 9). In this, she could well be representing Forster. West finds Hall's work sincere rather than creative, comparing it to "the earnest novels Miss Elizabeth Robins wrote in the 'nineties." Woolf's treatment of Robins, noted in chapter 3, engages in the same sort of dated dismissal. West also objects that the book is written sentimentally, to produce emotions in readers—something that she had faulted *Ulysses* for in "The Strange Necessity."

West favors making *The Well* accessible to adult readers, which she thinks would have been the result of its being marketed at the intended fifteen-shilling price by Cape. She joins a concerned mother who wrote to *Time and Tide* protesting the press coverage occasioned by the trial, which increased awareness of the book and lesbianism. West suggests that *The Well* probably would not have interested sophisticated adolescents had it not been so publicized. Via cheap, accessible media, lesbianism reached impressionable children, and not just the audience of "wondering adults" she deems appropriate (10–11). West's remarks suggest familiarity with the nature of obscenity law in England at the time. Rather than define "obscene," or concern itself with aesthetic quality, authorial intention, or the average, reasonable reader, the law protected a susceptible audience.[8]

The Well of Loneliness was largely composed and half of it is set in Paris, in the very milieu frequented and written about in *Ladies Almanack* by Djuna Barnes. Hall and Troubridge first visited the city in 1921 and were made welcome there by Natalie Barney at 20, rue Jacob. Barney's open avowal of lesbianism had come in *Pensées d'une Amazone*, published in 1920. The "Temple à l'Amitié" in the back garden was the focus for feminine associations and rituals, starting with antiwar gatherings held there in 1917. The rites of Sappho were introduced by Renée Vivien. As contrasted to other lesbians of the day, including Hall, Barney's society made lesbian practices normative. There was no need for expressions of guilt or the assumption of masks and codes. Shari Benstock suggests that Barney's lesbian aesthetic recuperated the pre-Raphaelite image of woman, severing it from cultural misogyny and celebrating feminine beauty (303). This seems particularly true of surviving photographs of Barney. Both Hall and Barnes would provide their different versions of Barney in their works of 1928, each opening out the discussion of lesbian sexuality in her own way. Hall's Barney character, Valerie Seymour, is unusual for having "created an atmosphere of courage" where storm-tossed victims may take refuge.

Hall's metaphors and plot develop an interpretation of the lesbian as victim and deviant—the "invert" hypothesized by Havelock Ellis, who was Hall's friend and the author of the introduction to the novel. Hall can be credited with attempting to arouse sympathy and create understanding for the cultural plight of lesbians. She is not a sparing crafter of sentences, as were Woolf and Barnes. This is shown in the first page, describing the ancestral home of her wealthy female protagonist, and the last, recording Stephen's acceptance of almost religious martyrdom. Particularly in portraying the lonely lesbian's relationships with horses and dogs, Hall seems to solicit the emotions of her readers in a way that Barnes never would, despite many interactions of humans with animals. Still, Hall's realistic style can be valued for its accessibility to a heterosexual middle-class audience whose attitudes she wished to change. She did this by involving them in the life story of Stephen Gordon, a talented, athletic girl who was born different, as only her father (a reader of Krafft-Ebing) and Miss Puddleton (her Oxford-trained tutor and a closeted lesbian) recognized. A second audience was the guilty and voiceless "inverts" whose suffering might be reduced through her efforts. One reason that Stephen suffers is that she is never told that the "invert" exists. Hence, contrary to West's analysis, Hall might very well have wanted young women, and not just inquiring adults, to have her book.

Hall ultimately offers a problematic, inconsistent view of lesbianism (see Lanser in Broe, ed. 166). For the presumed good of her youthful partner, Mary, whom she met while serving in the ambulance corps in World War I, Stephen pretends to be involved with Valerie Seymour. This prompts Mary to flee to Martin Hallam, Stephen's friend from her own youth, whose transformation into her lover had terminated the relationship for Stephen. Stephen sets aside her own rejection of this mate and the theory of inversion that suggests the unlikelihood of Mary's experiencing heterosexual love. That Mary was bisexual is another possibility. This marriage plot is only the last in Stephen's series of moves to protect Mary from prejudice and loneliness, much as the father or husband in patriarchy protects a presumed weaker female. Stephen's own father had acknowledged the improbability of her ever marrying; Miss Puddleton had aimed Stephen at a future enhanced by her own achievements. Stephen treats Mary more trivially.

The novel closes with an extraordinary passage that confronts both the essentialist needs of Stephen's dissatisfied womb and the invert's place in God's creation—a problem involving both guilt and indignation that concerns Stephen throughout the work. In her moment of self-sacrifice, Stephen is visited by the ghostly presence of the lesbian "strangers" she has come to know in Paris, "terrible ones . . . pointing at her with their shaking, white-skinned, effeminate fingers" in accusation. They take possession of her "barren womb," making it "fruitful," and her commanding voice. She ends voicing a plea to a legalistic, patriarchal God: "Acknowledge us, Oh God, before the whole world. Give us the right to our existence" (437).

We do not have any direct statement on *The Well of Loneliness* from Djuna Barnes. *Ladies Almanack* is her fictional alternative. Privately published, and sold largely by her friends in the streets of Paris, this work escaped the censors by its very mode of production. *Ladies Almanack* assembles the women of Barney's salon to engage in self-mocking internal debates—a tradition going back to Margaret Cavendish's seventeenth-century "Female Orations." The women of the *Almanack* participate in mythic improbabilities, such as all-female reproduction and the elevation of the immortal tongue of Dame Musset, which survived cremation. Year and life cycles provide a scaffolding for the book, which lacks a conventional plot. The chapters vary in length and manner, sometimes dispensing with characters altogether. Thus this work depends upon far less conventional processes of involving readers than does Hall's bildungsroman. Natalie Barney considered the work one of her lasting treasures, writing appreciatively of it in her final years, and urging republication, which finally did occur in 1972. Feminist debates about this work remain spirited and divided as to whether Barnes's work is lesbian celebration, lesbian betrayal, or verbal showpiece.[9] Karla Jay suggests that "the pity Hall hoped to evoke from the public in her novel is totally lacking in Barnes' cruel satire of her" ("The Outsider" 190). But pity may be less important than diverse discussion of the "undiscussable" subject. Barnes's work encourages debate within lesbianism to an extent that is not realized in Hall's.

Radclyffe Hall and Una Troubridge make a relatively short appearance in *Ladies Almanack,* evoked in "two British Women" who come forward at the start of March. Barnes preserves the essentials of their costumes— Troubridge's monocle and Hall's hat—often mentioned in accounts of the trial and cited in feminist analyses as the most notable item in the crossdressed, "mannish lesbian" look that she helped to turn into a cultural myth (see Newton):

> One was called Lady Buck-and-Balk, and the other plain Tilly-Tweed-In Blood. Lady Buck-and-Balk sported a Monocle and believed in Spirits. Tilly-Tweed-In-Blood sported a Stetson, and believed in Marriage. (18)

The women's proposals, like *The Well,* begin with an accent on English morals. They advocate marriage to sanction sexuality, avoid fornication, and provide security. Their arrangement provides for alimony should the relationship fail. The proposed lesbian marriage respects church and certificate, and appeals to judges and the House of Lords. The patriarchal conventionality of their marital and moral assumptions is a target in the debate. In Hall's defense, the long-term, legally sanctioned aspect of their plan survives in today's efforts to gain partner benefits from employers. The theme of marriage is important to *The Well.* The fact that Stephen could not offer marriage as security to her first love, Angela Crossby, was offered by Angela as the issue on which their relationship foundered. There is also an idealized marriage scene where two lesbians help celebrate the nuptials of one of Stephen's Parisian house staff.

The diverse representatives of lesbianism present in Dame Musset's establishment provide alternatives to the marital scheme of Lady Buck and Tilly-Tweed. Barnes's own character for Natalie Barney, Dame Musset, militantly suggests a duel between the dissatisfied lovers. Masie Tuck-and-Frill is more interested in problematizing love, along gendered lines:

> Love in Man is Fear of Fear. Love in Woman is Hope without Hope.
> Man fears all that can be taken from him, a Woman's Love includest that, and then Lies down beside it. A Man's love is built to fit Nature. Woman's is a Kiss in the Mirror. (23)

Masie has a wit with words, typically offering aphorisms and gendered juxtapositions. These were favorite stylistics of Barnes in her most concise writing. Masie also has formal resonance with Barney, whose *pensées* were epigrammatic.[10] Other interests and styles emerge in different situations. Bounding Bess does not particularly interest Musset, who considers her a "pedant," but she has a historical project that bears comparison to *Orlando* and *A Room of One's Own,* and a style suggestive of Rebecca West: "She was grand at History, and nothing short of magnificent at Concentration," and lectures on Catherine of Russia, Sappho, and the Destiny of Nations (32–33).[11]

Barnes's view of Barney is not so feminine as Shari Benstock's pre-Raphaelite image. As noted in chapter 4, Barnes's letters to Barney often bore as their salutation "Dear Dark Horse." She is the Amazon on horseback, enjoying the hunt and suggesting the duel. In the November illustration, she wears a military coat and poses as "wisdom" with her boot on the neck of "woman conquered." But that pose is quickly undermined. Musset, with the womanly wisdom of age fifty, "sat on the thorn of a Hedgerow (and never the wiser) that she might save a girl or so before she had wallowed in Love's rich welter, or troughed a mouthful at the Tarn of temptation." She cannot get a single girl to listen, though she has three encounters, in folktale form, with rural maidens. In this chapter, there is despair of any real threading the maze, to escape from human folly. Musset is the lesbian Ariadne, with added elements of Penelope:

> It is a Maze, nor will we have a way out of it, though we know of long that way. Much turning of the Spindle thins out the Thread of Despair, and much leaping of the Shuttle threads Trouble to a Purpose, yet we will none of it, and step the Treadle without Aim, and cast the Shuttle without food, and weave the air into a Mantle of Sickness. (58)

Barney's appropriation of Greek traditions, including the reconstructed work of Sappho at her temple in the garden, is overlaid by Barnes's interest in biblical materials, creating an element of the pope, or "a Monk in Holy Orders, in some Country too old for Tradition" (34), and finally a mourned saint, as another aspect of Musset.

Musset also encourages thinking about the erotics of the female body. Karla Jay has faulted her for claiming a clitoris that is similar but not equal to the penis, in the tradition of early sexology ("The Outsider" 187). Susan Lanser more optimistically substitutes Musset's cremation-proof tongue as a triumphant instrument of oral sexuality (189). The August chapter, which lacks an identified speaker, mocks the very discussion of lack:

> Some have it that they cannot do, have, be, think, act, get, give, go, come, right in anyway. Others that they cannot do, have, be, think, act, get, give, go wrong in any way, others set them between two Stools saying that they can, yet cannot, that they have and have not, that they think yet think nothing, that they give and yet take. . . . (48)

Musset's concupiscence for women's attractions builds to a glorious catalogue of beautiful female physicality, if we are willing to accept her memories of the best aspects of her many loves (65). Barnes challenges many lesbian visions, as Jay suggests, but she expands the field of possibilities, making simple definition or dismissal equally impossible.[12]

In *Orlando*, Woolf would negotiate her own lesbian sexuality with a fantasy biography celebrating the woman she loved, Vita Sackville-West. The novel offers the return of Knole, the family home denied Vita by male primogeniture in 1928, and a more experimental conception of Sackville-West's own poem "The Land," making it "centrally transparent" in ways that Sackville-West could not. Woolf's strategy for lesbian writing beyond the text spared Hogarth Press the incursion of the censors. Participation in lesbian relationships is virtually absent from the work, though implicit in its existence and its photographs. Rebecca West was greatly amused by the scandal in the Foreign Office over the appearance of Mrs. Harold Nicolson's photographs in the book. "Surely this is as funny as anything officialdom has done for years!" (West letter to Ratcliffe, n.d., Yale). It is notable that the photographs have been left out of several later editions. The lesbian subject is evident in its early conception, shared and approved by Sackville-West: "Suppose Orlando turns out to be Vita; and it's all about you and the lusts of your flesh and the lure of your mind (heart you have none, who go gallivanting down the lanes with Campbell)" (3 L 428–29).[13] For Sackville-West, as contrasted to Hall and Troubridge, monogamy was not the rule. A lesbian plot closer to Hall's might have resulted from the March 1927 plan of "Jessamy Brides" recorded in Woolf's *Diary:* "Two women, poor, solitary at the top of a house" resembling "the ladies of Llangollen" in which "Sapphism is to be suggested" (3 D 131).[14] Even in that early version, capacities of fantasy, rather than constraints of the social system, were anticipated, allowing one to "see anything," from Constantinople to Tower Bridge. Woolf's book is as un-

Plate 22. Vita Sackville-West.

From Virginia Woolf, *Orlando*.

conventional as Barnes's, possessed of characters but not of plot, moving into the fantastic yet relating to real people and literary forms, spoofing constantly but with serious intent. She celebrates the capacity of the woman she loves to triumph over cultural obstacles, rather than offering a cautionary tale about the problems of their lesbian love. Thus it seems appropriate that Rebecca West hailed *Orlando* not as a well of despair but as a "fountain of genius" (Scott, ed. 592).

In its own disarming way, *Orlando* makes a case for a more open discussion of sexuality and the abandonment of male accounts of female intellect and relationship. Orlando, by changing sex, visiting Eastern and gypsy cultures, and living through numerous historical periods, experiences sexuality vividly and comically as a social construct, while Hall's hero experiences her sexuality as a tragedy. Newly turned a woman, and in response to being run through by Pope's pen in his "Characters of Women," Orlando briefly resumes the clothing she had worn as a young man of fashion. She plays the gallant in meeting with a young prostitute with a head "of the most exquisite shapeliness." Her "feeling her hanging lightly yet like a suppliant on her arm, roused in Orlando all the feelings which become a man" (216–17). Woolf encourages us to think of multiple responses—possession of power over money, as well as erotic response. Woolf does not proceed to a love scene between a mannish lesbian and a feminine suppliant. Orlando decides that the prostitute's gestures are "put on to gratify her masculinity" (217). When Orlando's sex is revealed, affectations of speech and gesture can be dropped, and a new society of vivid discussion with the same sex is opened, in defiance of male stereotypes of women together.

Orlando offers various views of heterosexual love and its consequences. The young Orlando, who eschews conventional female marriage prospects in favor of the boyish and exotic Sasha, is betrayed in a political intrigue he cannot fathom. In Shelmardine, the female Orlando finds a frequently absent yet restorative husband, with a feminine inner self. "Shel" is accommodated in the loveliest of wave and bird metaphors—a far cry from the usual modernist metaphors of masculinity. As a result of their union, Orlando has the easiest childbirth in literature and is never tied essentialistically to maternity.

It is difficult to classify the amorous approaches of the Archduchess Harriet/Archduke Harry, cross-dressed or dressed to make a heterosexual match to Orlando's sex of the moment. In the first instance, the young male Orlando's enjoyment comes from discussions of the hunt and armor, topics for which Harriet, as a man, is prepared. Orlando responds to the disguised male's homosexual touch on his leg. Yet the false Harriet elicits a harpy, a foul face of lust, where love had seemed to flutter, and consequently Orlando flees in fear. The female Orlando has no sexual response to Harry when he offers his courtship. She uses a dead fly and a live toad to dispose of this would-be lover, who all too often takes on the role of a stalker. If s/he offers any sort of cautionary tale in this instance, it is to be certain that one's advances are wanted, regardless of the underlying dynamic of sex. Her use of fly and toad shows the difficulty of finding female strategies for dismissing men in polite society.

In *Orlando,* Woolf also dispatches the vision of woman offered by a male modernist in 1928—Lawrence's Lady Chatterley: "Surely, since she is a woman, and a beautiful woman, she will soon give over this pretence of writing and begin to think, at least of a gamekeeper (and as long as she thinks of a man, nobody objects to a woman thinking)" (268).

By rallying Woolf, West, and Barnes around *The Well of Loneliness,* we can appreciate the importance of sexuality as a subject matter for modernism, collecting a variety of useful attachments to the subject of lesbianism, with Barnes and Woolf playing around their own lesbian identifications. Miss Puddleton, Stephen Gordon's wise instructor in *The Well,* consoles her after Stephen comes across Krafft-Ebing in her recently deceased father's desk, interpreting for the first time her "inversion" as a mark of Cain:

> You've got work to do—come and do it! Why, just because you are what you are, you may actually find that you've got an advantage. You may write with a curious double insight—write both men and women from a personal knowledge. (205)

One of the most upbeat and most neglected characters of Hall's novel, "Puddle" might be dictating the design of *Orlando.* Rebecca West interpreted the merits of *Orlando* in a similar vein: "She is debating . . . how far one's sex is like a pair of faulty glasses on one's nose; where one looks at the universe, how true it is that to be a woman is to have a blind spot on the North Northwest, to be a man is to see light as darkness East by South" (595). Barnes achieves something comparable in the intermediate role of Dr. O'Connor, the male "invert" of *Nightwood,* who made his first appearance in Barnes's *Ryder* in 1928.

The case of *The Well of Loneliness* brought Woolf, West, and Barnes into a confrontation with the legal system, the shaping and limiting force of cultural institutions upon the "free" expression in art, and the sufferings of people marked by sexual difference from the heterosexual "norm." In the face of this, they grew playful. West positioned herself between judges who could and should be chided on their record of censorship and a group who had suffered from a lack of discussion and hence a lack of understanding, but she also challenged martyrdom as a personal strategy.[15] Woolf went to court and to the press, showing her capacity for activism, while she wrote her way through her own expression of lesbian love. Rather than rewriting the heterosexual marital script as a solution to lesbian persecution and loneliness, Barnes part-recorded, part-fantasized an energetic lesbian group capable of diverse expression, including gossip, self-satire, and the parody of religious and literary forms.

By 1928—a signal year for female modernist achievement—Woolf, West, and Barnes had become accomplished literary strategists. In the work that they brought to *The Well of Loneliness,* there are numerous achievements. One is a gauging of social institutions. They coped with legal structures to work around the censor, while simultaneously putting into question his authority. They anticipated different audiences, providing texts that could be read more or less personally. Genre structures also yielded to multiplication and combination, suitable to the complex perspectives pursued. Epigrammatic wit remained a primary weapon. They were passionate about discussion, particularly among women. This led to their most intimate and supportive attachments to one another.

Notes

Introduction

1. In *Writing beyond the Ending*, Rachel Blau DuPlessis places women's arti-
    sanal works at the center of an emerging feminine domestic aesthetic. This
    serves as a replacement for traditional patriarchal narratives which end in
    the marriage or death of the heroine. For a comprehensive summary of the
    feminist celebration of domestic arts by figures such as Judy Chicago, Alice
    Walker, Mary Daly, Robin Morgan, and Adrienne Rich, see Elaine Hedges's
    "The Needle or the Pen." She also offers a counter, antidomestic tradition,
    suggested in works by Genevieve Taggart, Edna St. Vincent Millay, and
    Sylvia Plath.

2. See Rabinowitz for a critique of readings that attend to figurative lan-
    guage, to the expense of more direct, realistic forms of writing, and aware-
    ness of the effects of history. He argues that close reading techniques, used
    in feminist as well as new critical theory, favor the canonization of works
    with complex figurative language, citing Woolf and Joyce as examples.
    While this study attends to modernist complexity, it grounds works in ev-
    eryday conditions and in history.

3. Jane Marcus, one of Hartman's critics, also uses the web as a model for
    feminist practice. She says of Procne, "The reading of the weaving is a
    model for a contemporary socialist feminist criticism. It gives us an aesthet-
    ics of political commitment to offer in place of current theories based on
    psychology or in formalism" (*Art and Anger* 215). Marcus's critique of
    Hartman for finding a universal story that "the truth will out" instead of a
    case of sorority and revenge for rape is in her essay "Liberty, Sorority, Mi-
    sogyny," in *Virginia Woolf and the Languages of Patriarchy*, 75–95.

4. Miller's essay begins by analyzing Roland Barthe's evocation of the text as
    "hyphology" or "the tissue and the spider's web" where he imagines the
    subject "dissolving in the constructive secretions of [her] web" (Miller
    270), a model which Miller finds erasing the "productive agency of the sub-
    ject" (271). See n. 3 (289) for her summary of Freud's version of weaving in
    his essay "Femininity."

5. West would later name one of her novels *The Fountain Overflows*, borrow-
    ing from William Blake's *Proverbs of Heaven and Hell*, and choosing the an-
    tithesis of "the cistern contains."

6. The pairing of tides and towers works nearly as well as the web in the scaf-
    folding as an enabling metaphor for this study. All of these women were

readers or contributors to the postsuffragist feminist periodical *Time and Tide,* one source of the impetuous sea. Marianne DeKoven has used the sea-change as a trope for modernism in her recent study *Rich and Strange: Gender, History, Modernism,* suggesting the value of the invasive, watery metaphor as an interpretive key to Woolf, Conrad, Chopin, Hurston, and others.

7. Quoted by Cohen (2–3).

8. In this instance, one might note that the "Sirens" episode of *Ulysses* closes with an extended anal monologue, based on Leopold Bloom's fart. In "Sexual Linguistics," Gilbert and Gubar used a memorable pun of resistance. Speaking for a group of critics uneasy with "feminologist re-Joycings," they refused to be "Mollified" ("Sexual Linguistics" 16). Molly Bloom has never offered a very alluring role model for feminists!

9. Jane Gallop has suspected Irigaray of using even metonymy as a "phallic conceit" (20). Diana Fuss, however, credits Irigaray with deconstructing metaphoricity and the binary drawn between metaphor and metonym (64–66). Barbara Johnson works with an awareness of the suspicions about metaphor, but demonstrates how it is inextricably connected to metonymy in Zora Neale Hurston's writing ("Gender, Theory, and the Yale School").

10. I thank Ann Ardis for this term, offered as she was reading a draft of this introduction.

11. Showalter grouped Woolf, West, Katherine Mansfield, and Dorothy Richardson as practitioners of a "female aesthetic" in work that she saw as replete with "self recrimination" (244), disputing an earlier idealization of "androgyny" as a feminine form by Caroline Heilbrun and others. In effect, she was agreeing with earlier critics such as the Leavises on Woolf.

12. Objections to Showalter's analysis were also registered by American critics, including Jane Marcus. Marcus had no difficulty detecting anger in Woolf's texts, while Showalter considered it lacking. I think this was because Marcus was more open to its more deeply encoded and performative expression in modernist, as opposed to realist, texts. Both Showalter and Marcus anticipate the postmodern interest in political praxis, however, and maintain a valuable attachment to women's history, including the suffrage movement. For a critique of Marcus, see London.

13. Among the recent publications to take this approach are Rita Felski's *Beyond Feminist Aesthetics,* Judith Butler's *Gender Trouble,* Pamela Caughie's *Virginia Woolf and Postmodernism,* and Bette London's "Guerrilla in Petticoats or Sans-culotte? Virginia Woolf and the Future of Feminist Criticism."

14. See, for example, the discussions of feminism vs. postmodernism in *Feminism/Postmodernism,* ed. Linda J. Nicholson, and the arguments of Rita Felski in *Beyond Feminist Aesthetics,* favoring the model of a feminist public sphere, and her article "Feminism, Postmodernism, and the Critique of

15. Related to this is an initial feminist resistance to the Rebecca West of the 1940s and 1950s, in favor of the young Rebecca.

16. As precedents for the turn to women modernists, see Toril Moi's *Sexual/Textual Politics*, Minow-Pinkney's *Virginia Woolf and the Problem of the Subject*, Shari Benstock's *Women of the Left Bank*, and Marianne DeKoven's *Rich and Strange: Gender, History, Modernism*.

17. For a fine overview of the textual aspect of "versioning," see Brenda Silver's essay, "Textual Criticism as Feminist Practice: Or Who's Afraid of Virginia Woolf Part II." The Derridean concept of *aporia* relates to the reading of gaps in texts for repressions.

18. For a summary of new historicists who give a more mixed account of women's entry into the public sphere, including war-related situations, see Felski, "Feminism, Postmodernism, and the Critique of Modernity" (49), where she cites in particular the work of Joan Scott on the French Revolution and of Nancy Fraser, commenting on the postwar work force.

19. West adopted the spelling Cicily in preference to Cicely.

20. Although she spent two summers in Devon at Peggy Guggenheim's residence, Hayford Hall, Barnes rarely took part in outdoor amusements. Woolf and West both had beloved country houses and enjoyed the alternation between London and the village.

21. West describes this lost uncle, her father's brother, in *Family Memories*: "Poor young Digby went out to India with the Royal Artillery and got cholera and was buried in the Frotwilliam burial ground, like many another English boy, at the age of twenty-five" (175).

PART ONE: BEGINNINGS
1. (Dys)functional Families

1. Woolf, West, and Barnes were all aware of Freudian theory, though not imaginatively subject to it. In *A Room of One's Own*, Woolf submits her imaginary Professor Von X to what she designates as Freudian considerations, thinking back to feminine insults he may have received in his cradle. *The Judge* is West's most deliberate exploration of infant psychology, offering a contrast in maternal nurture between two sons. Barnes parodies the psychoanalytic session, assigning the role of analyst to a homosexual in *Nightwood*.

2. The children by the first marriages were twelve to fifteen years old at the time of Virginia's birth.

3. Monk's House Papers/A13.

4. DeSalvo sees Vanessa's husband, Clive Bell, as Virginia's intended audience, noting that she sent him chapters a few at a time. I resist the negative motives DeSalvo attributes to Woolf. DeSalvo suggests that she wrote to make Clive envious of the sisters as "lovers" beneath the nursery table, or to deprive Vanessa of the saintliness attributed to her, by calling attention to her responsiveness to the widowed Jack Hills (Stella's husband). I should like to suggest that it is a work of many attachments—including one to the first child of the new generation.

5. See Miglena Nikolchina for a reading of Kristeva's concept of maternal abjection in the ink bottle murder (35–36).

6. This has been suggested to me by Carl Rollyson, who is at work on a biography of West. It is based on an interview with Winifred's daughter, Alison Macleod Selford. As a child, Winifred had found out with surprise that parents generally slept together and was humiliated to have disclosed that hers did not.

7. Victoria Glendinning was able to cite only West's account, her skepticism revealing the difficulty of establishing "truth" about this elusive, romantic character.

8. Sophie is given savage treatment in *Family Memories*.

9. Carl Rollyson is making new claims of paternal ideological influence in his forthcoming biography.

10. West's nine years of separation are an exaggeration. There were eight years between West and Lettie, six between her and Winifred.

11. There were other sibling nicknames. West invented the names "Frisk" for Lettie and "Podge" for Winnie, retaining the latter name for the less threatening middle sister into adulthood. West herself sometimes takes the rather common name Ann, using it even as a signature. This dates to a childhood misconception about the spelling of Antelope. Both the Stephen and the Fairfield families favored animal appellations. Virginia Woolf's family name, "Goat," is fairly well known.

12. Her books were *Child Guidance in America* (1928), *Catholics and the Public Medical Services* (1930), *Epilepsy* (1954), and *The Trial of John Henry Straffen* (1954). She was coeditor of the *Medico-Legal and Criminological Review*. Lettie shared her sister's interest in the housing of women workers and the welfare of mothers and children. Another common interest was the law. Letitia Fairfield was called to the bar, and combined this expertise with medicine.

13. Carl Rollyson interview with Alison Selford, as reported in his forthcoming biography of West. Scott interviews of Selford and Norman Macleod, July 1994. For another fictional representation of Lettie's early authority, see West's "Short Life of a Saint," a manuscript first published in the posthumous volume *The Only Poet*.

2. Edwardian Uncles

1. Woolf's own skepticism of Bennett's reviewing had begun in 1917 with her TLS review of his *Books and Persons*.

2. In *Covert Relations: James Joyce, Virginia Woolf, and Henry James*, Daniel Mark Fogel reports extensively on Woolf's writings about James and the intersections of their lives. Among the interesting comments made by James is "Virginia . . . writes reviews for the *Times*. . . . and the hungry generations tread me down!" (quoted 54–55), which suggests that the younger generation produced anxiety in the older, and not vice versa, which is more Fogel's interpretation. Fogel accepts the Oedipal model of Virginia Woolf advanced by Leonard Woolf, substituting James for Sir Leslie in the model. He usefully identifies a devotion to James held by Lytton Strachey and others of Thoby Stephen's Cambridge associates. The study tends to cull out James from many other writers Woolf reacts to (even in the same sentence), exaggerating his importance. West found more of Meredith than James in Woolf, who was able to convey "much more of the selves of her characters" (*Court and Castle* 219).

3. It was within Woolf's critical imagination to circle back to a former literary phase for a useful genre, to recall dead poets or even bring a Judith Shakespeare back to life (*Room*), giving them a second chance to create literature.

4. In 1928, West offered a belated explanation of a lifelong tendency toward fault finding, noted in the previous chapter (West letter to Walpole, 19 Sept. 1928, Texas). Walpole also labored under the lack of appreciation Virginia Woolf had for his writing. He was a full-fledged modernist to neither of them.

5. Wells first wrote this in a letter to Marsden (Princeton, n.d.). It was reprinted as an ad, along with other "opinions" by such well-known figures as Edward Carpenter, Havelock Ellis, Floyd Dell, and Mrs. G. Bernard Shaw (*New Freewoman*).

6. Wells destroyed most of her letters in his possession. Many of his, with West's gloss upon them, are available in Gordon Ray's *H. G. Wells and Rebecca West*.

7. In Wells's fiery metaphor there is an echo of the letter that survives only in several draft versions among West's papers. The fire metaphor occurs in the following accusation: "You want a world of people falling over each other like puppies, people to quarrel and play with, people who rage and ache instead of people who burn. . . . I can't conceive of a person who runs about lighting bonfires and yet nourishes a dislike of flame" (West letter to Wells, [1913], Yale).

8. Arling was the name she used after her divorce; she was Sachs before that, and Philips after a second marriage.

9. There was further drama in the letter to Arling, hinting at ESP or a psychic connection to the dying Wells. West had been "ill and apprehensive," mounting to a "state of hysteria" in the night, and asked her husband to drive to the head of the valley at 3 A.M., in order that she might walk the three miles home in solitude. She learned on her return that Wells had died at 3:45.

10. Anthony Burgess, "A Pre-War Idyll," *Atlantic* 255 (March 1985): 116–18.

11. A late interview provides a slap at Yeats, who she thought was in a perpetual fog ("Bookshelf" interview tape, Tulsa).

12. In a later version of the story, West told Jane Marcus that she had intended to evoke a libel suit from Bennett, presumably to make money in his defeat (conversation with Jane Marcus).

13. Her Henry James book and a monograph on Lawrence were equally timely.

14. In the upper-left-hand corner of the letter is a list of four women that concludes with "me." The others are Mrs. Fenwick, Mrs. Fitz, and Miss Parsons.

15. Her salutation in this letter is "Heart of my heart." Another supporter of Emma Goldman was Margaret Anderson, who did approve of her as an anarchist, as is clear in the *Little Review*. We return to Goldman in chapter 11.

16. On the Village reaction to lesbianism, see Lillian Faderman, who suggests that bohemian men controlled Village mores; "sexual love between women was never validated as equal to heterosexual intercourse" (82). Ann Larabee contrasts Barnes's dramas to the usual fare of the Provincetown Players:

> While Provincetown playwright Eugene O'Neill retreated into a Melvillean world of men asea on the psychosexual voyages of the S. S. *Glencairn,* the Provincetown women explored ways of making the female voice a transgressive agent against even liberal, progressive definitions of gender. But monogamy and heterosexuality remained firm, if slightly renegotiated, behavioral standards. (Broe, ed. 37–38)

3. Stretching the Scope of Suffrage

1. See especially chapters 7–9 of Marcus's *Art and Anger,* a section headed "Writing Practice: The Lupine Critic Writes a (Biased) History of Virginia Woolf Scholarship."

2. See the works by Andreas Huyssen, Jean-François Lyotard, and Peter Bürger listed in the bibliography. Bürger relies on M. M. Bakhtin's sense of political praxis. His work is frequently cited as a theoretical resource by feminists who detect a more political Woolf.

3. DeKoven suggests further that male and female writers were both ambivalent about the radical changes they advocated, but that they played this out

differently (4). Her idea that modernist women were apt to fear punishment for assuming control interests me. Of my three authors, West feared this most, as shown in her struggles with Walpole and Bennett, noted in chapter 2. DeKoven's finding that men feared a loss of hegemony supports Sandra Gilbert and Susan Gubar, who have offered an extremely negative collection and interpretation of anxious modernist "no-men." In their story of modernism, I find too little variation within the male category, and a neglect of male-figured modernisms as resources for issues and techniques that women writers could appropriate. The place of sexual politics, including suffrage, in male writing is one such indicator of difference among the men, and one that Woolf, West, and Barnes were keenly aware of.

4.   Born in January 1881, Gawthorpe was twelve years older than West.

5.   The observer, Richard Yaverland, is more interested in Ellen Melville, the young suffragette in the audience, and her attitudes toward the speakers, than in the women on the stage. The most charismatic speaker is an invincible older woman, Mrs. Ormiston, who reminds him of his mother and is suggestive of Emmeline Pankhurst. Richard's distaste for a younger suffragette who practices romantic poses, wears a "preposterous dress" (60), and spoke with "slow, pure gusto of the horrors of immorality" with phrases having "peculiar calm gross qualities" (65) embodies West's own critique of the sexual Puritanism of Christabel Pankhurst.

6.   Les Garner has been unable to locate conclusive evidence that Marsden was force-fed. She was imprisoned several times in 1909, an activist year that culminated with her challenge to the Home Secretary, Winston Churchill. Marsden defeated attempts to secure the hall where he was speaking from suffragettes, having climbed to the roof the day before. Speaking from a porthole in the ceiling, she defied Churchill on a supposed people's budget: "But it does not represent the women Mr Churchill." Marsden is compared to "one of those dainty little child angels the old Italian painters loved to show peeping down from the tops of high clouds or nestling amongst the details of their stately architecture" in Mrs. Pankhurst's recording of the event (Garner 39–40).

7.   West published two accounts of Marsden and her paper, the first written in 1926 at the request of the women's weekly *Time and Tide* and the second in 1970, as a book review of *Dear Miss Weaver,* the biography of Harriet Shaw Weaver, whose role as a publisher has been cited already. She was a devoted supporter of Marsden and James Joyce and took over editing the *Egoist* in 1914. West's letters to Marsden, Jardine, and Robinson offer contemporary impressions; there are discrepancies among the accounts. For example, West says in a letter that she met Harriet Weaver in the tube station, but in "Spinster to the Rescue" she says she met her only once, as she was closing the family home at Hampstead. It was probably more dramatically effective to cut the number of meetings, or her memory may have been de-

fective by 1970. The essay "The 'Freewoman' " in *Time and Tide* gives a colorful economic account of the failure of the *Freewoman,* neglecting the Smith boycott and the intermediate stage of the *New Freewoman.* It assigns West the title of "literary editor" when she is listed on the stationery as "Assistant Editor," the title she uses accurately in the later review, "Spinster to the Rescue." In this case, I suspect Woolf of spinning out the economic story that had involved her most (one that occurred at the *New Freewoman*) and of simplifying the intricate history for her audience at *Time and Tide.*

8.   In 1912 she gave a lecture, "Interpretations of Life," to the circle. It anticipated her preoccupation with binary arrangements, the topic which we will pursue with West in volume 2.

9.   Clarke prints more extensive versions of several letters I refer to, and deals comprehensively with the Marsden-Pound correspondence in the Princeton Marsden Collection. He focuses upon Pound's essay "The Serious Artist," probably solicited by Marsden as a leader for the *New Freewoman.* In his reading, Marsden may have influenced Pound as he turned to antisocialist, "anarchistic individualism." The discussion of Pound at the *Egoist* resumes in chapter 5.

10.   At one point Eliot consulted Woolf for advice on an article for this journal.

11.   In 1955, Leonard Woolf rejected with regret a life of Jane Harrison by Jessie Stewart, which he thought was "all over the place" (L. Woolf letter, 3 Aug. 1955, Sussex). It had been hoped that Hope Mirrlees would write one.

12.   Barnes's second skeptical article was "Part Victory, Part Defeat at Suffrage Aviation Meet."

4. Midwives of Modernism

1.   Woolf includes here authors on the Hogarth Press list. It is notable that Vernon Lee was disparaged in early versions of Eliot's "The Waste Land" as one of Flavia's favored writers (see chapter 7).

2.   This work was considered for publication at the Hogarth Press by Virginia and Leonard Woolf but rejected as unreliable. In her *Diary,* Woolf quotes the young Hunt overhearing a conversation about "intimate relations." Woolf notes that Hugh Walpole has told her about the extensive nature of Hunt's own intimate relations (4 D 27).

3.   The American title is *I Have This to Say.* Woolf wrote an unsigned review for *Nation & Athenaeum* (20 Mar. 1926, 870, 872) soon after the book came out.

4.   In her final years, Hunt suffered from advanced syphilis.

5.   Lynd's regular paper was the *Daily News.* He also wrote weekly for the *Na-*

tion and the *New Statesman.* Leonard Woolf admired his consistent production of good work.

6.   On Eliot, see " 'Prufrock: And Other Observations': A Criticism" (Scott, ed. 447-53); on Pound, see "The Reputation of Ezra Pound" (ibid. 468-76).

7.   As is well known, she took her term from William James—also a figure of departure for Gertrude Stein. See Sinclair's "The Novels of Dorothy Richardson" on the first three volumes of *Pilgrimage,* first published in the *Egoist* in April 1918; reprinted in Scott, ed. 442-48.

8.   Woolf did not have extensive experience of Sinclair. She did have one exchange on her with Lytton Strachey, in letters written in 1922. He wrote, "May Sinclair's book, 'The Life & Death of Harriet Frean'—has some merit, though nasty" (Woolf and Strachey 139). In her reply, she castigates Alice Meynell's criticism of Jane Austen and others, and seems surprised that Strachey would read Sinclair, but ends in flattering him: "And you read Miss Sinclair! So shall I perhaps. But I'd rather read Lytton Strachey" (140).

9.   H. D. is an ideal complement to the authors I am studying. I think of her launching out from Pound in *End to Torment,* from D. H. Lawrence and Richard Aldington in *Bid Me to Live,* and from Freud in *Tribute to Freud,* and her achievement of a mode that "regularly featured a woman speaking through a mythic mask, respeaking" masculinist classicism (Susan Stanford Friedman, "H. D.," in Scott, ed. 86).

10.   West's retelling of this story understandably became a source of embarrassment to Mew (West letter to Lynd, 28 July 1918, Tulsa).

11.   Mew's poem "The Fête," for example, dramatizes the excitement of an anticipated meeting of female lovers in clear physical terms. See Celeste Schenck, "Charlotte Mew," in Scott, ed. 317.

12.   See Marcus, "The Niece of a Nun" and "Virginia Woolf and Her Violin," both in *Virginia Woolf and the Languages of Patriarchy.* Marcus suggests various ways that the maternal model worked less well with her contemporaries. Additional work along these lines is Marianne Caws's *Women of Bloomsbury,* an interwoven study of three Bloomsbury women with various alliances to Bloomsbury men: Virginia Woolf, Vanessa Bell, and the painter Dora Carrington. Carrington lived in a *ménage à trois* with Lytton Strachey and her husband Ralph Partridge for the last sixteen years of Strachey's life; she took her own life soon after he died, despite Virginia Woolf's efforts to console her.

13.   Bell calls her "Miss Sheepshanks" and identifies her as "the daughter of the Bishop of Norwich." The Bell biography includes Woolf's "Report on Teaching at Morley College," from her 1905 notebook. His analysis of this material suggests that her teaching of history may have anticipated *Orlando,* at the same time proving rather difficult for the audience to follow. Bell does remark on her efforts to get to know her students. However, he makes the typical move of casting his aunt as a snob: "She must also have

felt a kind of revolted curiosity, the feelings of a lady for a pavement drab" (1 Bell 107).

14. See the entry on Mansfield in Blain, Clements, and Grundy, eds., *The Feminist Companion to Literature in English,* which cites this collection, along with early stories that appeared in the *New Age* as her most feminist work (712).

15. The vulgar view of Mansfield is elaborated by Quentin Bell, who states among other things that "she had given rein to all the female instincts, slept with all kinds of men. . . . She dressed like a tart and behaved like a bitch" (2 Bell 37). There is more on Woolf's attachment to Strachey in chapter 9.

16. Leonard Woolf did collect it in *Granite and Rainbow.*

17. The establishment founded there by George Gurdjieff was to attract many writers and editors, including Jane Heap and Margaret Andersen of the *Little Review.* Gurdjieffian philosophy was taken up by Jean Toomer, Nella Larsen, and other figures of the Harlem Renaissance.

18. See, for example, the first volume, where Holroyd suggests that Woolf was envious of Strachey's superior education and more rapid rise to fame (430), where his self-confidence is added to education as a source of envy and she is accused of making spiteful negative criticisms of his work, behind his back; and the second volume (368–69), where Woolf is described as malicious and envious when Strachey actively supported publication of Joyce's *Ulysses* by the Hogarth Press. She is again seen as jealous of Strachey's success when she offers negative criticism of his *Queen Victoria* (2.434). His 1994 "New Biography" quotes Woolf more extensively and is less judgmental (London: Chatto and Windus, 1994).

19. Richardson's great discontent with Duckworth for the lack of accessibility of the accumulating volumes of *Pilgrimage* to the public is expressed in numerous letters to Sydney Schiff (British Library).

20. To discredit her in her letters, West emphasized Richardson's old age (she was nearly twenty years West's senior) as a source of unreliability. In one report on Richardson to her friend Emily Hahn, West reported that Richardson had taken a "senile dislike to H. G. Wells and babbles to all comers about H. G.'s love affairs" (West letter to Hahn, 26 Jan. 1952, Lilly).

21. In her well-focused, pioneering study of a group of modernist women writers, Sydney Janet Kaplan concentrates on women's consciousness in Woolf, Dorothy Richardson, May Sinclair, Rosamund Lehmann, and Doris Lessing.

22. Ann Larabee suggests that the Provincetown Playhouse, which produced several important women writers and artists, including Susan Glaspell, Djuna Barnes, Edna St. Vincent Millay, and Marguerite Zoarach, existed in an atmosphere of "sex-antagonism" from its inception in 1917. She notes that "Barnes did not share the Provincetown Players' overall fascination with restoring besieged monogamous heterosexual relationships by hardening them into dramatic form" (Broe, ed. 38). See her "The Early Attic Stage

of Djuna Barnes" for a fine analysis of Barnes's plays of the Provincetown period.

23. In 1917, Sanger was listed with Margaret Anderson, Louise Bryant, Jane Heap, Elsa, Baroness Von Freytag-Loringhoven, and Mina Loy for the title of "modern woman" by the *New York Evening Sun.*

24. I borrow my title for this section from Shari Benstock's *Women of the Left Bank: Paris, 1900–1940,* which gives an invaluable census and a thorough grounding of the many women writers and artists on the scene, situated in their specific arrondissements and circles. Edith Wharton (the earliest figure in Benstock's study), Stein, Barney, and Beach were all Americans.

PART TWO: THE MEN OF 1914

1. The term appeared in Lewis's 1937 work, *Blasting and Bombardiering* (252).

2. See, for example, Lillian Robinson's "Treason Our Text: Feminist Challenges to the Literary Canon" and summaries by Suzanne Clark (33) and Karen Lawrence in her introduction to *Decolonizing Tradition* (3–6). Both Clark and Lawrence call attention to a multiple conflicts in canon formation, moving away from simple binary formulations.

3. For an idea of what Ellmann missed in terms of the women in Joyce's life, see Brenda Maddox's biography *Nora,* on Joyce's spouse, Nora Barnacle Joyce. I discuss limitations to Ellmann's interest in Lucia Joyce and his reliance upon Joyce's brother, Stanislaus, in *Joyce and Feminism.*

4. Kenner has cast a critical eye at the phenomenon of canonicity, particularly as a product of the academy. He sees the canon appropriately, I think, as "a narrative of some intricacy, depending on places and times and opportunities." By his own description, Kenner's earliest work on Pound, *The Poetry of Ezra Pound* (1951), came "at the threshold of two decades' academic expansion"—a time when a "new man" such as Pound was welcome to provide the subject matter of criticism. The Pound he brought was one who hadn't fit the "schoolroom movement" of New Critics with their formulas of "Wit, Tension, Irony" ("The Making of the Modernist Canon" 57–59).

5. "Make It New" is the title Ezra Pound gave to his collected essays in 1934, summarizing the series of directives through which he and other men of 1914 sought to shape the literary movement now generally termed "modernism." "Make It New" also appears in Pound's *Canto* LIII. Dennis Brown credits Pound with building the association of the four "men of 1914," both in his letters and in proposed meetings (80–83).

6. Recent studies which perpetuated into the 1980s the tradition set by Kenner in *The Pound Era* are Dasenbrock, Levenson, Longenbach, Quinones, Schwarz, Stead, and Sultan. Works that are heavily male in their coverage include Bergonzi, Bradbury and MacFarlane, Meisel, Menand, and Moore.

Kiely is exceptional in integrating Woolf in both his study of modernism and his collection. Symons centers on Joyce, Eliot, Lewis, and Pound, but devotes space to the female editors who were essential to modernism, and gives a final nod toward Gertrude Stein. Dennis Brown is aware of "sexist group solidarity" in the canonical group of Joyce, Lewis, Pound, and Eliot. See also my introduction to *The Gender of Modernism* and Rado, ed., *Rereading Modernism.*

7.   Lindberg suggests that Kenner conflates Pound unduly with the classicist, totalizing modernism of Eliot and his genealogical method of defining tradition (32, 37). Her Pound used metaphor in such terms as "imagism" and "vorticism," and in his readings of modernists. He chose marginal metaphoric texts and used metaphor to conduct "guerilla warfare" on Eliot's doctrine of "tradition" in his "Kulchur" writing of the 1930s (9). That Pound's metaphors are spermatic rather than architectural is a dubious gain but a worthwhile distinction. Also valuable are Lindberg's reattachment of Pound to the disruptive doctrines of Nietzsche and her association of his metaphors with Derridean dissemination.

8.   Kenner has an old resentment. In his view, it was the privileged of Bloomsbury who denied his complex men their place in England after the First World War (*The Sinking Island* 139). Lewis had suggested the same, though his pathos began with the onset of war and the loss of men such as the vorticist sculptor Henri Gaudier-Brzeska.

9.   Clive Bell writes "graceful twaddle," Roger Fry is basically an art dealer, and the philosophy of G. E. Moore can be mastered by turning to the end of his book to find his favored states of consciousness (Kenner, *Sinking Island* 125, 134, 161).

10.   Since Kenner has long been a favorite of the Joyce industry, both for his publications and for his featured papers at symposia, his objection cannot be commercial; it seems visceral.

11.   Cunningham lists the Virago classics for their revival of 1930s works by women. He does acknowledge homosexual bias against women writers, and is able to fit Sylvia Townsend Warner into a "Marxist decade."

12.   I am grateful to Ann Ardis for urging me to make more of this private/public distinction, as she reacted to an early draft.

5. Ezra Pound: Plunging Headlong into Female Chaos

1.   Dorothy arranged her own maternity of Omar Pound, independent of her husband, however. The arrangement of dual households was comparable to H. G. Wells's double *ménages.*

2.   Evidence of the growing importance of this sort of study in the academy is the multiple session on "Anthropology and Modernity" at the 1992 MLA Convention. The third session, subtitled "Exchange and Interchange," in-

cluded James Buzard's paper "Participant Observers: The Cultural Poetics of Eliot and Pound."

3. Eve Kosofsky Sedgwick initiated the terms needed for this sort of discussion in *Between Men: English Literature and Male Homosocial Desire*, focusing her work on the mid-eighteenth- to the mid-nineteenth-century novel. Although "male bonding" sometimes involves homophobia, Sedgwick proposes a continuum between homosocial desire and homosexuality (1). Wayne Koestenbaum's *Double Talk* provides an excellent study of Pound's collaboration with Eliot over *The Waste Land*.

4. See Bush, *Genesis* 103–107, 209–11, and 239.

5. On this episode, and Heap's role as an essayist and editor, see my essay " 'The Young Girl,' Jane Heap, and Trials of Gender in *Ulysses*."

6. Pound regards the "young ladies" Christabel and Sylvia Pankhurst with "envy" because in their martyrdom for an idea they "will have lived." But he says this in the context of a syndicalist disbelief in all political institutions, including the vote, blames the suffragettes for a lack of intellect, and concludes that Parliament might as well have one house for men and one for women.

7. It is possible that she would have written more had she not been suffering from an eye ailment.

8. Rachel Blau DuPlessis suggests that H. D.'s *End to Torment* (on her relationship to Pound) and *Notes on Thought and Vision* "take imagism apart" (*H. D.: The Career of That Struggle* 10). For a female-centered interpretation of *Asphodel*, relevant to the Cravens suicide, see Friedman, *Penelope's Web* (170–82). Friedman carefully follows H. D.'s progress in and beyond psychoanalysis. Freud had encouraged her to undertake a writing cure, and H. D. managed to write her way out of a long series of male attachments that included D. H. Lawrence as well as Pound and Aldington. *Bid Me to Live* relates most closely to Aldington and Lawrence.

9. Pondrom argues that Pound's first poem labeled as imagist, "Middle-Aged," fell short of imagist criteria. H. D.'s early work set the standard for his more developed imagism of "In a Station of the Metro" (88–89, 103–105).

10. It is unlikely that Pound knew anything about Moore's appearance, considering that she was an old friend of H. D. He may have pretended this for effect.

11. Pretending that the poets were really the "nagistes," he invited the massive Lowell to publicly bathe in a tub that he brought to a party she was giving. The stunt enacts the metaphorical assignment of the feminine to liquid. It was hardly calculated to encourage self-assurance among women who might care to take a managing hand in modernism.

12. Lowell published Lawrence under generous financial arrangements, even supplying him with a typewriter.

13. Dorcas societies were women's church groups that provided clothing for the poor, patterned on Dorcas, Acts 9:36–41.

14. Pound was capable of friendships with blacks and Jews. In a famous letter in which she denounces Pound's fascism, Cunard appreciates his support of her relationship with the black jazz musician Henry Crowder. For the letter see Scott, ed. 80–84.

15. Frank Kermode makes a strong argument for the romantic sources of imagism and vorticism (120–21).

16. Lindberg refers to this as a "spermatic reading economy" (22). Longenbach offers numerous examples of what he calls Pound's "fantasy of phallic creativity" ("Pound among the Women" 136ff.). Pound offered an early version of this characterization of woman as chaos in a letter to Marianne Moore, and echoed it in *Canto* XXIX, as Ron Bush has noted ("Ezra Pound" 353). I refer to Wayne Koestenbaum's excellent analysis of spermatic elements in Pound in chapter 3, with a consideration of the collaboration over Eliot's *The Waste Land*.

6. Wyndham Lewis: Above the Line of Messy Femininity

1. Virginia Woolf duly records the incident for her biography of Fry, quoting as I have from the circular letter and from Fry's response to it. Fry decided not to sue for libel, wanting to avoid more advertisement for the dissenters. Woolf ends, "The storm in a tea-cup blew over; though he noted bubbles from time to time" (*Roger Fry* 168). Her appropriation of Lewis's tea party language was probably deliberate. The bubbles included negative reviews for Omega in the *New Age*.

2. This instance of scaffolding amuses me, not just for feeding my central metaphor but also because it obscures a much-maligned male figure, always subservient to the corpulent Victoria, and made the object of mawkish sentimentality in long years of national mourning, one aspect of the discarded Victorian age. If scaffolded, of course, someone was taking pains to maintain it.

3. In placing Lewis, Jameson usefully identifies different subtraditions of modernism, though his assignments are debatable, particularly over the course of modernism that reaches to 1939. Jameson's design separates Lewis from a "hegemonic modernism" equated with Joyce. That tradition revolts against realism, exploring subjectivity through the internal monologue in a "newly autonomous realm of aesthetic language" (38).

4. Lindberg poses the same argument for Pound, as noted in the previous chapter.

5. Barry eventually put the children up for adoption.

6. Pound published a comparison of *Tarr* to Joyce's *A Portrait* in "Wyndham

Lewis," *Egoist* 1.12 (15 June 1914): 233–34, and he reviewed *Tarr* in the *Little Review* 4 (11 Mar. 1918): 35. Eliot compares *Tarr* and *A Portrait* for their formal accomplishments as novels in "*Ulysses,* Order and Myth." West's review appeared in the *Nation* (17 Aug. 1918).

7.   In contrast, H. D. has a positive evocation of a "jelly-fish" state of the "over-mind," and of a "jelly-fish" in the body or womb "with streamers or feelers floating up toward the brain" in "Notes on Thought and Vision" (written 1919; Scott, ed. 93–95). This suggests an intriguing counterimaginary.

8.   Glendinning suggests that the story was begun when West was still aspiring to be an actress, and that it was turned down by both the *English Review* and the *Blue Review* (39).

9.   This story, which can exemplify sex war, is their sole selection for West in their *Norton Anthology of Literature by Women*. They devote several pages of the first volume of *No Man's Land* to discussing it, noting that "for feminist modernists 'Indissoluble Matrimony' might have functioned as a witty exploration of the dynamics of sex antagonism, a paradigmatic (female) joke about the neurotic never-never-land inhabited by the lost boys who became the early twentieth century's no-men" (97). The story further exemplifies "male sexual paranoia," particularly as women entered the public sphere (98).

10.   The sketch hung on Rebecca West's wall until her death. It is now in the National Portrait Gallery in London.

11.   Garnett was the lover of Duncan Grant, and later the husband of Angelica Bell, the daughter of Grant and Vanessa Bell, Virginia Woolf's older sister.

7. T. S. Eliot: Playing Possum

1.   Commenting on the midwifery of "Sage Homme," Gilbert and Gubar suggest that because Pound "no longer has a suitable female muse, he might construct a male surrogate for her," but that the figure comes off "at best comic and at worst perverse, indeed potentially capable of inducing a kind of homophobic panic" (1 *No Man's Land* 161).

2.   This fragment has been treated repeatedly as a key to Eliot's attitudes toward religion and sexuality. See Gordon (*Eliot's New Life* 61–62), Ackroyd (52), and Gilbert and Gubar (1 *No Man's Land* 30).

3.   As will be developed in volume 2, Djuna Barnes was capable of tortured renditions of love that included mutilation of the beloved (e.g., her early play "The Dove," which ends with a bite to the shoulder) and the odd kiss of "Behind the Heart." Her own interest in saints receives fullest rendition in *Ladies Almanack*, which includes a martyrdom (see chapter 12).

4.   Twice in her life, Hale was left at loose ends by Eliot. She gave up her very

congenial post at Scripps College to come to him in England in 1934–35. She was between jobs and residences when he visited the U.S. in 1947, soon after Vivien's death. Gordon includes a letter from Hale to her friend Lorraine Havens that describes the situation in 1947 (Gordon, *Eliot's New Life* 170–71).

5. Lyndall Gordon has done the most to piece together the nature of the Hale and Trevelyan relationships in her *Eliot's New Life*. Strangely, she seems unaware of his warm correspondence with Djuna Barnes, intersecting as it does with visits to the U.S. in which he saw Hale, and surviving his marriage to Valerie Eliot, despite some troubled initial exchanges.

6. Letters tended to use the war as an excuse. Pound encouraged the step, according to Eliot's former secretary and second wife, Valerie ("Introduction," Eliot, *"Waste Land": Facsimile* ix). On the comparable symptoms of husband and wife, see Koestenbaum 118. Koestenbaum's assertion that Eliot confided his marital problems only to Pound is not borne out by what I have found in Woolf archives.

7. I am grateful to Nancy Gish for these insights.

8. Vivien enjoyed going dancing, as her diary reveals.

9. This is referred to by Dennis Brown (85–86). For published traces, see *"The Waste Land": A Facsimile* (4–21).

10. Gordon associates her with Emily Hale. Vivien Eliot has of course been associated with the neurasthenic voice of Part 2, "A Game of Chess," for some time.

11. The *Diary* makes it clear that an intimate sharing of experience (perhaps female experience) was possible with Mary Hutchinson, and that tensions were created by other of Eliot's friends, including the Schiffs and Ezra Pound.

12. Later letters use the more usual "Miss Weaver," and he dedicated *Selected Essays* to Weaver "in gratitude of her services to English letters."

13. While Joyce could be considered a prude in his personal affairs, it seems unimaginable to label his writing as prudish.

14. Eliot opens by congratulating the state of Virginia on being a region that has escaped "the influx of foreign populations that has almost effaced" tradition in the North (15). He declares that "the Civil War was certainly the greatest disaster in the whole of American history; it is just as certainly a disaster from which the country has never recovered, and perhaps never will" (16). In declaring the importance of unity in religious background for the survival of tradition, he says that "reasons of race and religion combine to make any large number of free-thinking Jews undesirable" (20).

15. Whether or not "feminine" is a positive value may depend on where it is evaluated. Eliot was writing for a journal Moore had edited, and he was far removed from 1914.

16. Eliot was aware of BLAST before coming to London in 1914, as he wrote

Conrad Aiken in parody of the blast and bless format from Germany in July 1914 (1 *Letters of T. S. Eliot* 40).

17. Gilbert and Gubar culminate a chapter titled "Tradition and the Female Talent" on the note that the " 'really new work' was women's work" (1 *No Man's Land* 162).

18. Andrew McNeillie, editor of the new volumes of Woolf's essays, remarks on the quality of her essays that her writing was "democratic in spirit: uncanonical, inquisitive, open, and unacademic. It is quite antithetical, it should be said, both to the 'great traditionalism' of F. R. Leavis, that dire scourge of literary journalism, and to the quest for the higher culture of T. S. Eliot, with whom in other important respects Virginia Woolf has much in common" (1 *E* ix). Levenson traces a male line of modernist descent from Hulme to Lewis to Pound and Eliot. In its last phase came a period of consolidation, when Pound and Eliot resisted democratization, dissemination, and supposed "vulgarization" (154). For a review that draws useful distinctions between Levenson and Gilbert and Gubar, see Pamela L. Caughie, "The (En)gendering of Literary History." Caughie notes that, whereas Gilbert and Gubar consider the battle of the sexes a motive force behind modernism, Levenson in his genealogy of a male set of modernists considers the loss of faith in religion, the rise of technology, and the spread of democracy as the essential threats. Gilbert and Gubar discuss "Tradition and the Individual Talent" (1 *No Man's Land* 154, 156, 162). Florence Howe contrasts Woolf and Eliot's "Tradition" in "Introduction: T. S. Eliot, Virginia Woolf, and the Future of Tradition" (see esp. 5). See also Pamela Caughie's list of contrasts and comparisons in *Virginia Woolf and Postmodernism* (188, 191n) and Patricia Waugh's *Feminine Fictions* (17–18).

19. Woolf noted his neglect of her writing on several occasions. In June 1925, she made up the excuse that often people don't get to books for weeks (3 *D* 27).

20. Gilbert and Gubar complain that Eliot published relatively few essays by Woolf, and that these were not important ones. "Character in Fiction" was surely one of her most important. "On Being Ill" was a deliberate departure from *TLS* style and an important study of altered states of mind. On the personal side, Woolf was writing about her frequent attacks of influenza—a problem shared by Eliot. His pursuit of articles from her was fairly flattering and vigorous, though I shall discuss her suspicions.

21. This title was first used in a short essay, written in response to Bennett's review of *Jacob's Room*, and published in the *New York Evening Post* in November 1923; it was resumed by the Hogarth Press when it republished the *Criterion* essay with slight revisions, as a pamphlet. Woolf had used "Character in Fiction" as the title of a paper delivered to the Cambridge Heretics Society in May 1924. In that version, Woolf's list of Georgians included Edith Sitwell and Dorothy Richardson in addition to Joyce, Lawrence, Forster, Strachey, and Eliot.

22. "You have freed yourself from any compromise between the traditional novel and your original gift" (1 *Letters of T. S. Eliot*).

23. She had seen him a few years earlier in a café.

24. Coleman reported to Barnes that she had taken out pages 29–31, 33–34, and 139–41. "These seem to be stories of the Doctor. However good they may be in themselves I know they will irritate Eliot; they hold up the book, and, in their place are boring (however charming they may be to one who is a devotee of the Doctor)." She also expressed her concern that the opening two chapters, featuring the Jew, Felix, his marriage to Robin, and the birth of Guido, were a detraction from the main theme and an unsuccessful scattering of passionate feeling (Nora's) on other characters. Some parts might be relocated in other chapters, and the chapter on the Jew used as a separate short story. Coleman also relied on George Barker, who was published by Faber, for reactions to her strategies with Eliot (Coleman to Barnes, 5 Nov. 1935, Maryland). In an earlier letter (27 Aug. 1935, Maryland), Coleman expressed in more detail her opinion that the "tragedy of Robin and Nora" was the central theme.

25. Coleman had discussed the closing incident, suggesting intimacies with a dog, arguing its sexual significance with Barnes (27 Aug. 1935). When Eliot suggested removing it, Coleman could summon the history of the various drafts to mind, recalling that it had not always been placed last, and predicting that Barnes would not want to take it out entirely but could restore it to this earlier position (Coleman letter to Barnes, 26 Jan. 1936, Maryland).

26. Through the years, Guggenheim was eager that Coleman's part in the publication be acknowledged. She criticized Sylvia Beach for failing to mention it in her autobiography, though Barnes pointed out that there was no occasion to, as *Nightwood* was not even mentioned.

27. See Koestenbaum (124). Koestenbaum notes the abundance of playful references to homosexuality in Pound's correspondence, urging his friend to play his sexuality straight: "Pound's gestures are paradoxical; he denounces instances of linguistic effeminacy, and yet the very act of intruding commentary is homosexually charged . . . 'I merely queeried the dialect. . . .' "

28. West's motives in her assault on the Midwest were undoubtedly complex but no doubt grounded in an awareness of the number of uppity exiles (Eliot and Pound included) who had come to London from that territory. As she was writing this essay, she was in the midst of a pitched critical battle with an Easterner, William Carlos Williams, over her assessments of Joyce, which we turn to in the following chapter.

8. James Joyce: Halting Female Pens with *Ulysses*

1. I have contributed two studies to this field: *Joyce and Feminism* and *James Joyce* in the Harvester Feminist Readings Series. See also *Women in Joyce*,

ed. Suzette Henke and Elaine Unkeless (Urbana: University of Illinois Press, 1982); Henke's *James Joyce and the Politics of Desire* (London: Routledge, 1990); Margot Norris's *Joyce's Web*; Kim Devlin's *Wandering and Return in Finnegans Wake* (Princeton: Princeton University Press, 1991); Christine van Boheemen's *The Novel as Family Romance* (Ithaca: Cornell University Press, 1987); and the special issue of *Modern Fiction Studies* 35.3 (1989), "Feminist Readings of Joyce," ed. Ellen Carol Jones.

2. The article was read to Joyce during one of his recurrent bouts with iritis. Padraic Colum may have been the reader. Nathan Halper learned of Joyce's reactions to West's essay through Colum. See Halper's "James Joyce and Rebecca West," *Partisan Review* 16 (July 1949): 761–63.

3. In *Joyce and Feminism* I considered Woolf, West, and Barnes as critics of Joyce, including many of the same incidents and passages. For Woolf see 121–24; for West, 118–21; for Barnes, 108–12.

4. See Gertrude Stein, "What Are Master-pieces and Why Are There So Few of Them." While it distorts Stein's form and meaning to make a brief quotation, suffice it to say that a modern crisis over identity figures into Stein's answer: "One might say it is impossible but that it is not impossible is proved by the existence of master-pieces which are just that. They are knowing that there is no identity and producing while identity is not" (Scott, ed. 499).

5. The list was shortened for publication in the *Criterion*. Edith Sitwell and Dorothy Richardson joined Joyce, Lawrence, Forster, Strachey, and Eliot in the earlier oral presentation to the Heretics Club.

6. In "The Strange Necessity: James Joyce's Rejection in England (1914–30)," Patrick Parrinder attempted to gloss the reactions of Woolf and West to Joyce in terms of a "genteel" English "dilution of pre-1914 international modernism" and "Bloomsbury values" of taste—having discovered "taste" as a common term in their analyses. The essay is very much of the Kenner and Leavis schools, failings of which were discussed in the introduction to Part Two. Parrinder fails to look into the serious formal concerns of both women in their reactions to Joyce.

7. This information comes from a conversation Colum had with Nathan Halper. See Halper 761. Joyce shared some of his most interesting observations on women with Harriet Weaver. He typically reserved his misogyny for male colleagues, and I suspect the chain of male auditors could have affected this account (see my *Joyce and Feminism* 157). Bernard Benstock sees Joyce's response as less severe. He reviews the references to West, supposedly made in retaliation, in *Finnegans Wake*, suggesting that he took her "robecca or worse" and married her into the involved framework of his last work (Bernard Benstock 229n). West took the *Finnegans Wake* insertions, together with hearsay of his conversations about her, as indications of "insane hostility" (Scott interview). West's letters to Richard Ellmann and Patricia Hutchins avow a real reverence for the genius of Joyce. For an ad-

mirable overview of the critical controversy of West on Joyce, see Austin Briggs, "Rebecca West vs. James Joyce, Samuel Beckett, and William Carlos Williams." Briggs quotes from West's letter to Ellmann and Hutchins's account. Joyce may have been under the impression that he had met her in the company of her publisher, George Doran, who apparently had an unpleasant visit with Joyce in Paris. She mentioned Joyce's misconception that he had met her in our interview.

8. I give a briefer and slightly different reading of this passage in *Joyce and Feminism* (119). For a fuller account of ALP's odyssey, see my *James Joyce* (100–103).

9. In view of the amount of work Beach did for this volume, one wonders why she was not listed as its coeditor, at least!

10. See Briggs for a detailed description of this confrontation, which continued with an exchange in the *New English Weekly* in 1932. As Briggs notes, she puts down his version of her Joyce criticism as an "amalgam of hysterics and stupidity"—another attribution of hysteria to a modernist male. Briggs also includes West's summary of the episode, offered in a letter to Richard Ellmann in 1958. He is doubtful of her claim that she never "meant to be offensive."

11. Their summary of "Oxen of the Sun" is as follows: "The 'Oxen of the Sun' chapter, after all, records the conception, incubation, and birth—'Hoopsa Boyaboy Hoopsa'—of a magical-sounding boy through a series of stylistic metamorphoses which seem to prove that (male) linguistic ontogeny recapitulates (male) linguistic phylogeny" (1 *No Man's Land* 260). They conclude sweepingly, "All these male modernists and postmodernists transform the female vernacular into a new morning of patriarchy" (261). Among the neglected elements in this analysis is that "Hoopsa Boyaboy Hoopsa" remains the vernacular of midwives, that the new day of *Ulysses* fails to leave any male in linguistic dominance, and certainly not Stephen Dedalus, whose "God of the creation, indifferent, paring his fingernails," far from being the Joycean credo they make it, went out with the youthful pomposity of Stephen in *A Portrait*.

9. Lawrence, Forster, and Bloomsbury: Male Modernist Others

1. The importance of the "Miriam Papers" has been trivialized by Harry T. Moore (51). For a discussion of Lawrence's literary "trespasses" into women's texts, see Simpson (143–63).

2. See also *Letters* 2.472–3.

3. In "A Propos of *Lady Chatterley's Lover*," Lawrence discusses the function of clothing in sexual vitality, finding that "the half-naked women of today certainly do not rouse much sexual feeling in the muffled-up men of today," because sex is not alive in them (497). I chose "Cocksure Women and

Hensure Men" and "Matriarchy" for inclusion in *The Gender of Modernism,* and this section of the chapter is derived largely from my introduction to the Lawrence selections (217–24).

4. Jane Marcus refutes the "feminine" gender label given to Bloomsbury homosexuals by the resentful Wyndham Lewis, allying them instead with patriarchy. See "Taking the Bull by the Udders" (*Virginia Woolf and the Languages of Patriarchy* 137).

5. In her memoir of Virginia Woolf, West reports, "The Bloomsbury Group did not like me, and I did not like them" (Noble, ed. 109). She makes an exception for Clive Bell, "a gay and kind companion" (109). On at least one occasion West shared a BBC radio broadcast with Bell. The "lunch conversation," scheduled for March 31, 1930, was titled "Living Dangerously" (BBC Written Archive).

6. An attachment that remains unspecified is Fry's love affair, from 1911 to 1914, with Woolf's sister Vanessa, though clearly Vanessa contributed to the intimate portrait.

7. Woolf suggested that Forster worked in two different traditions of the novel, and that he had difficulty moving from his talent for observation, in which he constructed a cage of social conditions for his characters, to a radiant symbolism. This left readers in doubt of both things (168–69).

8. The existing set of notes contains variants and false starts, and may represent versions of the talk given on two separate occasions, according to Michael Halls, former Modern Archivist of King's College Library, Cambridge, which holds the manuscript.

PART THREE: THE WOMEN OF 1928

1. In *The Essays of Virginia Woolf,* what has come to be known as "Mrs Bennett and Mr Brown" bears the name "Character in Fiction," the title it originally wore in Eliot's journal, the *Criterion,* in July 1924. When she reprinted it as a Hogarth Press pamphlet, Woolf used "Mr Bennett and Mrs Brown," which is the title she had given to a briefer review published in November 1923 in the *New York Evening Post.*

2. The travel genre was entered much more by all three authors. Woolf's *Orlando* and *The Voyage Out* merit consideration in the travel category. In works of mixed genre, West offers descriptions of contrasting parts of the British Isles (*The Judge*) and Yugoslavia (*Black Lamb and Grey Falcon*). West wrote on Spain for the *Freewoman* in 1913, and did a series on South Africa, "The Cauldron of Africa," for the *Sunday Times* in 1960. Barnes's journalism includes pieces that tour New York City, from the Bowery to Greenwich Village and Chinatown. See the collection *New York.*

3. The award ceremony of *Orlando* borrows from Hugh Walpole's awkward tribute at Woolf's *Femina* award, and may owe something to Forster's

struggle with perorations in "The Feminine Note in Literature," discussed in chapter 9.

> Fame! (she laughed.) Fame! Seven editions. A Prize. Photographs in the evening papers (ere she alluded to the "Oak Tree" and "The Burdett Coutts" Memorial Prize which she had won; and we must here snatch time to remark how discomposing it is for her biographer that this culmination and peroration should be dashed from us on a laugh casually like this; but the truth is that when we write of a woman, everything is out of place—culminations and perorations; the accent never falls where it does with a man). (o 312)

On the ceremony and Walpole's self-described "rotten speech" see Bell (2.137–38). The fictional episode refers to the awarding of the Hawthornden Prize for Vita Sackville-West's poem "The Land," published in 1926.

4. This is based upon a tax receipt among the files of her literary agent, A.D. Peters, Harry Ransom Humanities Research Center, University of Texas at Austin.

5. See, for example, Celeste Schenck's introduction to Charlotte Mew in *The Gender of Modernism* (316–21), her essay "Exiled by Genre: Modernism, Canonicity, and the Politics of Exclusion," and the volumes for Felski, Clark, and Ardis cited in the bibliography.

10. Arranging Marriages, Partners, and Spaces

1. The reporter is Quentin Bell. Casting Molly in the wifely role may have been congenial to him (2 Bell 83).

2. Later cat illustrations resemble domestic cats, with Jaguar sporting a Wellsian mustache. The Wells cat sheds tears in 1920 when he has no letter from Rebecca. One of the most humorous is titled "Egotists!" It shows the two cats facing away from each other, both saying "Should'v heard *my* speech." Beneath is the question "Can there be true love between such people?"

3. When Isabella Fairfield died, however, Wells expressed sympathy in kind letters to Lettie.

4. Faith Compton Mackenzie gave credence to rumors about Rebecca and Compton Mackenzie, forcing West to cut short a visit to their home on Capri over the winter of 1920–21. The visit to Capri brought her into the circle of one of Barnes's acquaintances, Romaine Brooks.

5. For example, she set up an interview for Anthony with Lord Beaverbrook, one of Wells's few surviving close friends (West letter to Beaverbrook, 11 Feb. 1949, House of Lords).

6. When Bernard Levin posed a question about Wells in his 1961 radio inter-

view for the "Bookshelf" program, West responded, "I cannot be bothered with this any longer" (tape at Tulsa).

7. Beaverbrook repeats Anthony's explanation that he had not completed the biography out of concern for giving Rebecca "pain" (Beaverbrook letter to West, 30 Oct. 1955, House of Lords). Like Rebecca, Anthony had many explanations for pain-inducing behavior. *Heritage* was not published in Britain until after Rebecca's death, no doubt to avoid a lawsuit. Charles Curran and Dorothy Thompson both encouraged Rebecca to view *Heritage* as fiction. Glendinning cites Anthony's introduction to the British edition of *Heritage* published after his mother's death as evidence that he did intend to hurt her (*Rebecca West* 205).

8. West wrote Alexander Woollcott in 1932 that Anthony "is so adolescent that it sticks out in Byronic lumps" but proclaimed him "an extraordinary being" (West letter to Woollcott, 9 Feb. 1932, Harvard). The most comprehensive report of her assessment of Anthony and her actions toward him that I have found is in a long letter to Emily Hahn, dated 26 January 1952. It starts out with a declaration that "Anthony is the charming and gifted person you know, but a lot else beside." Her story acknowledges the problems of being "very much the divorced parents' child." But she also recounts a history of abnormalities.

9. West chose as her amanuensis Gordon Ray, making a closed archive of Wells letters available for his *H. G. Wells and Rebecca West* (1974). She supplied her memory of events, and insisted that Ray should not consult Anthony. Presumably this was in return for Anthony's not consulting her about his late biography of Wells.

10. This is based on my interviews with Alison Selford, Norman Macleod, and Caroline Duan, July 1993. See also accounts of their aunt by Alison Selford and Norman Macleod in Rollyson. West's letters to her granddaughter Caroline reveal abiding concern that could prove meddlesome. Relevant correspondence will be published in the forthcoming *Selected Letters of Rebecca West,* ed. Bonnie Kime Scott.

11. Relatively little of Barnes's correspondence from the 1920s has survived, making the Barney archive in Paris particularly important to the researcher.

12. Blanch Ebling-Koning, former Curator of Rare Books and Literary Manuscripts at the McKeldin Library, University of Maryland, called attention to these flippant and provocative pieces at the Djuna Barnes Centennial Conference. See the guide to the conference exhibit, *Recollecting Djuna Barnes* (7–9).

13. She did not want a New York lesbian bookstore to be called Djunabooks (Doughty 149).

14. Interestingly, West's friend Dorothy Thompson did manage an interview of Hitler—much to the enhancement of her journalistic reputation.

15. I am grateful to Mary Lynn Broe for identifying these tendencies in a paper centering on "Behind the Heart" given at the Centennial Conference on Djuna Barnes, University of Maryland, October 1992. Both her observations on the text and the story itself have been published in the Djuna Barnes number of the *Review of Contemporary Fiction.*

16. For a discussion of Vita Sackville-West's nostalgic "semi-feudal, humanistic and agrarian order," as echoed in the work of a set of lesbians of her period, see Suzanne Riatt (11–13)

17. Jane Marcus embraced the lupine as emblem for a set of feminist critics who detected a more radical writer in Woolf than the identity suggested by her family biographer, Quentin Bell.

18. West's representation of Woolf's departure to death is reminiscent of Marion Yaverland of West's novel *The Judge,* who goes to her own suicide with great difficulty, lingering on her much-loved house and grounds.

19. In *The Judge* and *Harriet Hume,* Rebecca West depends upon the domestic interiors constructed by leading women characters to suggest their spiritual qualities, as will be discussed in volume 2.

11. Becoming Professionals

1. The essay is based on a 1931 lecture for the National Society for Women's Service, a fact that gives further dimension to its discussion of professions for women.

2. Her letters reveal that she knew little about riding, though she nearly got into trouble because her confident demeanor made people think she must be an expert.

3. West could be rather cutting in describing other women's grooming as well. She wrote to Woolf describing Elizabeth Jenkins at a Paris literary conference, which required a clarification. The first letter described her as a "disordered blonde" and recorded a supposed conversation: "What are you doing here with us? You are the Strand Cut, not Piccadilly" (West to Woolf, n.d., Sussex). Responding to Woolf's apparent inquiry about Miss Jenkins's character, West clarified that Jenkins was a "pile of battered blondness" in "brightly coloured but unsubstantial garments," but a "good girl" (West letter to Woolf, 26th, Sussex). The letter also discusses the rates paid by Mrs. Malony at her "deplorable rag," from which Woolf could receive enough to "buy Leonard diamond studs," yet noting that this was a "difficult market for literature to satisfy."

4. See, for example, her descriptions of Queen Adelaide (2 E 19-22), Lady Dorothy Nevill (an early review made over for the *Common Reader,* 201–205), and the Duchess of Newcastle (CR 70-79). In *The Voyage Out,* the aris-

tocratic lady, Mrs. Flushing, is adored by St. John Hirst for unscrupulously daring to behave as she does.

5. Writing across race is a new topic that deserves attention for all three authors. One manifestation is the phenomenon of both Toni Morrison and Alice Walker writing back to Virginia Woolf, who did provide them professional impetus. This topic is developed further in volume 2.

6. For an able summary, see Marcus, *Art and Anger* 260–61.

7. The major study is Diane Gillespie's *The Sisters' Arts*. See also Louise De-Salvo's *Virginia Woolf* and Jane Dunn's *A Very Close Conspiracy.*

8. See volume 2 for Vanessa's early memories of this relationship, as Virginia was coming into language.

9. This episode is now immortalized in Nigel Nicholson's *Portrait of a Marriage* and the BBC version of this work. Sackville-West and Trefusis lived together in Paris from November 1918 to March 1919, posing a severe threat to Vita's unusually open marriage to Harold Nicholson. West became an acquaintance of Trefusis in 1921.

10. This was a recollection of Muriel Bradbrook, shared with me when I was looking into college records of the event at Girton. As an undergraduate, Bradbrook had attended the lecture that became *A Room of One's Own.* She said nothing of her later negative criticism of Woolf, written for *Scrutiny,* which gained Woolf's attention, like that of another member of the Girton audience, Queenie Leavis.

11. Like Woolf, she received the *Femina Vie Hereuse* prize. Like West and Woolf, she was a contributor to *Time and Tide.*

12. In their early years together, Leonard and Virginia had animal names for one another—hers being mandrill.

13. In *The Court and the Castle* West says, "*Orlando,* the only successfully invented myth in English literature of our time, incarnates the development of poetic genius in England" (220).

14. At West's request, Woolf invited Ethel Smyth to tea to meet West in December 1933. They reminisced about Emmeline Pankhurst in a "screaming howling party" (5 L 2459).

15. The most recent effort in this direction is by Gloria Fromm: "One is almost tempted to say that she wrote fiction as a woman addressing women and nonfiction as a man speaking to men; and men were patently more important in her eyes than women, which means that fiction counted for less in the larger world of public affairs, the world inhabited by all the men who mattered to her" (50). As I have noted in "The Strange Necessity of Rebecca West," N. Gordon Ray's assumption that West had "private reservations" about the feminism of her early writing for the *New Freewoman,* and was only giving her readers what they paid for, is based partially on misrepresentation of that writing. In his introduction to *The Essential*

Rebecca West, Samuel Hynes attempts to lift West out of gender stereotypes, including the tradition of the woman novelist inhabited by Woolf.
He imagines that she shows us "how a free mind might play upon ideas"
(ix, xii). West had a much less naive sense of the power of the cultural
forces of gender, and Hynes overlooks this constant topic. Peter Wolfe and
Harold Orel both detract from her feminism.

16. Coincidentally, Emily Holmes Coleman served as Goldman's secretary in
1928, before she became a close friend of Djuna Barnes.

17. Concerning *Heritage,* Thompson advised West to "stop having fits, and
stop being wounded in your respectability. You are not, you never have
been, and you never will be 'respectable.' " Thompson advised her, on the
basis of her reputation, to be "*sovereign*" instead, rising above the situation
(Thompson letters to West, 27 and 28 Jan. 1956, Tulsa). Far from consoling
West in this instance, Thompson touched a nerve—quite likely over the
theme of respectability.

18. This letter is quoted at greater length in Peter Kurth's outstanding biography of Thompson, *American Cassandra.* His title evokes the same mythical
comparison that Jane Marcus made for West in her eulogy. He says in comparison, "Dorothy and Rebecca might have been sisters in their devotion to
the principles of enlightened individualism; in their abhorrence of communism as the 'nazism' of the nuclear age; in their resolute closing of the gap
that their personalities had set between them. Not since Rose Wilder Land
had Dorothy had a friend who understood her better" (387).

19. West had reviewed Thurber's *The Years with Ross,* and the women wrote
back and forth about a supposed plot to remove one of his supporters. In a
letter to West, Flanner expresses qualified admiration for McCarthy's "lapi-
dary writing" in *Venice Observed.* "I admire and enjoy her brain. How in-
delicate to think of her marital life with Wilson, with his harsh, manly,
sure voice and critiques as part of domesticity" (Flanner letter to West,
[1959], Tulsa). In *Darlinghissima: Janet Flanner's Letters to Natalia Danesi
Murray,* Flanner called West "a great gossip and repeater," and expressed
the opinion that "some of her ideas also are pretty odd" (257). Flanner actually preferred McCarthy's writing to West's. She told Murray that Rebecca
"lashed out with words like someone swimming or skating. Mary, on the
other hand, flew on them somehow" (313).

20. "The Art of Madness," *Little Review* (January 1920): 26.

21. The merits of Edna St. Vincent Millay have been argued as part of a suppressed sentimental tradition by Suzanne Clark. Millay was one of Barnes's
Greenwich Village set, though not a close friend.

22. West's correspondence with G. B. Stern and S. K. Ratcliffe suggests that she
had difficulty with its ending, its threatened proportions, and the previously noted potential for lawsuit from Beaverbrook.

23. Alfred Knopf tried to get West to expand her "World's Worst Failure" se-

ries into a book, and I suspect that *The Harsh Voice* was the delayed fulfillment of that suggestion. The "world" or cultural failures explored in "The World's Worst Failure" remain the ground for the later stories which Fromm dismisses as "women's magazine" fare.

24. Barnes used her own name for her article on James Joyce published in *Vanity Fair*. On the matter of pseudonyms, Rebecca West assumed hers for her early, radical works in socialist and feminist organs, wishing to protect members of her family from responsibility for her ideas. Once she took this name, she used it for novels, political writing, and *Vogue* alike. The only exceptions are unpublished poetry and a drama, which carry a male pseudonym, Richard Wynne Errington—perhaps betraying a separate gender category for these traditionally privileged genres, or her own uncertainty in them.

25. See, for example, "The Diary of a Dangerous Child—Which Should Be of Interest to All Those Who Want to Know How Women Get the Way They Are," *Vanity Fair* 18 (July 1922):56, 94, "Against Nature: In Which Everything That Is Young, Inadequate and Tiresome Is Included in the Term Natural," *Vanity Fair* 18 (August 1922): 60, 88, and "What Is Good Form in Dying; In Which a Dozen Dainty Deaths Are Suggested for Daring Damsels," *Vanity Fair* 20 (June 1923): 73, 102. The first of these records the adventures of Olga, a fourteen-year-old who is trying to decide whether to "place herself in some good man's hands and become a mother" or to be a wanton. She tends toward the latter, as she plans an assault on the man who has been courting her older sister, having summoned him with a love letter. She is also fascinated by the words "virago" and "vixen." We will return to "Against Nature" in volume 2.

26. BBC Written Archive, Reading.

27. Based on correspondence in the BBC Written Archive (Letter to Cecil G. Graves from Charles Bridge, 27 May 1936). Bridge suggested that "conditions make it important to do everything possible to increase British influence." When later called on to do a broadcast to Yugoslavia in the Serbo-Croatian language, West quipped, "If I were to speak in Serbo-Croat myself I fear we should lose whatever support we have in Jugoslavia" (West letter, 11 July 1940, BBC Written Archive). One talk was refused because of the anticipated reaction of the Foreign Office. She was told, "There is little hope of getting anything tough and bellicose passed" (E. M. Barker letter to West, 8 Sept. 1940, BBC Written Archive).

28. The BBC has three Rebecca West recordings, LPs 24660, 26401, and 28323. The last is the most notable as a unit, being "A Visit to a Godmother." This is an autobiographical account of her childhood, when she met the woman her mother had served as a musical governess, unexpectedly confronting class prejudice.

29. West was informed, as politely as possible, that her voice had not been deemed an asset: "Compared with the native gifts of mind and imagina-

tion this is a primitive, but none the less a first condition" (Christopher Salmon letter to West, 2 July 1936, BBC Written Archive). She was asked to break up a 1943 broadcast into a number of portions and make asides informing latecomers of her viewpoint.

30. A reading of the "frost and thaw" in *Orlando* was secured for the BBC in February 1929 (4 L 27).

31. West and her son Anthony were both analyzed. Barnes confided in a letter to Natalie Barney, "I prefer my knots." Woolf had many connections to psychoanalysts, including Alix Strachey and her sister-in-law, Karen Stephen. The Woolfs may also have deemed Virginia's "knots" essential to her creative powers.

32. Like many fugitive pieces it is now accessible in *The Essays of Virginia Woolf*, edited by Andrew McNeillie (3 E 376–79).

33. Gilbert Murray was a contemporary of Jane Harrison.

12. Rallying round *The Well of Loneliness*

1. As a contribution to the second women's movement of the century, Brittain published a volume representing the trial, providing both her responses and long citations of primary documents.

2. Galsworthy was a notable exception, causing great embarrassment to members of P.E.N., of which he was then president. Shaw declined to testify on the grounds that he was immoral himself. H. F. Rubenstein recalled that many popular writers also declined, reluctant to risk their reputations (Brittain, *Radclyffe Hall* 90–91).

3. In her *Epistemology of the Closet,* Eve Sedgwick argues against a "minoritizing view" of homosexuality, seeing it "as an issue of continuing, determinative importance in the lives of people across the spectrum of sexualities" (1)

4. Desmond MacCarthy was called to the stand and asked by Mr. Norman Birkett whether in his opinion the book was obscene. The question was disallowed. Justice Sir Chartres Biron refused to allow the same question to be put to thirty-nine other literary witnesses (Brittain, *Radclyffe Hall* 10–11), including the biologist Julian Huxley. Sir Chartres found that the book was an obscene libel. He ordered that seized copies be destroyed, and fined the defendants twenty guineas each. When Radclyffe Hall interrupted his judgment, at a point when he was referring to practices of women ambulance drivers (based on Hall's friends) in World War I, he threatened to have her removed (Brittain, *Radclyffe Hall* 100–101, 104). *The Well* won its 1929 trial against the charges of the infamous John S. Sumner, Secretary of the Society for the Suppression of Vice in New York—a case in which literary wit-

nesses were allowed to testify. Blanche Knopf had made and withdrawn an offer to publish; Alfred Knopf was the first American publisher (ibid. 154).

5. In disallowing the testimony, Sir Chartres stated, "A book may be a fine piece of literature and yet obscene. Art and obscenity are not dissociated at all" (quoted in Brittain, *Radclyffe Hall* 91).

6. Lovat Dickson notes that on one such evening, Hall got the idea for her story "Adam's Breed" from a lively conversation that West and May Sinclair participated in (114).

7. West became the lifelong intimate friend of Wilde's son, Vyvyan Holland. She advised him to allow publication of his father's letters, including unexpurgated ones to his homosexual partners. Holland dedicated his pictorial biography of Wilde to Rebecca West.

8. I am indebted to Leigh Gilmore for an excellent account of obscenity law in relation to Djuna Barnes and *The Well of Loneliness.*

9. For good arguments of all three views, see Lanser, Jay, and Michel in Broe, ed.

10. As Karla Jay has pointed out, even Barney was uncertain of Masie's real-life counterpart (394 n.14). For a description of Barney's style and her continuing debt to Renée Vivien, see Jay (118–20). Since Barnes did not read or speak French well, she might not have had a full appreciation for Barney's writing.

11. There is some chance that West wrote an anonymous review of Barnes's later work *Nightwood* for *New Statesman and Nation* (17 Oct. 1936). Jane Marcus detects the "tone" of West. See Marcus, "Mousemeat" 197–99. The review takes the book as evidence that "Lesbos has never been a happy island" (197). The charge of "pretentious" style that Wells leveled at West is used for some parts of the work. The review ends remarking that *Nightwood* is "an extremely moral work; and I was not surprised to learn that it appears under the aegis of the most eminent Anglo-Catholic poet of the present day" (199).

12. In a difficult explanatory note to the public edition published "before the compound eye" in 1972, Barnes described religious training, followed by games, and an odd protective reaction:

> Neap-tide to the Proustian chronicle, gleanings from the shores of Mytilene, glimpses of its novitiates, its rising "saints" and "priestesses," and thereon to such aptitude and insouciance that they took to gaming and to swapping that "other" of the mystery, the anomaly that calls the hidden name. That, affronted, eats its shadow.

The mystery and anomaly may be lesbianism, its name still heavily protected, even if bandied about.

13. Mary Campbell was one of Sackville-West's loves, overlapping with her affair with Virginia Woolf.

14.   As footnoted in the *Diary,* the Ladies of Llangollen were celebrated eccentrics who eschewed marriage and fled to Wales to live together. Borrowing upon the riding habit, they assumed a mixed costume including items of male apparel—the most notable item, top hats.

15.   West wrote in her diary, "If I were young again, I would deliberately (and against my nature) choose to be a Lesbian" (cited in Glendinning, *Rebecca West* 125). She apparently did not consider lesbian martyrdom inevitable in her youth.

Bibliography

Abel, Elizabeth. "Narrative Structure(s) and Female Development." In *The Voyage In: Fictions of Female Development,* ed. Elizabeth Abel, Marianne Hirsch, and Elizabeth Langland, 161–85. Hanover, N.H.: University Press of New England, 1983.

Ackroyd, Peter. *T. S. Eliot.* London: Hamish Hamilton, 1984.

Anderson, Margaret. *My Thirty Years' War.* 1930. Westport, Conn.: Greenwood Press, 1971.

Auerbach, Nina. *Communities of Women.* Cambridge, Mass.: Harvard University Press, 1978.

Barash, Carol. "Dora Marsden's Feminism, the *Freewoman,* and the Gender Politics of Early Modernism." *Princeton University Library Chronicle* 49.1 (Fall 1987): 31–56.

Barnes, Djuna. *The Antiphon.* In Barnes, *Selected Works of Djuna Barnes.* New York: Farrar, Straus and Cudahy, 1962.

———. "Behind the Heart." *The Review of Contemporary Fiction* 13.3 (1993): 17–21.

———. *The Book of Repulsive Women: Eight Rhythms and Five Drawings.* New York: Bruno Chap Books, 1915.

———. "The Confessions of Helen Westley." In Scott, ed., *The Gender of Modernism,* 40–45.

———. "The Dove." In Barnes, *A Book,* 147–64. New York: Boni and Liveright, 1923.

———. "Elsa Baroness Von Freytag-Loringhoven." *Transition* (December 1927): 19.

———. "The Girl and the Gorilla." *New York World Magazine* (18 October 1914): 9; rpt. in Barnes, *New York,* 180–84.

———. *I Could Never Be Lonely without a Husband: Interviews by Djuna Barnes.* Ed. Alyce Barry. London: Virago, 1987.

———. "James Joyce: A Portrait of the Man Who Is, at Present, One of the More Significant Figures in Literature." *Vanity Fair* 18 (April 1922): 65, 104; rpt. in Barnes, *I Could Never Be Lonely without a Husband,* 288–96.

———. *Ladies Almanack.* 1928. Elmwood Park, Ill.: Dalkey Archive Press, 1992.

———. "Lament for the Left Bank." *Town and Country* 96 (December 1941): 92, 136–38, 148.

———. Letters to Natalie Barney, Natalie Barney Collection, Bibliothèque Jacques Doucet, Paris.

———. Letters to Emily Holmes Coleman, Coleman Collection, Morris Library, University of Delaware.

———. Letters to family members, T. S. Eliot, Natalie Barney, etc., Djuna Barnes Collection, McKeldin Library, University of Maryland.

———. "Love and the Beast." Unpublished ms., Natalie Barney Collection, Bibliothèque Jacques Doucet, Paris.

———. *New York*. Ed. Alyce Barry. Los Angeles: Sun and Moon Press, 1989.

———. *Nightwood*. 1936. New York: New Directions, 1961.

———. *Ryder*. New York: St. Martin's Press, 1979.

———. "Vagaries Malicieux." *The Double Dealer* 3 (May 1922): 249–60.

Barnes, Zadel. See Gustafson, Zadel Barnes (Buddington).

Barney, Natalie. Letters to Djuna Barnes, Djuna Barnes Collection, McKeldin Library, University of Maryland.

———. *Pensées d'une Amazone*. Paris: Emile Paul Frères, 1920.

Bell, Quentin. *Virginia Woolf: A Biography*. 1972. 2 vols. London: Granada, 1976.

Bennett, Arnold. "Is the Novel Decaying?" In Bennett, *The Author's Craft and Other Critical Writings of Arnold Bennett*, ed. Samuel Hynes, 87–89. Lincoln: University of Nebraska Press, 1968.

Benson, Stella. Letter to Virginia Woolf, Woolf Collection, University of Sussex Library.

Benstock, Bernard. *Joyce-Again's Wake*. Seattle: University of Washington Press, 1965.

Benstock, Shari. *Women of the Left Bank: Paris, 1900–1940*. Austin: University of Texas Press, 1986.

Bergonzi, Bernard. *The Myth of Modernism and Twentieth Century Literature*. New York: St. Martin's Press, 1986.

Blain, Virginia; Patricia Clements; and Isobel Grundy, eds. *The Feminist Companion to Literature in English: Women Writers from the Middle Ages to the Present*. New Haven: Yale University Press, 1990.

BLAST: Review of the Great English Vortex. Nos. 1–2 (1914–1915). Ed. Wyndham Lewis. New York: Kraus Reprint Corporation, 1967.

Bradbury, Malcolm, and James MacFarlane, eds. *Modernism, 1880–1930*. Sussex: Harvester, 1978.

Briggs, Austin. "Rebecca West vs. James Joyce, Samuel Beckett, and William Carlos Williams." In *Joyce in the Hibernian Metropolis: Essays*, ed. Morris Beja and David Norris. Columbus: Ohio State University Press, in press.

Brittain, Vera. *Diary of the Thirties, 1932–1939: Chronicle of Friendship*. Ed. Alan Bishop. London: Victor Gollancz, 1986.

———. *Radclyffe Hall: A Case of Obscenity?* London: Femina Books, 1968.

Broe, Mary Lynn. " 'A Love from Back of the Heart': The Story Djuna Wrote for
　　Charles Henri." *The Review of Contemporary Fiction* 13.3 (Fall 1993): 22–32.
―――. "My Art Belongs to Daddy: Incest as Exile, the Textual Economics of Hay-
　　ford Hall." In *Women's Writing in Exile*, ed. Mary Lynn Broe and Angela In-
　　gram, 41–86. Chapel Hill: University of North Carolina Press, 1989.
Broe, Mary Lynn, ed. *Silence and Power: A Reevaluation of Djuna Barnes*. Carbon-
　　dale: Southern Illinois University Press, 1991.
Broe, Mary Lynn, and Angela Ingram, eds. *Women's Writing in Exile*. Chapel Hill:
　　University of North Carolina Press, 1989.
Brown, Dennis. *Intertextual Dynamics within the Literary Group—Joyce, Lewis,
　　Pound and Eliot: The Men of 1914*. London: Macmillan, 1990.
Brownstein, Marilyn. "Marianne Moore." In Scott, ed., *The Gender of Modernism*,
　　323–32.
Bruno, Guido. "Fleurs du Mal à la Mode de New York: An Interview with Djuna
　　Barnes by Guido Bruno." In Barnes, *I Could Never Be Lonely without a Hus-
　　band*, 383–88.
Bryher (Winifred Ellerman). *The Heart to Artemis: A Writer's Memoirs*. New York:
　　Harcourt, Brace, 1962.
Bürger, Peter. *Theory of the Avant Garde*. Minneapolis: University of Minnesota
　　Press, 1984.
Bush, Ronald. "Ezra Pound." In Scott, ed., *The Gender of Modernism*, 353–57.
―――. *The Genesis of Ezra Pound's Cantos*. Princeton: Princeton University Press, 1976.
Butler, Judith. *Gender Trouble: Feminism and the Subversion of Identity*. New York:
　　Routledge, 1990.
Carpenter, Humphrey. *A Serious Character: The Life of Ezra Pound*. London: Faber
　　and Faber, 1988.
Caughie, Pamela L. "The (En)gendering of Literary History." *Tulsa Studies in
　　Women's Literature* 8 (1984): 111–20.
―――. *Virginia Woolf and Postmodernism: Literature in Quest and Question of It-
　　self*. Urbana: University of Chicago Press, 1991.
Caws, Marianne. *Women of Bloomsbury: Virginia, Vanessa, and Carrington*. New
　　York: Routledge, 1990.
Christ, Carol P. *Diving Deep and Surfacing: Women Writers on Spiritual Quest*. Bos-
　　ton: Beacon, 1980.
Cixous, Hélène. "Castration or Decapitation?" *Signs* 7.1 (1981): 41–55.
Clark, Suzanne. *Sentimental Modernism: Women Writers and the Revolution of the
　　Word*. Bloomington: Indiana University Press, 1991.
Clarke, Bruce. "Dora Marsden and Ezra Pound: *The New Freewoman* and 'The Seri-
　　ous Artist.' " *Contemporary Literature* 33.1 (Spring 1992): 91–112.

Cohen, Ted. "Metaphor and the Cultivation of Intimacy." In Sacks, ed., *On Metaphor,* 1–10.

Coleman, Emily Holmes. Diary, Emily Holmes Coleman Collection, Special Collections, Morris Library, University of Delaware.

Cooper, Helen; Adrienne Auslander Munich; and Susan Merrill Squier, eds. *Arms and the Woman: War, Gender, and Literary Representation.* Chapel Hill: University of North Carolina Press, 1989.

Cunningham, Valentine. *British Writers of the Thirties.* New York: Oxford University Press, 1987.

Curry, Linda. "Tom, Take Mercy: Djuna Barnes' Drafts of *The Antiphon.*" In Broe, ed., *Silence and Power,* 268–86.

Dalton, Anne B. " 'This Is Obscene': Female Voyeurism, Sexual Abuse, and Maternal Power in *The Dove.*" *The Review of Contemporary Fiction* 13.3 (Fall 1993): 117–39.

Daly, Mary. *Gyn/Ecology: The Metaethics of Radical Feminism.* Boston: Beacon, 1978.

Dasenbrock, Reed Way. *The Literary Vorticism of Ezra Pound.* Baltimore: Johns Hopkins University Press, 1983.

DeKoven, Marianne. *Rich and Strange: Gender, History, Modernism.* Princeton: Princeton University Press, 1991.

Deleuze, Gilles. *The Deleuze Reader.* Ed. Constantine V. Bounder. New York: Columbia University Press, 1993.

de Man, Paul. "The Epistemology of Metaphor." In Sacks, ed., *On Metaphor,* 11–28.

DeSalvo, Louise. *Virginia Woolf: The Impact of Childhood Sexual Abuse on Her Life and Work.* Boston: Beacon, 1989.

Dickson, Lovat. *Radclyffe Hall at the Well of Loneliness: A Sapphic Chronicle.* New York: Scribners, 1975.

Doughty, Frances M. "Gilt on Cardboard: Djuna Barnes as Illustrator of Her Life and Work." In Broe, ed., *Silence and Power,* 137–54.

Dunn, Jane. *A Very Close Conspiracy: Vanessa Bell and Virginia Woolf.* London: Jonathan Cape, 1990.

DuPlessis, Rachel Blau. *H. D.: The Career of That Struggle.* Bloomington: Indiana University Press, 1986.

——. *The Pink Guitar: Writing as Feminist Practice.* New York: Routledge, 1990.

——. *Writing beyond the Ending: Narrative Strategies of Twentieth-Century Women Writers.* Bloomington: Indiana University Press, 1985.

Eder, Doris L. "Louis Unmasked: T. S. Eliot in *The Waves.*" *Virginia Woolf Quarterly* 2.1–2 (1975–76): 13–27.

Eliot, T. S. *After Strange Gods.* New York: Harcourt, Brace, 1934.

——. Introduction. In Pound, *Literary Essays of Ezra Pound,* ix–xv. Westport, Conn.: Greenwood Press, 1979.

———. *The Letters of T. S. Eliot*. Volume I: *1898–1922*. Ed. Valerie Eliot. San Diego: Harcourt Brace Jovanovich, 1988.

———. Letters to Djuna Barnes, Djuna Barnes Collection, McKeldin Library, University of Maryland.

———. Letters to Virginia Woolf, Virginia Woolf Collection, Sussex University Library, and Berg Collection, New York Public Library.

———. Preface. In *The Criterion*, vol. 1. Collected Edition. London: Faber, 1967.

———. "Review of Marianne Moore's *Poems* and *Marriage*." In Scott, ed., *The Gender of Modernism*, 146–49.

———. *Selected Prose of T. S. Eliot*. New York: Harcourt Brace Jovanovich, 1975.

———. "*Ulysses*, Order and Myth." *Dial* 75 (1923): 480–83; rpt. Ellmann and Feidelson, eds., *The Modern Tradition*, 679–81.

———. "*The Waste Land*": *A Facsimile and Transcript of the Original Drafts, Including the Annotations of Ezra Pound*. Ed. Valerie Eliot. London: Faber, 1971.

Eliot, Vivien(ne). (Feiron Morris). "The Dansant." *Criterion* 3.9 (October 1924): 72–78.

———. "Letters of the Moment—I." *Criterion* 2.6 (February 1924): 220–22.

———. "Letters of the Moment—II." *Criterion* 2.7 (April 1924): 360–64.

Ellis, Havelock. *Studies in the Psychology of Sex*. Volume 2: *Sexual Inversion*. Philadelphia: Davis, 1924–28.

Ellmann, Richard, and Charles Feidelson, eds. *The Modern Tradition*. New York: Oxford University Press, 1965.

Faderman, Lillian. *Odd Girls and Twilight Lovers: A History of Lesbian Life in Twentieth-Century America*. New York: Columbia University Press, 1991.

"Fairfield vs. the *Evening Standard* Co. Ltd," 1928-W.-No. 2589, High Court of Justice, 21 November 1928.

Felski, Rita. *Beyond Feminist Aesthetics: Feminist Literature and Social Change*. Cambridge, Mass.: Harvard University Press, 1989.

———. "Feminism, Postmodernism, and the Concept of Mothering." *Cultural Critique* 13 (Fall 1989): 33–56.

Field, Andrew. *Djuna: The Formidable Miss Barnes*. Austin: University of Texas Press, 1983.

Flanner, Janet. *Darlinghissima: Janet Flanner's Letters to Natalia Danesi Murray*. Ed. Natalia Danesi Murray. New York: Random House, 1985.

Fogel, Daniel Mark. *Covert Relations: James Joyce, Virginia Woolf, and Henry James*. Charlottesville: University Press of Virginia, 1990.

Forster, E. M. "The Feminine Note in Literature." Unpublished ms., EMF vi/9, King's College Library, Cambridge.

Forster, E. M., and Virginia Woolf. "The New Censorship." *Nation & Athenaeum* (8 September 1928): 629.

Foucault, Michel. *Discipline and Punish*. New York: Vintage, 1977.

————. *The Order of Things: An Archaeology of the Human Sciences.* New York: Random House, 1970.

Frank, Joseph. *The Widening Gyre: Crisis and Mastery in Modern Literature.* New Brunswick: Rutgers University Press, 1963.

Fraser, Nancy, and Linda J. Nicholson. "Social Criticism without Philosophy: An Encounter between Feminism and Postmodernism." In Nicholson, ed., *Feminism/Postmodernism,* 19–38.

Friedan, Betty. *The Feminine Mystique.* New York: Norton, 1963.

Friedman, Ellen G. " 'Utterly Other Discourse': The Anti-canon of Experimental Women Writers from Dorothy Richardson to Christine Brooke-Rose." *Modern Fiction Studies* 34.3 (1988): 353–70.

Friedman, Ellen G., and Miriam Fuchs. *Breaking the Sequence: Women's Experimental Fiction.* Princeton: Princeton University Press, 1989.

Friedman, Susan Stanford. *Penelope's Web: Gender, Modernity, H. D.'s Fiction.* New York: Cambridge University Press, 1990.

Fromm, Gloria G. "Rebecca West: The Fictions of Fact and the Facts of Fiction." *New Criterion* 9.5 (1991): 45–53.

Fry, Roger. *Letters of Roger Fry.* 2 vols. Ed. Denys Sutton. London: Chatto and Windus, 1972.

Fuss, Diana. *Essentially Speaking: Feminism, Nature and Difference.* New York: Routledge, 1989.

Gallop, Jane. *The Daughter's Seduction: Feminism and Psychoanalysis.* Ithaca: Cornell University Press, 1982.

Garis, Leslie. "Rebecca West." *New York Times Magazine* (4 April 1982): 30–36, 98–101.

Garner, Les. *A Brave and Beautiful Spirit: Dora Marsden, 1882–1960.* Aldershot: Avebury, 1990.

Gawthorpe, Mary. *Up Hill to Holloway.* Penobscot, Maine: Traversity Press, 1962.

Gilbert, Sandra M., and Susan Gubar. *No Man's Land: The Place of the Woman Writer in the Twentieth Century.* Volume 1: *The War of the Words.* New Haven: Yale University Press, 1988.

————. *No Man's Land: The Place of the Woman Writer in the Twentieth Century.* Volume 2: *Sexchanges.* New Haven: Yale University Press, 1989.

————. *The Norton Anthology of Literature by Women: The Tradition in English.* New York: Norton, 1985.

————. "Sexual Linguistics: Gender, Language, Sexuality." *New Literary History* 16 (1985): 515–43.

Gillespie, Diane F. "May Sinclair and the Stream of Consciousness: Metaphors and Metaphysics." *English Literature in Transition, 1880–1920* 21.2 (1978): 134–42.

—————. *The Sisters' Arts: The Writing and Painting of Virginia Woolf and Vanessa Bell.* Syracuse: Syracuse University Press, 1988.

Gilmore, Leigh. Panel presentation on pornography and the law. Djuna Barnes Centennial Conference, University of Maryland, October 1992.

Ginsberg, Elaine K., and Laura Moss Gottlieb. *Virginia Woolf: Centennial Essays.* Troy, N.Y.: Whitston Publishing Company, 1983.

Glendinning, Victoria. Afterword. In West, *Sunflower,* 268–76.

—————. *Elizabeth Bowen.* New York: Knopf, 1978.

—————. Introduction. In West, *Harriet Hume.*

—————. *Rebecca West: A Life.* London: Weidenfeld and Nicolson, 1987.

—————. *Vita: The Life of V. Sackville-West.* London: Weidenfeld and Nicolson, 1983.

Gordon, Lyndall. "Eliot and Women." In *T. S. Eliot: The Modernist in History,* ed. Ronald Bush, 9–22. Cambridge: Cambridge University Press, 1991.

—————. *Eliot's Early Years.* Oxford: Oxford University Press, 1977.

—————. *Eliot's New Life.* New York: Farrar Straus Giroux, 1988.

—————. *Virginia Woolf: A Writer's Life.* Oxford: Oxford University Press, 1986.

Gross, John L. *The Modern Movement: A TLS Companion.* Chicago: University of Chicago Press, 1992.

Gustafson, Zadel Barnes (Buddington). "The Children's Night." *Harper's New Monthly Magazine* 296 (January 1875): 153–64.

—————. Letters to Djuna Barnes, Djuna Barnes Collection, McKeldin Library, University of Maryland.

—————. *Meg: A Pastoral.* Boston: Lee and Shepard, 1879.

H. D. (Hilda Doolittle). *Bid Me to Live.* 1960. London: Virago, 1984.

—————. *End to Torment: A Memoir of Ezra Pound.* New York: New Directions, 1979.

—————. *The Walls Do Not Fall.* 1944. In H. D., *Trilogy,* 1–59. New York: New Directions, 1973.

Hall, Radclyffe. *The Well of Loneliness.* 1928. New York: Doubleday, 1990.

Halper, Nathan. "James Joyce and Rebecca West." *Partisan Review* 16 (July 1949): 761–63.

Hammond, J. R. *H. G. Wells and Rebecca West.* New York: St. Martin's Press, 1991.

Hanscombe, Gillian, and Virginia L. Smyers. *Writing for Their Lives: The Modernist Women, 1920–1940.* London: The Women's Press, 1987.

Haraway, Donna. "A Manifesto for Cyborgs: Science, Technology, and Socialist Feminism in the 1980s." In Nicholson, ed., *Feminism/Postmodernism,* 190–233.

Harrison, Jane Ellen. *Epilogomena to the Study of Greek Religion.* Cambridge: Cambridge University Press, 1921.

—————. *Themis: A Study of the Social Origins of Greek Religion.* Cambridge: Cambridge University Press, 1912.

Hartman, Geoffrey. "Virginia's Web." In Hartman, *Beyond Formalism: Literary Essays, 1958–1970*. New Haven: Yale University Press, 1970.

Hawkes, Ellen. "Woolf's 'Magical Garden of Women.'" In Marcus, ed., *New Feminist Essays on Virginia Woolf*, 31–60.

Hedges, Elaine. "The Needle or the Pen." In Howe, ed., *Tradition and the Talents of Women*, 338–64.

Herring, Philip. "Zadel Barnes: Journalist." *The Review of Contemporary Fiction* 13.3 (Fall 1993): 107–16.

Herzig, Carl. "Roots of Night: Emerging Style and Vision in the Early Journalism of Djuna Barnes." *Centennial Review* 31 (Summer 1987): 255–69.

Holroyd, Michael. *Lytton Strachey*. 2 vols. New York: Holt, Reinhart and Winston, 1967.

Howe, Florence, ed. *Tradition and the Talents of Women*. Urbana: University of Illinois Press, 1991.

Hunt, Violet. *I Have This to Say: The Story of My Flurried Years*. New York: Boni and Liveright, 1926.

Huntington, John. "Problems of an Amorous Utopian." In *H. G. Wells under Revision*, ed. Patrick Parrinder and Christopher Rolfe, 168–80. Selinsgrove: Susquehanna University Press, 1990.

Hutchinson, G. E. "The Dome." In Hutchinson, *The Itinerant Ivory Tower: Scientific and Literary Essays*, 241–55. New Haven: Yale University Press, 1953.

———. *A Preliminary List of the Writings of Rebecca West*. New Haven: Yale University Library, 1957.

Huyssen, Andreas. *After the Great Divide: Modernism, Mass Culture, Postmodernism*. Bloomington: Indiana University Press, 1986.

Hynes, Samuel. Introduction. In West, *Rebecca West: A Celebration*. New York: Viking, 1977.

Ingram, Angela. "'The Sacred Edifices': Virginia Woolf and Some of the Sons of Culture." In Marcus, ed., *Virginia Woolf and Bloomsbury*, 125–45.

Irigaray, Luce. *This Sex Which Is Not One*. Trans. Catherine Porter with Carolyn Burke. 1977. Ithaca: Cornell University Press, 1985.

Jackson, Dennis. "The 'Old Pagan Vision': Myth and Ritual in *Lady Chatterley's Lover*." In *Critical Essays on D. H. Lawrence*, ed. Dennis Jackson and Fleda Brown Jackson, 128–44. Boston: G. K. Hall, 1988.

Jacobus, Mary. *Reading Woman: Essays in Feminist Criticism*. New York: Columbia University Press, 1986.

Jameson, Fredric. *Fables of Aggression: Wyndham Lewis, the Modernist as Fascist*. Berkeley: University of California Press, 1979.

Jardine, Alice. *Gynesis: Configurations of Woman and Modernity.* Ithaca: Cornell University Press, 1985.

Jay, Karla. *The Amazon and the Page: Natalie Clifford Barney and Renée Vivien.* Bloomington: Indiana University Press, 1988.

——. "The Outsider among the Expatriates: Djuna Barnes's Satire on the Ladies of the *Almanack*." In Broe, ed., *Silence and Power,* 184–94.

Jehlen, Myra. "Archimedes and the Paradox of Feminist Criticism." *Signs* 6.4 (1981): 525–50.

Johns, D. B. "Ezra Pound and the 'Cosmic Male Principle.' " *Lit: Literature Interpretation Theory* 1.3 (1990): 171–82.

Johnson, Barbara. "Gender, Theory, and the Yale School." In *Speaking of Gender,* ed. Elaine Showalter, 45–55. New York: Routledge, 1989.

Jolas, Eugene. "Glossary: *Ryder* by Djuna Barnes." *Transition* 16–17 (June 1929): 326. New York: Kraus Reprint Corporation, 1967.

Joyce, James. *Finnegans Wake.* New York: Viking, 1939.

——. *Letters of James Joyce.* 3 vols. Ed. Stuart Gilbert (vol. I) and Richard Ellmann (vols. II and III). New York: Viking, 1965–66.

——. *A Portrait of the Artist as a Young Man.* New York: Viking, 1968.

——. *Selected Letters of James Joyce.* Ed. Richard Ellmann. New York: Viking, 1975.

——. *Ulysses: A Critical and Synoptic Edition.* Ed. Hans Walter Gabler. New York: Garland, 1984.

Kaplan, Sydney Janet. *Feminist Consciousness in the Modern British Novel.* Urbana: University of Illinois Press, 1975.

Kenner, Hugh. "The Making of the Modernist Canon." *Chicago Review* 34 (1984): 49–61.

——. *The Pound Era.* Berkeley: University of California Press, 1971.

——. *A Sinking Island: The Modern English Writers.* London: Barrie and Jenkins, 1988.

Kermode, Frank. *Romantic Image.* London: Routledge and Paul, 1957.

Kiely, Robert. *Beyond Egotism: The Fiction of James Joyce, Virginia Woolf, and D. H. Lawrence.* Cambridge, Mass.: Harvard University Press, 1980.

Kirchwey, Freda. "Freda Kirchwey on Wells as the Ideal Father." In *H. G. Wells: The Critical Heritage,* ed. Patrick Parrinder, 307–309. London: Routledge and Kegan Paul, 1972.

Koestenbaum, Wayne. *Double Talk: The Erotics of Male Literary Collaboration.* New York: Routledge, 1989.

Kristeva, Julia. *Desire in Language: A Semiotic Approach to Literature and Art.* Ed. Leon S. Roudiez. Trans. Thomas Gora, Alice Jardine, and Leon S. Roudiez. New York: Columbia University Press, 1980.

———. "From 'Oscillation between Power and Denial.'" Trans. Marilyn A. August. In *New French Feminisms: An Anthology,* ed. Elaine Marks and Isabelle de Courtivron, 165–67. New York: Schocken, 1986.

———. *The Kristeva Reader.* Ed. Toril Moi. Trans. Alice Jardine, Leon S. Roudiez, Seàn Hand, et al. New York: Columbia University Press, 1986.

Kurth, Peter. *American Cassandra: The Life of Dorothy Thompson.* Boston: Little, Brown and Company, 1990.

Lanser, Susan Snaider. "Speaking in Tongues: *Ladies Almanack* and the Discourse of Desire." In Broe, ed., *Silence and Power,* 156–69.

Laurence, Patricia Ondek. *The Reading of Silence: Virginia Woolf in the English Tradition.* Stanford: Stanford University Press, 1991.

Lawrence, D. H. *Lady Chatterley's Lover: A Propos of Lady Chatterley's Letter.* Ed. Michael Squires. Cambridge: Cambridge University Press, 1993.

———. *The Letters of D. H. Lawrence.* Vol. 2. Ed. George J. Zytaruk and James T. Boulton. Cambridge: Cambridge University Press, 1981.

———. *"Psychoanalysis and the Unconscious" and "Fantasia of the Unconscious."* 1921–1922. New York: Viking, 1960.

———. "Surgery for the Novel—or a Bomb?" In *Phoenix II: Uncollected, Unpublished and Other Prose Works by D. H. Lawrence,* ed. Warren Roberts and Harry T. Moore. London: Heinemann, 1968.

———. *Women in Love.* 1920. Harmondsworth: Penguin, 1976.

Lawrence, D. H., and Amy Lowell. *The Letters of D. H. Lawrence and Amy Lowell, 1914–1925.* Ed. E. Claire Healey and Keith Cushman. Santa Barbara: Black Sparrow Press, 1986.

Lawrence, Karen. "Introduction." In *Decolonizing Tradition.* Urbana: University of Illinois Press, 1992.

Levenson, Michael H. *A Genealogy of Modernism: A Study of English Literary Doctrine, 1908–22.* New York: Cambridge University Press, 1984.

Lewis, Wyndham. *Blasting and Bombardiering.* Berkeley: University of California Press, 1967.

———. *The Letters of Wyndham Lewis.* Ed. W. K. Rose. Norfolk: New Directions, 1963.

———. Letters to Sidney Schiff, Sidney Schiff Collection, British Library.

———. *Men without Art.* London: Cassell, 1934.

———. *Rude Assignment.* London: Hutchinson, 1950.

———. *Satire in Fiction.* In Lewis, *The Enemy: A Review of Art and Literature* 1; rpt. London: Frank Cass and Co., 1968.

———. *Tarr.* New York: Knopf, 1926.

Lidderdale, Jane, and Mary Nicholson. *Dear Miss Weaver: Harriet Shaw Weaver, 1876–1961*. New York: Viking, 1970.

Lindberg, Kathryne S. *Reading Pound Reading: Modernism after Nietzsche*. New York: Oxford University Press, 1987.

London, Bette. "Guerrilla in Petticoats or Sans-culotte? Virginia Woolf and the Future of Feminist Criticism." *Diacritics* 21.2–3 (1991): 11–29.

Longenbach, James. *Modernist Poetics of History: Pound, Eliot, and a Sense of the Past*. Princeton: Princeton University Press, 1987.

———. "Pound among the Women." *Review* 12 (1990): 135–58.

———. "The Women and Men of 1914." In *Arms and the Woman: War, Gender and Literary Representation*, ed. Helen M. Cooper, Adrienne Auslander Munich, and Susan Merrill Squier, 97–123. Chapel Hill: University of North Carolina Press, 1989.

Lyotard, Jean-François. *The Postmodern Condition*. Minneapolis: University of Minnesota Press, 1984.

Maddox, Brenda. *Nora Joyce*. London: Hamilton, 1988.

Mansfield, Katherine. *The Letters of Katherine Mansfield*. 2 vols. Vol. 2, ed. John Middleton Murry. New York: Knopf, 1930.

Marcus, Jane. *Art and Anger*. Columbus: Ohio State University Press for Miami University, 1988.

———. "Mousemeat: Contemporary Reviews of *Nightwood*." In Broe, ed., *Silence and Power*, 195–204.

———. "Rebecca West: A Voice of Authority." In *Faith of a (Woman) Writer*, ed. Alice Kessler-Harris and William McBrien, 237–46. Westport, Conn.: Greenwood Press, 1988.

———. "Still Practice, A W/rested Alphabet: Toward a Feminist Aesthetic." *Tulsa Studies in Women's Literature* 3.1/2 (1984): 79–97.

———. *Virginia Woolf and the Languages of Patriarchy*. Bloomington: Indiana University Press, 1987.

———. "A Wilderness of One's Own: Feminist Fantasy Novels of the Twenties—Rebecca West and Sylvia Townsend Warner." In *Women Writers and the City*, ed. Susan Merrrill Squier, 134–60. Knoxville: University of Tennessee Press, 1984.

Marcus, Jane, ed. *New Feminist Essays on Virginia Woolf*. Lincoln: University of Nebraska Press, 1981.

———. *Virginia Woolf and Bloomsbury: A Centenary Celebration*. Basingstoke: Macmillan, 1987.

Marsden, Dora. "Views and Comments." *New Freewoman* 1.1 (1913): 5.

McAlmon, Robert, and Kay Boyle. *Being Geniuses Together, 1920–30*. Garden City, N.Y.: Doubleday, 1968.

Meisel, Perry. *The Myth of the Modern: A Study of British Literature and Criticism after 1850*. New Haven: Yale University Press, 1987.

Menand, Louis. *Discovering Modernism: T. S. Eliot and His Context*. New York: Oxford University Press, 1987.

Meyerowitz, Joanne. "Beyond the Feminine Mystique: A Reassessment of Postwar Mass Culture, 1946–1958." *Journal of American History* 79.4 (March 1993): 1455–82.

Meyers, Jeffrey. *The Enemy: A Biography of Wyndham Lewis*. London: Routledge and Kegan Paul, 1980.

Michel, Frann. "All Women Are Not Women All: *Ladies Almanack* and Feminine Writing." In Broe, ed., *Silence and Power*. 170–82.

Michie, Helena. *The Flesh Made Word*. New York: Oxford University Press, 1987.

Miller, Nancy K. "Arachnologies: The Woman, the Text, and the Critic." In *The Poetics of Gender*, ed. Nancy K. Miller, 270–95. New York: Columbia University Press, 1986.

Minow-Pinkney, Makiko. *Virginia Woolf and the Problem of the Subject*. New Brunswick: Rutgers University Press, 1987.

Moi, Toril. *Sexual/Textual Politics: Feminist Literary Theory*. London: Methuen, 1985.

Moore, Harry T. *The Priest of Love: A Life of D. H. Lawrence*. New York: Farrar, Straus and Giroux, 1974.

Moscato, Michael, and Leslie LeBlanc, eds. *The United States of America v One Book Entitled "Ulysses" by James Joyce: Documents and Commentary—A 50-Year Retrospective*. Frederick, Md.: University Publications of America, Inc., 1984.

Mulvey, Laura. "Visual Pleasure and Narrative Cinema." In Warhol and Herndl, eds., *Feminisms*, 432–42.

The New Freewoman: An Individualist Review 1–13 (1913). New York: Kraus Reprint Corporation, 1967.

Newton, Esther. "The Mythic Mannish Lesbian: Radclyffe Hall and the New Woman." *Signs* 9 (1984): 557–75.

Nicholson, Linda J., ed. *Feminism/Postmodernism*. New York: Routledge, 1990.

Nikolchina, Miglena. "Born from the Head: Reading Woolf via Kristeva." *Diacritics* 21.2–3 (1991): 30–42.

Noble, Joan Russell, ed. *Recollections of Virginia Woolf by her Contemporaries*. London: Cardinal, 1989.

Norris, Margot. *Joyce's Web: The Social Unraveling of Modernism*. Austin: University of Texas Press, 1992.

O'Neal, Hank. "Reminiscences." In Broe, ed., *Silence and Power*, 348–61.

Orel, Harold. *The Literary Achievement of Rebecca West*. New York: St. Martin's Press, 1986.

Pankhurst, E. Sylvia. *The Suffragette*. London: Gay and Hancock, 1911.

Parrinder, Patrick. "The Strange Necessity: James Joyce's Rejection in England (1914–30)." In *James Joyce: New Perspectives*, ed. Colin MacCabe, 151–67. Bloomington: Indiana University Press, 1982.

Peterson, Shirley. "The Emancipation of the Heroine: The Suffragist in the British Novel (1907–1922)." Dissertation, University of Delaware, 1990.

Plimpton, George, ed. *Women Writers at Work: The Paris Review Interviews*. New York: Penguin, 1989.

Pondrom, Cyrena N. "H. D. and the Origins of Imagism." In *Signets*, ed. Susan Stanford Freidman and Rachel Blau DuPlessis, 85–109. Madison: University of Wisconsin Press, 1990.

Pound, Ezra. "Doggerel Section of Letter to Marianne Moore." In Scott, ed., *The Gender of Modernism*, 362–65.

———. *Literary Essays of Ezra Pound*. Edited with an Introduction by T. S. Eliot. New York: New Directions, 1968; rpt., Westport, Conn.: Greenwood Press, 1979.

———. "Others." In Scott, ed., *The Gender of Modernism*, 365–67.

———. *Pound/Joyce*. New York: New Directions, 1967.

———. Translator's Postscript. In Remy de Gourmont, *The Natural Philosophy of Love*, trans. Ezra Pound. New York: Collier Books, 1961.

Pound, Ezra, and Margaret Cravens. *Ezra Pound and Margaret Cravens: A Tragic Friendship*. Ed. Omar Pound and Robert Spoo. Durham, N.C.: Duke University Press, 1988.

Pound, Ezra, and Dorothy Shakespear. *Ezra Pound and Dorothy Shakespear: Their Letters*. Ed. Omar Pound and A. Walton Litz. New York: New Directions, 1984.

Quinn, John. Letter to Ezra Pound, Northwestern University Library.

Quinones, Ricardo. *Mapping Literary Modernism*. Princeton: Princeton University Press, 1985.

Rabinowitz, Peter. "Canons and Close Readings." *The Chronicle of Higher Education* (6 April 1988); rpt. in *Falling into Theory: Conflicting Views on Reading Literature*, ed. David H. Richter, 218–21. Boston: St. Martin's Press, 1994.

Rado, Lisa, ed. *Rereading Modernism: New Directions in Feminist Criticism*. New York: Garland, 1994.

Radway, Janice. *Reading the Romance: Women, Patriarchy and Popular Literature*. Chapel Hill: University of North Carolina Press, 1984.

Ray, Gordon N. *H. G. Wells and Rebecca West*. New Haven: Yale University Press, 1974.

Recollecting Djuna Barnes: A Centennial Exhibition. College Park, Md.: McKeldin Library, University of Maryland, 1992.

Riatt, Suzanne. *Vita and Virginia: The Work and Friendship of V. Sackville-West and Virginia Woolf.* Oxford: Clarendon Press, 1993.

Rich, Adrienne. *On Lies, Secrets and Silence: Selected Prose, 1966–1978.* New York: Norton, 1979.

Richardson, Dorothy. "Women and the Future." In Scott, ed., *The Gender of Modernism,* 411–14.

Ricoeur, Paul. "The Metaphorical Process as Cognition, Imagination, and Feeling." In Sacks, ed., *On Metaphor,* 141–57.

Robinson, Lillian. "Treason Our Text: Challenges to the Literary Canon." *Tulsa Studies in Women's Literature* 2.1 (Spring 1983): 83–98.

Rollyson, Carl. *Rebecca West: A Saga of the Century.* New York: Scribners, forthcoming.

Ruddick, Sara. "Private Brother, Public World." In Marcus, ed., *New Feminist Essays on Virginia Woolf,* 185–215.

Ruderman, Judith. *D. H. Lawrence and the Devouring Mother: The Search for a Patriarchal Ideal of Leadership.* Durham, N.C.: Duke University Press, 1984.

Sacks, Sheldon, ed. *On Metaphor.* Chicago: University of Chicago Press, 1978.

Salmon, Christoper. Letter to Rebecca West. BBC Written Archive, Reading.

Schwarz, Sanford. *The Matrix of Modernism: Pound, Eliot and Early Twentiety-Century Thought.* Princeton: Princeton University Press, 1985.

Scott, Bonnie Kime. *James Joyce.* Brighton: Harvester, 1987.

———. "Jellyfish and Treacle: Joyce, Lewis, Gender and Modernism." In *Coping with Joyce: Essays from the Copenhagen Symposium,* ed. Morris Beja and Shari Benstock, 168–79. Columbus: Ohio State University Press, 1989.

———. *Joyce and Feminism.* Bloomington: Indiana University Press, 1984.

———. " 'The Look in the Throat of a Stricken Animal': Joyce as Met by Djuna Barnes." *Joyce Studies Annual 1991,* 153–76. Austin: University of Texas Press, 1991.

———. "Refiguring the Binary, Breaking the Cycle: Rebecca West as Feminist Modernist." *Twentieth Century Literature* 37.2 (Summer 1991): 169–91.

———. "The Strange Necessity of Rebecca West." In *Women Reading Women's Writing,* ed. Sue Roe, 265–86. Brighton: Harvester, 1987.

———. "Uncle Wells on Women." In *Wells under Revision,* ed. Patrick Parrinder and Christopher Rolfe, 108–20. Selinsgrove, Pa.: Susquehanna University Press, 1990.

———. " 'The Word Split Its Husk': Woolf's Double Vision of Modernist Language." *Modern Fiction Studies* 32.3 (1988): 371–85.

———. " 'The Young Girl,' Jane Heap, and Trials of Gender in *Ulysses*." In *California Joyce*, ed. Margot Norris and Vincent Cheng, forthcoming.

Scott, Bonnie Kime, ed. *The Gender of Modernism*. Bloomington: Indiana University Press, 1990.

Sedgwick, Eve Kosofsky. *Between Men: English Literature and Male Homosocial Desire*. New York: Columbia University Press, 1985.

———. *Epistemology of the Closet*. Berkeley: University of California Press, 1990.

Shaw, George Bernard. Letters to Rebecca West, Shaw Collection, British Library.

Showalter, Elaine. "Feminist Criticism in the Wilderness." In Showalter, ed., *The New Feminist Criticism*, 243–70.

———. *A Literature of Their Own: British Women Novelists from Brontë to Lessing*. Princeton: Princeton University Press, 1977.

Showalter, Elaine, ed. *The New Feminist Criticism: Essays on Women, Literature and Theory*. New York: Pantheon, 1985.

Silver, Brenda. "Textual Criticism as Feminist Practice: Or Who's Afraid of Virginia Woolf Part II." In *Representing Modernist Texts*, ed. George Bornstein. Ann Arbor: University of Michigan Press, 1991.

Simpson, Hilary. *D. H. Lawrence and Feminism*. London: Croom Helm, 1982.

Sinclair, May. *Feminism*. London: Women Writers Suffrage League, 1912.

Singer, Alan. "The Horse Who Knew Too Much: Metaphor and the Narrative of Discontinuity in *Nightwood*." *Contemporary Literature* 25.1 (1984): 66–87.

Sitwell, Edith. *Selected Letters*. Ed. John Lehmann and Derek Parker. London: Macmillan, 1970.

Spender, Dale, ed. *Time and Tide Wait for No Man*. London: Pandora Press, 1984.

Squier, Susan. "The City as Landscape." In *City Images: Perspectives from Literature, Philosophy and Film*, ed. Mary Ann Caws, 99–119. New York: Gordon and Breach, 1991.

Stead, C. K. *Pound, Yeats, and the Modernist Movement*. London: Macmillan, 1985.

Sultan, Stanley. *Eliot, Joyce and Company*. New York: Oxford University Press, 1987.

Symons, Julian. *Makers of the New: The Revolution in Literature, 1912–1939*. London: Andre Deutsch, 1987.

Trilling, Diana. "Rebecca West's Judgment." *New York Times Book Review* (18 July 1993): 27.

Walker, Alice. *In Search of Our Mothers' Gardens*. New York: Harcourt, 1983.

Warhol, Robyn R., and Diane Price Herndl, eds. *Feminisms: An Anthology of Literary Theory and Criticism*. New Brunswick: Rutgers University Press, 1991.

Warner, Marina. "The Art of Fiction LXV: Rebecca West." *Paris Review* 23 (Spring 1981): 117–64.

Waugh, Patricia. *Feminine Fictions: Revisiting the Postmodern.* London: Routledge, 1988.

Wells, H. G. *H. G. Wells in Love.* Ed. G. P. Wells. London: Faber and Faber, 1984.

———. Letters to Rebecca West, West Collection, Beinecke Library, Yale University.

West, Anthony. *H. G. Wells: Aspects of a Life.* London: Hutchinson, 1984.

———. *Heritage.* London: Secker and Warburg, 1984.

———. Letter to H. G. Wells, West Collection, Beinecke Libary, Yale University.

———. "Mother and Son." *New York Review of Books* 31 (March 1, 1984): 9–12.

West, Rebecca. "Adela." In West, *The Only Poet and Short Stories,* 17–60.

———. *Arnold Bennett Himself.* New York: John Day Company, 1931.

———. *Black Lamb and Grey Falcon.* New York: Viking, 1941.

———. *The Court and the Castle: Some Treatments of a Recurrent Theme.* New Haven: Yale University Press, 1957.

———. *Cousin Rosamund.* New York: Viking Penguin, 1986.

———. *Ending in Earnest: A Literary Log.* 1931; rpt., Freeport: Books for Libraries, 1967.

———. *The Essential Rebecca West.* Harmondsworth: Penguin, 1983.

———. *Family Memories.* London: Virago, 1987.

———. *The Fountain Overflows.* Harmondsworth: Penguin, 1987.

———. "The 'Freewoman.' " In Scott, ed., *The Gender of Modernism,* 573–77.

———. *Harriet Hume: A London Fantasy.* London: Virago, 1980.

———. *The Harsh Voice.* Garden City: Doubleday, Doran, 1935.

———. *Henry James.* London: Nesbit, 1916.

———. "High Fountain of Genius." In Scott, ed., *The Gender of Modernism,* 592–96.

———. "Imagisme." *New Freewoman* 1.5 (1913): 86–87.

———. "A Jixless Errand." *Time and Tide* (15 March 1929): 282–86.

———. *The Judge.* 1922. London: Virago, 1980.

———. "Juvenilia: Poems 1897–1906." Ms., West Collection, Beinecke Library, Yale University.

———. "Letter from Abroad: Virginia Woolf Braces Herself against a Harsh Wind." *The Bookman* 70 (January 1930): 551–57.

———. *A Letter to a Grandfather.* London: Hogarth Press, 1933.

———. Letters to Dora Marsden, Grace Jardine, and Rona Johnson, Marsden Collection, Princeton University Library.

———. Letters to Sylvia Lynd, G. B. Stern, Bernard Lafourcade, and Jane Lidderdale, West Collection, McFarlin Library, University of Tulsa.

———. Letters to H. G. Wells, S. F. Ratcliffe, and Emanie Arling, West Collection, Beinecke Library, Yale University.

———. Letters to Lord Beaverbrook, Beaverbrook Collection, House of Lords Records Office.

———. Letters to Fannie Hurst and Hugh Walpole, Harry Ransom Humanities Research Center, University of Texas at Austin.

———. Letters to Emily Hahn. Lilly Library, Indiana University, Bloomington.

———. "Mr Setty and Mr Hume." In West, *The Essential Rebecca West*, 260–319.

———. "The New God." Unpublished ms., West Collection, McFarlin Library, University of Tulsa.

———. *1900*. New York: Viking, 1982.

———. "Notes on the Effect of Women Writers on Mr. Max Beerbohm." In West, *Ending in Earnest*, 66–74. 1931. New York: Books for Libraries Press, 1967.

———. "Notes on Novels: *The Romantic* by May Sinclair, *Larry Munro* by G. B. Stern, *Caliban* by W. L. George." *The New Statesman* 16 (20 October 1920): 50–51.

———. "On Making Due Allowance for Distortion." [Review of *Paleface* by Wyndham Lewis.] *Time and Tide* 10 (May 1929): 623–24.

———. *The Only Poet and Short Stories*. Ed. Antonia Till. London: Virago, 1992.

———. "Reply to D. H. Lawrence's 'Good Boy Husbands.' " In Scott, ed., *The Gender of Modernism*, 584–87.

———. *The Return of the Soldier*. 1918. London: Virago, 1980.

———. "Spinster to the Rescue." In Scott, ed., *The Gender of Modernism*, 577–80.

———. *The Strange Necessity*. 1928. London: Virago, 1987.

———. "The Strange Necessity." In West, *The Strange Necessity*, 13–198.

———. *Sunflower*. London: Virago, 1986.

———. *Sunflower* ms. notebook, West Collection, McFarlin Library, University of Tulsa.

———. "Tarr." *The Nation* 107 (10 August 1918). Rpt. in *Essays on Wyndham Lewis*, 67–69. Folcroft, Pa.: Folcroft Library Editions, 1971.

———. *The Thinking Reed*. 1936. London: Virago, 1984.

———. "Tradition in Criticism." In *Tradition and Experiment in Present-Day Literature: Addresses Delivered at the City Literary Institute*, 179–97. London: Oxford University Press, 1929.

———. *The Vassal Affair*. London: Sunday Telegraph, 1963.

[West, Rebecca]. *War Nurse: The True Story of a Woman Who Lived, Loved and Suffered on the Western Front*. New York: Cosmopolitan Book Corporation, 1930.

———. "The World's Worst Failure." In Scott, ed., *The Gender of Modernism*, 580–83.

————. *The Young Rebecca: Writings of Rebecca West, 1911–1917.* Ed. Jane Marcus. London: Virago, 1983.

Wickes, George. *The Amazon of Letters: The Life and Loves of Natalie Barney.* London: Allen, 1977.

Williams, William Carlos. "A Point for American Criticism." In *Our Exagmination round His Factification for Incamination of Work in Progress,* ed. Samuel Beckett, 171–85. 1929. New York: New Directions, 1962.

Wilson, Edmund. *The Twenties.* New York: Bantam, 1976.

Wolfe, Peter. *Rebecca West: Artist and Thinker.* Carbondale: Southern Illinois University Press, 1971.

Wood, Thelma. Drawings. Barnes Collection, McKeldin Library, University of Maryland.

Woolf, Leonard. *Letters of Leonard Woolf.* Ed. Frederic Spotts. San Diego: Harcourt, Brace, Jovanovich, 1989.

Woolf, Virginia. *Between the Acts.* 1941. San Diego: Harcourt Brace Jovanovich, 1969.

————. *The Collected Essays of Virginia Woolf.* 4 vols. Ed. Leonard Woolf. London: Hogarth, 1966–67.

————. *The Common Reader.* New York: Harcourt Brace and World, 1953.

————. *The Diary of Virginia Woolf.* 5 vols. Ed. Anne Olivier Bell. San Diego: Harcourt Brace Jovanovich, 1977–84.

————. *The Essays of Virginia Woolf.* 4 vols to date. Ed. Andrew McNeillie. San Diego: Harcourt Brace Jovanovich, 1986–94.

————. "Four Hidden Letters." *Virginia Woolf Miscellany.* Special Summer Issue (1994): 1–3.

————. "Friendship's Gallery." *Twentieth Century Literature* 25.3–4 (1979): 275–302.

————. *Granite and Rainbow.* New York: Harcourt Brace, 1958.

————. *Jacob's Room.* 1922. San Diego: Harcourt Brace Jovanovich, 1960.

————. Letter in ms. to Rebecca West, 1928. West Collection, McFarlin Library, University of Tulsa.

————. *The Letters of Virginia Woolf.* 6 vols. Ed. Nigel Nicolson and Joanne Trautmann. San Diego: Harcourt Brace Jovanovich, 1975–80.

————. "Life and the Novelist." In Woolf, *Granite and Rainbow,* 41–47.

————. *Moments of Being: Unpublished Autobiographical Writings.* Ed. Jeanne Schulkind. New York: Harcourt, Brace, Jovanovich, 1976.

————. Monk's House Papers, University of Sussex Library.

————. "Mr Conrad: A Conversation." In Woolf, *The Essays of Virginia Woolf,* vol. 3, 376–80.

————. *Mrs. Dalloway.* 1925. New York: Harcourt Brace and World, 1953.

———. "The Narrow Bridge of Art." In Woolf, *The Collected Essays of Virginia Woolf,* vol. 2, 218–29.

———. *Night and Day.* New York: Harcourt Brace Jovanovich, 1948.

———. "The Novels of E. M. Forster." In Woolf, *The Death of the Moth and Other Essays,* 162–75. San Diego: Harcourt Brace Jovanovich, 1970.

———. *Orlando: A Biography.* 1928. San Diego: Harcourt Brace Jovanovich, 1956.

———. *The Pargiters: The Novel Essay Portion of The Years.* Ed. Mitchell A. Leaska. New York: Harcourt Brace Jovanovich, 1977.

———. *A Passionate Apprentice: The Early Journals, 1897–1909.* Ed. Mitchell A. Leaska. San Diego: Harcourt Brace Jovanovich, 1990.

———. "Phases of Fiction." In Woolf, *Granite and Rainbow,* 93–145.

———. "Professions for Women." In *Collected Essays of Virginia Woolf,* vol. 2, 284–89.

———. "Reminiscences." In Woolf, *Moments of Being,* 25–59.

———. *Roger Fry.* 1940. Harmondsworth: Penguin, 1979.

———. *A Room of One's Own.* 1929. San Diego: Harcourt Brace Jovanovich, 1957.

———. "A Sketch of the Past." In Woolf, *Moments of Being,* 64–137.

———. *Three Guineas.* 1938. New York: Harcourt Brace and World, 1966.

———. *To the Lighthouse.* 1927. New York: Harcourt Brace and World, 1964.

———. *The Voyage Out.* 1915. New York: Harcourt Brace and World, 1948.

———. *The Waves.* 1931. San Diego: Harcourt Brace Jovanovich, 1959.

———. *Women and Fiction: The Manuscript Versions of "A Room of One's Own."* Ed. S. P. Rosenbaum. Oxford: Shakespeare Head Press, 1992.

———. *Women and Writing.* Ed. with introduction by Michèle Barrett. London: The Women's Press, 1979.

———. *The Years.* New York: Harcourt Brace Jovanovich, 1937.

Woolf, Virginia, and Lytton Strachey. *Virginia Woolf and Lytton Strachey: Letters.* Ed. Leonard Woolf and James Strachey. New York: Harcourt, Brace, 1956.

Index

Abel, Elizabeth, xxxiii, xxxv, 205

Ackroyd, Peter, 119–121, 126, 127, 273

aestheticism, xxxi, xxxiv, 35, 81, 98, 99, 100, 103, 129, 153, 178, 260, 272

aesthetics, xxvii, 39, 55, 61, 95, 171, 173, 177, 217, 248, 259

African Americans, xv, xxxviii, 72, 108–109, 215, 268, 272, 283

African culture and people, xxxviii, 9, 74, 85, 92–93, 109, 114, 135, 159, 215, 228, 246, 279

Aiken, Conrad, 114, 116, 118, 137, 275

Aldington, Richard, 33, 47, 55, 85, 88–89, 91, 93, 125, 152, 162, 267, 271

Americans, xxxviii, xliii, 21, 61, 70, 72, 84–85, 89, 90, 91, 94, 119–120, 124, 133, 140–141, 144, 195, 197, 224, 260, 276

anarchism, 10, 35, 39, 43, 47

Anderson, Margaret, 42, 71, 85–86, 89, 92, 185, 242, 264, 268

Anderson, Sherwood, 30

Andrews, Henry (West's husband), xli, 197–198, 224

androgyny, 92, 255, 260

Anglican Church, 23, 117, 126, 129, 136, 142, 184, 287

animals, xv, xx, xxvi, 5, 9, 12, 28, 74, 90, 105, 108, 109, 111, 114, 119, 122, 133–136, 154, 156, 160, 163–166, 167, 168, 192–193, 206, 207, 209, 221–223, 239–240, 244, 249, 252, 256, 262, 263, 273, 275, 279, 280, 282, 283, 286–287

Antheil, George, 90

anti-Semitism, 94, 125, 153, 274

aphorism, xxvii, 74, 211, 252, 253, 257

Archimedes, xxiv

architecture, xxvi, 82, 153, 170, 207, 259, 270

archives, xl, 12, 83, 175, 263, 276, 279

Ardis, Ann, 186, 260, 270, 280

aristocrats, xxviii, 63, 165, 215, 218, 247, 255, 282–283

Aristotle, 103, 104, 145

Arling, Emanie, 27, 28–29, 263

Athenaeum, 64, 85, 115, 130

Auden, Wystan Hugh, 83, 124

audience, 65, 141, 151, 236, 249

Austen, Jane, xxv, 20, 66, 80, 176, 177, 188, 267

authority, xxxvii, 11, 22, 83, 119, 144, 237, 246

autobiography, 3, 18, 39, 59, 162, 185, 197, 204, 227, 235

Bakhtin, M. M., xxxiii, 264

Barash, Carol, 41, 44, 88

Barker, George, 124, 276

Barnes, Djuna, xxii, xxvii–xxviii, xxx, xl, 33–34, 52–54, 70, 71, 74, 90, 108, 112, 116, 117, 120, 124, 126, 138–143, 156–161, 183, 185–186, 200–203, 228–233, 235, 239–240, 266, 281, 285; *The Antiphon*, 16, 17, 141; *Ladies Almanack*, 72, 74, 90, 185, 250–253; *Nightwood*, 16, 64, 70, 90, 133, 138–140, 183, 207, 256, 261, 276, 287; *Ryder*, 14, 16, 185, 200–201, 256

Barnes, Elizabeth Chappell (Barnes's mother), xxxviii, 14, 16, 17

Barnes, Wald (Barnes's father), xxxviii, xxxix, 14, 16, 17, 33, 215

Barnes, Zadel. *See* Gustafson, Zadel Barnes Buddington

Barney, Natalie, xxv, 16, 33, 72–75, 90, 112, 141, 200–202, 205, 207, 217, 229, 248–252, 269, 281

Barry, Iris, 91, 103, 272

BBC, 191, 234–236, 279, 283, 285–286

Beach, Joseph Warren, 21

Beach, Sylvia, 72, 151, 157, 200, 269, 276, 277

Beardsley, Aubrey, 20

Beaverbrook, Lord (William Maxwell Aitken), 30–32, 195–197, 227, 280–281, 284

Beckett, Samuel, 155–156, 278

Beerbohm, Max, 22, 28, 211

Behn, Aphra, 220

Bell, Angelica, 187, 189, 212, 273

Bell, Clive, xxv, xxxix, 94, 104, 115, 128, 172–173, 187–191, 211, 232, 262, 270, 279
Bell, Gertrude, 55, 220
Bell, Julian, 189, 217
Bell, Quentin, 35, 189, 267, 268, 280
Bell, Vanessa Stephen (Woolf's sister), xxv, xxxix, 4–5, 20, 62, 136, 187–191, 199, 205, 212–213, 218, 261–262, 273, 279
Bennett, Arnold, xxv, xxxvii, 20, 23, 27, 29–31, 55, 59, 109, 168, 173, 176, 199, 225, 263, 264, 275
Benson, Stella, xxv, 220–221, 234
Benstock, Bernard, 277
Benstock, Shari, xxxiv, 249, 252, 261, 269
Bergonzi, Bernard, 269
Bible, 20, 250, 252, 272
Biddle, Francis, 198
binary, 103, 108, 164, 199, 250, 266, 269
biography, xxxiii, xli, 6, 13, 57, 69, 74, 81, 89, 91, 112, 137, 162, 173–174, 183, 196, 200, 245, 280, 281
Blake, William, 20, 88, 259
BLAST, 89, 100–103, 107, 114, 274
Blavatsky, Mme Helena, 60
Bloom, Harold, xxxv, 67
Bloomsbury, xxxix, 80, 82, 94, 115, 124, 129, 137, 169–174, 176, 190–191, 267, 270, 277, 279
body, xviii, xliii, 17, 119, 131, 132, 161, 190, 221, 224, 227, 250, 252–253, 273
Boni and Liveright, 190, 200–201
Bookman, 143–144, 185, 188–189, 224, 233, 234
Bowen, Elizabeth, 64, 205, 217, 224
Bowles, Paul, 204
Boyle, Kay, xxv, xxxiv, 229–231
Bradbrook, Muriel, 283
Bradbury, Michael, and James MacFarlane, 269
Bradley, F. H., 127
Briggs, Austin, 155, 278
Brittain, Vera, 48, 62, 109, 197, 243–244
Brontë, Charlotte, 7, 124, 147, 176
Brontë, Emily, 177
Brontës, 20, 124, 188
Brooks, Romaine, 74, 200, 280
Brown, Dennis, 269, 270
Bruno, Guido, 19, 33
Bryher (Winifred Ellerman), xxxiv, 89, 94
Bürger, Peter, 264
Burgess, Anthony, 27, 264

Burton, Bhima Husted, xli–xliii
Butler, Judith, xxxiv, 260

Cambridge University, 51, 115, 152, 187, 189, 215–216, 219, 263, 275
Cameron, Julia, 36, 62, 185, 246
cannibals, 114, 204, 273
canon, 80–83, 92, 128, 132, 137, 269, 275
Cape, Jonathan, 30, 125, 199, 235, 236, 244, 246
Carpenter, Edward, xl, 39, 247
Carpenter, Humphrey, 91
Carrington, Dora, 267
Carter, Huntly, 47, 88
Case, Janet, 50, 62, 146, 170
categories, 20, 91, 175, 247, 265
Cather, Willa, 30
Catt, Carrie Chapman, 53
Caughie, Pamela, xxxvi, 260, 275
Cavendish, Margaret, 250
Caws, Marianne, 267
censorship, xxxvi, 46, 140, 150, 169, 184, 199, 201, 242, 247, 253, 257
Chambers, Jessie, 162, 278
Chaplin, Charlie, 154, 195
character, 23, 131, 250, 255, 263
Chaucer, Geoffrey, xxv, 20
Chekhov, Anton, 67
Chicago, Judy, xv, 259
childbirth, 14, 54, 72, 189–190, 230, 255, 275
China, 220–221
Chodorow, Nancy, xxxvi
church (building), xxviii, 61, 72, 135, 153, 157–158
city, xviii, xxxviii, 81, 84, 118, 190–192, 207
Cixous, Hélène, xxix, 95
Clarion, 26, 39, 45, 192, 194
Clark, Suzanne, xxix, xxxiv, 186, 269
Clarke, Austin, 29, 266
class, xxiv, xxxviii, 10, 35, 106, 135, 213–216, 221, 268
classicism, 81, 82, 98, 145, 152–153, 161, 171, 184, 218–219, 220, 267, 270
clothing, xli, 6, 105, 119, 141, 155, 171, 200, 207, 211, 228, 234, 255, 282, 288
Cocteau, Jean, 30, 121, 157
Coleman, Emily Holmes, 17, 70–71, 112, 138–140, 160, 187, 201–202, 217, 229–232, 284
Colette, xxv, 72, 74
Colum, Padraic, 155, 277

commodification, 82, 88, 179, 201, 235, 270

Communism, 31, 32, 71, 227

Conrad, Joseph, 32, 80, 237–239, 260

country settings, xxxix, 37, 81, 84, 116, 123, 191–192, 198, 228, 261

Cravens, Margaret, 84, 90, 271

Criterion, 115, 120, 124, 129, 131–132, 140, 277, 279

Cunard, Nancy, xxv, 91, 94, 103, 185

Cunningham, Valentine, 82, 270

Curran, Charles, 196, 281

Daily Eagle (Brooklyn), 52, 186

Daily Express, 30, 31

Daily Herald, 23, 44

Daly, Mary, xv, 259

dance, 20, 95, 108, 119, 120, 195, 274

Dante Alighieri, 104, 128

Davies, Margaret Llewelyn, 50, 52, 216

de Gourmont, Remy, 87, 98

DeKoven, Marianne, xxxv, 35, 259, 260, 261, 264, 265

Deleuze, Gilles, 209

Dell, Floyd, 70, 263

de Man, Paul, xxix

Derrida, Jacques, xxix, xxxii–xxxiii, xxxv, 261, 270

De Salvo, Louise, xxxiii, 4, 5, 261

Despard, Charlotte, 42

Dial, 127, 186

dialogue, xxxiii, 20–21, 70, 129, 234, 237–241, 255

Dickinson, Violet, 20, 61, 62, 63

Dodge, Mabel (Luhan), 71, 162

domestic focus, xvi, xxviii, xxix, 5, 14, 20, 41, 42, 49, 54, 150, 154, 166, 191, 198, 207, 213, 225, 234, 259, 272, 282, 284

Doran, George, 195, 199, 278

Dostoyevsky, Fyodor, xxv, 68, 108, 178–179

Duckworth, George (Woolf's half-brother), 4, 7–8, 187–188

Duckworth, Gerald (Woolf's half-brother), 4, 7–8, 19, 68, 268

Duckworth, Stella (Woolf's half-sister), 4, 6–7, 12, 262

DuPlessis, Rachel Blau, xv, 47, 91, 259, 271

Earhart, Amelia, 183

economics, xxxviii, 42–43, 85, 88, 104, 106, 133, 188, 194, 209, 215, 266

Edinburgh, 9, 12, 36, 188

editors, 44, 65, 71, 84, 85, 115, 125, 138–140, 171, 191

education, xxxviii–xxxix, 5, 13, 14, 25, 27, 41, 42, 48, 60, 62–63, 82, 84, 124, 177–178, 205, 216, 221, 267

Edwardians, xx, xxii, xxxvi, 8, 19–34, 35–36, 42, 58, 62, 66, 68, 149, 173, 177, 180, 211, 263–264

Egoist, 46–48, 55, 85, 89, 104, 113, 125, 127, 129, 265, 267

Eliot, Charlotte, 122–124, 135

Eliot, George, 124, 147, 176

Eliot, T. S., xvi, xxii, xxv, xxvi, xxxi, xxxiv, xxxvi, xxxvii, 48, 51, 58, 59, 64, 65, 67, 79, 80, 81, 85, 90, 95, 97–98, 103, 104, 107, 108, 112, 113–114, 146, 169, 174, 184, 190, 211, 230, 232, 235, 236, 266, 267, 270, 272–276; "Tradition and the Individual Talent," 126–130; *The Waste Land*, 97–98, 116, 121–122, 130–131, 143, 145, 266, 271

Eliot, Valerie, 118, 142–143, 274

Eliot, Vivien Haigh-Leigh, 113, 115–116, 126, 118–121, 128–129, 134, 260, 274

Elizabethans, xxv, 20, 139, 171

Ellis, Edith Lees, 46, 247

Ellis, Havelock, xl, 46, 175, 247, 263

Ellmann, Richard, xli, 80–81, 269, 277, 278

empire, xxxviii, 81, 114, 189, 220, 261

English Review, 32, 85, 273

Epstein, Jacob, 99

Ernst, Morris, 156

essentialism, xxxi, xxxiii–xxxiv, 48, 69, 167, 177, 206, 250

Evening Standard, 29–32, 196

exile, 21, 94, 160, 276

experimental writing, xxxi, xxxiv, xxxviii, 21, 53, 88, 132, 156, 184, 186, 218, 219, 236

Faber (publishers), 64, 86, 90, 115, 133, 140, 141, 190, 235, 276

Fabian Society, 13, 31, 36, 37, 39, 87, 234

Fadiman, Clifton, 139

Fairfield, Charles (West's father), xxxix, 8–11, 13, 27–28, 215, 262

Fairfield, Isabella (West's mother), xxxix, 8, 11–12, 44, 45, 188, 193, 194, 280

Fairfield, Letitia (West's sister), 9, 12–13, 28, 36–37, 196, 217, 262, 280

family, xxxiv, xxxviii–xxxix, 3–18, 19, 61, 70, 84, 112, 153, 189, 217–218, 261–264
fantasy, 4, 8, 16, 31, 205, 253
fascism, xxxvi, 3, 10, 82, 85, 129, 184, 198, 202, 235, 272
fathers, xxxv, xxxix, 6, 9, 41, 82, 113, 194, 250
Faulkner, Percy, 17–18, 200
Faulkner, William, 81
Felski, Rita, 186, 260, 261
feminine, xxiv, xxix, 29, 60, 92, 98, 102, 103–107, 111, 117, 121, 124, 127, 133, 145, 156, 161, 164, 205–208, 234, 238, 241, 255, 259, 271, 280
feminism, xliii, 13, 20, 25, 27, 29–30, 36, 44, 46, 47–49, 59, 62, 65, 68, 79, 84, 87, 120, 145, 170, 177, 178, 184, 216, 224, 227, 228, 268, 283–284
feminist criticism and theory, xxii, xxiv, xxxi–xxxvi, 35, 91, 145, 164, 238, 250, 251, 259–261, 264–266, 269, 275, 278; French, xxii–xxiv, xxxii, xxxiv, 89, 97, 122
Field, Andrew, 202
Flanner, Janet, xxv, xxvi, 75, 228, 284
Flint, Frank, 85, 87
Fogel, Daniel Mark, 263
Ford, Charles Henri, 187, 202, 204
Ford, Ford Madox (Hueffer), xxv, xxxvii, 32–33, 43, 44, 55, 56–58, 72, 74, 85–86, 88–89, 107, 229
form, 48, 53, 130–131, 147, 237, 277
Forster, E. M., xxv, xxxvii, 23, 35, 80, 146, 169, 243–246, 248, 275, 279–280
Foucault, Michel, xxxii
fragmentation, xxvii, 67, 100, 103, 120, 149
Frazer, James, 120
Freewoman, 25, 36, 39, 42, 265
French language and culture, xxxviii, 87, 191
Freud, Sigmund, xxxv, xl, 3, 59, 67, 79, 160, 162, 179, 184, 246–247, 259, 261, 263, 267, 271
Friedan, Betty, 232
Friedman, Susan Stanford, xxxiii, 91, 267
Fromm, Gloria, 32, 233, 283, 285
Fry, Roger, xxv, xxxix, 80, 94, 100, 102, 135, 136, 137, 149, 173–174, 190–191, 245, 270, 272, 279
Fuss, Diana, 260

Gallop, Jane, 260
Galsworthy, John, 23, 27, 59, 286
Garland, Madge, 213, 233
Garner, Les, 26, 88, 265

Garnett, Edward, 112
Gaudier-Brzeska, Henri, 94, 98–99, 270
Gawthorpe, Mary, 28, 36–39, 265
gaze, xviii, xxx, 97, 211, 333
gender, xxix, 44, 79, 80, 83, 107, 113, 118, 122, 153, 162, 163, 176, 183–184, 238, 284
Gender of Modernism, xx, xxii, xxiii, xxxvii–xxxviii, 270, 280
generations, xxxii, xxxiv, xxxvii, xliii, 6, 13, 21, 23, 62, 130, 163, 170, 184, 211, 262
genre, 184, 257, 263
Germans and German culture, xxxviii, xli, 32, 106, 108, 114, 116, 191, 198, 207, 221, 227
Gide, André, 81, 142
Gilbert, Sandra, and Susan Gubar, xxix–xxx, xxxv–xxxvi, 107, 119, 161, 164, 260, 265, 273, 275, 278
Gilbert, William, and Arthur Sullivan, 120
Gillespie, Diane, 283
Gilligan, Carol, xv, xxxvi
Gilman, Charlotte Perkins, 43
Gladstone, William Ewart, 9, 29
Glaspell, Susan, 268
Glendinning, Victoria, xv, xxxvi, 13, 25, 224, 235, 262, 272, 281
Goldman, Emma, 31, 71, 225, 264, 284
Good Housekeeping, 232–233
Gordon, Lyndall, 117, 273–274
Grant, Duncan, 50, 169–170, 187, 273
Greek culture and language, xxxviii, 5, 50–51, 55, 125, 152–153, 156, 159, 178
Greenwich Village, xxxviii, 19, 33, 70–72, 75, 93, 200, 204, 279, 284
Guggenheim, Peggy, 70, 139–140, 200, 229–230, 261
guilt, 10, 12, 227, 249
Gunther, John, 195, 227
Gurdjieff, George, 60, 67, 268
Gustafson, Zadel Barnes Buddington, xxxviii, xxxix, 14–18, 52, 53

Hahn, Emily, 196, 197, 228, 268, 281
Hale, Emily, 117, 119, 124, 142, 273–274
Hall, Radclyffe, xxv, xxxvii, 57, 72, 242–246, 251, 286–287; *Well of Loneliness*, 75, 140, 242, 244–245, 249–250
Halper, Nathan, 277
Hanscombe, Gillian, and Virginia L. Smyers, xxxiv
Hapgood, Hutchins, 70
Hardy, Thomas, xxv, 55, 61, 176, 212

Harper's, 16, 235
Harris, Frank, 33
Harrison, Jane, 50–51, 55, 62, 93, 266
Hartman, Geoffrey, xviii, 259
Harvard University, 114–115, 137
Hastings, Beatrice, 103–104
Hawkes, Ellen, 205
H. D. (Hilda Doolittle), 51, 55, 59, 60, 84–85,
    90, 94, 109, 117, 125, 162, 267, 271, 273
Head, June, 195, 224
Heap, Jane, 70, 86, 142, 185, 200, 202, 217,
    228, 242, 244, 268, 269
Hedges, Elaine, 259
Hegel, Georg Friedrich, 144
Heilbrun, Caroline, 260
Hemingway, Ernest, 32
Herring, Philip, 14
heterosexuality, xl, 26, 90, 107, 117, 122, 164,
    202, 225, 227, 242, 249, 250, 255, 257, 264,
    268
hierarchy, 104, 163
Hinckley, Eleanor, 124, 129
Hiss, Alger, 32
history, xx, xxiv, xxvi, xxviii, xxxiv–xxxv,
    xxxvi–xxxvii, 21, 23–24, 63, 89, 93, 109,
    131, 165, 170, 172, 184, 211, 223, 241, 245, 252,
    255, 259, 260, 266, 267, 275
Hitler, Adolf, 198, 202, 281
Hoare, Peter, 143
Hogarth Press, 68, 72, 115, 128, 133, 150–151,
    186, 190, 218, 233, 253, 266, 268, 275, 279
Holroyd, Michael, 67, 268
Holtby, Winifred, 48, 62
Homer, xxvi
homosexuality, xl, 86, 94, 113, 116, 124, 125,
    128, 139, 169, 175, 187, 242, 244, 246, 247,
    256, 271, 273, 276, 279, 286, 287; homopho-
    bia, 80, 100, 169, 247, 273
Hulme, T. E., 85–86, 98–99, 103, 116, 275
Hunt, Violet, 32, 55–58, 59, 85–86, 107, 192,
    211, 225, 266
Hurst, Fannie, 195, 196, 217
Hurston, Zora Neale, xx, 260
Hutchinson, Mary, 115, 123–124, 185, 274
Huxley, Aldous, 63–64, 115, 144, 168, 223, 232
Huyssen, Andreas, 186
Hynes, Samuel, xli, 284

Ibsen, Henrik, xxv, xxvi, 36, 61, 62, 175
illegitimacy, xl, 48, 196–197
illness, 118–119, 132, 196, 199, 217, 262, 266

imagism, 59, 85, 87–88, 91–94, 97, 100, 152,
    237, 270, 271
indecency, 149–150
incest, xxxix, 4, 7, 9–10, 16–17, 33, 163, 170,
    188, 204
India, xxxviii, 189, 220, 261
individualism, 39, 126, 266
interviews, 19, 20, 29, 53, 159–160, 234, 239,
    264
Irigaray, Luce, xxiv, xxx, xxxiii, 79–80, 136
Irish culture, xxxviii, 10, 150, 159, 161, 178

Jack the Ripper, 45, 52
Jakobson, Roman, xxx
James, Henry, 20–22, 55, 58, 80, 128, 130, 263,
    264
James, William, 267
Jameson, Fredric, 103, 108
Jardine, Alice, xxix, xxx
Jardine, Grace, 41, 265
Jay, Karla, 250, 252–253, 287
Jehlen, Myra, xxiv
Jenkins, Elizabeth, 282
Jews, 139, 153, 189, 195, 225, 276
Johnson, Barbara, 260
Jolas, Eugene, 157
journalism, xxxix, 9, 31–32, 33, 49, 54, 85, 89,
    151, 184–186, 199, 200, 212, 224, 232–236, 275
Joyce, James, xviii, xxii, xxv, xxvi, xxx,
    xxxi, xxxiv, xxxvi, 43, 47, 65, 67, 72, 74,
    79, 80, 81, 86, 90, 95, 97, 107, 111–112, 124,
    125, 126–127, 130, 132, 143, 145–161, 162, 172,
    200, 230, 242, 259, 260, 265, 268, 270, 272,
    274, 275, 276–278, 285; *Ulysses*, xxvi, xxvii,
    60, 86, 111, 130, 132, 133, 145–146, 149, 152–
    153, 160, 242; *A Portrait of the Artist*, 43,
    104, 145, 160, 272–273, 278
Joyce, Lucia, 95, 269
Joyce, Nora Barnacle, 159, 269
Joyson-Hicks, William, 244, 246
Jung, Carl, 163, 179

Kenner, Hugh, 80–83, 84, 111, 156, 169, 269,
    270, 277
Kermode, Frank, 272
Kipling, Rudyard, 30
Kirschwey, Freda, 27
Knopf (publishers), 284, 287
Koestenbaum, Wayne, 86, 95, 113–114, 271–
    272, 274
Koteliansky, S. S., 67, 163, 168

Krafft-Ebing, R. von, 249, 256
Kristeva, Julia, xviii–xx, xxxiii, xxxvi
Kryemborg, Alfred, 92
Kurth, Peter, 227–228

labor, 16, 37, 39, 42, 48–49, 194, 262
Lacan, Jacques, xviii, xxx, xxxiii, 165
Ladies' Home Journal, 232, 235
language, xv, xxix, xxx, xxxiii, xxxvi, 3, 22,
    84, 92, 131, 136, 157, 161, 167, 173, 197, 218,
    224, 245, 252, 259, 260, 272, 276, 278
Laser, Susan S., 249, 252–253
Larabee, Ann, 264, 268
Latin (language), xxxix, 16, 79, 133, 178
law, 48, 107, 244, 248, 250, 256–257, 262, 264,
    281, 286–287
Law, Bonar, 31
Lawrence, D. H., xxii, xxxvii, 41, 51, 57, 63,
    65, 67, 79, 80, 93, 124, 126–127, 144, 145, 149,
    162–169, 209, 242, 264, 267, 271, 275, 278;
    Lady Chatterley's Lover, 165–166, 242, 256,
    278
Lawrence, Emmaline Pethwick, 39
Lawrence, Frieda, 162–163
Leaska, Mitchell, 7–8
Leavis, F. R., 35, 80, 82, 148, 216, 260, 275, 277
Leavis, Queenie, 80, 215–216, 260, 283
Lee, Vernon, 55, 186, 266
Lehmann, Rosamond, xxxiv, 60, 268
Lemon, Courtenay, 19, 200, 202
lesbians, xxxiii, xxxiv, 46, 60–61, 71–75, 89,
    90, 140, 174, 184, 190, 205, 216–231, 241–257,
    275, 276, 281–282, 283, 286–288
Levenson, Michael, 86, 269, 275
Lewis, Sinclair, xxv, 194, 227
Lewis, Wyndham, xxiv, xxv, xxxvii, 55, 69,
    79, 85, 89, 94, 98–114, 124, 130, 133, 146, 156,
    161, 169, 238, 272–273
Lindberg, Kathryne, 82, 270, 272
Little Review, 42, 59–60, 70–71, 85, 89, 92,
    159, 185, 228
Locke, John, xxix
London, xxxviii, xxxix, 36, 51, 84–89, 113–
    115, 137, 194, 261
London, Bette, 260
London, Jack, 14
Longenbach, James, 86
Lowell, Amy, xxxiv, 43, 88, 93–94, 100, 271
Loy, Mina, 71, 74, 75, 91, 157, 200, 202
Lubbock, Percy, xxvii, 146–148, 173

Lynd, Robert, xxv, 58, 199, 266–267
Lynd, Sylvia, 58, 152, 199, 217, 225
Lyotard, Jean-François, 264
Macaulay, Rose, 185, 212
MacCarthy, Desmond, 137, 169–170, 188, 211,
    286
MacCarthy, Mary, 188
machines, 81, 97, 105
MacKenzie, Compton, 194, 280
Macleod, Winifred Fairfield, 8, 197, 262
male modernists, xxxvi, xxxvii, 151
Mallarmé, Stéphane, 173
Manchester University, 40–41
Manichaeanism, 153, 157
Mann, Thomas, 81
Mansfield, Katherine, xxv, 43, 62, 64, 65–68,
    115, 125–127, 162, 173, 177, 186, 221, 241, 260
Marcus, Jane, xxxiii, 143, 171, 224, 259, 260,
    279, 282, 287
Marinetti, F. T., 102
marriage, 3, 18, 25, 28, 90, 107, 118, 163, 187–
    188, 189, 197–198, 225, 251, 259
Marsden, Dora, xxv, 25, 36, 39–45, 46, 48, 51,
    52, 60, 86–88, 150, 186, 233, 265
martyrs, 39, 246, 257, 273
masculine, 32, 69, 79–80, 82, 87, 92, 94, 97–
    99, 100, 103–107, 111, 169, 183, 255, 272
mastery, xxix, xxxi, 81, 134, 151, 277
maternal, xxxix, xl, 6, 48, 54, 72, 88, 107, 113,
    117, 122, 163–164, 165, 189, 194, 197, 201,
    204, 216, 217, 227, 230, 262, 267, 285
Matheson, Hilda, 191, 236
McCall's, 186, 200
McCarthy, Mary, 284
McCarthy, Senator Joseph, 227
McLuhan, Marshall, 81
Meikle, Wilma, 69, 194–195
Men of 1914, xxii, xxxvi–xxxvii, 35, 59, 74,
    79–83, 112, 115, 128, 129, 145, 162, 242
mental illness, 7, 133, 139, 189, 225
metaphor, xv, xviii, xx, xxiv, xxvi, xxviii–
    xxx, 26, 44, 66, 72, 79, 82, 88, 94–95, 107,
    113–114, 141, 147, 149, 153, 170–171, 176, 179,
    184, 204, 206, 217, 238, 249, 255, 263, 269,
    270, 271
Mew, Charlotte, 60–61, 267, 280
Meyers, Jeffrey, 103, 112
Michie, Helena, xxx
Millay, Edna St. Vincent, xxxiv, 232, 259, 284
Miller, Nancy K., xv, xx, xx, 259

Milton, John, 147
mind, 53, 66, 68–69, 146, 148, 154, 179, 212, 245, 273
Minow-Pinkney, Makiko, 261
Mirrlees, Hope, 51, 185, 266
misogyny, 103, 115, 116
Mitchison, Naomi, 215
Moi, Toril, xxxi, 261
Monnier, Adrienne, 72, 229
Monroe, Harriet, 85–86, 94
Montaigne, Michael de, 20
Moore, G. E., 176, 270
Moore, Harry T., 164, 269, 278
Moore, Marianne, xxii, xxv, 75, 91–94, 127, 271
Morley, Frank, 90, 138–140
Morley College, 61, 62, 170, 267
Morrell, Lady Ottoline, xxxvi, 50, 63–64, 126, 140–141, 168–169, 221
Morrison, Toni, 283
mothers, xxxii, 5–6, 42, 44, 60, 93, 107, 122, 153, 163–165, 194, 197, 200, 205, 217, 227, 248
Muir, Edwin, 138–139, 143
multiculturalism, 81, 177, 255, 270–271, 279
Murray, Gilbert, 239, 286
Murry, John Middleton, xxv, 65–67, 85, 115, 125, 163
music, xxxviii, xxxix, 9, 12, 84, 160, 235, 272
Mussolini, Benito, 85, 216
myths, xv, 103, 223, 250, 267

Nation, 27, 133, 232, 267
Nation & Athenaeum, 237, 245
nature, 1, 16, 102, 105, 121–122, 174, 205–206, 251, 285
Negoe, Peter, 112, 138, 202
New Age, 39, 79, 85, 88, 104, 268, 272
new critics, xvi, xxvii, xxxi, 35, 80, 81, 116, 126, 129, 146–147, 269
New Freewoman, xli, 20, 25, 42, 45–46, 51, 70, 84, 86, 266, 283
New Republic, 185, 211, 234
new woman, xviii, 72, 192, 196
New York American, 185, 199, 234
New York City, xli, 33, 71–72, 75, 195, 196, 229, 279
New Yorker, 75, 196, 234
New York Evening Post, 186, 279
Nicholson, Harold, 187, 219, 253, 283
Nicholson, Linda, 260

Nietzsche, Friedrich, 42, 102, 104, 154, 184, 270
Nikolchina, Miglena, 262
1928, xxxvi–xxxvii, 27, 55, 56, 143, 146, 151, 172, 183–186, 191, 194, 199, 201, 202, 212–213, 218, 225, 233, 235, 240–241, 242, 249, 256

obscenity, 242, 245, 248, 286–287
O'Neal, Hank, 212
O'Neill, Eugene, 70, 264
Orage, A. R., 39, 42, 85
Orel, Harold, 284
other, xviii, xxxiii, 26
Ovid, 160
Oxbridge, xxxviii, 41, 152, 170
Oxford University, 115–116, 121, 123, 152, 168, 225, 249

Paglia, Camille, xxxi
Pankhurst, Christabel, 36, 37, 42, 265, 271
Pankhurst, Emmeline, 36, 37, 42, 265, 283
Pankhurst, Sylvia, 36, 39–42, 52, 271
Paris, xxxiv, xxxviii, xli, 18, 32, 72, 74–75, 90, 104, 155–160, 200–202, 248
Parrinder, Patrick, 277
Pater, Clara, 170
Pater, Walter, 95
Patmore, Brigit, 32, 43, 57, 58, 124
Pavlov, Ivan, 154, 237
P. E. N., 211, 219, 224, 286
performance, xli, 26, 27, 33, 130, 135, 143, 154, 204, 211, 212, 240–241
Peters, A.D., 280
phallicism, xxxiii, 79, 95, 98, 103, 111, 165–166, 169, 260, 272
philosophy, 20, 42, 48, 61, 127, 139, 185
photography, 13, 28, 36, 62, 176, 196, 211, 249, 253
Picasso, Pablo, 72, 149
Pinker, James, 27
plants, xxviii, 73, 105, 116, 164, 183, 191, 205–207; flowers, 7, 66, 97, 122, 133, 205
Poetry, 85–86
politics, xxxviii, 9, 33, 35, 81, 196, 245, 255, 259, 260, 264, 271
Pondrom, Cyrena N., 91
Pope, Alexander, xv–xvi, xviii, 120, 255
postmodern, 153, 186, 260, 261
Pound, Dorothy Shakespear, 43, 84, 89, 95, 96, 185, 270

Pound, Ezra, xvi, xxii, xxxi, xxxvi, xxxvii, 43, 45, 47, 51, 55, 59, 67, 70, 72, 74, 75, 79–82, 84–99, 100, 104, 112, 113–115, 119, 124, 143, 152, 169, 232, 237, 242, 272, 274, 276
primitive, 60, 99, 108, 149, 163, 166, 168
professionals, xv, 34, 44, 50, 209–211, 282, 286
Protestants, 29, 93, 156; Calvinist, 12, 18
Proust, Marcel, 80, 121, 124, 144, 154, 162, 173, 178, 287
Provincetown Players, xxxviii, xli, 36, 70, 268
psychoanalysis, 9, 12, 59, 71, 79, 82, 196–199, 236–237, 261, 286
psychology, 57, 59, 69, 97, 108, 119, 130, 134, 139, 147, 148, 156, 160, 161, 178, 183, 236, 247
publishers, xxxvii, 19, 24, 31, 35, 44, 66, 68, 113, 125, 129, 131, 133, 138–141, 145, 150, 151, 182, 183, 185, 190, 198, 199, 229, 230, 241, 247–248, 284–285
Puritans, xxviii, 22, 124–125, 139, 152, 156, 184, 201, 265
Pyne, Mary, 70, 202

Quinn, John, 84, 86, 159, 242, 244

Rabelais, François, xxv, 20, 159, 161
Rabinowitz, Peter, 259
race, 3, 72, 109, 114, 121, 126, 283
racism, 92, 94, 108, 114, 121
radio, 184, 186, 191, 199, 220, 235–236, 279, 281, 286
rape, xviii, 106, 212, 259
Ratcliffe, S. K., 31, 197–198, 284
Ray, Gordon N., 263, 283
Ray, Man, xix, 210, 211
readers, xxvii, xl, 39, 132, 139, 146–148, 173, 178, 223, 237, 245, 250
Rhondda, Lady, 48, 49
Rhys, Jean, 33
Rich, Adrienne, xv, 259
Richardson, Dorothy, xxv, xxxiv, 19, 43, 59, 60, 65, 68–69, 162, 260, 268, 275, 277
Robins, Elizabeth, 36, 48, 52, 61, 66, 150, 185, 248
Robinson, Lillian, 269
Robinson, Rona, 41, 43, 265
Rollyson, Carl, 167, 262, 281
Rosetti, Christina, 127
Ross, Harold, 196, 284
Ruddick, Sara, 5
Ruderman, Judith, 165

Russell, Bertrand, 63–64
Russian culture, 81, 108, 179, 252

Sackville-West, Vita, xxv, 50, 185, 205, 213, 218–220, 223–224, 236, 254, 280, 282, 283
St. Sebastian, 116–117
salon, 70, 71, 72, 111, 169, 250
Sand, George, 176
Sandburg, Carl, 94
Sanger, Margaret, 71–72, 192, 269
Sappho, 72, 93, 177, 244, 248, 252, 253
scaffolding, xviii, xxii, xxiv–xxviii, xxx, xxxii, 3, 19
Schenck, Celeste, 186, 267, 280
Schiff, Sidney, 115, 119, 123, 268, 274
Schiff, Violet, 110, 274
science, 39, 41–42, 82, 97, 130, 162, 245
Scott, Bonnie Kime, xx, xxii, 145–146, 206, 262, 269, 270, 271, 276–280, 281, 283
Scrutiny, 80, 215–216, 283
Sedgwick, Eve, xxxiv, 175, 271
sentimentality, xxxiv, 8, 102, 105, 126, 151–152, 230, 232, 248, 272, 284
sex and sexuality, xxxvi, xxxviii, xl, 11, 18, 25, 42, 43, 46, 57, 62, 64, 65, 67, 93, 94, 97–98, 103–106, 113, 124, 127, 153, 161, 163–165, 184, 192, 196, 198, 218–219, 221, 251, 255–256, 262, 268, 275, 278
Shakespear, Olivia, 85
Shakespeare, William, xvi, xxv, xxvii, 5, 172, 230
Shaw, Charlotte, 28, 43, 263
Shaw, George Bernard, xxxvii, xli, 10, 20, 27–29, 33, 43, 62, 143
Sheepshanks, Mary, 62, 267
Showalter, Elaine, xv, xxxi, xxxiv, 35, 189, 260
Silver, Brenda, 261
Simpson, Hilary, 164
Sinclair, May, xxv, xxxiv, 43, 55, 57, 58–60, 64, 69, 70, 85–86, 123–124, 236, 267, 268, 287
Sitwell, Edith, xxvi, 72, 109, 204, 275
Smyth, Dame Ethel, 50, 64, 165, 190–191, 217, 221–223, 283
socialism, xxxv, 10, 23–27, 39, 52, 59, 63, 107, 215
Solano, Solita, 72, 75, 142, 202
Spain, xxxviii, 26, 279
Spencer, Herbert, 9
Spender, Dale, 49
Spender, Stephen, 124

Spoo, Robert, 91
Spotts, Frederic, 188
Squier, Susan, xxxv
Stanton, Elizabeth Cady, 16, 52
Stead, C. K., 269
Stead, W. D., 16
Stein, Gertrude, xxxv, 72, 74, 80, 94, 148, 157, 267, 269, 270
Stephen, Adrian (Woolf's brother), 4–5, 188–189
Stephen, Caroline Emilia (Woolf's aunt), 61
Stephen, Sir Leslie (Woolf's father), xxxix, 188–189, 237
Stephen, Julia Princep Duckworth (Woolf's mother), xxxix, 4–5, 50, 217
Stephen, Laura (Woolf's half sister), 4–5
Stephen, Thoby (Woolf's brother), 4–5, 62, 170, 187–189, 217, 263
Steptoe, Lydia (Djuna Barnes), 120, 235
Stern, G. B., xxv, 57, 60, 195, 199, 217, 224–227, 233, 284
Sterne, Laurence, 148
Stevens, Wallace, 81
Strachey, Lytton, xxv, 51, 65, 67, 80, 111, 115, 132, 136, 146, 169, 171–172, 174, 187–189, 263, 267, 275
Strachey, Pernel, 51, 62
Strachey, Ray, 51
suffragism, xxxvi, xli, 16, 28, 35–54, 59, 61, 87–88, 102–103, 108, 109, 150, 178, 184, 194, 260, 264–266, 271
suicide, 26, 90, 136, 192, 206, 228, 241, 245, 267, 271
symbolism, 100, 166, 173, 175, 279

technology, 99–103, 105, 122, 162
temperance, 16
Terry, Ellen, 36
Theatre Guild, xxxviii, 200, 233
Thomas, Dylan, 202
Thurber, James, 284
Thompson, Dorothy, 232, 284
Time, 196, 227
Time and Tide, 37, 48, 62, 197, 224, 233, 244, 246, 248, 260, 265–266
Times Literary Supplement (TLS), 24, 115, 132, 146, 185–186, 188, 232, 263
Todd, Dorothy, 213, 223, 233
Tolstoy, Count Leo, xli
tradition, xxvi, xxvii, 108, 127, 136, 144
transition, 157, 160, 228, 229

travel, 21, 26, 166, 168, 185, 194, 195, 215, 219–220, 279
Trevelyan, Mary, 117, 142, 274
trials, 156, 198, 244–246, 251, 262, 286
Trilling, Diana, 82
Troubridge, Una, 246, 248
Twain, Mark, xxv, 20
Valéry, Paul, 80–81
Vanity Fair, 68, 151, 157, 159, 186, 200–201, 232, 235
Verenal, Jean, 116, 121
Victorians, xx, xxviii, 3, 4, 6, 19, 25, 60, 61, 95, 138, 172, 188, 246, 272
violence, 36, 106, 121, 143, 251
Vivien, Renée, 72, 248, 287
Vogue, 186, 223, 232–233, 235
von Arnim, Elizabeth, 25–26, 192
Von Freytag-Loringhoven, Elsa Baroness, 160, 200, 214, 215, 228–229, 269
vorticism, 81, 88, 94–95, 100–103, 106, 107, 112, 173, 270

Walker, Alice, xv, xxvi, xxxi, 259, 283
Walpole, Hugh, 22–25, 174, 223, 263, 265, 266, 280
war, xxxvi, 112, 136, 216–217; World War I, xxxvi, xli, 31, 63, 66, 99, 103, 104, 106–107, 109, 112, 116, 144, 163–166, 171, 211, 234, 248, 249, 270, 274, 286; World War II, 31, 108, 136, 184, 194; Civil War (U.S.), 9, 16, 207, 274
war between the sexes, xxx, 161, 167, 273
Ward, Mrs. Humphry, xxiii, 25, 43, 50, 176
Warner, Sylvia Townsend, 270
Waugh, Patricia, 275
Weaver, Harriet Shaw, xxvi, xliii, 43, 47, 80, 90, 125, 150, 151, 265, 274, 277
web, xv, xvi, xviii, xx, xxvi–xxviii, xxx, xxxii, xxxiii, xxxvi, xl, 21, 51, 95, 131, 154, 161, 252, 259
Wells, Catherine (Jane), 192
Wells, H. G., xl, 19, 20, 22–27, 31, 33, 37–39, 41, 43, 44, 55, 68, 69, 72, 89, 136–137, 149, 173, 188, 192–196, 206, 219, 263–264, 268, 270, 280, 287
West, Anthony, xl, 11, 13, 56–57, 194–198, 227–228, 280–281, 284
West, Dame Rebecca, xxi, xxii, xxvii, xxxviii, xl, xli, 24–33, 35–49, 64, 69, 72, 80, 86–89, 102, 107–110, 143–144, 146, 166–168, 183–185, 191–199, 218, 221–228, 233–235, 253,

West—*continued*
255, 259, 263–266, 273, 276, 283, 285, 287;
Black Lamb and Grey Falcon, 69, 279, 235;
Family Memories, xli, 10–12, 262; *Harriet
Hume*, 184–185, 206, 223, 282; "Indissol-
uble Matrimony," 107, 109, 273; *The Judge,*
xvi, xxviii, 37, 64, 261, 265, 282; "The
Strange Necessity," 128, 151–157, 184, 225,
236, 246, 248
Westley, Helen, 70, 200, 239
Wharton, Edith, 72, 269
White, Antonia, 229
Wickham, Anna, 72, 74
Wilde, Oscar, 14, 20, 240, 246, 287
Wilde, Speranza, 16
Williams, William Carlos, xxv, 81, 84, 153,
155–156, 276, 278
Wilson, Edmund, 80, 284
Wolfe, Peter, 284
Women's Social and Political Union
(WSPU), 36, 39, 42, 45, 50, 52, 62
Women Writers' Suffrage League, 59, 62
Wood, Thelma, 74, 201–203, 207
Woodhull, Victoria, 16
Woolf, Leonard (Woolf's husband), 65, 134–
136, 151, 185, 188, 206, 244–245, 263, 266,
267, 268, 282, 283
Woolf, Virginia, xvi, xvii, xx, xxxi, xl, xliii,
20–24, 49–52, 68–69, 108–112, 128–138, 143–
151, 153, 168–169, 183–185, 187–192, 199, 204,
216–224, 232–233, 259, 266–268, 272, 275;
Between the Acts, xxvii, 23, 24; *Jacob's
Room*, 20, 21, 66, 130, 172, 275, 279; *Moments of Being*, xxvii, 5, 7; *Mrs. Dalloway,*
130, 191; *Night and Day*, 51–52, 66, 170–171;
Orlando, 120, 178, 183–184, 191, 216, 223,
236, 252–256, 267, 279, 283; "Phases of Fiction," 66, 132, 179, 233, 235; *A Room*, xv,
xxviii, xxxi, xxxvi, xxxviii, 19, 47, 50, 51,
55, 61, 64, 66, 131, 147, 151, 154, 206, 209,
224, 252, 261, 263; *Three Guineas*, 24, 62,
173, 178, 221; *To the Lighthouse*, xvi, xxvii,
82, 173, 191, 246; *Voyage Out*, xii, xxvii,
xxxix, 171, 279, 282–283; *The Waves*, 220–221
Woollcott, Alexander, xxv, 195, 198–199, 232,
281

Yeats, William Butler, 29, 60, 80, 97, 143,
159, 264
Yugoslavia, xxxviii, 198, 235, 240, 285

BONNIE KIME SCOTT, Professor of English and Women's Studies at the University of Delaware, is general editor of *The Gender of Modernism*; she is also author of *Joyce and Feminism* and *James Joyce* (feminist readings series) and editor of *New Alliances in Joyce Studies*. She is presently editing the selected letters of Rebecca West.